INQUIRY
BY DESIGN

REVISED EDITION

JOHN ZEISEL

INQUIRY
BY DESIGN

Environment / Behavior / Neuroscience in Architecture, Interiors, Landscape, and Planning

REVISED EDITION

FOREWORD BY JOHN P. EBERHARD

W. W. NORTON & COMPANY
New York • London

Copyright © 2006 by John Zeisel
Foreword copyright © 2006 by W. W. Norton &
Company, Inc.
Copyright © 1981 by Wadsworth, Inc., Belmont,
California 94002
Copyright © Cambridge University Press 1984

All rights reserved
Printed in the United States of America
First Edition

For information about permission to reproduce
selections from this book, write to Permissions,
W. W. Norton & Company, Inc., 500 Fifth Avenue,
New York, NY 10110

Composition and book design by Abigail Sturges
Manufacturing by Fairfield Graphics
Production Manger: Leeann Graham

Library of Congress Cataloging-in-Publication Data
Zeisel, John.
    Inquiry by design : environment/behavior/neuro-
science in architecture, interiors, landscape, and
planning / John Zeisel ; foreword by John P. Eberhard.
– Rev. ed.
            p. cm.
    Includes bibliographical references and index.
            ISBN 0-393-73184-7 (pbk.)
            1. Environmental psychology – Research.
2. Architectural design – Psychological aspects. I. Title.

BF353.Z44 2005
720'.1'9—dc22

2005051290

W. W. Norton & Company, Inc., 500 Fifth Avenue,
New York, N.Y. 10110
www.wwnorton.com

W. W. Norton & Company Ltd., Castle House,
75/76 Wells St., London W1T 3QT
0 9 8 7 6 5 4 3 2 1

CONTENTS

Observing Behavior Update
Overview

Pre-Interview Analysis and Interview Guide
Objectives of Focused Interviews
Basic Characteristics of Focused Interviewing
Probes
Group Focused Interviews
Focused Interview Update
Overview

Qualities
Organization
Coding Open-Ended Reponses
Precoding Responses
Visual Responses
Questionnaires Update
Overview

Topics
Format
Overview

Qualities
Using Archives
Document Files
Types of Data
Plan Annotation
Behavioral Plan Analysis
Data Archive Update
Overview

Neuroscience and E-B Concepts
Neuroscience/Design Arriving at Different Design Criteria
E/B/N Performance Criteria Design Guidelines
Overview

ACKNOWLEDGMENTS

*To everyone living with Alzheimer's disease and their care partners,
who taught me so much about the purity of the human mind.*

Many people patiently supported and contributed to this revision of *Inquiry by Design*. Jacqueline Vischer's focus on writing and her dedication to E-B set a high standard to meet. Adam, Evan, Isabelle, and Alexander were patient with my early fumbling explorations into new universes of the brain, creativity, and lessons that can be learned from an ever-growing collection of innovative objects. My partner at Hearthstone Alzheimer Care, Joan Hyde, has played a crucial role in developing many of the ideas about Alzheimer treatment and design presented here. Also at Hearthstone Alzheimer Care, Sharon Johnson, Sean Caulfield, Dan Colucci, and Sue Blackler have all enthusiastically engaged—or so it seems—in the organization's evidence-based innovative practice approach to management as well as design.

Marilyn Albert, Daniel Shachter, Kenneth Kosik, Howard Eichenbaum, and Mark Baxter are owed thanks for solidifying my commitment to the path of neuroscience in design by generously inviting me to participate in a Mind-Brain-Behavior (MBB) working group at Harvard University. Appreciation goes out to the many members of EDRA—the Environmental Design Research Association—who provided helpful advice as well as hundreds of articles I read for the methods updates sections. Nick Watkins provided invaluable assistance screening abstracts and articles as part of this effort.

The exceptional thinkers and professionals whose case studies are highlighted at the end of chapters, are owed inestimable thanks not only for their contributions to this book, but for their steadfast pursuit of excellence in E-B studies. These include my colleagues and friends Clare Cooper-Marcus, Fank Duffy, Henry Sanoff, Jacqueline Vischer, Jay Farbstein, Min Kantrowitz,

Mark Francis, and Karu Bowns. John Eberhard, who exemplified critical research and design thinking when we first met and discussed E-B as part of the AIA's Research Advisory Panel, is now a colleague and fellow adventurer in the domain of neuroscience and design at the Academy of Neuroscience for Architecture. Wayne Ruga, founder of the Symposium for Health Care Design and the Caritas Project, has been a constant and steadfast model for and supporter of my exploring new ideas. Marc Maxwell, AIA, has been central to the ideas in this book and to the case studies I have been involved in. Marc's personal and professional commitment to E-B research, design, and process has been unsurpassed in my experience. He represents the best intellectual and personal attributes of any architect.

Thanks to Irwin Altman I wrote the first edition of *Inquiry by Design*—a prerequisite to this revision. At an EDRA conference a long time ago, Irv suggested I go away to a mountaintop to conceive and write the book I wanted to write. He commented on drafts critically yet gently. He knows how to use his belief in others to get them to do what he wants them to do—and what they want to do, too. Many mountaintops later, I still understand the power of this approach.

FOREWORD

JOHN P. EBERHARD

If we allow discoveries in neuroscience and cognitive science to butt up against old philosophical problems . . . we will see intuitions surprised and dogma routed.

— PATRICIA CHURCHLAND

For centuries, architects have recognized that the buildings in which we live, learn, work, and worship influence how we feel and act, setting the stage for quiet reflection, invigorating interaction, or inspiration. Recently, neuroscientists began to extend that intuitive understanding by showing how our brains are fine-tuned to our environment and how they respond and adapt to information—including awareness of our orientation in space—that reaches us through our senses. Fred "Rusty" Gage, the Salk Institute neuroscientist who discovered neurogenesis in the early 1990s, said in his 2003 AIA Convention keynote address: "As neuroscientists, we believe that the brain is the organ that controls behavior, that genes control the blueprint, the design, and structure of the brain, but the environment can modulate the function of genes, and ultimately the structure of our brain. Changes in the environment change the brain and therefore they change our behavior. Architectural design changes our brain and our behavior."

Can the tools of brain science demonstrate a neurobiological basis for what architects have believed intuitively? Conversely, can brain research learn about what moves and delights us from the challenges of designing exceptional spaces? This book represents an important first step in answering these questions. The parallel Zeisel draws between design, research, and creativity as well as the Environment/Behavior/Neuroscience (E/B/N) paradigm he proposes are likely to play a significant role in anchoring the developing field of neuroscience and design.

We already have good examples of this reward from health care. For example, we know now that certain levels of light and noise in neonatal care units can interfere with critical sensory development in premature infants. We know that specific features of their physical environment can support healthy behavior among people with Alzheimer's disease. This book helps the reader look deeper into such environments and their effects and provides hope that designers will be able to draw on such examples for future health care design.

It will be neither quick nor easy to recast the intuitions of architects as testable scientific hypotheses. Questions of study design, identification of the outcomes to be measured, validation, and funding all must be addressed. Brain-imaging techniques and other tools of neuroscience can help us measure aspects of brain physiology and behavior that offer clues to the answers we seek. For example, heart rate, perspiration, and levels of certain hormones and chemicals can be useful markers of emotional response, and imaging modalities such as functional magnetic resonance imaging (fMRI) and positron emission tomography (PET) can zero in on the brain regions that could be involved in given responses. Devices that track eye movements might be useful in finding out where people's attention is focused when they enter a space and what types of architectural elements have "enduring interest," as opposed to initial novelty. Much has been studied and written about what contributes to a "healthy" building, and we have begun to learn how a workplace's spatial organization and environmental attributes can affect productivity. The last chapter of *Inquiry by Design* describes specific steps to take in translating such a neuroscience approach into environmental design practice and research.

Meanwhile, social and behavioral scientists have studied the effect of lighting on children in classrooms and almost universally report that learning improves when artificial light is reduced and daylight increased. The benefits include better grades and fewer absences (presumably correlated with enhanced learning) and improvements in student behavior as reported by teachers. But notably missing is definitive research that investigates how lighting levels correlate with cognitive functioning in children of various ages. Research on how the brain develops over the first two decades of life could hold clues. Such research shows that the different brain regions and systems develop on different schedules. For instance, postnatal development in the hippocampus continues until about 4 to 5 years of age, but development of the visual cortex continues until ages 7 to 11. The prefrontal cortex, where higher cognitive functions such as planning and reasoning occur, is not fully mature until young adulthood. Age-appropriate environments that take into account these different developmental stages could be beneficial, but first we need more information and ways to test the effect of specific environmental features on learning. The links this book makes between the social sciences, neuroscience, and design can be used in E/B/N research and practice to achieve our ultimate goal—healthier buildings, interiors, landscapes, and cities.

Architects have known intuitively the value of their design decisions on the quality of human experiences. Social and behavioral scientists have added an overlay of research that sharpens our understanding of how design impacts these experiences. Now it is going to be possible to use neuroscience research to answer the critical question of why this happens. Why do patients in a hospital respond better to certain colors? Why is the cognitive ability of children in a classroom impacted by background noise? Why do Alzheimer's patients respond to sunlight?

Zeisel's *Inquiry by Design* contributes to the knowledge base architects and programmers need to more precisely define the design criteria for architectural spaces that support the brain and to identify the research instruments that will enable us to more accurately measure how well these criteria are met.

PREFACE

After twenty-five years of progress in the field of environment-behavior (E-B), its original goals and fundamental methods remain strong and are the focus of much research creativity and application. E-B has profoundly influenced the practice of architecture, design, landscape, and planning through practitioners who have either directly studied it or who are more aware of popular trends towards people-centered and evidence-based design. With programs and courses in universities throughout Europe, North America, China, Russia, Korea, Japan, Australia, South America, and beyond, E-B is also well established in education, having found a home in social and psychological sciences departments, and in schools of architecture, interior design, landscape, planning, and industrial design.

There is today a 30-year body of E-B knowledge on which to build, including comprehensive textbooks and multivolume edited series that have been published since *Inquiry by Design* first appeared in 1981 (Gifford, 2002; Bechtel and Churchman, 2002; Bell, Greene, Fischer, and Baum, 2000; Zube, Marans, and Moore, 1997; Altman et al., 1980–1984).

These books reflect the breadth and depth of the field as it moves into the twenty-first century. Many excellent research-based books have also been published over the past quarter century on specific topics such as therapeutic gardens; offices of the future; Alzheimer's design; design for assisted living, playgrounds, housing, elderly housing; design for health; design programming; post-occupancy evaluation; design methods; and creativity. The case studies that end the chapters in this edition reference many of these topics.

Methodological developments have occurred primarily in the creative application of techniques described in this book and in technical advances, rather than in the discovery of new methods. Observing people and environments, asking questions in interviews and questionnaires, and using data and plan archives remain primary methods in E-B research. Computers now enable E-B researchers to carry out surveys online, gather relevant existing research through broad Web-based calls for information—the Environmental Design Research Association (EDRA) facilitates such searches—analyze databases with GIS mapping software, and easily examine design alternatives with auto-CAD. Miniaturization has led to handheld data gathering and input devices, sometimes using barcode systems.

Advances in applying research in design are evident in design firms and research consulting practices. The dozen selected case studies in this edition highlight practice accomplishments. Carried out by exceptional professionals in the field—Clare Cooper-Marcus, DEGW & Frank Duffy, Henry Sanoff, Jacqueline Vischer, Jay Farbstein, Min Kantrowitz, Mark Francis, and Karu Bowns—as well as by the author, all studies have resulted in impressive buildings and places, and useful information. Each case study represents an E-B intervention in design, employs between two and ten skillfully coordinated research methods, and results in high quality evidence-based information and intriguing design. The cases span the research and design cycle of basic research, programming, evidence-based design, post-occupancy evaluation (POE), and improved design. The cases that include all these stages over the life of a design and building project impressively demonstrate how each E-B intervention contributes to significant innovation in methods, approach, and design concept.

The cases represent a broad range of designed environments and research approaches: a residence and center for education and health care of multiply handicapped students; offices demonstrating new forms of work and teamwork; a powerful psychological interview technique used to uncover housing desires, needs, and traumas; an exceptional university building; innovative postal service delivery methods; and combined headquarters/manufacturing plants. Standing alone, these projects deserve attention. As illustrations of how research and design can be brought together creatively in practice, they deserve even more celebration! I have been fortunate to have contributed to the program design and evaluation of congregate housing for the elderly, Alzheimer's assisted living treatment residences, a historic corporate headquarters renovation, and a newsroom remodeling. In each case, remaining faithful to the methodological guidance this book provides has served the projects well.

This book has two parts. In Part One, I discuss design, research, and what researchers and designers can achieve if they work together. More specifically, I address such questions as: What can designers do better by organizing their inquiry as research and their design as inquiry? What goes on in researchers' and designers' minds when they apply their skills? How can a model of these cognitive processes be used to improve the way research and design are carried out? How are research and design activities similar? How are they different? How can researchers and designers exploit their differences to get something out of working together? On what immediate problems can the two professions work together? What are some possible long-range benefits to this collaboration?

In Chapter 1 I present a description of design that people can compare against their own experiences and use to organize and achieve their own design ideas. Chapter 2 explains the research component and emphasizes its often-overlooked creative and inventive qualities. Chapter 3 addresses one reason researchers and designers may choose to work together: to better control the effects of their decisions, especially when the effects lie in the realm of the other discipline. Chapter 4 discusses a second reason: for a professional in one discipline to define and approach their own problems in new ways, by learning the conceptual tools of the other. Chapter 5 characterizes research as a set of activities designed to help solve problems in specific situations. Research *quality* is explained in Chapter 6 as the degree to which the research can be shared, used, and improved upon by other people.

In Chapter 7, the last chapter in Part One, and in Chapter 14, the last chapter in Part Two, I suggest that if neuroscience is formally integrated with the social and psychological sciences in E-B studies, a great deal more can be achieved. These chapters reflect scientific advances of the last quarter of the twentieth century in exploring how brains are structured, develop, and work. Chapter 7 proposes that interrelated sets of neurons and functions in our brains employ and deal with physical environment cohesively as an *environment system*. The chapter goes on to describe the significant role that *physical environment* plays in critical brain functions, including memory, learning, perception, and spatial orientation. Neuroscience research also indicates that our brains are particularly well suited to designing things—concepts, tools, languages, and places. Our brains may well have evolved to be creative in every sense of the word—to imagine new ideas, put into practice what we invent, and critically examine the results of our actions.

In Part Two, I describe how to carry out E-B research to achieve specific purposes. Six research methods are explained: (1) observing physical traces, such as paths across a lawn or decorations on a living-room wall, to see how people have affected their physical surroundings (Chapter 8); (2) observing behavior in its environmental context to see how people use physical settings (Chapter 9); (3) engaging in focused interviewing to find out how individuals and groups define specific environmental situations they have experienced (Chapters 10 and 12); (4) using structured questionnaires to gather data about individuals' perceptions, attitudes, and aspirations that can be applied to groups (Chapters 11 and 12); and (5) employing archival methods—for example, analyzing documents such as newspapers and institutional records—to turn data recorded for other reasons into information useful in solving E-B problems (Chapter 13). Also in Chapter 13 (6), plan annotation, a special E-B behavioral technique for analyzing plans, is described in greater detail than in the first edition.

The descriptions of design and research as well as the six basic E-B research methods have been left intact with their original references. This deserves an explanation. Many colleagues advised me to update the text with more recent case examples. Reading more than 300 articles and reports to find new examples convinced me that updating would essentially mean merely replacing older examples with more recent ones, *without* changing the basic description of design, research, or methods. I feel strongly that replacing the classic illustrative examples with more recent ones would neither substantially improve the clarity of the methods descriptions, nor highlight any better that the text reflects quite fundamental thinking. That said, a new methods "*update*" section, which discusses the many exciting advances that have been made in the use of methods, analysis of data, and applications in design and planning, ends each chapter in Part Two.

Chapter 14 presents the Environment/Behavior/Neuroscience (E/B/N) approach as an enriched way of understanding E-B concepts such as place, territory, personalization, and wayfinding. The chapter uses neonatal care unit design and learning environments as examples of how to generate E/B/N hypotheses and performance criteria design guidelines. The chapter ends with a case study explaining the unique contributions and differences an E/B/N approach makes in design and programming an Alzheimer's assisted living treatment residence. Employing this paradigm emphasizes how environments can support natural brain development and functioning, whether for those with Alzheimer's disease, premature babies, or students in schools.

This revised edition reflects several major present trends and future directions of E-B. First, practical research applications are being developed for the design and construction of significant and innovative physical settings—for buildings, interiors, parks, planning projects, and objects. Second, E-B research and consultants are increasingly employing evidence-based design, a major concept of this book, when constructing environments to improve productivity, quality of life, learning, teamwork, and memory. Third, designers who employ E-B research systematically and regularly help to contribute to a shared body of E-B knowledge. Their designs and design decisions, which will eventually be evaluated, will further augment E-B research and its overall evolution and progress. Finally, the contributions that neuroscience can make in design is another major trend that is likely to expand the present discipline of E-B beyond the bounds of imagination.

PART ONE

RESEARCH
AND DESIGN

CHAPTER 1

DESIGN: IMAGES, PRESENTATIONS, AND TESTS

Inquiry is the creation of knowledge or understanding; it is the reaching out of a human being beyond himself to a perception of what he may be or could be, or what the world could be or ought to be.

— C. WEST CHURCHMAN
The Design of Inquiring Systems

During a physical design project, an individual or team generates ideas for changing the existing physical environment and presents them in a form to guide construction. Design begins when an individual or team first thinks about the project—for example, a building, an open-space plan, or an object. It includes a stage when detailed working drawings of a project are given to contractors instructing them how the designers expect the project to be built. It includes a stage when contractor and designer negotiate changes in design to respond to problems that arise during construction. The process formally ends when construction is completed. Designers conventionally break down this process into contractually binding stages: programming, preliminary design, final design, working drawings, and construction supervision.

Design is difficult to describe because it includes so many intangible elements such as intuition, imagination, and creativity—which are also essential to research. Nevertheless, several analysts have done a remarkable job of articulating parts of this process (Hillier and Leaman, 1974; Korobkin, 1976; and others). Their descriptions apply to a prototypical design process that, in an architect's office, might go something like this:

> Posed with a design problem—let us say for a new elementary school—an architect gathers information about the specific site and about elementary schools generally. She does this by visiting the site, having discussions with clients and users, and studying books.
>
> Through a series of trials, she generates a preliminary mental image of an "elementary school," responding to the information she has gathered, her personal experiences, and mental images of schools she knows and likes.

She draws rough sketches or diagrams to begin fleshing out this image and reviews them with people in the office, with the client, and by herself. She may even build rough working models.

Stepping back from her presentations, she asks herself whether they do justice to her concept and the information she has. She might feel she needs to gather more data to assess them adequately. Through this process, the architect tests and refines her concept and her information. She repeats these steps several times within days, hours, or even minutes until she feels she has begun to generate a clearer mental image, one that corresponds to both her sketches and the information.

Up to this point, each sketch might be different from previous ones, yet influenced by studies of previous sketches. The architect may even have developed several alternative but equally fruitful concepts. Concept sketches and diagrams at this stage include ideas about overall building image, major spaces, and relationships among building components. She shows these to her clients and may share them with the building's eventual users. Both groups may have been consulted earlier in the process as well. Now they may suggest revisions, discuss alternatives, or request that the designer pursue a whole new direction.

After the appropriate groups improve and approve concept sketches, the architect and her team think about and then draw schematic drawings—the first step in moving from concept to building. Schematic drawings begin to present specific room relationships, room sizes, door and window locations, and where facilities will be located.

As the architect designs schematic drawings, she repeatedly checks to make sure they are true to the agreed-upon concept, to government regulations, and to performance standards dictated by theory and empirical work. She simultaneously develops and refines the overall design concept, paying attention to how its individual parts relate, how the whole building "hangs together," and how the building fits in context.

This process of design development results in "presentation drawings": plans, sections, elevations, and perspective renderings that give clients an idea of what the final product will be. Such drawings specify what attributes the building will have, from dimensions to material to color. When client groups review presentation drawings, they may once again respond with suggestions for improvement. At this point the designer negotiates with clients in order to make decisions that meet their needs.

After presentation drawings are approved, the architect and her team articulate their ideas in "working drawings" that detail for the contractor how each part of the building is to be built—from foundation to doorknobs. While working drawings are being drafted, each decision is checked again to see that it meets legal regulations, such as building and safety standards, and that it reflects the initial design concept. Major conceptual design shifts made this late in the process can be costly.

When the design team feels that working drawings adequately present its ideas, regulatory personnel have checked that working drawings meet legal standards, and specialist consultants have reported that their criteria have been met, the working drawings are complete. At this point a contractor is hired to construct the building.

The contractor constructs the building according to the drawings and written specifications in documents. If he does not understand a specification, has difficulty securing materials, or for some reason feels a change is necessary, he reports the problem to the architect. When both agree that a change is required, the architect issues an official change order. At this late stage, modifications in design are carried out with great care.

In most cases architects remain involved in projects during construction until specifications have been officially fulfilled and the project is considered built.

Architects may return informally to their buildings after occupancy to learn from what they have done or they may carry out a formal post-occupancy evaluation (POE) of the building. This information is useful for future design.

WHY DESCRIBE DESIGN?

Describing the design process may help designers and teachers of design understand their own behavior and thereby improve their design ability. Analysis is also useful for researchers and designers who want to work together.

Although outsiders can directly observe behavioral and representational parts of designing, they cannot directly observe the cognitive design processes that take place inside the designer's mind and brain. Research evidence for describing what happens when designers think is therefore necessarily indirect and inferential or introspective. Evidence includes personal experience (Jones, 1970; Korobkin, 1976), participant observation (Zeisel, 1975), stream-of-consciousness reports by designers actively designing (Foz, 1972), and analysis of successive design drawings (Foz, 1972). Some design theorists look to other disciplines to provide illuminating analogies: linguistics (Hillier and Leaman, 1974), artificial intelligence (Foz, 1972; Hillier and Leaman, 1974), and biological evolution (Hillier and Leaman, 1974). In Chapter 7 I look to the neurosciences and find descriptions of creativity, memory, and even phantom limb reactions that provide insight into designers' mental processes.

Design methodologists' theoretical, personal, and practical reasons for analyzing design result in their emphasizing different elements and using different analogies to describe how parts of the process fit together. In a particular situation one description may be more helpful than another to designers or researchers in achieving their ends. Comparing such descriptions is likely to provide both a useful, multifaceted picture of design and interesting problems for further study.

FIVE CHARACTERISTICS OF DESIGNING

Physical design inventively mixes together ideas, drawings, information, and many other ingredients to create something where nothing was before. Design can also be seen as an ordered process in which specific activities are loosely organized to make decisions about changing the physical world to achieve identifiable goals. However one thinks about design and for whatever purposes, five characteristics emerge as useful tools for understanding what designers do.

Five Design Characteristics

I. Three Elementary Activities

The complex activity called "designing" interconnects three constituent activities: imaging, presenting, and testing.

II. Two Types of Information

Information used in designing tends to be useful in two ways: as a heuristic catalyst for imaging and as a body of knowledge for testing.

III. Shifting Visions of Final Product

Designers continually modify predictions about their final result in response to new information and insight. The design process is thus a series of conceptual shifts or creative leaps.

IV. Toward a Domain of Acceptable Responses

Designers aim to reach one acceptable response within a range of possible solutions. This domain of acceptance is measured largely by how well a product is adapted to its environment and how coherent constituent parts of the product are with one another.

V. Development through Linked Cycles: A Spiral Metaphor

Conceptual shifts and product development in design occur as the result of repeated, iterative movement through the three elementary design activities.

I. Three Elementary Activities

Designers working on an actual project do not just sit down and "design"; it is not a one-dimensional activity. Rather, like other developmental processes, such as writing a book or bringing up children, design is a complex activity more usefully thought of as including several analytically distinct elementary activities: imaging, presenting, and testing.

The first activity I will discuss is imaging (Korobkin, 1976). I might have said "The first activity in design is imaging," but this would have reinforced the false popular idea that using one's imagination is the most important element in creative action and that any design process must begin with an act of imagination. In reality, the starting point for any developmental process is among its least important aspects (Bruner, 1973, p. 160; Popper, 1972, pp. 34, 72, 104).

• *Imaging.* Imaging is the ability to "go beyond the information given," as Bruner (1973) calls the process of seeing something where nothing seems to have been before. This activity, often called "real creativity" by laypersons, might most accurately be called "imaging" after the verb *to image*, which the *Oxford English Dictionary* defines as

> to form a mental image of: to conceive (a) something to be executed: to devise a plan, and (b) an object of perception or thought: to imagine, to picture in the mind, to represent *to oneself*, as in Coleridge, 1818, "Whatever is admitted to be conceivable must be imageable," and in Browning, 1855, "Image the whole, then execute the parts. . . ."

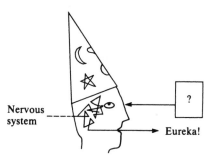

Black-box designer. (From *Design Methods: Seeds of Human Features*, by J. C. Jones. Copyright 1970 by John Wiley & Sons Ltd. Reprinted by permission)

Imaging means forming a general, sometimes only fuzzy, mental picture of a part of the world. In design as well as in other types of endeavors, images are often visual; they provide a larger framework within which to fit specific pieces of a problem as they are resolved.

How a designer's image is formed has been the topic of much discussion but little empirical research until the neurosciences focused on imaging in the brain. The concept is well expressed in Jones's picture (1970, p. 46) of a "black-box designer," reflecting his interpretation of how Osborn (1963), Gordon (1961), Matchett (1968), and Broadbent (1966) describe design.

Designers use their visions of eventual solutions to define better the design problem they are working on and to guide their search for answers. Comparing a design against a mental image makes visible where the design can be improved and perhaps where the image itself might be modified (Foz, 1972). One hypothesis about the nature of images is that they are deductive constructs akin to the "conjectures" that Popper (1963) describes as essential to scientific progress; that is, these visions of a "solution in principle" developed early in a design process parallel researchers' working hypotheses (Hillier, Musgrove, and O'Sullivan, 1972). Working hypotheses are refined during scientific exploration; images are developed during design activity.

Images, however, are more than just a person's internalized pictures. They represent subjective knowledge, used to develop and organize ideas in such areas as visual perception and learning (Bruner, 1973), language (Polanyi, 1958), child development (Piaget and Inhelder, 1969), and economics and politics (Boulding, 1956).

Although the neurosciences now allow us to understand better the internal process of imaging, in studying imaging in design we are constrained to observing its external manifestations: (1) how designers present their images to others and to themselves and (2) how their observable behavior changes while developing internal images of situations.

• *Presenting.* Sketching, drawing plans, building models, and taking photographs are some of the many ways designers externalize and communicate their images. It takes skill not only to present an idea well but also to choose the mode of presentation best suited to a particular time in the design process. Designers present ideas to make them visible so that they themselves and others can use and develop them. For each presentation, the designer must choose and then organize only some elements from a larger number. Presenting includes both variety reduction, in that "more and more specific drawings . . . exclude more and more detailed design possibilities" (Hillier, Musgrove, and O'Sullivan, 1972), and opportunity expansion, in that new problems for further design resolution are made explicit.

Of course, if images and their presentations were identical, it would not be possible to use one to clarify the other. Rather, designers present not images themselves but the implications of images (Simon, 1969: 15). The importance of "representation" may be stated in an extreme way by asserting that "solving a problem simply means representing it so as to make the solution transparent" (Simon, 1969, p. 77). Whether or not this conscious oversimplification is tenable, "a deeper understanding of how representations are created and how they contribute to the solution of problems will become an essential component in the future theory of design" (Simon, 1969, p. 77).

In a pilot study of how architects with different design experience solved a short two-hour sketch problem, the more experienced architects tended to be better able to make decisions in the form of presentations (Foz, 1972). They did not agonize over decisions, as did beginners. Skilled designers used "three-dimensional representation . . . more often, more quickly, more realistically" (1972, p. 72). In other words, the more experienced designers could quickly sketch out an idea, draw it, or build a model—even though that presentation may not have been perfect. They knew that soon after they would return to the model with a fresh eye to evaluate and improve it.

• *Testing.* Appraisals, refutations, criticisms, judgments, comparisons, reflections, reviews, and confrontations are all types of tests. After presenting a design idea in any form, designers step back with a critical eye and examine their products (Hillier et al., 1972; Korobkin, 1976), sometimes in groups and sometimes alone (Christopherson, 1963). Design testing means comparing tentative presentations against an array of information like the designer's and the clients' implicit images, explicit information about constraints or objectives, degrees of internal design consistency, and performance criteria—economic, technical, sociological, and neurological.

An interesting dimension of design testing is that designers look both backward and forward simultaneously: backward to determine how good a tentative product is, forward to refine the image being developed and to modify the next presentation. While reviewing, criticizing, and analyzing any presentation, designers are preparing the way for the next creative leap.

Although testing contributes to design innovation, it also makes a designer's task more manageable in the face of the potentially infinite number of alternative responses to any problem (Jones, 1970). Testing in design makes it "possible to replace blind searching of alternatives by an intelligent search that uses both external criteria and the results of partial search to find short cuts across the unknown territory" (Jones, 1970, p. 55).

Testing is a simultaneous feed-back and feed-forward process, adjusting the relation between a design product as it develops and the many criteria and qualities the product is intended to meet. Without testing there can be no improvement.

In sum, imaging, presenting, and testing are elementary activities constituting a complex process called "design."

II. Two Types of Information

During a project, designers define problems that require them to add to what they know. Gaps in knowledge may be specific (what is the lightest readily available building material in Brazil?) or general (what about life in Brazilian universities is applicable to the university I have been asked to design there?). Among the problems designers face are technological, chemical, economic, cultural, psychological, esthetic, social, and ecological ones to cope with the great amount of information needed. Some designers and researchers propose that design information must be explicitly formulated and rationally organized to make it easily retrievable.

Many practicing designers and some design methodologists react to this by pointing out that proposals that fit discrete bits of scientific information into an artificially rationalized design process hinder design creativity and overlook more important information needs that designers have (Hillier et al., 1972; Rapoport, 1969a).

Korobkin (1976) elegantly resolves this debate, asserting that knowing what different forms of information are useful to designers, and when in the design process, can stimulate design innovation. Korobkin groups information in the design process into two categories:

- *Image information* . . . provides a general understanding of important issues and of physical ideas pertinent to their resolution.
- Test information . . . [is] directly pertinent to evaluating the good and bad points of a given hypothesis design.
  This distinction is not necessarily one of information content. It primarily clarifies different purposes that the information serves (1976, p. 20).

Designers use "image information" heuristically as an empirical source for basic cognitive design decisions: What is the meaning of a school in a child's life? What is life like for a person with a disability? What do teenagers define as their neighborhoods in suburban areas? Image information conveys a feeling or a mood of some environment. It cannot be used to evaluate isolated specifics of a design concept. Test information drawn from the same body of knowledge

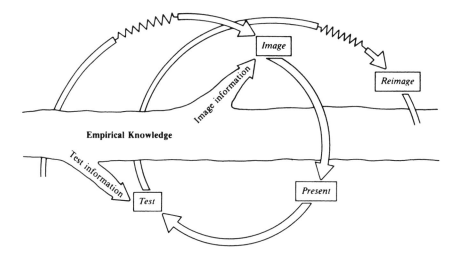

is useful to evaluate specific design alternatives. For example, is it easier for most older people who use wheelchairs to push themselves up from the toilet with a horizontal grab bar or to pull themselves up on a slanting grab bar? (For most, a horizontal bar is easier [Steinfeld, 1975, p. 98]).

Using information in this twofold way is remarkably efficient and contributes directly to design as a learning process. It also provides an important link to understand the relation between how research and design are carried out, in that "information which has been used heuristically [to help generate conjectures], can also be used to test the new conjectures" (Hillier, Musgrove, and O'Sullivan, 1972).

III. Shifting Visions of Final Product

What happens when designers test the responses they present? What do designers image? How do designs develop once conceived? Discussing questions like these sheds light on the dynamics of design.

As we have seen, designers form images of future products they intend to design. One reason designing is so intriguing is that "the final outcome of design has to be assumed before the means of achieving it can be explored: designers have to work backwards in time from an assumed effect upon the world to the beginning of a chain of events that will bring the effect about" (Jones, 1970: 9–10). Designers must predict the future and then figure out how to get there! Of course, such predictions are not precise; they are fuzzy predictions that the design process makes less approximate.

Images rarely appear fully formed in one cataclysmic blinding vision. Most images are developed and refined by means of a series of modest "creative leaps." The process by which such leaps are made has been called many things: variety reduction (Hillier and Leaman, 1974), reworking sub-objectives

(Archer, 1969), restoring balance (Sanoff, 1977), hypothesis refinement (O'Doherty, 1963), and transformation (Schon, 1974). Testing triggers creative leaping. Testing a tentative design response against quality criteria within the situation and its context to find out where the presentation is strong and where it is weak forces the designer to respond creatively.

Making tacit attributes of a design explicit through testing helps designers re-image and re-present their designs with greater precision (Schon, 1974). Testing makes contradictions apparent (1) among elements of a design at a particular stage of development and (2) between the design and previously accepted requirements it was intended to meet. Designers use this activity in the design process to learn from themselves: "New [design] options are versions of earlier ones growing out of the thinking that went into the rejection of earlier ones" (Schon, 1974, pp. 17–18). Critically analyzing tentative design responses and adding new information can progressively improve designs (Asimow, 1962; Guerra, 1969). Testing is essential to design as inquiry.

Designs develop cumulatively. Concepts originating in general form are developed to an acceptable level in a series of presentations, tests, and re-images. But what does "an acceptable level" mean? What is optimization (Markus, 1969) or fit (Alexander, 1964)? When do designers stop reducing variety? What is the goal of the design process?

IV. Toward a Domain of Acceptable Responses

Built buildings, constructed parks, manufactured objects, and enacted regulations may be seen as preordained, perfect end points that people reach by designing. To improve the way we design, however, it may be more useful to see final design products as unique responses to particular problems that fall within a set of alternatives controlled by our imagination, available technological knowledge, ethical values and personal skills, resources in the actual design situation, and our definition of quality.

Adjusting any of these values influences available alternatives. Using our imagination, increasing our substantive knowledge, or finding additional time and money resources broadens the range of possibilities. Paradoxically, no matter what designers do to control it, there is an infinite array of equally good potential responses in any *domain of acceptable responses* (Archer, 1969, p. 83).

If we think of design as a process of choosing the single best solution from among all possible alternatives, we run into difficulties. First, among an infinite number of possible alternatives there will be an infinite number of best ones. Second, for complex problems there may be no such thing as a best solution— and any problem can be as complex as one wants to see it.

> When we come to the design of systems as complex as cities, or buildings, or economies, we must give up the aim of creating systems that will optimize some hypothesized utility function; and we must consider whether differences do not represent highly desirable variants in the design process rather than alternatives to be evaluated as "better" or "worse." Variety, within the limits of satisfactory constraints, may be a desirable end in itself, among other reasons, because it permits

us to attach value to the search as well as its outcome—to regard the design process as itself a valued activity for those who participate in it (Simon, 1969, p. 75).

After such a discussion one may well ask how a designer decides what is acceptable. On what basis does she test and improve her designs? How does she decide on a final design to be built? In other words, what are their criteria for acceptability and quality?

Acceptability and quality criteria. These difficulties become clearer when we see designing not as an abstract intuitive process, but as a set of activities taking place in response to actual problems in actual situations. In the so-called real world, designers make decisions about practical, substantive attributes of the objects they design. These might be material properties like weight, elasticity, and strength; properties of the physical setting of the object like light, degree of urbanization, and soil conditions; or administrative properties of the object like cost, marketability, and construction scheduling. Designers use such attributes, along with available real-world resources, to test and improve their ideas and to decide when to end this process for any particular project.

Two sets of attributes describe designed objects in actual settings. First is *contextual responsiveness*, or the degree to which objects respond to external conditions. In southern climates, for example, do buildings protect users from direct sun while allowing breezes to provide natural cross-ventilation? In different cultures do building forms respond to the cultural expectations of residents (Brolin, 1976)? Second is *internal coherence*, or the degree to which components of a design object are consistent with one another (Archer, 1969, p. 101; Jones, 1970, p. 30). For example, in a northern climate do material selection, room arrangement, and site orientation each contribute to protection from the cold, or does one decision—say, to plan open spaces—counteract the effects of others?

The use of responsiveness and coherence as criteria to evaluate designed objects constitutes a significant link between design and science, as Simon points out:

> Natural science impinges on an artifact through two . . . terms . . . : the structure of the artifact itself and the environment in which it performs; and symmetrically, an artifact can be thought of as a meeting point—an "interface" in today's terms— between an "inner" environment, the substance and organization of the artifact itself, and an "outer" environment, the surroundings in which it operates (Simon, 1969: 6).

A complementary, two-sided approach to improving and evaluating the acceptability of a designed object underlies the work of architect and design methodologist Christopher Alexander. Identifying the importance of design appraisal, he describes acceptable designs as those that achieve a degree of "fit" between a "form in question and its context." To Alexander the artifact of design is form and context seen as one, not form alone.

This deceivingly simple idea has profoundly influenced design theory. The term *form* as Alexander (1964) uses it can be replaced by *internal coherence*, and *context* can be replaced by *external responsiveness*:

- *Form [Internal Coherence].* Indeed, the form itself relies on its own inner organization and on the internal fitness between the pieces it is made of to control its fit as a whole to the context outside (p. 18).
- *Context [External Responsiveness].* The context is that part of the world which puts demands on this form; anything in the world that makes demands of the form is context (p. 19).
- *Fitness [Acceptability].* Fitness is a relation of mutual acceptability between these two. In a problem of design we want to satisfy the mutual demands which the two make on one another (p. 19).

A difficulty still remains, however. How do designers decide to stop developing a product? When do they accept it as ready to be built?

- *Stopping.* Changing an environment has effects and side effects. Some may be visible beforehand, others not. Choosing to stop making one's product better means deciding one is willing to risk unintended side effects. What is considered an acceptable mix of knowing and risk in any actual situation reflects conditions like established professional norms, available resources, personal preferences, costs and rewards, and perceived competition.

Actual settings in which people design provide tools for making these decisions. The process of improving a design may stop, for example, when the allotted time and money have been spent and a design review team in the office judges that the product meets office standards. If the designer has an agreement with a client group that it has final say on the project, the group may make the decision to stop.

There are innumerable ways designers can use their surroundings to help them decide when a project is acceptable enough. What is significant is that *go rules* and *stop rules* are different. Quality criteria to improve a design constitute the go rules that keep the process going. One cannot rely on the same criteria to set limits—to stop the process. Stopping is the result of someone applying stop rules, declaring, for example, that there is no more time or money, and deciding that he or she is willing to live with the project's potential and as yet unseen side effects.

V. Development Through Linked Cycles: A Spiral Metaphor

The metaphor of design as a spiral process can be used to model how the various design elements fit together. A spiral process reflects the following characteristics of design: (1) designers backtrack at certain times—move away from, rather than toward, the goal of increasing problem resolution; (2) designers repeat the same series of activities again and again, resolving new problems with each repetition; and (3) these apparently multidirectional movements together result in one movement directed toward a single action.

- *Backtracking.* Throughout a design project, a designer returns to problems already studied to revise or adjust earlier tentative decisions (Archer, 1969, p. 95). For example, a landscape architect designs a park assuming the final budget will support construction of both a wading pool for children and a dec-

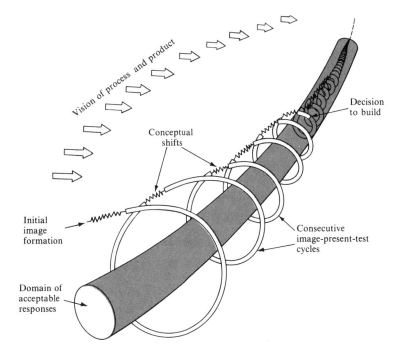

Design development spiral.

orative fountain. Later, finding that the larger playing field he wants costs more than expected, he combines the fountain and a wading pool into a single water project that meets both purposes.

It would be more efficient to focus on problems to resolve early in the process that do not have to be reexamined later, but this is seldom possible. Each decision designers make, even if they think it is final, has consequences for future steps in the process and, as we have seen, for past ones as well. Problems arise that earlier decisions did not foresee and that cannot be resolved unless a previous decision is revised (Jones, 1970: 68). Backtracking is not only unavoidable, it is essential to improve design quality (Amarel, 1968). One can hope that later knowledge will not necessitate radical changes in earlier decisions, but this does occur. Not surprisingly, a highly valued skill among designers is the ability to foresee the impact later design decisions will have on earlier ones.

Testing can be seen as a form of backtracking. "Whenever the designer pauses to evaluate what he has done . . . [he occasions] . . . feedback loops, shuttle action, and other departures from linearity indicated in most models of the decision sequence. These are introspective and retrospective acts; for he looks back to earlier decisions" (Markus, 1969, 112). In sum, backtracking to adjust earlier decisions is an integral part of design, and a spiral metaphor indicates this activity.

• *Repeating activities with shifting focus.* In each cycle of a design proj-ect, the designer presents, tests, and re-images responses to a set of related prob-lems. Each repetition focuses on a different problem. For example, in one cycle a designer may focus on architectural style, in another, on kitchen hardware. A decision in one cycle may determine the context for a decision in the next (for example, a decision about architectural style may limit the range of choices for hardware), but this does not mean that foci are necessarily sequential by size. Designers may find it more efficient to examine very large, very small, and then very large questions than to progress linearly from large to small or from small to large questions. For example, urban design decisions about street width may be followed by decisions about street hardware, which in turn are followed by decisions about the modes of transportation the streets will allow.

Design decisions in different cycles also vary by subject: physical elements like materials or room sizes at one point; at another, systems like heating or plumbing; and at still other times, psychological and social issues like territory or privacy.

Imaging, presenting, and testing are not equally important in each cycle. Designers tend to spend more time developing images in earlier cycles and more time presenting them in later ones. Testing can take place so quickly that design-ers appear to skip it entirely in a cycle; for example, when designers "think with their pen," testing can take place almost simultaneously with presenting and re-imaging. In such cases neither actor nor observer may be able to differentiate the activities—but all three must take place in each cycle for the process to progress.

The time designers spend in image/present/test cycles varies. One cycle may last days or weeks before a conceptual leap and eventual re-imaging take place. Another may last only seconds. And each activity in a cycle does not begin and end at a discrete point. Where one activity ends and another begins is not clear; each contains remnants of the previous activity and roots of the next.

One way to envision re-cycling and repetition is to think of design as a conversation among three activities: imaging, presenting, and testing. The dis-cussants remain the same, but the intensity and topics of the conversation change as time passes.

• *One movement in three.* Designers are like good hunters and trackers. They appraise their goal not by rushing straight at it but by continually read-justing their position to gain new perspectives on their prey. Backward move-ment, repetitions at different levels, and progressively linked cycles combine into one movement toward the goal of an acceptable response.

Growth and learning are essential parts of design. Once started, the process feeds itself both by drawing on outside information and by generating additional insight and information from within: "In the course of cycling the loop, the designer's perception of his real world problem, his concept of the design solution, grows" (Archer, 1969, 96).

The many adaptations, revisions, and conceptual shifts that take place during design are guided by a designer's vision of the design process leading to action. Something is built.

OVERVIEW

Farmers design when they figure out where and when to plant various crops. Lawyers design when they prepare a strategy for a client's defense. "Everyone designs who devises courses of action aimed at changing existing situations into preferred ones" (Simon, 1969, p. 55).

What architects, interior designers, landscape architects, industrial designers, and physical planners do can be seen as applying basic principles of action to solving a particular type of problem. Physical design as a formal set of disciplines presents opportunities for self-consciously analyzing design.

This chapter proposes that to organize our own design behavior to achieve the ends we want, it is helpful to see design as a loose ordering of three activities: imaging, presenting, and testing. Using a spiral metaphor to describe design enables people to identify some things they can do to use design as a way to grow and learn.

The next chapter describes research—its goals and uses, the way ideas develop, and the role individual researchers play in the process. Similarities between design and research are not pointed out explicitly in every case, yet it should be clear that there is a close kinship between design images and research concepts, design presentations and research hypotheses, and tests in both disciplines.

CHAPTER 2

RESEARCH: CONCEPTS, HYPOTHESES, AND TESTS

A cobblestone is more real than personal relationships, but personal relationships are felt to be more profound because we expect them yet to reveal themselves in unexpected ways, while cobblestones evoke no such expectation.

— MICHAEL POLANYI
Personal Knowledge

Research provides deeper insight into a topic, better understanding of a problem, more clearly defined opportunities for and constraints on possible action, measurement of regularities, and ordered descriptions. Designers face many problems in which they use environment-behavior (E-B) research to control the effects of what they do. What street layout, sign system, and landmark location in a new town will make it easy for residents to feel at home? Why do teenagers vandalize isolated buildings in parks that they themselves could otherwise enjoy? Does high-density living make people friendlier or meaner? What does density actually mean?

What is research? It is more than just searching (which can be haphazard) or solving problems (which can remain merely pragmatic). Researchers want to use their experience systematically to learn something that will help identify and solve new problems. Presented with a problem, researchers draw on theory, training, accumulated knowledge, and experience to generate tentative ideas about how to solve it. Exploratory hypotheses serve as the basis first for observing and gathering data about the topic and then for describing and understanding it. Making visible the implications of the data leads to improved hypotheses, further data gathering, and so on until the problem is sufficiently redefined and a tenable solution found.

In the course of their work, investigators develop concepts, formulate hypotheses, and test their ideas. During a research project, investigators carry out these activities in various sequences and combinations and in various ways. This complex activity is called "research."

```
┌─────────────────────────────────┐
│  Doing Research                 │
├─────────────────────────────────┤
│                                 │
│  Developing Concepts            │
│                                 │
│      Characteristics            │
│      Approaches                 │
│      Preconceptions             │
│                                 │
│  Formulating Hypotheses         │
│                                 │
│      Classifying hypotheses     │
│      Explanatory hypotheses     │
│                                 │
│  Empirical Testing              │
│                                 │
│      Observing                  │
│      Sampling                   │
│                                 │
└─────────────────────────────────┘
```

Anyone can become a researcher by doing normal, everyday things in an orderly way and for interesting purposes that can be generalized. The orderly way to do research can be learned rationally and impersonally. The ability to develop interesting concepts—to go beyond the information given—can also be learned, but it is a creative ability to be learned as one learns a skill.

DEVELOPING CONCEPTS

In a research project investigators aim to define a concept with which to order information. A research concept does not pop out of the data; it is formed slowly. Investigators may have a faint vision of it when their project begins. They may glimpse it when they start to analyze a particular bit of data. They may realize how to organize their study findings only when the last piece of information becomes clear.

In the beginning of a project, emerging concepts are visions defining what data to gather. In the middle, information clarifies the concepts. At the end of a successful research project, clearly stated concepts summarize increased insight and define areas where further research can increase precision.

Characteristics

Creative researchers invent and discover. In E-B studies innovation has given us concepts to order what we see: personal space (Sommer, 1969), the hidden (spatial) dimension (Hall, 1966), urban villages (Gans, 1962), and the image of the city (Lynch, 1960). Sommer, Hall, Gans, and Lynch carried out research to its full creative potential, giving others new images with which to illuminate part of the world.

The concept of personal space explains why low lighting levels in bars bring couples closer together, why others get upset when we read over their shoulders, why psychiatric clients feel that counselors who sit far away are not receptive, and why passengers waiting in airports feel uncomfortable when seats bolted to the floor prohibit adjusting their seating arrangements. The concept of city images helps us understand why most of us see cities in terms of elements such as the Eiffel Tower and London Bridge (which Lynch calls "landmarks"), Harvard Square and Times Square (which he calls "nodes"), the Charles River and Lake Michigan ("edges"), the Los Angeles freeways and the Amsterdam canals ("paths"), and Greenwich Village and Chinatown ("districts").

Polanyi concisely defines the intangible activity of discovery by which an investigator describes something he cannot see:

> How can we concentrate our attention on something we don't know? Yet this is precisely what we are told to do: "Look at the unknown!"—says Polya (1945)— "Look at the ends . . . *Look at the unknown*. Look at the conclusion!" No advice could be more emphatic. The seeming paradox is resolved by the fact that even though we have never met the solution, we have a conception of it in the same sense as we have a conception of a forgotten name . . . *we should look at the known data, but not in themselves, rather as clues to the unknown, as pointers to it and parts of it.* We should strive persistently to feel our way towards an understanding of the manner in which these known particulars hang together, both mutually and with the unknown (1958, pp. 127–128).

Explanatory concepts tend to be *holistic*; they describe entities that cannot be analyzed into the sum of their parts without residue. Personal space is not merely the sum of body movements, cultural habits, and attitudes toward one's own body. A designer's office cannot be fully defined by describing the people there, the settings, the rules, the services, and the output. The holistic character of concepts is like that of a chord in music: "The musical chord . . . as long as it is a chord, is utterly different from its component tones. It does not even have tones until it is analyzed. Indeed, one cannot say that it is a synthesized whole until this is done; otherwise it is an elementary phenomenon" (Barnett, 1953, p. 193).

By reasonably extending creative research concepts, investigators generate new problems to study and new hypotheses. For this reason such a concept is sometimes called a *generating formula*: "a formula capable of summing up in a single descriptive concept a great wealth of particular observations" (Barton and Lazarsfeld, 1969, p. 192). Gans's "urban village" concept is just such a formula. In describing the group of people living in Boston's primarily Italian West End neighborhood during the 1960s, Gans points out an essential contradiction in their lives. Social relations among residents are almost like those in a rural village: people know one another well, they get their news from friends at local bars, and they know who does and does not "belong." But economic and political life are embedded in an urban context: residents work in the city, they elect representatives to the city council, and university students from the city come to the West End to live.

Summing up this neighborhood in the term *urban village* raises a host of questions: If village residents hold mainly local values, how do they react to the constant influx of outsiders? Does the village nature of the neighborhood result in tighter social control over crime? What pressures does the urban context exert on family life? With this generating formula in mind, one can recognize urban villages in other cities as well. Before Gans's invention these districts were not clearly identifiable.

Approaches

How do researchers develop concepts? One approach to this murky task is to move in two directions simultaneously, becoming both as intimate as possible with data and as distant as possible from them at the same time.

Intimacy for one researcher may mean stewing over a particular photograph or staring at a sketch of a childhood home a respondent has drawn to find what sense can be made of it. Another investigator may look intently at data arranged on a Geographic Information System (GIS) map or read through a large number of completed questionnaires from beginning to end, getting a feel for what to ask the data. These methods enable an investigator to focus her attention on particulars of diverse phenomena until she begins to see them as a coherent whole, just as a musician practices a piece until it comes together for him. The term *indwelling* is used to refer to these methods, to make clear that they are attempts to become as close as possible to the data—to dwell in them (Polanyi, 1967, 16).

When researchers achieve such internal awareness, they cannot necessarily articulate it—either verbally or diagrammatically. Another step, such as using *analogies* as organizing principles, is required to articulate the tacit knowing that indwelling can bring. Analogies enable researchers to use related past experience to articulate how they envision fitting data together. In analogies "there is a sameness of relationship—but a substitution of its parts. These parts may be things, or they may be behaviors or ideas. In any event, there is a change of the content . . . but a retention of its shape or form because of the retention of relationships" (Barnett, 1953, 267).

Thinking of analogies to summarize a large body of information temporarily enables investigators to picture and use what they do not know by substituting known elements for gaps in their knowledge. For example, the idea of map reading may help someone describe the way people envision the future, and the idea of a theater lobby may help someone else describe the channeling operations carried out in a hospital emergency room. Analogies are holistic mental models that, although not derivable from the data, can be used to organize them.

Discovering scientific images and generating scientific concepts demand inspiration, imagination, and intuition:

> True discovery is not a strictly logical performance, and accordingly, we may describe the obstacle to be overcome in solving a problem as a "logical gap," and speak of the width of the logical gap as the measure of the ingenuity required for solving the problem. "Illumination" is then the leap by which the logical gap is

crossed. It is the plunge by which we gain a foothold at another shore of reality. On such plunges the scientist has to stake bit by bit his entire professional life . . . .

Established rules of inference offer public paths for drawing intelligent conclusions from existing knowledge. The pioneer mind, which reaches its own distinctive conclusions by crossing a logical gap, deviates from the commonly accepted process of reasoning, to achieve surprising results (Polanyi, 1958, 123).

Preconceptions

Researchers do not approach problems with empty minds. Each researcher knows something about his particular problem from related empirical work and theories. Personal experience also influences how we look at the world: early family life, school, trips, friends, professional training, and books. As we think and talk, we draw on a mental picture of our topic that is either vague or clear, and is held either consciously or subconsciously (Korobkin, 1976). When our topic is a physical environment, we call our mental picture a "cognitive map"; when it is less tangible and more conceptual, a related term—*cognitive image*—can be used (Boulding, 1973). The more we think we know about a topic, the more detailed is our cognitive image of it. The preconceived images with which investigators begin research projects can distort what researchers see, bias explanations, and limit how concepts develop. But they do not have to.

Made explicit as a first step in research projects, preconceptions can be helpful. For example, in a study of how people work and feel in open-plan offices, one researcher might begin with a preconception that everyone will be miserable because there is no privacy. Another investigator expects everyone to be smiling and happy because the lack of walls brings people together. These preconceptions, or advance guesses, no matter where they come from, can be used as reference points for future observations.

Explicit preconceptions like these can sensitize researchers to see and to be surprised by what they see. In our hypothetical open-plan office, because both researchers thought about workers' happiness, both will look for indicators of attitudes: smiles or frowns, backslapping, chatting, angry looks, fights. Both researchers will be able to improve their pictures of the situation. Each preconception made explicit at the beginning of an investigation serves as a useful sensitizing tool and as a beacon pointing out realms for fruitful data gathering.

FORMULATING HYPOTHESES

To improve concepts and preconceptions, investigators confront them with empirical evidence and other concepts. This is possible if concepts are testable and presented tangibly—whether they be statements about possible resolutions to an investigator's problem, diagrams, drawings, or even buildings.

Investigators initially formulate exploratory hypotheses based on theory and previous empirical data; then they use preliminary, unfocused investigation to decide what specific data they will use to confront these hypotheses. As data are gathered and made more visible, descriptive hypotheses are developed with which investigators seem to say, "This is what I think I see." More detailed information determines the tenability of such hypotheses. The more-tenable ones help investigators organize, simplify, and explain ever-greater amounts of related information in explanatory hypotheses that enable investigators to make explicit the holistic conceptual framework they have been developing.

Complex and sophisticated possible solutions to a problem—that is, hypotheses—can be thought of as conceptual models analogous to the physical models that designers use. Designers' models, often constructed of lightweight wood, clay, fiberboard, or colored paper, are scaled reductions of the intended final product. Physical models represent abstract attributes of a concept: massing of buildings, openness of space, or clustering of elements. Sometimes they represent what the actual final building might look like. Constructed early in the process, designers' working models are usually inexpensive and easily dismantled, so that they can change rapidly as designs develop, just as hypotheses change quickly under the influence of newly gathered information when a research project develops.

Models represent the intended resolution of problems in mathematical, symbolic, physical, or some other form. Investigators and designers can therefore learn from models by observing what happens to them under different conditions, as if they were the final research or design concept. Developing and testing working hypotheses and working models allows researchers to make major adjustments in approach before such changes would mean destroying the whole project and starting from scratch.

The following discussion points out some important types of hypotheses, moving from simpler to more sophisticated ones.

Classifying Hypotheses

Classifying hypotheses orders available information so that researchers can more clearly define their problem and decide how to study it further. Explanatory hypotheses, described later, address the roots of a problem and identify possible solutions.

• *List of types.* A simple way to order information is to classify it into a list of types. When Weiss and Bouterline (1962) wanted to understand why exhibits at the Seattle World's Fair differentially interested visitors, they started by noting how much time visitors spent at each of thirty-three exhibits in five pavilions. Because they felt that describing each exhibit separately would not lead to better general rules about how to design interesting exhibits, they grouped the exhibits into seven major types: (1) participation exhibits, with which visitors somehow interact; (2) demonstration exhibits, where a person acts as a guide or teacher; (3) models of objects or complex phenomena (subdivided into full-scale, small-scale, and complex teaching models); (4) panel exhibits with still or moving lights; (5) filmstrips that include a voice narration and tell a story; (6) totally housed exhibits that separate visitors from outside distractions; and (7) animal exhibits. These rough exhibit types over-

Motive \ *Consequence*	Instantaneous Damage Demanding Immediate Attention	Cumulative Damage Demanding Eventual Attention
Conscious	Malicious Vandalism (Example: Window broken in principal's office)	Nonmalicious Damage (Example: Hockey goal painted on blank wall with spray paint)
Not Purposeful	Misnamed Vandalism (Example: Window broken at basketball court)	Maintenance Damage (Example: Lawn eroded by shortcuts)

Substructure of property damage.

lap at times; nevertheless, the list enabled the researchers to ascertain that certain demonstrations, filmstrips with story lines, and animal exhibits held visitors' interest the longest. Further explanation of why these "types" work the way they do could be useful in deciding how to convey public information effectively.

   • *Substructures.* Investigators also organize information by structuring it within a descriptive ordering system. This organizing system may be constructed by juxtaposing several attributes that describe the research problem. For example, degree of legibility and impact on behavior might describe how a sign system works. The organizing principle may also be a system of nested physical parts; for a hospital the parts might be beds, rooms, nursing stations, wards, floors, and buildings. Juxtaposed attributes or parts form a multi-celled table, or matrix, in which each cell represents one of a total set of possible combinations of variable values (Barton & Lazarsfeld, 1969).

   Such a table can be used to identify dimensions of a problem for further study. For example, Zeisel (1976a) redefined the term *vandalism* and identified fruitful research avenues by substructuring the problem of school property damage. Interviews and a literature review showed the research team that the broad term *vandalism* means different things to different people. The team realized that to remedy discrete and manageable problems, they had to introduce more-precise terms. They began by listing the ways that people used the term: all property damage; vicious kids attacking a building because they hate it; graffiti; desecration of religious buildings.

   Further analysis was organized according to two attributes: whether "vandals" are conscious of the damage they do and whether the damage requires immediate repair if the school is to continue working adequately. Combining these two dimensions generated a substructure clarifying different kinds of vandalism and providing direction for the rest of the study.

Explanatory Hypotheses

Investigators, look at the implications of their problem organization and at the data they gather, to develop tentative answers to the questions "How did something occur?" and "Why did someone do something?" Some answers come from subjects who describe why they think they did something and give details about their motives and the intended consequences of their actions. For instance, an office worker may tell the researcher that she moves her desk away from the window to avoid glare on her computer screen.

In designing a housing project in South Carolina, architect Brent Brolin provided pairs of houses set back alternately closer to and further from the street with adjacent driveways for each pair of houses instead of a driveway on the same side of every house (Zeisel, 1971). He intended to increase the chances that neighbors would run into each other and possibly become friendly and to make a street that residents would feel is less regular and more attractive. Each of these conscious intentions can be turned into a hypothesis and tested. Do neighbors with adjacent driveways meet more than other neighbors? Are they more friendly? Are streets perceived as irregular? Tests of conscious intentions explain part of the story. Building on them, researchers can generate hypotheses having to do with unforeseen and unintended consequences of actions. Explanations of actions that refer to an actor's intent can be called *manifest* explanations; explanations that refer to unforeseen effects can be called *latent* explanations (Merton, 1957).

Latent explanations, once formulated, are also testable. But they are harder to formulate because they are unexpected by participants and often are based initially on a researcher's theoretical expectations rather than empirical observation (Zeisel, 1978).

Gans's *Levittowners* (1967) provides a basis for hypotheses about the possible latent effects of adjacent driveways. Gans found that next-door or across-the-street neighbors do tend to meet often. But he also found unexpected consequences of contact between neighbors in Levittown: The contact is not always as friendly as planners might predict. When neighboring children ride bikes, roller-skate, and play together on driveways, they sometimes fight.

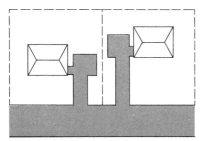
Adjacent driveways

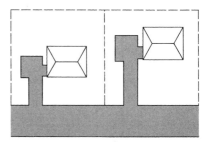
Parallel driveways

Layout of driveways in Spartanburg, South Carolina housing project.
Site design by Brent C. Brolin.

Children soon forget fights and go back to playing; parents do not. Parents expect the aggressor—usually the neighbor's child—to be punished in the same way they would punish their own child.

Levittown neighbors—although earning roughly equivalent salaries—came from different cultural backgrounds with different attitudes toward child rearing and punishment. Some parents believed more in hitting children, others more in disciplining children verbally. Gans found neighbors fighting because they were not satisfied that a child had been sufficiently punished or were unhappy that the punishment was too severe. Brolin's shared driveways, by bringing neighbors together, might also drive them apart.

Research that generates and tests both manifest and latent explanations is likely to provide new insights into a problem.

EMPIRICAL TESTING

You may test hypotheses by confronting them with empirical data and other hypotheses. If no data have yet been gathered, you might carry out empirical research specifically to test a set of hypotheses. If all data in a study have been collected, however, hypotheses are tested by reassessing those data from another point of view—by analyzing and ordering them in new ways. Testing hypotheses leads to their replacement, improvement, and refinement and to reformulating them for further testing.

Part Two of this book describes observation and interview techniques that can be used to help develop and test hypotheses about E-B problems. This section focuses on methodological questions useful in organizing such research, no matter which technique one uses.

Observing

When a patient goes into a hospital for "observation," doctors and nurses do more than just look. They also measure temperature and blood pressure, they take X rays, and they make specimen analyses.

As used here, the term *observation* is similarly broad. It means looking at phenomena connected to a problem by whatever means necessary: looking with one's eyes, asking questions, using mechanical measurement devices, and so on.

Single observations. One observation is the simplest research datum: a smile, a park, a movement, an answer to a question, an event. Single observations that surprise the observer tend to indicate interesting research avenues because such observations conflict with exploratory hypotheses formulated from theory, from other empirical research, or from common sense.

As a researcher it is useful to keep your mind open to things you do not see—to be surprised by what does not happen. Given some direction, commonplace observations of things most people do not notice become strange and problematic. "The ability to take a commonplace fact and see it as raising problems is important because it can lead to . . . enlightenment" (Barton and Lazarsfeld, 1969, 168).

Whyte's research on how people use open spaces, plazas, and streets in New York City (1980) provides an illuminating example. Whyte wanted to provide city planners with information to help them design pedestrian zones to accommodate the large diversity of needs of various users like pedestrians, window-shoppers, people watchers, and peddlers. During preliminary research on busy sidewalks, he noticed that pedestrians chose to converse in places where they most disrupted other pedestrian traffic—in the middle of traffic and near crosswalks.

This seemingly common observation raised problems: Was it a freak occurrence or part of a recurring pattern? What type of conversation was taking place? Why were speakers apparently so unreasonable that they would not get out of the way? Further research led to the hypothesis that finding a more convenient place to stand would commit the talkers to continue for a long time. Standing precariously in traffic made it easy for either person to break off the conversation at any moment.

• *Regularities.* One way to test a hypothesis developed from a single observation is to look for other observations like it—for example, other people conversing in traffic. This is particularly relevant if the problem you are studying aims to do something that affects such a pattern: designing sidewalks to accommodate regular uses or designing schools to avoid major types of nonmalicious property damage.

Looking for a regularity and not finding it makes visible another regularity—its absence. If, for example, Whyte had first observed one couple speaking near a wall and looked for this as a pattern, he would have naturally been led to notice the recurrence of in-traffic conversations. When investigators find no other observations like the first, this too is useful. For example, in other U.S. cities, a planner may find no park as large as New York's Central Park. If she is studying problems associated with designing urban environmental legislation, it may be helpful to know why no landscape architect since Olmsted has achieved this unique feat.

A surprising regularity or unique event raises questions: Why does it occur? What effect does it have? What does each one mean? How can others use it? What can be done to change or accommodate it? To improve one's answers to such questions, it is often helpful to look not for more of the same, but at other things connected to it—namely, its context.

• *Contexts.* To test an explanatory hypothesis of an observed event, researchers use its context—how the event is both linked to it and isolated from it. The context of Whyte's sidewalk talkers included others around them, their motives and attitudes, their destination, time of day, and location. Although not everything in an event's context is significant to solving a researcher's problem, some things are likely to be.

For example, a team of researchers in Baltimore studied an urban rowhouse neighborhood with small playgrounds adjacent to the backyards and stoops in front of the houses. They wanted to know whether these playgrounds were used, and if not, why not. They observed more people using the front stoops than the playgrounds in back (Brower, 1977). To understand why, the research team looked to the context. Brower noticed that when residents sat on the stoops, they talked together, visited each other, watched strangers passing by, and supervised children playing on the sidewalk. On the basis of these findings, he developed, tested, and refined the hypothesis that residents felt their neighborhood network included people who lived on the vehicular and pedestrian street in front of the houses rather than the people on the physical block whose backyards were next to the common playground areas.

In sum, testing your hypotheses against empirical data requires that someone first make interesting observations that shed light on your problem. To do this, no matter what observation techniques and methods you use, it is essential to see significant single events, to perceive regularities over events, and to take into account the context of your problem. This approach will help you use the real world to improve the way you look at it, what you know about it, and the actions you take in it.

Sampling

When you test an idea by gathering empirical evidence, you *may* be able to examine every instance in which the idea is relevant. For example, when studying the 212-unit Charlesview housing development, Zeisel and Griffin (1975) used the "census technique" to test the hypothesis that residents were more likely to decorate and personalize enclosed front yards than non-enclosed backyards. They observed every front and back yard and found that, of the forty-nine residents with enclosed front yards, over 80 percent planted grass and flowers or kept furniture there, whereas fewer than 10 percent decorated their backyards.

It is not always possible, however, to observe every instance in which your hypothesis might apply. You may not have the resources to find all the people or situations that have a certain characteristic. The group you want to study may be too undefined, as were the crowds of New Yorkers Whyte (1980) observed on sidewalks. Or you may want to say something about the likelihood of future events, which are clearly impossible to observe.

Such natural limitations lead researchers who want to generalize to take a sample of people, places, or events in order to say something about a larger group. Generalizing always entails some error, however, as researchers may generalize too much, too little, or in the wrong way.

Festinger, Schachter, and Back (1950) probably generalized too much. They observed that married MIT students living in apartments or houses with locations that forced the students to cross paths with certain neighbors tended to choose those neighbors as friends more often than neighbors living the same physical distance away whose paths they did not have to cross. These researchers and others used these observations to develop a more general principle—that physical distance, together with "functional distance" (the likelihood of daily chance encounters), leads to increased liking among residential neighbors. It took Gans (1967) to point out that the generalization probably holds only when housing residents are homogeneous in background and interests—as were most of the married MIT students Festinger and his team studied. Gans found that neighbors in the planned community of Levittown tended to choose as their friends those neighbors they considered most compatible, whether they lived adjacent to them or across the street.

Certain sampling procedures can help to reduce errors that you know you will have when you test hypotheses and generalize the results. *Randomizing* procedures help control error from sources you do not anticipate. *Matching* or *stratifying* procedures are used to reduce the chance of errors from conditions that previous knowledge says are likely to influence your results. Randomizing and matching procedures can be combined to reduce overall generalization error in a particular situation.

• *Randomizing.* E-B researchers often study diverse groups of people, places, and environments they know little about relative to the hypothesis being tested. For example, if you wanted to study people buying tickets at an airport in order to plan an airline terminal, you probably would not know in advance what influences their ticket-buying behavior: their age, cultural background, or how they feel that day. Randomizing procedures are used to disperse such characteristics in the sample as they are dispersed in the population, so that the generalization error they cause is reduced. Interestingly, you do not have to trace how a characteristic is dispersed to control its effects.

Randomizing is not only a useful idea, but also a surprising one. If you draw a random sample from a large group, you can generalize or project results from the sample onto the group within statistically definable limits. For example, from a randomly selected sample of 1,500 people, political pollsters can predict within an accuracy of 3 percent how 70 million people will vote. Another surprising attribute of randomizing is that the accuracy with which you can project from randomly chosen sample data to a population depends mostly on the absolute size of the sample, not on the ratio of the sample size to the size of the population. In other words, generalization error from a suitable sample of 1,500 will be the same whether you project your results to a town with a population of 50,000 or to a city with a population of 5,000,000.

"Random" in this context does not mean haphazard, helter-skelter, or unsystematic, as it does in everyday usage. Its meaning is actually closer to "unpredictable" or "by chance." Specifically, the word "random" as used in statistics is a technical term describing the process by which a sample is chosen. The principle of random sampling is simple: selection of the sample group must be left to chance, so that every member of the population and every combination of members has the same opportunity of being selected.

A common-sense way to select a random sample is to put names or numbers of elements on pieces of paper, drop them into a hat, and have someone choose a few with his eyes closed. But this procedure can be inexact: If some pieces of paper stick together, that group of elements has a higher chance of being selected than any other group; if the hat is not thoroughly shaken, numbers or names put in last have a higher chance of being chosen. We could go on for quite some time thinking of things that can and do go wrong when sampling is carried out manually.

Researchers who want to select random samples for actual projects can use a computer-generated table of random numbers. In E-B research, the simple device of taking every nth name from a list will often suffice as a "systematic" random sampling procedure, assuming that the interval n is unconnected to what you want to test. If there is no list, you can make one—for instance, by observing every tenth person in line at a ticket agent's counter.

• *Matching.* When you want to observe a sample from a larger population with which you are familiar, and you think that a characteristic of the larger group will affect what you observe, you can match the sample to the larger group on that characteristic. For example, suppose you are interested in what the residents of a neighborhood feel about having a playground located near their homes. You are likely to get different answers when interviewing women, especially those with children, than when interviewing men. Stratifying the proportion of men and women you include in the sample to reflect the proportion of men and women actually living in the neighborhood will reduce error when you project from your sample to the whole neighborhood.

The same principle applies when observing behavior over time. You would get a very unusual picture if you observed airline ticket counters only on Friday afternoons and Monday mornings, the peak traffic hours. Because experience says that air traffic varies with the cycles of the day, week, and year, you want to be certain to include all periods of the day, days of the week, and possibly months of the year in the random sample of times you choose to observe.

Researchers carrying out experiments match groups before observing them, constructing experimental groups in which an experimental change is introduced and control groups in which no planned change is made. For example, an experiment might be designed to test the hypothesis that people's reactions to interviews vary with an increase in the size of the interview room. If the researchers think that age and professional experience with interviews could affect the study results, they would match the two groups to make certain that the experimental group did not comprise mainly older doctors and lawyers while the control group contained mostly college freshmen. Otherwise, should the researchers find a difference between the groups, they would not know how to generalize the results: Is the observed difference due to the experimental manipulation or to the different makeup of the groups?

• *Combining randomizing and matching procedures.* When researchers want to reduce generalization error from both known and unknown causes, they use a mixture of randomizing and matching (or stratifying) procedures to select their sample. For example, suppose the population you want to find out about contains five important subgroups. After dividing the population into these subgroups, you would randomly select individuals from each subgroup for your sample. Similarly, after grouping the times of day, week, and year, you would use randomizing procedures to decide what particular times you were going to observe.

When researchers test a hypothesis by confronting it with empirical data, they will want to generalize these results to new situations. Using randomizing and matching procedures to organize empirical tests enables them to reduce, estimate, and control the errors inherent in making generalizations.

OVERVIEW

Research is essentially a creative endeavor requiring a subtle blend of personal skill and impersonal order. Relying only on order in research minimizes individual responsibility and risk. Although it shows that you know how to play the game, it also limits the contribution research can make to new knowledge.

This chapter stresses the importance of personal knowledge (Polanyi, 1958) and skill in developing concepts, formulating hypotheses, and testing them. The chapter also proposes that researchers can achieve the results they want by systematically presenting and testing concepts as they are developed. The methodological principles presented for organizing research are intended to enable the investigator to control his or her own research activities and their consequences.

The next chapter discusses reasons designers and researchers work together, occasions they have for cooperation, and problems they resolve by doing so.

CHAPTER 3

RESEARCH AND
DESIGN COOPERATION

And the Lord said, Behold, the people is one, and they have all one language; and this they begin to do: and now nothing will be restrained from them, which they have imagined to do.

— *Genesis 11:6*

People look to cooperate with others when they want to do more than they can do alone.

An architect is commissioned to design an open-plan office building that the clients can periodically reevaluate and redesign as their needs change. The designer has no problem designing a quality office building. But he has no tools in his arsenal to assess the effects periodic redesign might have on the clients' organization.

An environment-behavior researcher is funded to study impacts of physical environment on hospital patients' self-confidence. She has no problem documenting the state of knowledge about this issue, studying people in existing settings, and developing research hypotheses to test. But she has no tools in her arsenal to predict how using her information will change designs.

Research and design cooperation grows out of the variability of social reality: boundaries of problems change, situations differ, viewpoints are flexible, and people grow. The solutions that designers or researchers provide to their own problems have side effects in the other discipline. Cooperation is fostered when designers or researchers decide they want to use the other discipline as a tool to improve their control over side effects—that is, to solve more broadly defined problems than they can solve alone.

PURPOSES OF COOPERATION

Researchers' Purposes

One reason researchers work with designers is to increase the control they have over testing hypotheses. Researchers who want both to generate and to improve knowledge want to test it. When applied environment-behavior researchers happen to find actual physical settings that are well suited to testing their ideas, they usually adjust their hypotheses and research goals to learn what these available settings allow them to learn. The more involved researchers are in making decisions about the setting in which ideas will be tested, the more they can learn.

Research and Design Cooperation

Purposes of Cooperation

    Researchers' purposes
    Designers' purposes

Occasions for Cooperation

    Programming
    Design review
    Evaluation research

Researchers who want their information to be used by and useful to others want to know about the types of problems designers have that E-B studies can help solve. What types of E-B design problems do landscape architects face most often? What unsolved design problems have the most critical behavioral side effects for designers? Do clients ask designers questions about the impact of rules on behavior in physical settings? What commonsense and generally accepted perspectives about people have the greatest chance of being revised on the basis of research? When researchers choose to study E-B problems and eventually present problems and their solutions to designers, one measure of success is the degree to which designers find the problems relevant to their concerns. Researchers work with designers to find out what these concerns are—that is, to identify problems that designers may not see themselves but will realize immediately when research makes them apparent.

Researchers who want to share their information with designers want to know how designers work. Understanding how architects make decisions enables researchers to present research information in a form that meets decision makers' schedules. The clearer the process of using information in design is to researchers, the easier it is to modify that process so it can better accommodate new types of information. The boundaries between decision-making and information development can be examined and, for certain purposes, improved. When meshing like this takes place, there is a greater chance that research information will be tested in practice.

The research and design case studies that end each chapter in this book demonstrate not only how research contributes to improved design, but also how involvement in design increases consultants' knowledge. There is also precedent for applied research activity among non-environmentally oriented behavioral scientists who presently make decisions or advise others who make decisions in hospitals, schools, social work agencies, policy-making offices, and many other settings where people understand that behavioral research information and perspectives are useful. Investigators learn from such situations partly by making hypothetical predictions, evaluating outcomes, and modifying their hypotheses. They are also able to identify interesting problems and research issues in such settings. By working with decision makers, they learn how to organize their information to respond to the needs of those who use it. Methodological and substantive advances in science are significantly helped by the exchange and use of information between basic and applied scientific settings (Lazarsfeld, Sewell, and Wilensky, 1967).

Designers' Purposes

Designers have a different problem: Although their main objective is to change physical settings, they want to control the behavioral effects of the design decisions they make. They want their buildings, open spaces, and objects to meet the social, psychological, and developmental needs of those who use them. This is not easy in our increasingly complex society, where designers often build for strangers and strange groups. The gap between decision maker and user is too great to be overcome by designers using only a personal perspective. If government regulations or the free market would ensure that users' needs were taken into account, there would be no problem. But this is not the case.

The gap that designers face between themselves and those who put their designs to use has developed historically. In primitive societies everyone could and did build his own house, "designing" according to one model of a building. This model was developed and adjusted over generations to satisfy cultural, climatic, physical, and maintenance requirements (Rapoport, 1969b, 1–8).

As trades became increasingly specified, what Rapoport calls *vernacular design traditions* emerged. Everyone still knew the traditional rules of construction, organization, and style, but craftspeople knew them in greater detail. Because craftspeople and clients shared an "image of life" (Rapoport, 1969b, 6), they could work together to introduce individual variation into accepted residential and ceremonial building models while still respecting the traditions that the models embodied.

Since the Industrial Revolution several new ways to design and construct buildings have developed. In the marketplace, users affect decisions through selective buying. The gap between designer and user has grown, but market research and the sensitivity of builders to market conditions can narrow it, resulting in open-market buildings that embody commonly held values even though users did not participate directly in the design. One example is the Levittown development tract (Gans, 1967), which included such design elements as pitched roofs, picture windows, and large front lawns.

In another tradition, designers contract with individual clients who request styled, one-of-a-kind buildings. Clients pay for the building, criticize it during design, and eventually use it personally. To determine clients' needs, designers negotiate with them to reach an agreement on design. In such settings clients may delegate considerable authority to the professionals they pay because they want to benefit from the special expertise these professionals have: expertise about such things as style, methods, and materials.

The most dramatic postindustrial development in environmental design began when people concentrated around factories in cities and new technology enabled construction of large buildings. Governments, factory owners, corporations, and other often well-intentioned groups of people contracted with designers to construct settings and objects for masses of people to use daily: parks, furniture, schools, hospitals, appliances, playgrounds, offices, dormitories. In mass design like this, designers have two clients: those who pay for what is built and those who use it (Madge, 1968). The user client has no choice and no control. This situation presents designers with a problem: no matter how much they negotiate with paying clients, it is difficult to plan for the needs of user clients, who are neither well known nor readily available to plan with.

To solve or at least improve the user client problem, designers, adminis-

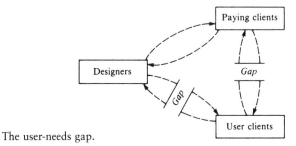

The user-needs gap.

trators, researchers, users, and others have developed mechanisms that change the boundary between designers and user clients. Citizen-participation techniques that include user clients as members of design teams, giving them control that is traditionally reserved for paying clients, is one way to change the boundary. Flexible building frameworks, with partitions and even alternative façades (Habraken, 1972; Wampler, 1968), provide user clients with more direct control over their surroundings by enabling them to adapt a structure themselves. Each design case study in this book highlights inventive techniques a team of designers and an E-B consultant has employed to change the boundaries among designer, researcher, paying client, and user clients. E-B research changes the boundary by making more visible to designers the needs, desires, and reactions of users to their surroundings, thus enabling designers to better negotiate with users and understand the effects decisions will have on them. Solving the user client problem offers both researchers and designers opportunities to learn from users and from each other.

OCCASIONS FOR COOPERATION

The day-to-day practice of design offers at least three occasions for research and design cooperation: (1) *design programming* research for designing a particular project; (2) *design review* to assess the degree to which designs reflect existing E-B research knowledge; and (3) *post-occupancy evaluation (POE)* of built projects in use. Each occasion contributes to the fund of *basic E-B knowledge*, improving our general ability to solve design and research problems (Conway, 1973; Zeisel, 1975, 20).

Design Programming

Design contracts may specify that either the client or the client together with the designer is responsible for stating clearly what the building (or other setting) is expected to do. This document is called the "program" and the process of preparing it "programming."[1]

Programs reflect a broad array of concerns affecting design decisions. Economic, cultural, stylistic, ecological, structural, sociological, and psychological concerns are just a few. Strictly *quantitative programs* specify design goals

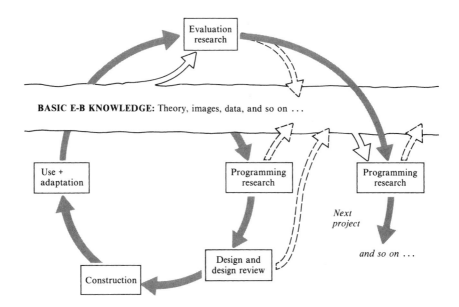

Occasions for research/design cooperation in the design-process cycle.

and requirements in terms of amount of floor space, minimum room dimensions for certain uses, types of spaces, specific materials and hardware, maximum cost estimates, and minimum window area in proportion to floor area. In programs such as these, the level of performance for design concerns generally remains implicit. For example, a landscape architect's program might specify that particular park benches will have a certain durability, ease of maintenance, and economy not necessarily detailed in the program.

Performance programs, on the other hand, make explicit what conditions a design decision is intended to meet—its performance—allowing designers to decide on particular responses (National Bureau of Standards, 1968). For example, a behavioral performance program developed for the cancer radiation clinic at the National Institutes of Health (NIH) included the criterion that patients and their companions be easily able to handle other aspects of their lives, such as work and family, while they wait to be treated. But the program did not tell designers whether to accomplish this by having Internet-ready work cubicles, private rooms for cell phone use, or by other means. (Conway, Zeisel, and Welch, 1977). Performance programs are intended to make user needs visible rather than to delimit designers' options. E-B research is particularly helpful to designers in determining cultural, social, and psychological performance criteria.

User-needs programming research is not limited to the contractual stage of a design project called programming. Such cooperation continues to be useful in solving E-B problems raised throughout the design process, whenever designers are faced with making trade-offs—deciding the relative importance of the effects of decisions.

Although it is often uncertain who the specific users of a particular physical setting will be, people design particular settings for particular residents with particular problems. Designers and researchers at Oxford, New York, for example, prepared a behavioral program and designed a residence for present and future older veterans, many of whom are ill or handicapped (Nahemow and Downes, 1979; Snyder and Ostrander, 1974). If the present residents who participated in the research change or are replaced by new and different residents, results may eventually become irrelevant. Additionally, if a planned setting is new, as many are, you do not even have the questionable benefit of working with present users.

One way to resolve this seeming paradox is to locate and study settings, users, and problems representative of future ones, generalizing from these to the probable future setting and its users. There are two types of representative groups: those who will immediately use the new setting (commonly called "users") and those who merely represent the type of persons actual users are likely to be.

When designers and investigators know the people who will inhabit a setting, as at Oxford, they assume that although present users will eventually move out, the second and third waves of inhabitants will resemble them. In programming a school, for example, designers assume that although particular administrators, teachers, students, maintenance workers, and parents will change, the patterns of reactions and needs of such groups change relatively slowly. They also assume that changes that certainly will occur in the situation will in some way include the initial users of the setting: as the starting point for change, as catalysts, as limits, or as some part of the context for change. In this way, by identifying tendencies for change among users—for example, trends in methods of teaching or new types of care administered to mental patients—designers and investigators can plan for change. Predictions are more accurate when they reflect knowledge of the present.

Designers sometimes do not have a group of actual residents to plan with and study. They may know only the project site (urban/rural, north/south), the type of setting (park, school, plaza), and general characteristics of future users (incomes, ages, culture, health needs, lifestyle stages). They can then choose a representative substitute user group to work with from people with similar problems in similar settings.

For example, when investigators programmed a cancer clinic, they carried out case studies in four large urban cancer-therapy clinics, interviewed users, observed their behavior, and documented physical traces (Conway et al., 1977). They observed at each location during different days and at different times of day. They assumed that the people, settings, and situations there represented the types of people, settings, and situations for which the clinic was being designed—that the information they gathered was generalizable to the larger group from which future users would be drawn.

Design Review

In a design project designers use the existing information from their program and from available research to generate and test design ideas. Testing ideas through a *design review* process provides another occasion to link design and research.

• *Design review problem: how to present information.* As many practicing designers and others involved in design can attest, it is not always apparent how basic research findings are helpful to solve design problems (Reizenstein, 1975). Consequently, much basic research goes unused, untested, and unimproved in applied design situations. A fundamental problem E-B researchers face is to make apparent how basic research information can be helpful to design decision makers: user clients, paying clients, design professionals, and administrators. The way this task is carried out affects how various design-team members can help change design decisions, and it affects the likelihood that useful knowledge can increase and be developed further.

Researchers who want their information to be helpful to designers and to be improved by its use in design projects present information so that (1) people who affect decisions can share it, (2) design-team members can use it in their interaction during the design process, and (3) users of the information can question and confront it (Argyris, 1977). At least as important is that E-B information be presented so that it draws out the knowledge about a particular problem that participants bring to design and design review. The more participants in a design process combine research information with what they know about themselves, other participants, the setting, and its context, the more they can tailor information to do what they want.

A helpful way to approach solving these problems is to ask where research information fits in the designer's cognitive process. Design, according to the formulation in Chapter 1 and the neuroscience discussion in Chapter 7, comprises at least three primary activities—imaging, presenting, and testing. Research information can influence design through these activities. When designers and others participating in a design process meet at the beginning of the project, they use research information to help develop shared images. When presenting ideas about settings and behavior, people use research to show how they expect decisions about physical things to influence behavior. And to test their design decisions and the information used to make decisions, people need to have questions that encourage them to confront what is presented with outside information. The following techniques are aimed at achieving these ends.

• *Presentation technique: shared E-B images.* Designers formulate problems so that better design responses can be developed without expending more resources. Images suited to a problem can be used to decide which resources are useful to solve it and which are not. For example, seeing housing for older people on an urban site mainly as a building-design problem has different consequences than seeing it as a problem of designing part of an urban context. The first image of the problem would indicate that information about available services and nearby facilities is not useful. If eventual users of the building do not use the surrounding area heavily, there is no new problem. If they do use it, however, this image turns out to have unwisely excluded useful information from consideration, and eventually more resources will have to be expended to improve the now problematic solution.

Choosing "a 'point of view' of the problem that maximally simplifies the process of finding a solution" is essential for researchers as well as designers (Amarel, 1968, 131). This is one impetus researchers have to formulate information in such a way that it helps designers when they develop an image for their problem. The words that researchers use to describe problems, concepts,

Negotiating a shared image. (From Zeisel, 1975b)

and analyses can be interpreted differently by different people. For example, what do you think of when you hear the words *privacy*, *territory*, and *invasion of personal space?*

Mathematics provides opportunities for greater precision and less misinterpretation. But mathematical expression is not always useful in making decisions. A numerically expressed measure of annoyance at having one's privacy invaded does not necessarily help designers design an open-plan office.

Research presented so that it "paints a picture" of an idea for design-team members begins to help them go beyond the information—to build on it, develop it, and transform it so that it applies to the particular decision being made (Korobkin, 1976). Pictures of familiar settings, drawings, verbal scenarios of typical situations, cartoons, diagrams, and films all express information and encourage groups of people to discuss what they see. Such discussions in turn can enable participants to negotiate shared group images useful to their problem (Zeisel, 1976b). If designers are planning a school with citizens, for example, it is essential that each group understands what the other means if they are to be able to design together. Research presented holistically as well as analytically can be used to develop shared images of both people's behavior and physical settings.

• *Presentation technique: annotated plans.* Designers who want to provide places for people and behavioral scientists who want to understand how physical environments relate to people are interested in the same topic (although visually different dimensions), whether called "behavior settings" (Barker, 1968; Bechtel, 1977; Wicker, 1979), "man-environment systems" (Archea and Esser, 1970), or simply "places" (Canter, 1977; Moore, Allen, and Lyndon, 1974; Zeisel, 1975). This often-overlooked identity of interests provides researchers and designers an obvious common ground on which to share information.

Plan annotation is a technique for presenting behavior information together with traditional symbolic design information: diagrammatic and schematic plans. Annotated plans are design drawings on which information about the relation between the planned environment and behavior is written in words and other easily understood symbols. This technique is further elaborated in Chapter 13. Depending on the phase of design in which a plan is annotated, this information includes data used as background for making the design decision; behavioral expectations held by the designer; and behavioral hypotheses for future testing. As an example, a team of architects and researchers designing a cancer-treatment center for the U.S. National Institutes of Health used annotated plans to present explicit predictions about what they supposed the eventual relation between setting and behavior would be (Conway et al., 1977). One E-B prediction presented in the annotated plan was that if the receptionist can see and be seen by patients in corridors, all users will feel comfortable with letting patients walk around more freely.

Plan annotation encourages people to look closely at the behavioral rationale behind each decision: to confront and question both their decisions and the information on which those decisions are based. As you annotate plans

Visual images used to communicate E-B concepts—
photographs, cartoons, perspectives

Personal space: Social distance—a zone used widely in public settings.
Photo © Jim Pinckney. (From Altman, 1975)

you not only present, you begin to test what you know. You become engaged in linking research information to particular design decisions (Epp, Georgopulos, and Howell, 1979). You find out both what you know and what you do not know, in a structured way.

   • *Presentation technique: design review questions.* Throughout any design process, some decisions are made so rapidly that designers are unable to look up relevant research data to justify or question the decision. This would not be a problem if intuitive decisions had no unintended negative side effects—but most do.

   Even when research data are arrayed systematically and extensively, it may not be easy to locate appropriate data to test a particular design decision. Designers may have to wait until they are faced with unresolvable technical dilemmas or with users who react in contradictory ways before they realize that somewhere information had been available to test and inform a much earlier decision.

   Information-utilization problems are confounded still further when, at various stages of design, users and paying clients participate as design review-

Territorial behavior: Janitors have jurisdictional right in others' territories and ofter ignore the occupant as they go about their work. Drawing by Chas. Addams © 1942, 1970, The New Yorker Magazine, Inc. Reprinted by perrmission. (From Altman, 1975)

"Window to the world": Older people need a place to view life around them. (From Zeisel et al., 1978)

ers; these may include community school-board or housing-board members, corporate officials, or just citizens concerned about their community. If professional designers do not know what questions to ask, how should user clients be expected to? User clients have an additional problem. Before testing designs with research information, they must test the information by comparing it with their own lives, answering the question "Do these issues actually describe the needs of people like me?"

Korobkin (1976) suggests that one form of research presentation for environmental design be a series of questions to be used during reviews of developing designs. This technique helps to involve every member of a design process in testing and improving design ideas. In the early stages of a design project, questions aim to make sure designers focus on issues that research has shown to be salient to the problem being addressed. For a dormitory, questions might raise issues of privacy, quietness, independence, and supervision; for a school playground, issues of teenagers hanging out and potential property damage. "Accountability questions" like these (Korobkin, 1976) are formulated in general terms: "How has the design addressed teenage hanging-out behavior (or students' needs for privacy or the potential problem of property damage to nearby facilities)?"

When designers want to identify data, problems, and issues that bear on making detailed design decisions, more-specific design review questions are appropriate. For example, in their behavioral guidelines for design of low-rise housing for older people, Zeisel, Epp, and Demos (1978) first summarized existing published research by describing a series of E-B problems that older people face when they live in and move around housing projects. For the issue "pathfinding" they developed the following description:

> Finding one's way around a housing site can be difficult for both residents and visitors when pathways are not clear, when there are no identifiable landmarks, and where entrances are not marked. As a result, careful consideration must be given to site "legibility" so that the giving and following of directions from one place to another on site can occur with ease. People must know where they are on the site and where they are going at all times. Pathfinding confusion also arises when streets or paths which are at the back of one unit are at the front of another unit; when there is no distinction made between areas for resident use and areas open to the general public; and when buildings seem to have two "front" sides. It is important to resolve these issues because clear pathfinding opportunities add to older residents' sense of security (86).

Following each description of an issue is a series of design review questions to identify behavioral problems related to the issue. For "pathfinding" these questions include:

- Is the site organized to provide clear unit addresses within the conventional address system of streets, entries and units?
- Is it easy for residents to describe to friends how to find where they live?
- Are units and clusters designed and located so that it is easy for residents and visitors to orient themselves?
- Is there a clear and consistent distinction between front door and back door of units?

- Are natural and built landmarks utilized to help give individual identity to different clusters and different parts of large sites? (88)

Design review questions included in important evidence-based design volumes (Cooper Marcus and Barnes, 1999) have no right or wrong answers; they simply raise issues for discussion. By answering the questions, every member of the design team gains greater control over design decisions. This holds for designers as well as users and other clients. They all contribute to improving a design. Users gain a special additional benefit from design review questions. Assessing how well each question corresponds to their own lives makes apparent to them knowledge and experience they may not know they have. They are put in the position not of individual clients being asked to express personal desires and tastes but of knowledgeable participants whose ability to tailor the research to a particular situation is valuable to design.

Post-Occupancy Evaluation (POE)

Another occasion for designers and researchers to cooperate is after a building or other setting has been occupied—when it is in use. POEs answer questions like: What were the designers' original intentions, and how did they try to implement them? What is there in the design that influenced use of the setting in ways the designers did not intend? How did position, expertise, and know-how of design-team members affect decisions during design? Answers to such questions can be used to reorganize design teams, improve designers' control over the effects of future design decisions, and test theories on which design decisions are based.

One problem in POE research is how to reconstruct design decisions. Investigators can better use POE results to improve the process of making design decisions in the future if they can identify and make visible the design decisions that led up to the setting being evaluated. If designers and researchers collaborated throughout the design process—programming, design, and construction—making the process visible is less of a problem; it is more of a problem if behavioral information was not made explicit during design.

An explicit behavioral performance program and annotated plans on which designers have presented behavioral expectations provide a solid footing for evaluation researchers to reconstruct the behavioral components of a design process. For example, in the NIH cancer-treatment center designed with research, the program and annotated plans could be translated into testable hypotheses, as in Table 3-1 (Conway et al., 1977).

The more inventive evaluators are, the more hypotheses they will generate from any stated intention, and the more they will profit from their study.

In a POE of a setting for which no behavioral program or written explanation of design decisions was prepared at the time decisions were made, investigators have greater difficulty reconstructing the how and why of decisions. The problem is further compounded when decisions were made by designers who no longer work for the firm, or by one of several unidentifiable

UNOBTRUSIVE CARE: Residents will not feel they are in a facility in which others are caring for them because the office is small and out of the way.

HEALTH: Residents will frequently use main stairs near entry and it will be healthy for them.

PREVIEWING: Residents will stop at the midway stair landing to decide if they want to join activity below.

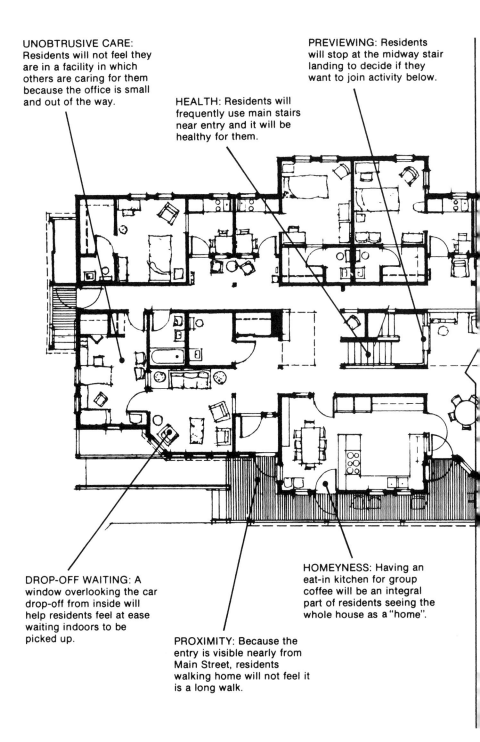

DROP-OFF WAITING: A window overlooking the car drop-off from inside will help residents feel at ease waiting indoors to be picked up.

PROXIMITY: Because the entry is visible nearly from Main Street, residents walking home will not feel it is a long walk.

HOMEYNESS: Having an eat-in kitchen for group coffee will be an integral part of residents seeing the whole house as a "home".

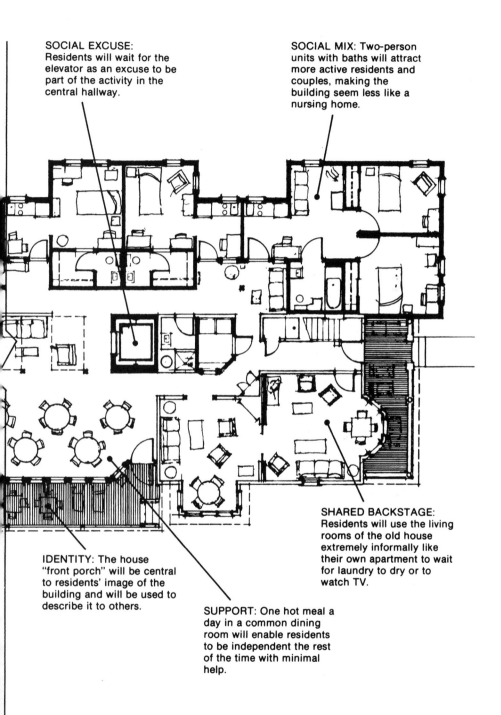

SOCIAL EXCUSE:
Residents will wait for the
elevator as an excuse to be
part of the activity in the
central hallway.

SOCIAL MIX: Two-person
units with baths will attract
more active residents and
couples, making the
building seem less like a
nursing home.

SHARED BACKSTAGE:
Residents will use the living
rooms of the old house
extremely informally like
their own apartment to wait
for laundry to dry or to
watch TV.

IDENTITY: The house
"front porch" will be central
to residents' image of the
building and will be used to
describe it to others.

SUPPORT: One hot meal a
day in a common dining
room will enable residents
to be independent the rest
of the time with minimal
help.

Annotated plan stating environment-behavior hypotheses to be evaluated.

Table 3-1. Behaviorial hypotheses derived from annotatd design features of a cancer center

Design Decision	Annotated Intention	Testable Hypothesis
Stairs and elevators are adjacent, making available only one possible path for patients.	That patients clearly undersand how to get into and out ot the setting.	Environments offering only one option for direction are more easily comprehending than several options.
Receptionist desk overlooks and is visible from all patient areas and corridors.	That patients are not afraid of being lost when they walk down corridors to treatment. That staff in not worried about patients getting hurt or upset, consequently limiting patient movement.	Environments enabling patients and staff to see each other will be more reassuring to both groups than settings in which this is not possible.

draftspeople instructed to solve a design problem as they saw fit. Often so much time elapses during a design and so many people work on a design project that asking decision makers what they intended creates a *Rashomon* problem of recall (Keller, 1978). To determine behavioral intentions of design decisions in a Planned Unit Residential Development in New Jersey, Keller (1978) faced problems like these and therefore used maps, models, official statements, and commercial advertisements in addition to interviewing designers and planners.

Table 3-2. Behavioral hypotheses derived from design features of the St. Francis Square housing development

Design Feature	Assumption about Behavior
Fenced patio or balcony attached to each unit—with access to most patios from the living room of apartment only.	Mothers of small children will not object to them entering the apartment via the living room after they have been playing on the patio.
Service facilities like common drying yards are provided in each court—visible in two courts from every apartment.	Residents in these two courts will use the common drying yards, since they are within view of all the apartments.

From *Sociology and Architectural Design*, by John Zeisel. Copyright 1975, Russell Sage Foundation, New York. Reprinted by permission.

Analysis of physical plans can be used to identify a design team's implicit assumptions about behavior, and knowing the assumptions helps to structure a focused interview with a designer on the subject of his intentions. For example, in Cooper and Hackett's POE of St. Francis Square (1968), they noted specific design features, and inferred the assumptions stated in Table 3-2.

When Cooper later investigated these behavioral predictions, she found that drying yards, underused by residents, were turned into handball courts. She assumed this was due to nearby drying machines and "the fact that people felt their clothes might be damaged or stolen if they left them unattended in a communal yard" (1970, 20)—even though the yards were visible from the apartments.

If you want to be sure not to miss significant design decisions, you will analyze plans at small and large scales of design decision making. In housing, you will look at the range of decisions from hardware and apartment unit to site plan (Cook, 1971, 1973; Cooper, 1970); in town planning, from building and street layout to location of the town center (Brolin, 1972); in institutional buildings, you might include hardware, offices, and internal services as well as site location (Zeisel and Rhodeside, 1975). POE research organized on the basis of systematic plan analysis is likely to include essential design questions—especially small-scale ones—that might otherwise be overlooked.

Architect's rendering of interior street in the Charlesview housing development. (Courtesy of Sy Mintz Associates Architects/Planners, Inc.)

Other useful sources for understanding designers' behavioral implications are presentation drawings on which designers label places and insert sample furniture layouts or equipment and renderings that present places in perspective drawings as designers see them, often including people. Visual documents like these are particularly fruitful because they represent a designer's overall image of life in the future setting (Montgomery, 1966; Zeisel and Griffin, 1975).

When you have made design decisions and intentions explicit and have translated them into testable hypotheses, a POE can be extremely instructive. In her Twin Rivers study, for example, Keller (1976, 1978) evaluated planning decisions for a Planned Unit Residential Development intended (1) to create microcommunities within the overall development, (2) to make the community self-sufficient, and (3) to induce residents to take up walking as a major mode of locomotion.

The Twin Rivers planners tried to create microcommunities by dividing the development into four roughly equal areas, two on one side of a highway and two on the other. Keller found, however, that residents did not identify with the four intended subdivisions; instead two larger identification areas developed, divided by the highway. Meanwhile, loyalty and local pride centered in smaller areas around people's homes. To help engender community feelings, Keller concluded, the size of formal subdivisions must reflect a better understanding of how people develop community feelings and how different types of communities interact.

To create a self-sufficient community, planners wanted to provide all the services necessary to support residents within the Twin Rivers development. At the same time, they could not provide services before enough residents were living there to support the services economically. This internal contradiction resulted in a sparseness of available facilities for earlier residents, forcing them to leave Twin Rivers for religious services, health care, movies, and concerts. Community feelings, of course, developed slowly because residents depended so much on support from surrounding towns. Planners can avoid such catch-22 situations only by identifying secondary consequences like these and modifying their objectives before it is too late.

Finally, the Twin Rivers planners believed that if houses, shops, and schools were accessible to residents on foot, walking would become a "major mode of locomotion." The POE pointed out, however, that residents were part of a car culture and drove even to nearby locations, citing as reasons bad weather, no time, and the lack of anything interesting to look at on pedestrian paths. Perhaps the most obvious reason for car use was that whenever residents had multiple destinations (which was most of the time), a car was clearly more efficient. One lesson Keller draws from these findings is that rather than thinking they could banish the car and car culture by providing pathways, Twin Rivers planners should have developed a shared image of the residents' lifestyle with residents themselves.

Post-occupancy evaluation research, as this example shows, holds special potential for building a body of tested E-B knowledge.

DESIGN CASE STUDY

THE CAPTAIN CLARENCE ELDRIDGE CONGREGATE HOUSE

Hyannis, Massachusetts

The following case study demonstrates how full project team cooperation between researchers and designers can result in an elegant building that adds to both new design and knowledge and new environment-behavior research approaches. The Captain Clarence Eldridge House is a congregate house designed and constructed in 1980 for twenty seniors. Such group living arrangements with formal support services gave rise to Assisted Living Residences as a housing type. Designed and built to demonstrate how a certain degree of shared living could house seniors in public housing with greater mutual awareness and care, and at lower construction cost, the building was intended from its inception to serve as a model for other similar buildings. Environment-behavior research was integral to the project's programming and design because the model needed to include a sound rationale for decisions, not merely one person's whimsy. The research and design team worked as one to define the attributes of this new "congregate" type of living, select the site, develop the design program, and design the building. The team of Korobkin-Jahan Architects as designers, Donham & Sweeny Architects as architects of record, and John Zeisel as team coordinator selected as the site a corner lot one block from Main Street in Hyannis, Massachusetts. An important factor in site selection was that residents could walk to Main Street, with its shops and restaurants, without crossing any streets. The intent was that the safety of walking to downtown

The Captain Clarence Eldridge House.

Hyannis would encourage residents to use local shops and restaurants. The team enlarged the original 2,000- square-foot 1890s whaling captain's house on the site to 10,000 square feet while maintaining its residential character. The Captain Clarence Eldridge House is now home to twenty seniors living in a socially cohesive setting.

The owner, operator, and immediate client for design of "Eldridge House," as local residents and neighbors refer to the building, is the Public Housing Authority for Barnstable County. The Housing Authority selected the combined design/research team because the Authority's Executive was particularly interested in housing innovation and the Authority's volunteer Board of Directors comprised college professors, a building inspector, and others who wanted to be clients for something new and exciting. Funding for Eldridge House was provided through a state government program whose chief architect, Stephen Demos, was also an environment-behavior researcher and author (Zeisel, Epp, and Demos, 1978).

The Eldridge House design program called for a single building to house twenty frail seniors in a house-like environment, with each resident having some private space and all residents sharing common areas such as living and dining rooms; but it did not specify precisely what would be private and what would be shared. This was left to the team to propose.

• *The Critical Programming Dilemma* revolved around a seemingly simple question: What spaces were to be private and what spaces were to be shared? Because the original design program did not answer this question, it became the

Front porch as seen from community kitchen.

Original house entry foyer viewed from living room.

primary programming question for the research and design team. From the beginning of the programming effort it was clear that bedrooms were to be private and that there would be a common living room, dining room, and serving kitchen. Unresolved questions included: Would each individual living and sleeping space have its own kitchen and dining area? Its own bathroom? Would adjacent residents share a toilet, sink, and shower? What about bathtubs?

The team began its programming by generating alternative scenarios and sketches with several private-shared space alternatives. Focus group interviews were carried out with five groups, each including more than ten seniors presently living in public housing units managed by the same housing authority.

The original flawed focused interview question was: "What should be private and what shared in the new housing being planned?" The team quickly learned from the first group interview that the term "shared" was the wrong term to use when discussing certain common areas. None of the respondents saw themselves sharing a bathtub merely because someone else might have bathed there previously or might bathe there later. They no more shared the bathroom than a hotel room occupant "shares" the room with all previous and future occupants. The phrases "used in common" or "used by others as well" fit the respondents' frame of reference better, and uncovered what the team needed to know to make decisions about this critical issue.

How bathrooms were treated throughout the building was more important than how kitchen or dining areas were allocated. Having one's own toilet was more important than having control over any other room. Few focus group participants wanted to have their toilet used in common with others. As they aged, participants further explained, they increasingly needed to use the toilet at a moment's notice, and they were afraid that a common toilet room might already be in use when they needed it.

Bathing, however, was different. The focus group consensus was that common bathtubs and showers were more acceptable than common toilets because they are employed less frequently and their use could be more conveniently planned and scheduled. When the research and design team tested with the focus group a European model of toileting and washing—namely toilet and sink separate from bathtub or shower—approval was unanimous and the design solution became evident: Provide a private toilet and sink within each living space, along with several full bathtub and shower rooms accessible from common hallways.

The enlarged building is designed to look like an oversized turn of the century Cape Cod house, with the roofline, windows, and general exterior appearance of the 8,000-square-foot addition mirroring the original 2,000-square-foot original design. The final building comprises seventeen one-bedroom and three two-bedroom dwellings and looks very much like an extremely large single-family house with a wraparound front porch, clapboard siding, and paneled doors. On the first floor, with six living units are, a common kitchen, atrium piano area, living room, dining room, laundry, a mail area, a bathing room, a shower room, and a small office.

An open atrium connecting the two floors enables those on each floor to see activity on the other. The original building's front door on a busy street serves as the formal front door for the new building and leads into a hallway. Most residents use the informal "back" door—closer to Main Street with its shops— leading past the common kitchen into a mailbox area at the foot of the common stairs.

• *The Design Process:* The team developed the design and the user-needs program concurrently and interactively. As research inquiry was carried out, design inquiry was as well. As the design process generated new issues that need-

View of dining room from "previewing" landing.

Residents meeting in common kitchen.

ed resolution, the programming process followed up on them. For example, while the principle of a common "congregate" area was established early in the program, design options for this "congregate" area included a large interior room, a two-story atrium, a cluster of several spaces, or an outdoor garden. With these questions raised in design, research data were gathered to help select the best answer.

When the physical setting itself delineates parameters for the subject of inquiry, environment-behavior teams do better posing questions to themselves in drawings rather than verbally. In this case, the parameters were an existing building, the size and shape of the site, and the location and nature of the adjacent street and nearby Main Street. Even this verbal description lacks the completeness you can see in the following sketches.

• *Inquiry by design:* In addition to answers designed into the building, the interactive research and design effort generated questions that the building included as physical hypotheses and experiments. The questions were:

1. Because older people tend to live alone, should the house be all single studio apartments or should there also be apartments for two people? If so, how many and in what configuration? While the single-person studios each have a small kitchen area, what should the two-person apartments have in terms of a cooking area?

2. Most of the apartments are located on the second floor, away from the common spaces. Should the downstairs apartments be completely separated from the common areas like the apartments upstairs, or should they be more open and connected to the downstairs common dining room and atrium?

3. Is the common kitchen a place where a staff person is in charge—preparing and serving meals alone—or would residents participate in the life of the kitchen, using it as many families do, to sit, have coffee or tea, and chat?

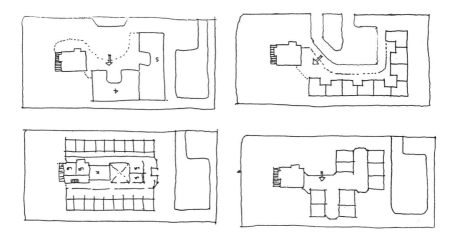

Sketches of alternative building concepts.

Because the research either did not clearly indicate a "right" direction, or it indicated an option to which only a minority might be attracted, the team designed hypotheses and experiments into the building to be tested in use. Only introducing an alternative by design would demonstrate how great the demand would be for a totally new option. Later research on the designed-in experiments indicated that each experiment proved to be positive when it contributed something to the setting beyond its original intention. What were these hypotheses and experiments?

The first hypothesis related to the fact that in addition to fourteen single-person apartments, Eldridge House included three two-person apartments. The hypothesis being tested was that, although they represented only a minority of potential residents, there was the possibility of elderly couples moving in, siblings or old friends who wanted to live together, and possibly even people who did not know each other but wanted companionship in their old age. For this reason, two traditional two-person apartments were included in the plan at the southeast corner of both floors. But this alone did not raise any truly probing questions through design which would significantly add to our knowledge.

To raise such questions, the plan included one completely unique two-person apartment—at the northwest corner of the second floor. Two bedrooms were designed each with their own front door for personal identity of each resident, and each with their own toilet room, but in this apartment the two residents share a full kitchen with place for a small kitchen table and two chairs next to a window overlooking the street and back door. From this kitchen there was also a view through an internal window into the common atrium on the second floor, to avoid isolating the residents in this apartment. Since the building was first occupied in 1980, one couple lived there using one bedroom as a bedroom and the other as a living room, friends and sisters have lived there each in their own bedroom while sharing breakfast together in their eat-in kitchen, and unrelated residents have lived there.

Although programming research showed that primarily single people would live at Eldridge House, offering these two-person options by design provided the entire house with more residents who were more social and couples who have sometimes been younger than other residents. The hypothesis that two-person apartments would broaden the resident population, adding to the social life of the entire house, has been confirmed. If it had not, renovations might have been necessary.

The second hypothesis related to apartment location on the first floor. Although the research found that most respondents wanted privacy in their apartments, some felt frail and were afraid of being isolated. While there was no clear direction to provide some more and some less private apartments, the team included in the design two apartments on the first floor that opened directly onto the common atrium and dining room. When a resident comes out of one of these apartments, she can see over a half-wall and be seen by others in the dining room. Once again, only trying it would tell us if this option solved the isolation problem for those residents who felt that way. Over the years, there have regularly been residents who were more social, who wanted more contact with others, and who selected these apartments.

The final hypothesis related to the common kitchen on the first floor that provides a place for shared meals to be prepared, and serves as the hub of the house. It is the first room you see when you come in the "back door," it gives the house its interior "house-like" quality, and it provides a place for residents

View of common kitchen, dining room, "previewing landing,"
and apartment "front porches."

to sit together and chat without going into each other's apartments. But what would the cook think? Wasn't it her realm?

From the beginning, residents used the kitchen as they would their own kitchen in their own home. They set up a coffee maker there and were ready to serve a cup to visitors if someone should come by. They sat and played cards together there, and often met with the part-time administrator and care staff in the kitchen rather than in the office. There have been cooks who would have preferred "their own" space, but for the most part this type of person has not worked at the facility. The kitchen's message to everyone—residents, cook, and visitors—is that this is everyone's room, and that the meals prepared there are for the entire Eldridge House "family."

E-B Post-Occupancy Evaluation

Being a prototype meant that the building had to be a post-occupancy evaluation site if it was to serve its purpose. The team visited the building often during its first year of operation, usually with curious visitors and journalists. Each visit served as the chance to carry out an informal walk-through POE. The building was the subject of a master's POE thesis by a Harvard University psychology student who also attended architecture courses (Vanderburgh, 1981), was one of the central study sites for a federally funded study of congregate housing compared to nursing home care (Zeisel, Welch, and Epp, 1984), and was included in Victor Regnier's seminal evaluation and book, Assisted Living Housing for the Elderly (1994).

What did these more and less formal POEs uncover? What information did this conscious inquiry by design yield?

1. The elderly residents of Eldridge House tend to walk to Main Street regularly because, not having to cross any streets, they feel physically safe in making this short trip. One of the benefits to residents' quality of life is not only how residents use Eldridge House, but also how they do not use it. From the beginning, when team members would drop in to meet with a resident, she was always "out for a walk" or just on her way "to town." An unexpected side effect of this connection between the Eldridge House and Main Street is that the town of Hyannis decided shortly after completion to make the adjacent street one-way and to install a new sidewalk so Eldridge House residents could travel even more safely to Main Street.

2. Several design factors combined to "turn the building around." The "back door" next to the kitchen became the Eldridge House front door. Although located on a side street, the back door was closer to Main Street than the formal "front door" and the taxi drop-off and the parking areas are located there. Overlooking the steps and ramp leading to the back door is a window from the common kitchen. Residents playing cards and having a cup of coffee there serve as informal guardians, providing a feeling of security and safety for all residents using that door. The back door also leads directly to the mailboxes, and from that area you can see into the dining room and decide if you want to join an activity or pass by it. As a result of all these factors, it was decided

to give the building address as the "back" rather the "front" door. The building was officially turned around.

3. With a single central shared kitchen, it was difficult to make it a "backstage service area." One side effect was that residents played a greater part in selecting how meals would be prepared and served than if the kitchen had been less central to their lives. Eldridge House residents select their own cook, participate in meal selection, and even in laying the table. The kitchen location and design seem not only to create this opportunity, but almost to suggest that this is what it was designed for.

4. To encourage residents to feel at home in their apartments, each apartment has a kitchenette with a small window onto the interior hallway. While most residents do not cook entire meals there, they do like to sit there to feel at home. In fact many have breakfast there on their own rather than go to the common dining room. It provides them the chance to get up and make themselves ready for the day without confronting other residents who, although friendly, are often unwelcome encounters early in the morning. As a group, the residents decided that they would hire a cook to shop, prepare, and clean up only for lunch from 10 A.M. to 2 P.M., rather than serve three meals a day. The cook became a member of the large Eldridge House family.

The individual kitchenettes were originally planned almost as symbols of home rather than as an actual place to have meals. One unintended negative side effect of residents having breakfast and other snacks in their own kitchens is that the storage provided was inadequate. Some residents installed small cupboards that, no matter how small, made the kitchenette spaces even more inadequate. Future kitchenettes need to be more than symbolic if they are to be useful at all for residents.

5. In the design special effort was made to provide each resident with her own apartment "front door." Each apartment door is inset, creating a small interior "porch" in front of it that residents can decorate and otherwise "present themselves" to others. In addition to general hall lighting, next to each door there is a small lighting fixture just outside the front door, allowing the resident to control the ambience of his or her front porch. In addition, each apartment has an operable double hung window between the kitchenette and the front porch, and every front door is a "Dutch door" opening separately on the top and the bottom. Thus each resident can decide how much privacy they want at any time during the day.

What effect did this have? While no recent research has been carried out on this question, a year or so after occupancy a resident chastised the author when he asked how this combination of environmental design factors worked: "Don't you know, when we want visitors to drop in, we turn on the light and open the top of the Dutch door. When we want privacy everyone can tell." Each porch is individually decorated with furniture, as are the windows from the kitchenettes, which have curtains and display mementos.

6. The major innovation in social imagery that the POE studies uncovered was the two-level definition of "home" that residents developed. Throughout this description I have used the term "apartment," but residents refer to the place they live as their "home," not their apartment. "Would you like to see my home?" they

ask when inviting you to see where they live. At the same time they refer to the entire Eldridge House as their "home." They see no contradiction between these two homes—the building with a grand porch near Main Street and the place that is theirs with its own front porch and kitchen window. By not designing either scale clearly as "home," and employing residential imagery both inside and out, residents have developed their own "double home" image of where they live.

The uniqueness of Eldridge House at the time of its development, its overt and easily understandable research basis, and its high visibility through publications because of its design have made Eldridge House a true inquiry by design.

This evidence-based design case study is based on the contributions of Lenny Jones at the Barnstable Housing Authority; Stephen Demos of the Massachusetts Executive Office of Communities and Development; Korobkin-Jahan Architects, designers; Donham and Sweeney Architects, architects of record; and John Zeisel, research and design team coordinator.

OVERVIEW

People from different disciplines work together because they want to, not because they must. When researchers and designers cooperate, each uses the other to do more than either can do alone: researchers to have designers use and improve their information; designers to have E-B researchers help narrow the gap between them and their anonymous user clients.

The practical side to multidisciplinary professional cooperation is that designers make decisions about real environments for real clients and expect that applied E-B research can mesh with design—on a day-to-day operational basis. Occasions for cooperation in design include (1) programming research, in which investigators work with and study representative groups of potential users to arrive at a behavioral program; (2) design review during the design process, when researchers and designers test and modify their ideas in the light of available E-B knowledge; and (3) post-occupancy evaluation (POE) research of built projects in use in order to improve future designs and design processes.

Applied design research poses problems: How do you find out about users of an as-yet unbuilt setting? How do you present research information so that designers can use it? How do you reconstruct a past design process? How do designers present their decisions so that researchers can use them to improve a body of knowledge? Techniques invented to answer these questions represent practical ways to link applied E-B research to professional environmental design.

Cooperation enables people who work together to achieve more than the sum of each working separately. Even when people are through working together to solve shared problems, something remains: a knowledge of the other's discipline and point of view; new ways to define problems; an improved knowledge of how to cooperate with others. These and other side effects of cooperation are the topic of the next chapter.

CHAPTER 4

SIDE EFFECTS OF COOPERATION

I see in science one of the greatest creations of the human mind. . . . It is a step at which our explanatory myths become open to conscious and consistent criticism and at which we are challenged to invent new myths.

— KARL R. POPPER
Objective Knowledge

Designers and researchers working together to make places to live, work, and play better suited to people's needs also enrich and improve themselves. Through cooperation they take advantage of the other's difference to order what they do in a new way, extend their skills to do new things, and replace old ways with new options. Each uses the other to improve his or her own ability to contribute.

People use research and design skills jointly whenever they identify problems, observe the world around them, develop concepts, decide to act, develop plans for what to do, and do it. Disciplinary boundaries were erected to help us isolate and develop one or another of these activities in order to better achieve particular ends. For example, designers who want to control how others—such as contractors—carry out their instructions have highly developed methods for presenting plans. Researchers who want to be able to share their observations about the world with others have highly developed methods for observing.

Differences between the structure of research and design, their content, their emphases, and their values provide a basis for the two fields to borrow from each other, to incorporate new elements, to rely on each other, to invent shared methods, and generally to broaden themselves. Particularly rich chances for mutual improvement can be found in the following differences: (1) Designers, more than researchers, work on problems requiring them to make *high-risk* decisions. (2) Researchers have a longer tradition of rigorously and critically *testing* their knowledge in order to improve it (3) Researchers tend to emphasize *explicit* knowing, while designers tend more to accept *tacit* knowing.

Opportunities for Researcher and Designer Growth

Risk Taking

Intradisciplinary
Interdisciplinary
Transdisciplinary

Critical Testing

Appropriateness
Testable designs
Reactions

Tacit and Explicit Knowing

Theories
Hypotheses
Exemplars
Models

RISK TAKING

Throughout a design project, decisions are made—for example, when to present drawings to a client or how to specify a particular construction detail. Researchers make similar decisions—what research design to choose and when to publish an empirical report. In making a decision, people weigh what they think are the possible effects of the decision against the risks of unintended consequences they are willing to take.

Designers and researchers weigh knowing against risking under different conditions: different professional norms, degrees of visibility, costs and rewards, and so on. It is hard enough within one disciplinary framework to determine what is tenable knowledge and what action the problem at hand demands. When two or more disciplines are involved, the potential for problems is even greater. There are difficulties of communication, and difficulties of deciding who has the power and responsibility. There is an inherent difficulty that pressures to take action in one discipline may be inconsistent with the pressures in another, creat¬ing a tug-of-war for control between participants. In designing the Oxford veter¬ans' residence, for example, when the architects felt pressured to begin developing concept sketches, they asked the researchers to tell them what they had found so far. The researchers complained that their findings were merely exploratory. The designers argued that any findings they had would be acceptable because those were the best knowledge about the problem available at that time (Ostrander and Groom, 1975).

Decisions made in actual multidisciplinary situations are determined by the procedures that participants have expressly or implicitly agreed on for resolving disagreements. When researchers work for designers or designers for researchers in a traditional consultant relationship, for example, *intradisciplinary* procedures are used. One person works within the discipline of the other. The member of the primary discipline retains responsibility for the outcome of the process and has final authority in making decisions—for example, whether to spend resources to carry out further research on a problem. A researcher working for a designer in such a situation might say "Although my scientific norms say I ought to study the problem longer, I will stop because the designers in charge decided that I have provided them with enough information on which to base their decision." In intradisciplinary settings, consultants learn how other people solve problems, and consultants influence the solution to the degree that they visibly contribute to the decision maker's definition of the problem. The better suited the contribution is to the accepted problem definition, the more the consultants control the effects of their input.

Some problems can be solved by dividing them into sub-problems so that team members from different disciplines can separately apply their own professional standards. For example, if a client wants a building both built and evaluated, a design and research team might decide to carry out the two sets of tasks separately but in parallel. Investigators decide when POE research is needed and when findings may be published; designers decide when design concepts are sufficiently informed and when buildings go into construction. These procedures are *interdisciplinary* because they rely for their success on how well participants construct links between two or more separate disciplines. Responsibility for each part remains separate, but team members have joint responsibility for the quality of the links.

Possibly the most rewarding procedures to use are ones in which team members jointly decide what to do throughout a project. Employing such *transdisciplinary* procedures, the criteria the team use neither wholly reflect any one discipline nor join different disciplines. They are new procedures developed by team members who respect each other's disciplinary norms, rewards, and sanctions and who are willing and able to reevaluate their own norms in the light of the team's common goals.

The flexibility a team has to institute transdisciplinary decision-making procedures is controlled by the real setting in which the team works, by clients, and by members' energies. Team members making transdisciplinary decisions benefit by engaging in tasks that are not part of their normal work; for instance, designers may assess the validity of research methods and researchers may generate design images. They all benefit by carrying out entirely new tasks; for example, designers may analyze their own completed plans to identify implications for behavior they were not aware of while designing and from these formulate research hypotheses. Each team member benefits by inventing new types of shared presentation methods and by increasing the number and types of tools he or she can use separately, such as behaviorally annotated plans and behavioral design performance programs.

To researchers one of the greatest benefits is that they are able to share in making, and taking responsibility for, risky decisions. Such training is invaluable, especially if it leads to the ability to be a bit more daring in carrying out research projects. This skill is not always nurtured in scientists' training, but it is an important one to develop:

> We must commit ourselves to the risk of talking complete nonsense, if we are to say anything at all within any [deductive] system (Polanyi, 1958, p. 94).
>
> Give me a fruitful error any time, full of seeds, bursting with its own corrections. You can keep your sterile truth for yourself (Pareto, cited in Gould, 1978, p. 22).
>
> The "better" or "preferable" hypothesis will, more often than not, be the *more improbable* one (Popper, 1972, p. 17).

By learning how to choose "bold" hypotheses (Popper, 1972, p. 53), researchers may be able to increase their chances of eventually making significant contributions to scientific knowledge.

CRITICAL TESTING

Science may be thought of as continual criticism of necessarily incomplete knowledge (Popper, 1972). Scientific researchers rely mainly on explicit test procedures to decide whether an assertion is tenable enough to be included in a growing body of shared knowledge. They are not unfamiliar, however, with using tacit criteria to assess, for example, the elegance of an argument.

Designers who use tests to improve their knowledge rely mainly on tacitly understood criteria, having only a weak tradition of explicit shared tests. In itself this is not a problem. It is a problem only for designers who want to make empirically testable assertions and then have no way to test them: "Designs which are unevaluated are just assertions no matter how they are derived. Testing and evaluation are the only way of deciding whether a design is a success and of building up a *body of knowledge*" (Rapoport, 1969, p. 146). This statement could easily be adopted as the keystone for all research and design endeavors. Rapoport rightly assumes that design is potentially a developing body of knowledge. Designers who want to contribute to it can use collaboration with researchers to develop new test procedures and to improve the testability of designed objects.

Effective environment-behavior tests (1) are appropriate to their subject matter, (2) are used on testable presentations, and (3) provide results that participants do not disregard.

Appropriateness

Designers and researchers sometimes mistakenly think they add to knowledge by making assertions (a building; a hypothesis) that they justify by referring to the past rather than by testing. Justifications take different forms (de Zeeuw, 1978). One is *personal judgment*: "I say this building works or this hypothesis is sound because So-and-So says so." Le Corbusier, Talcott Parsons, Paul Goldberger, and Freud are frequently used "So-and-Sos" in E-B debates. *Intersubjective* justifications assert that a group of people agrees with one's point of view: important designers, scientific peers, or the public. Such authorities may be appropriate for judging how beautiful a group considers a design to be, for example, or how well it fits certain postmodern design beliefs.

Personal judgment and intersubjectivity, however, are inappropriate when used to test whether a building leaks or whether it satisfies psychological and social needs. These situations offer designers a chance to take advantage of developed research procedures.

Testable Design Presentations

The less testable hypotheses are, the less meaningful they are for researchers who want to solve a problem. If drawings, plans, and even buildings are presented in such a way that assertions can be empirically tested, knowledge and action can be improved. For E-B questions this implies that designers and researchers develop a body of shared knowledge by making explicit some of the behavioral expectations they hold for planned buildings, the operational procedures they see being used to test their expectations, and the theories on which their expectations are based.

Two pitfalls peculiar to design can make buildings untestable. The first is that designs are often presented *ceteris paribus* ("all things remaining equal"): "As designed, this building will be a success using the following criteria . . . all things remaining equal." Presenters using a *ceteris paribus* clause take responsibility for the success of a building under a range of conditions; but, conversely, when conditions vary at all, they can insulate themselves from test results by saying "All things did not remain equal."

Buildings may also be presented *fait accompli*—after all chances are past for effective criticism, testing, or sanctions. Although testing can theoretically still take place, in reality the presentation goes unchallenged.

Reactions to Test Results

A reasonable degree of "methodological tolerance" (Lakatos, 1970, p. 157) helps maintain fresh ideas in a developing body of knowledge. Tests applied too harshly run the risk of nipping in the bud young ideas that with hindsight may prove to have been the beginning of important shoots. However, the suspended judgment necessary in such situations does not give either researchers or designers license to submit fuzzy and incoherent ideas. Rather, it provides temporary license to present and develop tacit aspects of their work without fearing ruthless criticism because certain parts of the whole are still unclear.

Methodological tolerance is an attitude toward constructing and applying tests to nurture new ideas. It is not an appropriate response to agreed-on test results after receiving them. In multidisciplinary work both researchers and designers have a natural tendency to retreat into their own disciplinary shells and say "*Your* test results are not relevant for me." Severe arguments are avoided when collaborating designers and researchers both understand that if they want to improve what they know, they must see problems made visible by test results as opportunities for further learning.

TACIT AND EXPLICIT KNOWING

It is expected that scientific procedures are formulated in such a way that they can be shared in a broader community. Many people interpret this to mean that scientific knowledge is explicitly held. In fact, among philosophers of science there is an ongoing debate about the role of objective knowing and tacit knowing in science (Kuhn, 1970; Polanyi, 1958). There is a similar debate among designers and design researchers about the need for "objective," systematized design knowledge.

When scientists and designers work together, they learn about different types of knowing useful in both fields. Scientists can test the usefulness of such expressions of tacit knowing as exemplars and models. Designers can see what they might gain from testable theories and hypotheses.

Explicit Knowledge

Theories about a subject summarize past experience in a set of statements, using quality criteria to ensure that the statements are internally coherent, that they are explicitly transferable to other people, that they can be connected to new experience by testing, and that from them one can derive new testable statements about unknown experience.

Theories in social science form the basis of research programs carried out by generations of investigators, such as Parsons' theory of action (Parsons & Shils, 1951) and Lewin's field theory (Lewin, 1951). Environment-behavior researchers have few formal macrotheories to develop; Barker's ecological psychology (Barker, 1968) is unique in its theoretical completeness. There are however, important middle-range theories (Merton, 1957) summarizing empirical evidence in E-B research—for example, Hall's *proxemics* (Hall, 1966). Altman (1975) astutely responds to the need for formal theory in environmental design by proposing a "boundary-regulating" theory to combine previous research on privacy, personal space, territory, and crowding. Although design disciplines have not traditionally emphasized formal theory, cooperation between designers and researchers serves as an opportunity to develop E-B theory.

Hypotheses are explicit provisional suppositions or conjectures explaining empirical research that serve as starting points for further investigation and can be made more or less tenable by this research. In other words, hypotheses, like theories, are explicit and testable guesses about the world.

Theories comprise hypothetical statements. Some hypotheses refer to directly observable phenomena (like the height of a door or the percentage of teenagers using a park), some refer to indirectly observable, deduced phenomena (like the relation between the weight of chairs in a room and inhabitants' feeling of control over their environment). As the case studies in this book make evident, designs, sketches, and even buildings may be seen as hypotheses adding to a body of knowledge if they serve as starting points for further research and if the conjectures they make are testable.

Tacit Knowledge

Tacit knowledge is knowledge we use that we cannot make explicit, as when we recognize that someone is angry or is feeling pity without being able to describe just what it is about the person's face that expresses the mood (Polanyi, 1967). It is therefore not codified in explicit "rules, laws, and criteria for identification" and is "learned by doing . . . rather than by acquiring rules for doing" (Kuhn, 1970, pp. 191–192). In research, tacit knowing is often considered intellectually inferior to other types of knowing. One reason may be that forms of expressing tacit knowledge are so poorly understood, exemplars and models among them.

Exemplars are typical examples that members of a group agree exhibit certain qualities common to a class of objects, processes, or ideas. Students study exemplars to gain new knowledge—to "grasp the analogy between two or more distinct" situations and thus assimilate "a time-tested and group licensed way of seeing" (Kuhn, 1970, p. 189), learning to apply the analogy to new, similar situations when they arise.

> One of the fundamental techniques by which the members of a group, whether an entire culture or a specialists' sub-committee within it, learn to see the same things when confronted with the same stimuli is by being shown examples of situations that their predecessors in the group have already learned to see as like each other and as different from other sorts of situations (Kuhn, 1970, pp. 193–194).

In science, laboratory experiments carried out to demonstrate methodological principles are exemplars of a way of doing things. In an E-B seminar, students may be asked to analyze in detail Cooper's *Easter Hill Village* (1975) as an exemplar of the principles necessary to carry out a competent post-occupancy evaluation study. Professors teach architecture and art history students to recognize styles by showing them examples of buildings representing a style while describing the style's specific characteristics. In some business and law schools, established wisdom is conveyed by the "case study" method: descriptions of situations are read and discussed by students under the direction of a leader who points out exemplary methods of resolving problems in the cases. Exemplars like these are frequently used in the sciences, arts, and professions.

Models for a subject are representations—sometimes analytic, sometimes more poetic—that imply that one can learn how the subject acts by treating the model "as if" it were the subject itself. Models express primarily tacit knowledge. In science, models include such statements as "The molecules of a gas behave like tiny elastic billiard balls in random motion" (Kuhn, 1970, p. 184). In modern architecture, models run rampant, the most famous probably being

Le Corbusier's dictum that "the house is a machine for living in" (1965, p. 100).

Models differ from analogies in that a model, in addition to communicating similarities of whole shapes and ratios among some parts, implies that doing something to the model will have the same consequences as doing something to what it represents. Models provide designers with ways to learn about things they do not know by providing the chance to generate questions and try out answers on things they do know. If gas molecules behave like elastic billiard balls, what happens if the billiard table is made smaller? What happens if pairs of elastic billiard balls are glued together? In a machine for living, what are measures for operational efficiency? What happens if the energy source for the machine is stopped? And so on.

The following programming case study demonstrates how a team in which designers, research consultants, and the client work in a truly cooperative way results in an award-winning design while developing evidence-based office-planning principles (Zeisel and Maxwell, 1992; Zeisel and Maxwell, 1993).

CASE STUDY

THE H-E-B CORPORATE HEADQUARTERS
San Antonio, Texas

The San Antonio, Texas, headquarters of the H-E-B Food and Drug Company houses an extremely successful U.S. company that employed 21,000 workers at 148 stores in 1982, 40,000 workers in 200 stores in 1992, and 60,000 workers at 277 stores in 2000. The headquarters complex is located on an eleven-acre site in downtown San Antonio, and includes an historic former U.S. military arsenal. After the fall of the Alamo in the Mexican-American War, U.S. forces used this arsenal and its stables.

In 1992, a decade after the complex was programmed and constructed, it served as the physical center for managing 100 percent growth in corporate sales. During the same period, a 40 percent growth in headquarters staff was accommodated in only 10 percent additional occupied area, without compromising the overall quality or design of the facility.

The Client's Participation on the Program-Design Team

The client fully participated, making certain the program findings and analysis were incorporated into the master plan for the complex, its architecture, and space planning. The client's sophistication, philosophy, and complexity contributed to the positive tenor of this effort. Because H-E-B stresses quality in business, personnel, customer service, and in the products it sells in its stores, as a client it understood how to effectively employ the quality control aspects

H-E-B Headquarters viewed from San Antonio Riverwalk.

of programming. This was further supported by the fact that H-E-B, with its many stores and shopping centers, is also a sophisticated building owner. Among its divisions, the organization includes a real estate department, a store planning and design department, and a construction arm.

H-E-B knows how to participate in complex projects. The company's organizational structure includes accounting, advertising, publicity, printing, human resources, purchasing, marketing, planning, design, and real estate, all under one roof and leadership structure in addition to its hundreds of stores.

The president and chairman of family-owned H-E-B, Charles Butt, championed the programming-design process (1989) and encouraged upper management's participation in the programming process. Vice presidents served as experts for their particular departments during programming, while the controller generated accurate staffing counts and projections that served as the basis for large-scale space programming and allocation.

A three-part team of client, programmer, and architect emerged in the project. The three maintained a dynamic tension during the entire process, through construction and move-in, leading to efficient, effective, and quality decisions.

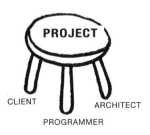

Programming

Programming research employing observation, focused interviews, question-naires and measurement progressed hand in hand with design inquiry employing diagrams, sketches, models and plans. Programming methodology employed at H-E-B was carried out on a "fast track" with master planning and design starting at the same time as programming. Multiple data gathering techniques blended together in a seamless multiple-method approach, resulting in a set of office planning rules of thumb that guided project planning and design.

FAST-TRACK PROGRAMMING AND DESIGN

It is generally thought that programming must precede design to be effective. It seems to make sense that designers ought to know what a project requires in order to design to meet its needs. In practice, however, design in most projects begins when programming begins. This project demonstrates how design and programming carried out in tandem rather than sequentially can be more robust and mutually beneficial.

Like its design, the H-E-B program was developed as an iterative spiral of research, reports, and decisions. With design carried out in the same iterative way as programming, the H-E-B program-design process resulted in two interlocking spirals, a sort of double helix in which programming and design decisions that needed to draw on each other were carried out at the same time, and both processes moved forward without interruption.

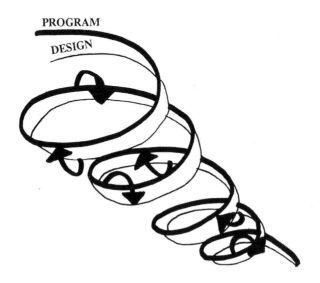

Interactive programming-design spiral.

Regulatory, financial, and organizational objectives dictated that design begin immediately and not be delayed until a "final" program was written. The existing historical buildings presented the architects with spatial and formal design challenges and opportunities that needed to be solved during feasibility studies and master planning, independent of programming. These included creating a courtyard in the complex, demolishing unused Quonset huts, and restoring the historic stables and arsenal buildings. The architects decided to complete the courtyard by adding what was later called the "north" building, a new building with a facade that fit into the historic context. The architects also decided to bring light and views into the large non-office buildings by selectively cutting portions out and creating atria within the buildings.

Three streams of activity in the H-E-B program-design process continually fed each other. The architects in the design stream determined the overall direction for planning and design—the parti, as architects call it—namely, the courtyard scheme for the new complex. The programming stream focused on defining the planning and design problem; namely, how to consolidate a complex and a disparate group of departments into a cohesive organizational whole that was the right size for H-E-B (Stubbs, 1989). Members of the client's management and decision making stream, managed the relocation of this large organization from Corpus Christi to San Antonio, coordinated all the consultants involved in the project, made the financial and development decisions needed to keep the project moving, and determined the number of employees who would eventually move into the new headquarters.

The programming effort employed a multiple-method environment-behavior data collection approach adapted to the needs of the project. These methods included:

- Physical environment observation of existing conditions
- Behavioral observation of work in existing settings
- Questionnaires
- Interviews
- Archives review, and
- Photographic documentation

Rules of Thumb / POE Hypotheses

For the H-E-B designers to translate the Design Program into a physical work place environment, more than numbers and diagrams were needed. The program therefore included a set of evidence- and theory-based planning and design principles responsive to what the programming effort determined were the organization's style and culture. These "rules of thumb," developed before planning and construction took place, represented principles based on translating program research into design directives. Once built, these became knowledge embodied in the buildings-in-use. As such they are the potential subjects for ongoing research and the source of as-yet unmined future knowledge.

PROGRAM RULES OF THUMB FOR H-E-B DESIGN/ HYPOTHESES FOR FUTURE POE

Planning Principles
- Facility purposes from goals and objectives
- Gross space locations from functional analysis
- Gross space allocations include growth

Individual Workspace Planning
- Workspaces reflect both rank and tasks
- Minimize workspace area differentials

Workgroup Planning
- Workgroup as basic planning unit
- Workgroups sized to minimize growth disruption
- Dedicated workgroup circulation
- Daylight/environmental quality for all employees

Common Amenities
- Conference space proximity/control for higher-rank employees
- Conference areas for growth and expansion
- Conference room allocation by workgroup task need
- Common amenities allocated for workgroup tasks

Each rule of thumb is explained below, along with the resulting planning and design decisions.

PLANNING PRINCIPLES

• *Design purposes from goals and objectives.* The more architects and designers are clear about what an owner wants a building to achieve—its purposes—the more effective their trade-off decisions about that building will be. Some dimensions of purpose are derived from the building type. A post office, store, or headquarters, each has unique purposes. Other dimensions of purpose are more specific to a client, owner, manager, or user group. The client's goals and objectives for the building—how they will eventually judge the building's success or failure—determine its purposes. Major purposes for the H-E-B headquarters were determined to be:

- supporting corporate administration
- consolidating all administration in one place
- developing a high class yet modest public image
- matching headquarters image to service quality in stores
- accommodating corporate and headquarters staff growth.

• *The functional basis for planning decisions.* Headquarters programming is organizational analysis. The more the program and the resulting buildings reflect a thoughtful theory of organizational structure and function, the more the complex will support the organization's operations. The organizational approach employed at H-E-B aimed to support four areas of the organization: dealing with the outside world, getting the job done, integrating departments and personnel, and recognizing employees' need to maintain contact with other parts of their own lives (Parsons, 1964; Merton, 1957).

• *Gross space allocation for growth.* The more gross square footage allocated per person in planning reflects an organization's growth and expansion plans, the longer will be the period before the facility must be reprogrammed and redesigned. To accommodate growth without leaving large spaces empty within each workspace, an additional allocation of 12 percent was built into the space allocation at H-E-B, creating a spatial generosity within workgroups. This number is derived from design inquiry indicating that workgroup space planned for seven people will neither seem overly spacious with 12 percent too much space, nor crowded when an eighth employee is added—a 12 percent increase.

INDIVIDUAL WORKSPACE PLANNING

• *Workspace allocation by both rank and task.* When the workspace allocated to an individual employee reflects both rank and task needs, space use will be most efficient and support both the individual's and the organization's work goals. Each employee's space at H-E-B reflects both the employee's managerial level within the organization—clerical, supervisor, manager, up to president—and additional space needs based on the specific tasks that an employee carries out.

Precise workspace allocations were critical during the space planning phases of the project. As opposed to gross space allocations per employee, square footage assignments were made based on the needs of particular positions—considering the tasks, furniture, equipment, and storage required to perform the work associated with each employee.

• *Minimize workspace differentials.* The quantitative difference in workspace allocation between the lowest-rank employee and the highest-rank employee of an organization reflects the organization's attitude toward its own hierarchy. The difference between the smallest and largest workspace in the H-E-B complex is kept to a minimum: 190 square feet. As with workspace allocations, additional square footage was assigned as required by the tasks assigned to the workgroup or individual.

WORKGROUP PLANNING

• *The workgroup as basic planning unit.* When workgroup areas are used as the basic planning and design unit, space use is both most efficient and effective from the individual employee's and the organization's perspectives. Workgroups provide the basis for territorial privacy without requiring totally enclosed workspaces for each employee. Within each workgroup, as few as six and as many as fourteen individuals perform similar or closely related tasks, and their proximity is essential to achieving the group's organizational mission. H-E-B space planning was organized around identifiable workgroups.

• *Workgroups sized to minimize disruption for growth.* Workgroups of six to fourteen employees planned as cohesive areas give the greatest opportunity for incremental growth without major design shifts, and reduce the negative spatial impact of such growth throughout the organization. The workgroup planning unit is most adaptable to small-scale incremental growth.

• *Dedicated workgroup circulation.* If circulation within a workgroup is planned primarily for employees in the workgroup or others doing business with them, workgroup efficiency and effectiveness will be greatest, noise and traffic disturbances will be minimized, and employees will be able to concentrate better. This can be accomplished if separate shared circulation is provided for others to get from their workgroup area to such places as toilets, elevators, cafeterias and other workgroups. Foot traffic—circulation—within a workgroup is dedicated to that workgroup in the H-E-B plan.

• *Daylight/environmental quality for all employees.* When clerical and other lower-rank employees can see windows and daylight when seated at their workspaces, this offsets some of the negative effects of their having less space to work in than others. As a planning principle, shared access to daylight often requires tradeoffs. At H-E-B, lower-level employees were given access to daylight even at the expense of private, enclosed offices with windows for others.

COMMON AMENITITES

• *Conference space proximity/control for higher rank employees.* Although workspaces for employees of different rank are similar in size, those in managerial positions are located closer to conference rooms and have greater control over their use. If conference spaces are located near the workspace of higher-rank employees, and if these employees or their staff schedule conference space use, higher-rank employees have greater effective territory.

• *Conference rooms to absorb expansion and growth.* If conference rooms and enclosed offices are the same size, workgroup growth can take place by judiciously converting these rooms to individual workspaces. This use can be either temporary or permanent as the needs of the organization dictate. This enables quicker realignment of space within workgroups as the organization's staff grows, making less renovation and construction necessary during periods of growth.

• *Conference room allocation by workgroup task need.* When conference rooms are allocated by workgroup need, overall space can be saved. The different ways conference rooms can be located are: dedicated to a workgroup, located within a workgroup but used by more than one workgroup, in a neutral area shared by several workgroups as well as for meetings by non-headquarters personnel. The H-E-B plan employed all these types of conference spaces.

• *Common amenities allocated for workgroup tasks.* By virtue of the tasks they need to perform, different workgroups have different needs for shared amenities. When these amenities are allocated to workgroups by virtue of need rather than by right, space efficiency and use of shared amenities is greatest. Shared amenities include such things as copiers, printers, mailrooms, break areas, storage rooms, restrooms, and conference facilities. At H-E-B these amenities were distributed throughout the facility, located near workgroups and departments that had an identified need for them. Not every workgroup that requested a particular amenity received it within their workgroup, but all were located within convenient proximity of the facilities necessary to the efficient fulfillment of their assigned tasks.

POE and Programming

In December 1988, six years after initial planning and programming, the company had doubled its sales, while the physical facility had undergone very few changes and no expansion. After five years of rapid corporate sales growth, during which no additional office space or major reconfiguration was required or made, many groups had put off filling approved staff positions because they did not have space for another workstation.

After a series of on-site meetings with various executives it became clear that H-E-B had successfully utilized the facility during this period. Groups had more or less grown in place to fill the available space and amenities such as conference rooms had been absorbed into work space for expanding groups.

The Maintenance Department had also proposed a number of interventions to add even more workstations. One particular proposed change included building new closed offices along an interior sunlit atrium that brought daylight into a very dense open-office area. While this seemed like a reasonable solution to the immediate need for more managerial offices, the change would have diminished the quality of the entire surrounding area, which was occupied by a number of workgroups. H-E-B, concerned that quickly planned interventions would compromise the original programming, planning, and design parti of the complex, requested an evaluation.

The post-occupancy evaluation included a structured walk-through in conjunction with a series of interviews with officers and directors. These methods uncovered that while the overall high quality of the planning, design, and ultimate building had endured, it was now being squeezed by the success and growth of the organization. Because several new organizational priorities and relationships had developed, the physical complex was no longer fully synchronized with the evolving corporate structure. In the initial planning and programming effort, much energy had been expended to match the needs of the corporation to the needs of workgroups within the building complex. In the reprogram, H-E-B was committed to reiterating the original good fit between corporate priorities, organizational structure, the buildings, space planning, and individual workgroup allocations.

This case study was based on the work of Hartman-Cox Architects; Chumney & Associates, associated architects; John Zeisel, programmer and design reviewer; Marc Maxwell, AIA, re-programmer and renovation architect.

OVERVIEW

Collaboration among disciplines is rewarding to participants when it helps them improve their results by providing more useful information, better products, or greater payment. But collaboration can also be rewarding for its own sake when it improves participants themselves—when they come out of it with more skills than when they began.

This chapter proposes that among the skills researchers and designers can learn from working together are how to evaluate the risk of making decisions in different situations, how to use critical testing to build a body of shared E-B knowledge, and how to use both tacit and explicit knowing.

The next chapter is more concrete than this chapter. It describes how to design your research project so that you can efficiently use available resources to solve your problem.

CHAPTER 5

RESEARCH METHODOLOGY: APPROACHES, DESIGNS, AND SETTINGS

A great discovery solves a great problem, but there is a grain of discovery in the solution of any problem.

— GEORGE POLYA
How to Solve It

An environment-behavior research project begins with the definition of a problem. You assess what you know about it and what you want to know, and you envision what you might do with the results. Then you commit yourself to a way of working: focusing on a particular problem and deciding on the research design and setting that will best solve your problem.

Decisions to Be Made About Research Methodology
Research Approaches
Diagnostic
Descriptive
Theoretical
Action
Research Designs
Case study
Survey
Experiment
Research Settings
Natural
Contrived

By answering these questions for yourself, you can design the methodology for your research project to achieve what you want: What do I want to find out? What design will give me useful information to solve my problem? What setting will use my resources effectively?

Your chosen combination of research approach, research design, and research setting in which to carry out your research indicates your preferred methodology. The more the methodology you develop is appropriate to your subject matter, the more employing your results in practice will result in the outcomes you want.

As discussed throughout this book, your choice of methodology and methods is independent of whether you want to collect quantitative or qualitative data. Each approach, design, setting, and set of methods can comprise either qualitative or quantitative data collection depending on the study's purposes and uses. An experiment is a good example of this flexibility. A design-research team planning a healing garden might change one element in such a natural setting—for example, adding a bench—and then employ qualitative participant observation techniques to understand the effects of this change on people's feelings and behaviors. Qualitative research before, during, and after the change provides the experimental data necessary to decide whether the team wants to make the bench a permanent addition. Another team that wants to develop international guidelines for user-responsive parks might employ the same research design but in a quantitative quasi-experiment. Pre- and post-test measures in such a study requiring a higher level of certainty might include questionnaires, behavior counts, and other quantitative data collection methods and analysis. As you read this chapter, keep in mind that both qualitative and quantitative methods are appropriate for each approach, design, and setting.

RESEARCH APPROACHES

Beginning with little knowledge about your study object, you might choose to carry out a reconnaissance mission (Gans, 1962) to find out about it generally: its purposes, its parts, and the relations among its parts. Alternatively, you may want to describe the object or some of its parts more thoroughly. In either case your main objective is improving your understanding of the study topic. However, your main objective may be to use the findings of your study to refine theoretical knowledge or to influence real-world decisions and their consequences. If your aim is to understand a topic, you might engage in a *diagnostic* or *descriptive study*; if it is to refine a particular theory or improve action, you might undertake *theoretical* or *action* research.

Research projects generally combine several approaches sequentially. Researchers begin with a diagnostic phase and then decide to describe further certain of the traits they have uncovered. They use theories when they make such decisions and when they formulate hypotheses they want their data to test. Ideally, applied research influences action. Examining each approach separately can help you select the mix most relevant to your problem.

Diagnostic Studies

Diagnostic studies help you deepen your understanding of a setting; they provide suggestive evidence on a broad realm rather than "rigorous safeguards on the trustworthiness and specifiability of findings" (Hyman, 1955: 67). They make the tradeoff between precision and breadth in favor of breadth. They offer insight into the structure and dynamics of a whole situation, possibly even setting the stage for further research. Gans' *Urban Villagers* (1962) is just such a study.

Gans lived in Boston's West End neighborhood for eight months in 1957 and 1958 just before the low-rise buildings were torn down and replaced by high-rise, high-income housing. In *The Urban Villagers* Gans diagnoses the West End, identifying its purposes, its parts, and the relations among them. He identifies what to him are the constituent parts of an urban village—an area where immigrants "try to adapt their nonurban institutions and cultures to the urban" (1962: 4). He describes what it was like to live there: family life, politics, social services, the mass media, and consumer goods. He compares West Enders with other Americans and concludes that their ethnic differences are less striking than their socioeconomic similarities. He comments on urban redevelopment, criticizing the definition many redevelopment officials then held of a "slum."

In his methodological appendix to the book, Gans points out that he had no rigorous hypotheses to test in his study and that in fact his findings were themselves hypotheses. His evidence, more "illustrative than documentary" (1962: 347), leads to after-the-fact sociological interpretation rather than tested knowledge. He describes his study as

> an attempt by a trained social scientist to describe and explain the behavior of a large number of people—using his methodological and theoretical training to sift the observations—and to report only those generalizations which are justified by the data. . . . Properly speaking, the study is a reconnaissance—an initial exploration of a community to provide an overview—guided by the canons of sociological theory and method but not attempting to offer documentation for all the findings. . . .
>
> Many of the hypotheses reported here can eventually be tested against the results of more systematic social science research (1962: 349–350).

For trustworthiness of findings, diagnostic studies rely on the consistency, clarity, and coherence of the insights they develop in the situation being studied. Researchers who want more precise measurement of particular attributes of a group or situation may carry out a descriptive study based on conceptual frameworks developed in diagnostic ones.

Descriptive Studies

Descriptive studies describe and measure as precisely as possible one or more characteristics and their relations in a defined group. Developing clear concepts and translating these into something that can be counted as a manifestation of the concept are particularly crucial problems in descriptive research. Rainwater's study of fear among residents of the Pruitt-Igoe housing project in St. Louis (1966) is a descriptive study. On the basis of a large survey Rainwater describes the feelings of a particular group of people about their homes. He shows that their feelings about the street are dominated by fear of social, psychological, and physical attacks from the outside world and that they consequently see their homes as havens from such abuse.

In an equally interesting but less well-known descriptive study, Altman, Nelson, and Lett (1972) interviewed 147 sailors about their and their families' activities at home. Their complex questionnaire requested the sailors, among other things, to draw floor plans of their homes, to label rooms, and to describe in detail how each room was used, by whom, and whether doors were left open, closed, or locked. The investigators recognized sets of relations in their data:

> . . . two characteristic family styles of use of home environments. One family pattern . . . seemed to be characterized by a cluster of environmental behaviors which were [open, accessible, informal, sharing, overlapping, and socially interactive. The other type of] families had firmer environmental boundaries between members, a more formal approach to use of space, and a lesser degree of family interaction and role sharing (1972, p. 2).

Their description of family styles began to uncover possible explanations for their findings:

> There was a bare suggestion that family size/density may be important. Other directions potentially worthy of exploration may concern family integration-disintegration, e.g., marital discord and harmony, presence of emotionally disturbed, delinquent, etc., children. Thus, the matter is totally open as to dynamics associated with these differences. [However,] because this study was inductive and normative in goal, no real explanation of these stylistic differences could emerge from the data. Future research can fruitfully address this question in terms of underlying factors associated with these behavior patterns (1972, p. 3).

Altman et al. recognized that different types of research projects can and must build on one another if a body of environmental design knowledge is to be established.

Theoretical Studies

Theoretical studies test specific hypotheses suggested by experiences elsewhere or primarily derived from more comprehensive theory. Such studies tend to increase general insights and to focus more on the conceptual framework of a problem than on the precise nature of the group they are observing.

A clear example of a theoretical environmental design study is *Social Pressures in Informal Groups* (Festinger, Schachter, & Back, 1950), carried out among married Massachusetts Institute of Technology students living in one dormitory complex. Festinger's research team wanted to test, among other hypotheses, the theoretically derived notion that the closer similar people live and the more chances an environment offers them to meet, the more likely they are to become friends. The research team chose these dormitories because they provided a naturally occurring experimental setting in which to test its theoretically derived ideas. All students living there were married, many were supported by the GI Bill, and all were assigned haphazardly to an apartment unit. Thus, the population was both homogeneous and apparently randomly placed throughout the site. Important for Festinger's natural experiment was the fact that the dorms were designed with two different building types on two sides of the dormitory site.

Festinger et al. found in both types of housing that proximity alone did not lead to greater friendship. Rather, placement of front doors and pathways was crucial: The more chances neighbors had to meet each other on the way in or out, the greater the likelihood that they would become friendly. As mentioned in Chapter 2, the researchers called this dimension of environment "functional distance."

Action Research Studies

In *action research studies* changes are made and analyzed that have direct and lasting consequences for people beyond the research subjects. An example is the

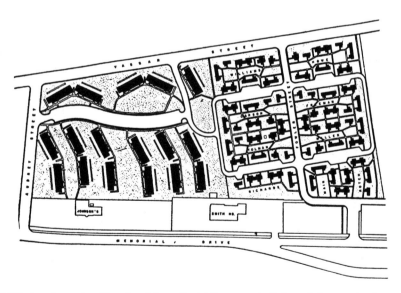

M.I.T. dormitory site. (Reprinted from *Social Pressures in Informal Groups*, by Leon Festinger, Stanley Schachter, and Kurt Back, with the permission of the publishers, Stanford University Press. Copyright 1950, renewed 1978 by the Board of Trustees of the Leland Stanford Junior University.)

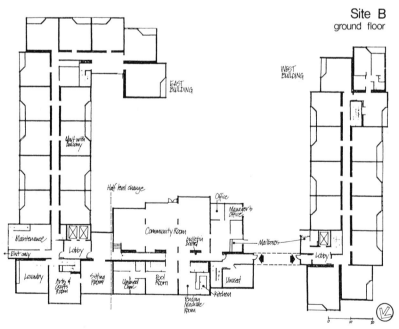

Relation between social spaces and path from entrance to elevator in two high-rise buildings for older people. (From Howell, Sandra C., *Designing for Aging: Patterns of Use*. Cambridge, MA. MIT Press (1980). Reprinted by permission.)

construction and evaluation of the Twin Rivers new town where residents were expected to walk more and drive less (Keller, 1978). Changes there included special pathways and stores located near housing, and consequences resulted for inhabitants. Action research projects aim to improve future actions by understanding earlier, similar changes in such things as physical environments, management rules, policies, and the way decisions are made.

To assess the side effects of an action, investigators can compare the consequences of different actions taken in roughly similar situations. Howell and Epp studied social spaces in high-rise housing for older persons (Howell & Epp, 1976; Howell, 1980). They located two nearby buildings whose designs differed primarily in whether or not residents were required to pass by social spaces as they walked from entrance to elevator. On the basis of observed differences in behavior at these and similar sites, Howell and Epp made visible for designers both positive and negative consequences of such decisions in the future.

For example, they found that if a building forces its residents to interact in social spaces when they do not want to and provides social spaces that make residents feel they are in a "goldfish bowl," residents are more likely to fight and less likely to use social spaces. This happened in building B, where the arrangement of entry, social spaces, and elevator forced residents to see others whenever they came or went. In building A residents were encouraged but not forced to interact and could engage comfortably in private meetings in the activity rooms. They consequently used these spaces more.

Comparative action research settings may occur naturally or may be created analytically by careful sampling. For example, a survey of the consequences for low-income families of moving into new public housing (Wilner et al., 1954) established matched samples of people who did and did not move, thereby assessing consequences over a ten-year period of a major E-B policy while it was being implemented.

Action research studies are particularly prevalent among the works of environmental researchers and designers who see planning and evaluation research as essential to effective decision making.

RESEARCH DESIGNS

What research design an investigator chooses to study a problem with depends on the way the problem is defined, what the investigator wants to know, the nature of the object being studied, previous knowledge the study is based on, and type of results desired. Researchers use a *case study* design when they want to develop intensive knowledge about one complex object, because case studies are designed to understand an object as a whole. Investigators who want to learn about classes or types of elements embedded in a diverse group use a *survey* design. *Experiments* are useful to test the effects of actions by observing differences between a situation in which an action is taken and another in which it is not taken.

Case Study

Investigators use case studies to describe and diagnose single, internally complex objects: individuals, buildings, episodes, institutions, processes, and societies. In case studies investigators delineate boundaries of an object and then observe such things as the elements it comprises, relations among elements, the development of the object, and contextual influences.

A case study is appropriate when investigators are interested mainly in information specific to the particular study object and context, rather than information easily generalizable to a large population.

Some benefits of this approach can be seen where a research/design team was asked to design a residence for older veterans in the small, rural town of Oxford, New York (Nahemow & Downes, 1979; Snyder & Ostrander, 1974). At Oxford, psychologists Ostrander and Snyder wanted to provide information about one institution—its residents, staff, and setting—in order to design another institution for essentially the same constituents. They had carried out similar projects on the needs of older people, which provided them general direction for asking questions, but at Oxford they were particularly interested in what this specific situation was like and what was important to the lives of users of this institution. This situation was prototypically appropriate to a case study.

In case studies, multiple research techniques, especially participant observation, are often needed for investigators to get sufficient data about different aspects of an object. At Oxford the researchers lived in the facility for several days in a row, observed and recorded physical traces, observed and mapped resident and staff behavior, analyzed health records, carried out an interview survey with all residents, and tested mock-ups of proposed room arrangements. By comparing the various types of data, they gradually began to see what was important in the daily lives of the people there.

Two examples of insights by the investigators at Oxford are that some older persons lived a twenty-four-hour lifestyle and that there was a link between physical mobility and friendship. While living at Oxford, Snyder and Ostrander observed that a number of residents heated food in cans on radiators and kept food chilled on their windowsills, although a communal eating hall served meals on a regular schedule. (Institutional rules prohibited hot plates or refrigerators in rooms.) When interviewed, residents explained food in their rooms by complaining that the cold meals served on Sundays were not sufficient. But it was clear to observers that food was prepared in rooms on other days and at other times as well. Investigators saw clues to a more plausible reason for this activity when they got up in the middle of the night and found some residents reading in the library (3:00 A.M.) and others taking showers (5:00 A.M.). Insomnia kept the residents up! Further probing in focused interviews revealed other activities that reflected a twenty-four-hour resident lifestyle that was independent from the institution's main 6:00 A.M. to 7:00 P.M. schedule. As a result, final design proposals included such things as all-night activity rooms, kitchenettes accessible to small groups of residents, and individually regulated temperature controls, all intended to accommodate residents' need for greater self-reliance.

Use of multiple techniques also enabled these researchers to see a special problem of residents: those with less mobility had fewer friends. This insight was sparked when investigators analyzed administrative records, finding a higher percentage of residents confined to wheelchairs than observed in the hallways and a strikingly high percentage of residents with degenerative disabilities. They had a hunch that these percentages were important. Observation of behavior and physical traces, as well as interviews, pointed out why wheelchair residents were so isolated: between the one ward on which many of them were located and most communal areas there were physical obstacles such as stairs, and aides assigned to help them were too weak to overcome these obstacles. The link between disability and social isolation gave particular force to design proposals for barrier-free access to all communal areas.

The design and research team at Oxford was particularly explicit about why it made certain design decisions. One set of design decisions was made to increase residents' control over their environment and in turn to increase residents' self-reliance and self-respect. These decisions included one-story buildings, rooms clustered around community spaces, a glass-enclosed "street" connecting clusters, and individual rooms easily convertible from singles to doubles.

Each design decision at Oxford is as much a research hypothesis as any verbal or mathematical formulation might be. It is a proposed response to a problem. Although acceptable for the moment, it is open to further testing and refinement. Future post-occupancy evaluation researchers will be able to build on and improve these hypotheses linking environment, behavior, and psychological states.

When case studies are carried out on topics that have been studied before and about which some theory exists, results may be generalizable beyond the particular situation examined. Another way to make a case study more generalizable is to choose a setting that is in many ways typical of other settings—for instance, a hospital whose size, facilities, services, and setting are like those of many other hospitals.

Survey

A survey design is useful when investigators want to find out in detail about a phenomenon, such as housing satisfaction, or about a class of elements, such as single-family homes located in a neighborhood with many kinds of dwelling units. Using a survey, investigators—such as census takers—can study groups of elements dispersed over a broad geographic area. The U.S. Housing Survey census gathers physical-trace data on buildings and their condition much as the population census finds out about people. Survey researchers who study large populations often choose to gather easily quantifiable data, which are less time-consuming to analyze than qualitative data. For this reason frequent research methods used in surveys are mail questionnaires and interviews. Yet, as the housing census makes clear, quantifiable survey data in E-B research can also be gathered by systematically observing physical traces or even behavior.

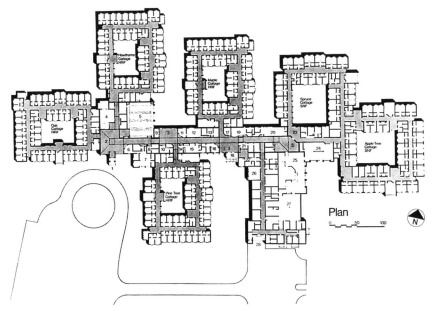

Plan of Oxford veterans' home. New York State Veterans Home, Oxford, New York. Completed 1979. Architects: The Architects Collaborative, Inc., Cambridge, MA. Used by permission.

To study school property damage in Boston, a team of sociologists, planners, psychologists, and architects used a multiple-method survey design. The goal of the study was to provide guidelines for Boston architects to use in designing schools that would decrease property damage and maintenance costs (Zeisel, 1976a). Zeisel and his colleagues used a survey design to explore the general phenomenon of property damage: They examined all sorts of damage that occurred at public schools, throughout the city. They wanted to discover how frequently different kinds of damage occurred and how various types of damage correlated with elements of physical settings. The resulting guidelines were intended to be applicable to any Boston school, not to one particular building.

Team members could not assume the problems at one school to be typical of those at others, nor did they have the resources to visit every school in Boston. They therefore used random sampling to identify a number of schools to visit, making sure the selected schools included both old and new ones, those in primarily white and black neighborhoods, and schools 1 in various school districts. The logic of sampling is central to surveying. Using such devices, investigators try to ensure that conclusions from the sample of a phenomenon—in this case property damage in the selected schools—are as similar as possible to conclusions they would draw were they to study the entire population from which the sample was chosen.

Limits to generalization are determined by such things as sample size, size of the population, and sampling techniques, as well as the salience of questions asked. Survey researchers, trying to be extensive in their studies, often expend a great deal of their resources to gather data with a low per-unit cost, using methods like questionnaires, interviews, and counts of physical traces and behaviors. These methods yield easily quantifiable data that are useful in making statistical generalizations about a larger population. To use these methods effectively, however, it is essential to ask questions and count behaviors or traces central to the study topic. If salient attributes are overlooked, they cannot be counted after costly data collection is complete.

To keep from overlooking salient attributes (as far as possible), survey investigators often carry out qualitative diagnostic explorations before settling on final quantitative data-collection instruments. The less the investigator knows about the subject, the greater emphasis is put on preliminary diagnostic studies. Just before the major data-collection effort, drafts of techniques are pre-tested to see whether they are understandable and whether any essential topics have been omitted. Various data-collection techniques are often employed so that each technique can be used to check on the others' completeness.

In Zeisel's survey of Boston schools, for example, investigators used observation of physical traces, observation of behavior, interviews, questionnaires, and records analysis. During an initial walk-through with custodians at each school, the researchers recorded physical damage in field notes and photographs. This information served as the first indication that custodians dealt with four kinds of property damage: (1) malicious damage resulting from attacks on the school; (2) misnamed vandalism, whose consequences look the same as malicious damage but are caused by acts not intended to do harm, such as hitting hockey pucks against a glass door for fun; (3) nonmalicious damage, such as graffiti, resulting from conscious action not meant to hurt the school or anyone in it; and (4) maintenance damage, such as paths worn across lawns, the consequence of unconscious behavior and design that is unresponsive to user needs. The first type of damage assumes malicious behavior but the last three do not.

Investigators then carried out focused interviews with groups of students in various neighborhoods to redefine the four categories so they would reflect students' points of view. A survey of maintenance records was made to determine the most frequently reported type of damage (window breakage) and how often custodians differentiated between malicious and nonmalicious damage (seldom).

After investigators analyzed all these data, they designed a structured questionnaire and sent it to maintenance superintendents in every school district in Massachusetts to find out how they spent most of their repair budget (on windows), whether they felt damage was increasing or decreasing (increasing), what they had already done to reduce the risk of future damage (fire and theft alarm systems), and how often they differentiated malicious from nonmalicious damage (seldom).

The multiple-method survey convinced the investigators and the city of Boston that the design guidelines they developed would make visible to architects a variety of design opportunities for reducing property damage in future schools.

Experiment

An experimental design is appropriate when investigators want to measure the effects that an action has in a particular situation. An experiment answers the question "What difference does it make?" What difference does it make if residents of a building participate in making management decisions, for example, or if students live in single rather than double rooms?

In an experiment you want to be able to focus observations on a small number of attributes at one time. To do so, you need control, so that you can be as certain as possible that the effects you observe result from experimental changes rather than the way the changes are administered or the effects are observed.

Control is used to achieve experimental knowledge built on the principle that "knowledge is knowledge of differences" (Runkel & McGrath, 1972). More precisely:

> Basic to scientific evidence (and to all diagnostic processes including the retina of the eye) is the process of comparison, of recording differences, or of contrast. Any appearance of absolute knowledge, or intrinsic knowledge about singular isolated objects, is found to be illusory upon analysis. Securing scientific evidence involves making at least one comparison. For such a comparison to be useful, both sides of the comparison should be made with similar care and precision (Campbell & Stanley, 1966: 6).

In experiments researchers organize their operations so as to control various factors. For example, to measure changes caused by the action they introduce, they may observe the situation both *before and after* the action. And to make sure that changes observed are not the result of other characteristics of the situation, they may also observe an equivalent one in which the experimental action is not taken. This comparison may be created by randomly assigning participants to both situations. The participants assigned to the situation in which the action is not taken are called a *control group*.

Experimental design in applied behavioral science research often seeks to approximate the control of a laboratory experiment but does not, because of real-world restrictions. Campbell (1974) distinguishes research projects in which randomized assignment is absent by calling them *quasi-experiments*. Environment-behavior studies often employ quasi-experimental research design (Marans and Ahrentzen, 1987). One classic quasi-experimental study is Carp's evaluation of Victoria Plaza, a housing project for older people in Austin, Texas (1966). As best she could, Carp controlled and identified differences between residents and a nonresident control group. She first interviewed and tested all 352 older persons who had applied for housing to the Austin Housing Authority—before any of them knew whether they would be accepted to Victoria Plaza. Of these persons, 204 were accepted and became residents; 148 either were rejected or withdrew their application. One year after the resident group moved in, Carp re-interviewed 190 residents and 105 nonresidents, treating the latter as a control group. This means she first compared the groups to determine whether they were significantly different in their initial interviews and then compared how they had changed or not changed during the year.

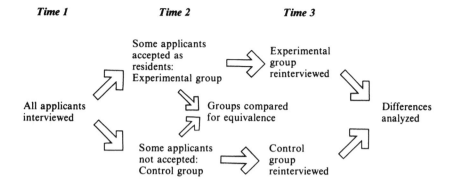

Before moving in, the two groups turned out to be significantly similar on such items as age, income, education, self-evaluation, health, and condition of present housing. The housing authority's procedures, however, tended to select for residence more people who said housing was a major problem for them and who seemed to be slightly more mentally alert and cheerful. For some research purposes, it might be preferable to select residents and nonresidents randomly; this is not always possible in real-world settings. In addition, since Carp was interested in how a real-world setting works, it would have gone against her intentions to control the assignments artificially. She overcame this problem by comparing the two groups after selection, taking small differences into account in her analysis and assuring herself that there were no significant differences on traits that might reasonably be expected to confound results. And what were those results?

Among the more interesting results was that while residents showed a decrease in desire for medical services (from 7 percent to 1 percent), nonresidents doubled their stated need for these services (from 13 percent to 27. percent). Carp concludes that either the new housing actually affected residents' physical well being or it improved their morale so that they did not feel as much of a need..

Not surprisingly, almost none of the residents felt that housing was a major problem after living in Victoria Plaza a year, while among nonresidents the percentage feeling this way increased from 27 to 29. A significant side effect of residence is also interesting: Before tenants were selected in 1960, only about a quarter of both residents and nonresidents felt they had "no major problems." In 1961 this figure jumped to nearly three-quarters for residents, while the proportion among nonresidents remained near a quarter (see Table 5–1).

Table 5-1. Percentage of Victoria Plaza residents and nonresidents reporting "no major problems"

Residents	Nonresidents	
In 1960, before moving	25	27
In 1961, post-occupancy	74	29

From *A Future for the Aged: Victoria Plaza and Its Residents*, by F. Carp. Copyright 1966 by University of Texas Press. Reprinted by permission.

Of course not all the effects of the housing move were good. Carp found that residents who started getting together with neighbors socially after moving in also felt more than nonresidents that they had to "keep up with the Joneses"—to buy new furniture and clothes. Residents became "house proud" in their new building, sometimes even dipping into capital. Although they felt living this way was worth it, many were worried: among residents the percentage who considered money to be a major problem increased from 65 to 89; among nonresidents it remained at 60.

Carp's experimental design was not as controlled as some laboratory experiments in physics—but then she wanted to shed light on the effects of an actual E-B setting. She did this as best she could in a real-world situation. Experiments also have limitations, and Carp discusses how these affected her research. For example, because she had to stay out of the picture to avoid influencing the results of the experiment, the extent to which her findings can be generalized to other older people may be limited. Her groups were initially self-selected (they wanted to move in) and were screened by eligibility requirements (excluded were younger persons, more prosperous ones, and those with serious handicaps). Once again this reinforces a major methodological point: Each investigator has to select his or her research design on the basis of his or her particular needs and purposes.

RESEARCH SETTINGS

Whether a research project is to be a case study, a survey, or an experiment, investigators can decide where they are going to study their problem. Will you slosh in the rain watching events in natural settings? Or will you sit indoors, observing subjects in contrived settings?

Natural Settings

Natural settings offer researchers the unique opportunity to observe people in settings they choose to come to, engaged in activities a contrived setting could not recreate: patients decorating walls of hospital rooms with get-well cards, customers expressing ethnic attitudes in neighborhood bars, teenagers roughhousing around schools.

Natural settings are particularly appropriate for diagnostic studies in which investigators want to find out what is actually going on—what elements, relationships, and dynamics are salient. You cannot fully observe a situation and its context if certain portions are excluded from study, as they might be if the situation were transferred to a contrived setting.

Gans' *Urban Villagers* (1962) and *Levittowners* (1967), Cooper's *Easter Hill Village* (1975), and Keller's study of Twin Rivers (1976) are all environment-behavior community case studies carried out in natural settings. Each of these investigators found a residential complex, neighborhood, or new town in which interesting E-B questions were answerable: Does proximity affect friendship? Does residential history affect residents' satisfaction with a new home (Cooper, 1975)? How far will residents walk to stores in our automobile society (Keller, 1978)?

In locating sites to carry out such studies, investigators look for situations, settings, and events that reflect theoretically relevant questions. A prepared investigator will be on the alert for research opportunities that present themselves suddenly: a change in train schedules, an accident, a new town being planned nearby, or an amenable building committee.

In natural settings you can carry out an experiment by manipulating a part of a physical environment, a particular social behavior, or a policy. For example, in a hospital an investigator might change a wall or a window in a randomly selected set of similar patient bedrooms, estimating effects by comparing before-and-after observations in rooms with and without changes. In one ingenious natural experiment, researchers had well-dressed and badly dressed men cross against a red light at a traffic intersection to see how the implied class difference of clothes influenced other people to break the law (Lefkowitz, Blake, and Mouton, 1955). In natural experiments like this one or like Carp's quasi-experimental study of Victoria Plaza, investigators are seldom able to control the situation by experimental methods like randomly assigning participants to different groups. In this project they assumed that at about the same time of day and at the same street corner, most people would vary randomly on attributes that might affect their responses to well-dressed or sloppily dressed men. (Pedestrians followed the well-dressed jaywalker more often.)

In natural policy experiments, investigators work with "experimental administrators" to collect baseline data, to help decide the location and timing of policy implementation, and to measure aftereffects both where policy is and where it is not implemented (Campbell, 1969). For example, the U.S. government wanted to determine the effects of a housing-allowance program under which people who cannot afford market-rate dwellings are given a direct monetary allowance. The government ran a large-scale natural E-B experiment in several selected areas around the country to determine the actual consequences of this policy. Among their findings were that increased spending ability did not necessarily lead low-income people to move into higher-income neighborhoods. Rather, social cohesion among residents and exclusionary practices among landlords led to higher prices being charged and paid for housing in what remained predominantly low-income areas. Such an experiment is costly, but less costly than if the program were implemented nationwide in a way that did not produce the desired results.

Surveys can also be conducted in natural surroundings, but the location for data gathering may be unimportant for the study itself. For example, Fried (1963) studied how people reacted to being forced out of Boston's ethnic West End neighborhood by urban renewal; he interviewed these people wherever they happened to have moved in the Boston area. The focus of the study was not the respondents' location, rather, it was their attachment to the place where they used to live—which by then was a demolished pile of rubble. Fried found that most residents experienced intense suffering because they felt that they had lost both their friends and the place with which they identified. For a smaller group the forced move had a positive effect. Dislocation presented an opportunity to move up the social and economic ladder, which living in the West End did not encourage. The setting that tied together Fried's respondents could be reconstituted only through data analysis.

Contrived Settings

Contrived settings are planned and controlled research environments in which one can observe people and gather data from them. One such setting is the experimental laboratory, in which investigators control the setting, choose participants randomly, effect controlled changes, and measure some attribute of the subjects after those changes. People in such situations usually know they are subjects in a research project, but not always. For example, to determine effects of room attractiveness on behavior, investigators had their assistants administer tests to subjects randomly assigned to rooms that were decorated differently—one "beautiful" and one "ugly" (Mintz, 1956). In addition to measuring subjects' test scores, however, for three weeks they observed how long it took the two assistants to administer the same test in different rooms. In thirty-two pairs of testing sessions, the examiner sitting in the "ugly" room finished before the one in the "beautiful" room twenty-seven times. The two examiners finished first the same proportion of times when they were in the "ugly" room, and the proportions remained the same during each of the three weeks of the experiment. This last observation led the investigators to conclude that the environmental effects were not merely initial adjustment reactions on the part of examiners. Although the assistants knew they were participants in the project, they did not realize they were actually its subjects.

Contrived settings can also be used to carry out surveys. For example, to determine teenagers' responses to particular types of property damage, Zeisel (1976a) showed slides to invited groups and interviewed them as groups about their reaction, finding that the teens defined most of the damage as nonmalicious. Altman et al. (1972) individually administered their survey questionnaires to sailors who were also together in a contrived setting.

Such contrived surveys, or "judgment tests" (Runkel and McGrath, 1972), may be carried out to determine people's reactions to videotape material as well. For example, using response meters in addition to questionnaires enables each subject to express a judgment, such as excitement or dislike, during the film by pressing a button. Responses recorded by a central computer are automatically correlated to the moment in the video when the judgment is made. Such methods, well known to test reactions to advertisements, can easily be transferred to assessing visual presentations of virtual or real environments.

In many people's minds natural settings are associated with diagnostic case studies and contrived settings with descriptive or theoretical experiments, much as they think white wine must be served with fish and poultry, red with other meat. Both beliefs are oversimplifications that inhibit researchers (and diners) from choosing the combination of elements that will best solve their problem and meet their needs.

The following programming and design case study of the *Star Tribune* newsroom in Minneapolis demonstrates the results of an interactive action research approach to space planning.

CASE STUDY 3

TEAMWORK SPACE AT THE STAR TRIBUNE NEWSROOM
Minneapolis, Minnesota

The *Star Tribune* is the largest newspaper in Minnesota, with a daily distribution of over half a million. Of the newspaper's 2,200 employees, 380 editors, reporters, photographers, computer graphic designers, and copy editors work in the "newsroom" where daily stories and weekly features are generated, written, and organized on the newspaper's pages.

In a traditional newsroom an editor decides a story needs to be written and assigns a reporter to gather information for the story. When the editor and reporter decide a photograph might enhance the story or graphic material might explain a particular aspect, the editor assigns a photographer or graphic designer that task. Photographers and graphic designers tend to leave the larger framework of the story to the editor and reporter. When the reporter's, photographer's and graphic designer's work is complete, a copy editor finalizes the story and a graphic designer lays it out for the paper.

Afternoon huddle at the *Star Tribune*.

On a daily basis, all the section editors—city news, international news, business, sports, and features—meet at about 10 A.M. to plan what the major stories will be for that day and where they will fall in the paper as a whole. At about 4 P.M. the group meets again to reexamine, modify, and firm up their morning decisions—finalizing the paper for the day. At the Star Tribune these meetings were called "huddles."

The majority of people in the newsroom work on computers most of the time—reporters, editors, copy editors, and graphic designers. Even photographers work on computers, digitally manipulating photographs. Ergonomic workstations are essential to such work because constant keyboard use carries with it a high risk of carpal tunnel syndrome—damage to the channel in the wrist carrying nerves and tendons between the hand and arm.. Ergonomics is the study of the relationship between the shape and function of the body carrying out a task and the design of the body-environment interface to maximize efficient energy transfer and minimize strain. Although it was originally developed in areas such as tool, airplane cockpit, car seat, and space station design, the design of work environments relies heavily on ergonomics.

Redesign of the newsroom was not the only project at the Star Tribune. Each newspaper has a distinct "look." The New York Times originally had a staid look with no color. In the 1990s the Times added color photographs on its front page and revised the size and typeface in its masthead. The New York Daily News has a much brasher look—large name at the top with full-size photographs and gigantic scale type announcing major breaking stories. The Star Tribune, like many papers, also had a "look" that had not changed for years.

In the early 1990s the Star Tribune launched several simultaneous initiatives with the assistance of consulting advisor Robert Lockwood (1992). The editor-in-chief and publisher hired Lockwood to redesign the "look" of the paper. Lockwood organized an integrated team of reporters, editors, photographers, and graphic designers who together developed alternative formats and "looks" for review by the editor-in-chief and the publisher.

At the same time, deciding that the traditional way to generate, investigate, write, edit, and illustrate stories was too linear for the dynamic shape of news at the turn of the millennium, the paper's editor, Tim McGuire, initiated a grand effort to "restructure the newsroom." He felt that the Star Tribune needed to implement an organization focused on teamwork in order to stay competitive with other newspapers and other media. More specifically, he directed a small group of newsroom staffers to develop a reorganization plan for the newsroom that was structured around traditional news areas (such as city news, international news, business, sports, etc.), but no longer employed the assembly line, relay race sequence: editor–reporter–photographer–graphic designer–copy editor. Instead, teams comprising all these professionals were to work together to develop, investigate, and present stories.

The editor's goals for this effort were:

1. To become a more reader-focused newspaper.
2. To become more journalistically excellent.
3. To become more diverse in the newspaper and in the newsroom.

4. To enrich job satisfaction.
5. To become faster, more flexible, and more efficient, especially when it comes to adding new initiatives and dropping old ones.
6. To gather, prioritize, and present the news no matter the channel.
7. To build community and communities.

The clearest way to explain the reason the editor wanted more teamwork is to give an example of news in which a photographer or graphic designer might be better suited than a reporter to be the central figure in presenting a story. When the Space Shuttle Challenger exploded over Cape Canaveral the initial story needed no text. A full-size front-page photograph of the horrifying disaster "told" the whole story. When there was a major nation-wide gas shortage in the 1980s in the United States, one newspaper told the story with graphics alone. The front page was a large graph: Across the top was the length of time cars were waiting at gas stations; along the side were the names and addresses of all the service stations in the city.

The newspaper's first environmental design initiative began with its decision to respond to the needs of its newsroom employees for a more ergonomic workplace; to purchase new "ergonomic" workstations to replace all the old-fashioned wooden desks staff had been sitting at for decades. In 1995, major changes were underway at the Star Tribune with an Ergonomics Committee overseeing the ordering of new furniture, a newspaper Redesign Team planning the paper's new "look," and a Restructuring Committee reorganizing the staff into content-based teams.

Design was also taking place, but in an unintended way. The Ergonomics Committee had the firm supplying the furniture develop an "installation plan," a computer generated arrangement intended to maximize the number of workstations the space could accommodate. In a related effort which was not identified as related until later on, the Restructuring Committee developed a complex organizational plan of multi-task teams, the basic component of each team being workgroups comprising one or more of each of the professionals in the newsroom.

But there was a problem! The paper's redesign effort could move forward without much reference to the restructuring efforts. But if the restructuring and ergonomics efforts were not closely aligned, the paper would end up with an organic "teamwork organization" forced to fit into a "linear workstation" layout. It would be extremely difficult, if even possible, for teams to work together if the work area layout did not respond to the varying team goals and work styles, different size teams, and different time constraints—features is a weekly effort, city is a changing effort depending on the news, and sports tends to peak in the evening and on weekends.

The architecture critic for the Star Tribune, Linda Mack, a participant in a monthly environment-behavior brown-bag luncheon group, was the first to identify this potential problem. She convinced the Ergonomics Team that a revision to the planned layout was imperative if the new ergonomic workstations were going to support the health of the "restructured" organization, as well as the individual health of each employee. Through her contacts at the informal luncheon seminar, she contacted John Zeisel—an environment-behavior specialist—for advice. The specialist organized a team of himself and an interior designer, Jenny Anderson-Eisenmann, and proposed that the newspaper take a new evidence-based design direction. The team was interviewed and selected to redesign the newsroom so that it would be responsive to the forthcoming restructured team-centered organization.

The Newsroom E-B Research Effort

The multi-method E-B interior design programming effort was structured to create a design program for the entire newsroom that reflected and balanced:

- Project goals of each organizational interest group
- The structure and function of the newsroom as a whole
- The teamwork needs of each news group
- The work needs of each employee

In order to determine project goals the E-B team carried out a series of focus interviews with both individuals and groups. Interviews were conducted with the editor, the newsroom managing editor, the Restructuring Committee, the Ergonomics Committee, and a group of editors that was overseeing the Ergonomics Committee, the Ergonomics Sponsors.

In addition, the E-B team examined archives: the editor's printed announcements, the restructuring team's documents, and the plans developed for the newsroom by the furniture contractor.

- *To understand the structure and function of the newsroom* as a whole, the E-B team employed *observation of behavior and observation of physical traces. Behaviors observed* included the way team members carried out their individual tasks, the frequency of their coming and going, the amount of time they spent at their desks, and the amount of time talking to others one-on-one

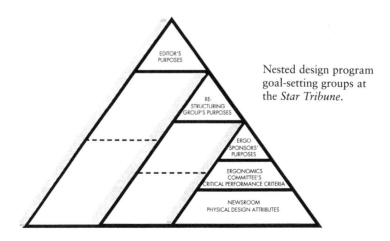

Nested design program goal-setting groups at the *Star Tribune*.

EDITOR'S PURPOSES

RE-STRUCTURING GROUP'S PURPOSES

ERGO SPONSORS' PURPOSES

ERGONOMICS COMMITTEE'S CRITICAL PERFORMANCE CRITERIA

NEWSROOM PHYSICAL DESIGN ATTRIBUTES

Impromptu work meeting in individual work area.

Focused team meeting around surface connecting two team members.

or in groups. The E-B team analyzed the observed behaviors in terms of the individual, the specific teams, and the newsroom as a whole—for example how the morning and afternoon huddle team assembled, conferred, and disbanded.

One of the most pleasant and interesting methods employed was observing physical traces and documenting them photographically. The newsroom environment is a visually exciting one with each reporter, photographer, editor, and graphic artist assembling material and mementos in their workspace that reflect their unique skills, their interests, and the stories they cover. Because so few outsiders come to the newsroom it is more a backstage than a front-stage

Editor working in private with view of team space.

Personalized work space.

environment. Employees dress informally and use their work environments to display informal and often humorous messages. Observation of physical traces also determined storage needs, specifically the large amount of books, papers, and photographs assembled in piles on each employee's desk.

• *To understand the teamwork needs of each news group,* the E-B team brought each news team into a conference room one at a time for a group focus interview. The following props were assembled: small scale table models of the furniture already purchased and being installed, cardboard disposable instant cameras with twelve exposures, and a flip chart.

The E-B team asked each news team:

• What other type of team exemplifies members' view of their newsroom team —a baseball or soccer team, a team of volunteers, the team that flies the Space Shuttle, an America's Cup sailing team?
• How would team members describe the way they work together: what are the team's structure and dynamics?
• Would the team organize the scale-model parts in a way that they collectively felt reflected the structure and dynamics of their team?

The E-B team recorded the responses to these questions on the flip chart and photographed the organized models the news teams constructed.

Handing each team member a disposable camera, the E-B team then asked each person to photograph places the employee felt expressed the feeling she would like to see in the newly redesigned newsroom—in her workspace, in her team space, or in the newsroom as a whole. When the teams met again two weeks later, the E-B team discussed the photographs and shared their analysis of the data provided in the first group interview.

Once these data were gathered and analyzed, the E-B team presented its design program in the form of a news story, deciding that the best way to convince its client was to present its findings and design intentions employing the client's own graphic and written format.

The E-B-Researched Design Program

The design program consisted of the following elements:

• The project goals
• Critical performance criteria for the project
• An overall "urban design" design concept and scheme
• "Urban" elements available to all employees
• News team locations in the "urban plan neighborhoods" of the newsroom
• Teamwork layout principles and layouts for each team
• Teamwork elements
• Workstation trade-offs

• *Project Goals.* Each of the major participants and participant groups had their own definition of what the goals were for the newsroom redesign effort—the editor-in-chief had a broad business view, the Restructuring Team members saw work style as most significant, and the Ergonomics Team members focused on physical health issues. To develop a unified design concept, the design program first had to consolidate these diverse views into a single list of goals. The final goals identified were:

• Higher quality newspaper
• Smoother idea-to-newsprint process
• Journalists achieving their potential
• Job satisfaction/quality of life among all employees

- Accommodation to long-term industry change
- Ergonomics and health
- Productivity and creativity
- Diversity within community
- Organization of continual change

Critical performance criteria for the project: Related to these general goals was a set of performance criteria that was used both to generate the initial design concept as well as assess the degree to which plans met the intended goals as they progressed in the design and implementation process. In the minds of those who were going to use the newsroom, it was critical that its planning and design create and support the following conditions.

- Health and safety
- Reduced stress
- Focus on creativity
- Better work product
- Celebration of craft
- Human place to live
- Aesthetics and fun
- Individuality and teamwork
- Human contact and synergy
- Environment of change and learning

The E-B-Researched Newsroom Design

The newsroom's design responded to the data collected and to the demands of the scale of the newsroom: a single space for 325 people.

- *Research-based urban design concept.* Such a large space required a major organizing principle to serve not only as a focal point for the design process, but more importantly to provide a naturally mapped environment around which the many users can easily develop their own cognitive maps. In the newsroom, an "urban" analogy emerged as the major research-based planning concept.

After identifying that a major problem newsroom employees faced was disorientation in the large 50,000-square-foot space, the design team decided to organize the entire newsroom as a city—with boulevards, streets, neighborhoods, front porches, parks, coffee shops, newsstands, and alleys. Cities generally have a natural and understandable organization—either organic, developed over time like European cities, or grid-structured, like Midwestern American cities. In either case, it is the major features of cities—town halls, squares, rivers, parks, and so on—that provide orientation cues for everyone. The research findings of planner Kevin Lynch (described in Chapter 4) provided an inspiration for the newsroom design. The organizing plan centered on Lynch's five urban elements: landmarks, pathways, nodes, districts, and edges.

- *Landmarks.* The E-B design team implemented several landmarks in the newsroom city There is a "forum" as in ancient Rome where the wise citizens met

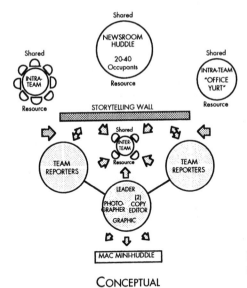

CONCEPTUAL

Focus group output: evolution
of team space design.

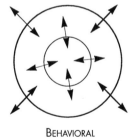

BEHAVIORAL

TEAM BEHAVIORAL DIAGRAM

Δ   Team core of leader, copy editors, graphic design
and photographer work intensely together
Δ   Central core works at intervals with outer ring of
reporters
Δ   Reporters work with community

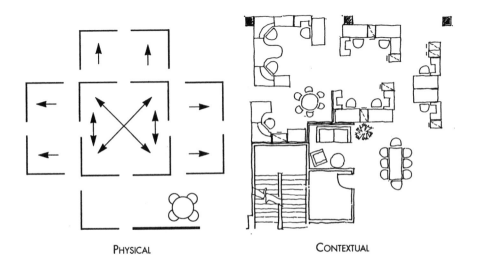

PHYSICAL   **CONTEXTUAL**

to make policy. The Star Tribune forum, located at the single spot most visible from all work areas, serves as the place for the morning and afternoon meetings. Other landmarks include a coffee shop located at the end of Park Avenue, Central Park at the intersection of Park Avenue and the Sports Street, the Library, and the open amphitheatre conference area at the other end of Park Avenue. Each of these landmarks helps employees orient themselves in space. Minor landmarks were created in three places by the erection of newsstands where the previous day's newspaper is laid out for inspection and employee comment.

• *Pathways.* The newsroom city is organized on a grid system with pathways of different size running parallel to one another. The largest pathways are avenues, there are smaller streets, and then alleys that are located within the work neighborhoods. The simplicity of the pathway scheme, and the fact that each pathway ends up at a landmark, serve to further orient employees.

• *Nodes.* When pathways intersect they create nodes—such as where Park Avenue meets the Sports Street. The more each such intersection is celebrated with a design element, the more it helps orient users of the space. Central Park is located at the most important such intersection, with comfortable colorful armchairs, a coffee table, natural light from the adjacent windows, and plants. But even more important than the physical Park is the fact that the major news section neighborhoods are located adjacent to the Park, and each of the section editors has a large circular desk extension facing the Park. This serves one of the major performance criteria of the space's success—increased informal interaction among employees from different sections.

• *Districts.* Each of the newspaper's sections constitutes its own neighborhood—where the editors, writers, photographers, and graphic artists work together as a team. There are neighborhoods for city, national, and international news; for sports, business, and culture; and there are administrative neighborhoods as well. Each neighborhood houses one of the teams that participated in a group focused interview during programming research. The results of the interview—types of organization as well as layouts tailored to the particular workgroup approach—were implemented organizing the workstations and selecting specific workstation extensions. Choices were made among tables in the center of the work neighborhood, shared tables attached between two workspaces, privacy barriers between workspaces, and large round extensions that serve as small conference tables attached to a particular workspace.

• *Edges.* Along pathways, edges that define neighborhoods. The major edge-related design decision in this case was to locate as many shared files as possible in cabinets along the edges of major pathways. Because reporters and others had formerly stored so many books, articles, and papers on their desks, and continue to do so, shifting to a team-based storage system was a large effort—but only by achieving this was enough space saved to enable the park and coffee shop to be included in the floor plan. Edges of neighborhoods were planned either to offer a hard edge—privacy for those within those teams—or a soft edge—welcoming interaction with passersby. The precise edge condition chosen reflected the degree of interaction the team said it needed to get its job done most effectively.

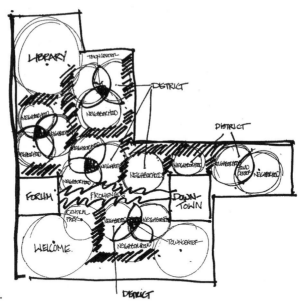

Conceptual plan.

Final plan.

In sum, the *Star Tribune* newsroom posed a complex set of interrelated planning and design problems: scale, numbers, way finding, teamwork, effectiveness, and efficiency. The research-based approach resulted in a design that simultaneously addressed and resolved a great many of these problems.

This case study was drawn from the teamwork of designer Jenny Anderson-Eisenmann, ASID and environment-behavior specialist John Zeisel, Ph.D.

OVERVIEW

Research methodology comprises commitments to a particular problem and a way of working on it. The first steps that you take when planning a methodology for a research or research-based design project have important consequences not only for the way you allocate time, money, and energy but also for what you observe later on. This chapter describes some ways to approach research problems and makes visible the consequences of certain choices, so that people involved in research projects can choose strategies suited to achieving what they want. This chapter proposes that investigators can avoid costly revisions in their research if they self-consciously answer the following questions: What do I want to find out? What research design will give me useful information to solve my problem? What setting will use my resources effectively?

The next chapter examines criteria researchers can use to evaluate and thus improve the quality of their research.

CHAPTER 6

RESEARCH QUALITY

Personal knowledge in science . . . commits us, passionately and far beyond our comprehension, to a vision of reality. Of this reality we cannot divest ourselves by setting up objective criteria of verifiability—or falsifiability, or testability, or what you will.

— MICHAEL POLANYI
Personal Knowledge

People devised research to improve the way they observe the world around them and to increase their control over the consequences of their actions. When research is applied to design, the better the observations, data, and analysis are, the better the design can be.

To achieve these ends it is useful to differentiate what you know from what you do not know—that is, to identify problems present-day knowledge cannot solve. If what you know and do increasingly solves recognized problems and identifies new ones, your knowledge has improved.

When other people can understand your research methods and results, those others can help you identify your progress. When you can compare your research conclusions with other interpretations of the same data, you can identify your own progress. When you know how to transfer what you learn to new situations without unconsciously creating more unseen problems than you solve, you can improve your own action.

Investigators can maintain these conditions by continually asking themselves the following questions: Have I carried out my research in such a way that it can be shared with others? Have I presented my research results in such a way that they can be tested in comparison with other researchers' results? Have I clearly identified what problems my research results can and cannot solve?

Fundamental to continued learning is an open mind. Paradoxically, this is not easy for researchers to maintain if at the same time they want to use developed theoretical perspectives and build on a body of scientific knowledge. The difficulty is that working within a theoretical perspective sometimes limits researchers in identifying problems.

Investigators who share a theoretical perspective—also called a paradigm (Kuhn, 1970) or a research program (Lakatos, 1970)—make assumptions about some problems in order to focus attention on others that they feel are important. They may use this approach to direct research to answer questions and explain empirical results in ways that provide further insight into the theory rather than identifying additional problems. "Don't study that topic, you won't learn anything interesting from it" can actually mean, "It won't help develop the theory."

When investigators regularly question their assumptions, they keep their minds open and provide themselves with new problems to solve. One simple way to do this is to think about seemingly obvious observations as hypotheses

---

Criteria of Research Quality

Shared Methods

    Intersubjectivity
    Reliability
    Validity

Comparable Presentations

    Tenability
    Testability

Controlled Results

    Specifiability
    Generalizability

---

rather than facts. For example, saying, "It may be a street corner" instead of "It is a street corner" generates questions whose answers will be new knowledge: What, precisely, is a street corner? Is this really one? How do different people define street corners? How do street corners differ?

Creative investigators know how to keep avenues open for exploration. Using shared methods, presenting findings comparably, and knowing how to use results to solve problems all help make research explorations learning experiences.

SHARED METHODS

When a group of people jointly understand a set of research methods and use them to solve problems, they can identify ways to improve the quality of their research. For this to occur, investigators make *explicit* their methods, the way they use these methods, and the conclusions drawn from using them. As a result of the sharing this explicitness makes possible, members of the group can (1) use one another as measuring sticks to establish the acceptability of a method to the group, its *intersubjectivity*; (2) test a method against shared expectations about how it ought to perform in use, its *reliability*; and (3) assess how well a method can be used to inform action in the real world, its *validity*. A high degree of intersubjectivity, reliability, and validity among techniques excludes from the sphere of scientific observations those that are idiosyncratic, murky, inconsistent, or reflect only one person's unique perspective.

Intersubjectivity

When researchers assess one another's investigatory methods, they judge such things as how appropriate the methods seem for solving a particular problem, how reliability and validity of methods have been controlled, and how consistent the methods are with accepted theory. A group of scientists judge, for example, the extent to which the application of a method fits their scientific attitudes about how a phenomenon ought to be studied. Does a researcher employ only nonvisual interview techniques to find out about people's perception of a city, or does he use an array of techniques better suited to more recent theoretical developments about cognitive maps and images (Downs and Stea, 1973)?

Investigators might question the efficiency of using participant-observation techniques to measure national attitudes toward environmental legislation or using survey research to determine the salient characteristics of toddlers' play behavior in order to design one daycare center. This type of assessment is meant to guard against a common occurrence: Investigators accustomed to using a particular technique sometimes find themselves applying that technique to every problem they encounter.

Intersubjective judgments, which are based on attitudes shared by a group, can be a limiting criterion in scientific inquiry. However, when the scientific community at large shares in research through publications and discussion, there is hope that diversity of opinion will reward the innovative as well as reasonable and appropriate use of research methods.

Reliability

A perfectly reliable research method would consistently yield the same results if it could be used repeatedly in a situation that did not change at all. In solving actual research problems, the reliability of a method is greater when, after repeated use, little variability of results can be attributed to the method. For example, the more a set of categories for recording behavior used repeatedly or by different persons leads to similar records in the same situation, the more reliable it is considered to be.

We can think of assessing the reliability of a method in the same way we think of assessing the reliability of a child's memory about an event. We cannot recreate the event, but we can test his memory of it in order to share in his experience.

For example, a child returns with his sister from the drugstore and reports that he saw a friend of ours there. We could wait a short while and then ask him to describe again whom he saw, to see whether the two reports are the same. We might ask his sister what happened and compare reports. Or we might ask the child to describe the beginning and end of the event to see whether the two reports agree.

Reliability tests used in research parallel this type of questioning. One method (test-retest) compares results from the same technique used with the same group after enough time has elapsed for the subjects to forget their answers to the first test. Another method (alternate forms) compares the results of two techniques that are the same type of tool, yet are designed to be as different as possible; one technique considered reliable is tested against the other. A third method (split-half) compares the results of two parts of the same technique applied to the same group at the same time. For example, results of twenty-five questions in a fifty-item test of housing satisfaction are compared with results from the other twenty-five; each set of questions is considered a repetition of the other.

When research techniques are used to observe changes, reliability tests minimize the chance that changes recorded are actually due to repetitious use of the measuring technique or to the way it is applied. Reliability tests uncover such things as shifts in results as the technique gets older or worn by use, shifts in results over time because initial application affected respondents' responses to the next application, and results reflecting systematic errors in the technique.

Unfortunately, it is usually quite difficult to distinguish between measurement error (unreliability) and actual change in an object. The problem arises because most topics deal with things that are continually changing. Therefore, constant results ought not to be expected even with perfect reliability. When a research technique is test-retested for reliability—say, a standardized semantic differential scale measuring perceptions of a new building—it is highly likely that some attribute of the context or respondent will have changed, however slightly. If investigators in such a situation measure no change at all (false constancy), they do not congratulate themselves for using reliable techniques; it is likely that their unreliability is covering up actual changes. Instead they begin to refine their measures to respond to the real change that is likely to have taken place.

Using multiple research techniques to study a problem also increases reliability and decreases the chance of falsely constant results. Collecting different kinds of data about the same phenomenon with several techniques counterbalances bias inherent in any one technique with the biases of the others. "Triangulation" of methods to increase reliability assumes, of course, that techniques are not biased in the same way (Webb et al., 1966).

We want to make methods more reliable so that when we talk about comparable research data we can assume we are talking about the same thing. Testing for reliability helps to establish and stabilize a shared memory among researchers—a shared set of categories for structuring and recording experience.

Validity

Investigators use research findings to achieve real ends such as making design decisions. The more a method increases their and others' control of action, the more valid the method is considered to be. Most variability in research results can then be attributed to actual changes, not the research methods used.

Validity can also be seen as a criterion applied to the report of a child returning from a trip to the drugstore. We want to be able to act on what the child tells us. If he has reliably reported that a special friend of ours is working at the drugstore, we want to be able to trust that our walking to the store will have the consequences we want—namely, that we will find our friend. If we do, the child's report can be called valid as well as reliable.

If the child reports that a friend whose funeral we just attended was the store clerk, we would immediately discount the story as invalid. But if the report is possibly valid, we could test its validity by, for example, asking his older sister (who is more familiar with our friend) whether the store clerk really was the friend. Or we might phone the store and ask for our friend, assuming that her presence now means the child actually saw her earlier. We could also try to remember more about our friend—does she have a relative who owns a drugstore; is she a trained pharmacist? This way we could construct other evidence to back up the child's report. We might also analyze the report to see whether the attributes the child uses to describe our friend all match the person we expect to find when we arrive at the store.

These everyday practical tests parallel formal ones for assessing the validity of research methods. *Concurrent validity* tests compare results from one technique with results of another technique that has been accepted as valid. For example, proposed new measures for ascertaining housing satisfaction are considered valid if results agree substantially with measures of satisfactory housing that other planners have already used successfully.

• *Predictive validity* tests compare results of one technique with those of another that measures a phenomenon the first is expected to predict. Answers to housing-satisfaction questionnaires, for example, might be expected to correlate with (that is, predict) the amount of time residents spend fixing up their homes. If this theory is applied, and results from questions about satisfaction correspond to results from questions about time spent, the satisfaction questions could be considered valid. This test assumes correct theoretical assessment of the relationship between satisfaction and time spent. It assumes that there are no other significant conditions influencing time spent improving the house that might confuse the comparison.

• *Construct validity* relies on correlation between the results of a technique and a network of theoretically related concepts. In other words, the property the technique measures is considered part of a more comprehensive construct whose other parts are in turn assumed to have been validly measured: Tests of design creativity are considered valid, for example, only if they correlate with measures of performance, achievement, and mental quickness.

• *Content validity* tests determine whether different parts of the same technique show the same results—for example, whether different sets of items on a design-creativity test show the same creativity quotient. This test is related to, but not the same as, the reliability test for internal consistency; it presents a similar problem when results are not consistent. It is difficult for investigators to know whether the two halves of the technique measured different concepts or measured several dimensions of one concept.

In general, the more methods that are used simultaneously to observe different traits of a complex phenomenon, the more chance there is to validate the techniques a researcher has, as long as all the methods are related to what the researcher wants to do. Investigators can compare techniques systematically by comparing the extent to which several techniques differentiate traits from one another while showing similar results when measuring the same trait—thus establishing the "convergent and discriminant validity" of the techniques (Campbell and Fiske, 1959).

In sum, validity tests are used to find out whether methods explain what is needed to act on the world with desired results, while reliability tests make certain that investigators using and reusing a set of methods collect comparable data. Intersubjectivity keeps scientists and designers who use research focused on a set of shared approaches and theories and ensures that they "speak the same language." Fundamental to being able to share and thus improve research methods is making as explicit as possible what methods are used, how they are used, and how results are interpreted—in other words, making the methods comparable.

COMPARABLE PRESENTATIONS

To see whether research results are an improvement on what we know, it is essential that alternative explanations of data can be compared. When we say that research hypotheses are *testable*, we mean that they are presented in such a way that they can be confirmed or disconfirmed by empirical data. When a hypothesis is confirmed, its *tenability* increases.

Testing a hypothesis is an attempt to show that a plausible rival hypothesis does or does not do a better job of explaining results. "A better job" means that one hypothesis explains what the other hypothesis explains and more (Popper, 1972). The tenability of a hypothesis is increased both when it is tested and not disconfirmed and when plausible rival hypotheses are disconfirmed. The more rival hypotheses that are disconfirmed, the greater is the tenability of the hypothesis (Campbell and Stanley, 1966). Mere replication of the same test findings does not necessarily increase the tenability of a hypothesis.

In testing a hypothesis the more you can present it so that the test will prove its inferiority, then the more important are results of the test. In other words, the greater the risk investigators take of being wrong, the more they can value the times they are right. Of course, being right merely means one has not been shown to be wrong, this time.

Three problems limit the testability of a hypothesis: (1) its wording, (2) the problem of defining data that can confront the hypothesis, and (3) the problem of getting necessary data (Galtung, 1967).

The Wording Problem

Statements considered true or false merely on the basis of their construction are customarily called *analytic*. Examples are "All boys are young males" (true) and "Girls are boys" (false).

Several types of statements are untestable in the sense that testing them gives us no new answers; nothing can be learned from testing them. A hypothesis that building a park will increase, decrease, or not change the feeling of neighborliness among adjacent residents is a *tautology*—a statement that is analytically true. A hypothesis that if there are more tall modern buildings in a city, the degree of city pride among residents will be simultaneously higher, lower, and the same is a *contradiction*—a statement that is analytically false. It is not useful to test such statements.

Problem of Defining Data

Some hypotheses do not analytically restrict researchers from imagining empirical data with which to confront them, but use terms or references that exclude them from being empirically testable. Examples are easy to think of: city planning is a necessary profession; territoriality is an innate drive among men and women; the Seagram's building in New York City is beautiful. One can imagine no data to test these hypotheses as worded, although they are not analytically true or false. In research terms, they are examples of *indecision*.

The following diagram presents tenability as a variable, taking into account tautologies, contradictions, and undecidable statements.

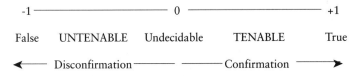

Tenability: Degree of hypothesis confirmation.

Adapted from *Theory and Methods of Social Research*, by J. Galtung. Copyright 1967. (New York: Columbia University Press, 1967.) Reprinted by permission of Universitets-forlaget, Oslo, Norway.

For tests of hypotheses to lead to greater or lesser tenability, the hypotheses must be worded so they lie on the line within (-1, +1), not including 1, -1, or 0. The terms *true* and *false* are left to describe analytic statements because "we cannot imagine a synthetic hypothesis that we cannot also imagine being confirmed to an even higher degree, or even more disconfirmed" (Galtung, 1967, p. 33).

Problem of Collecting Data

Conceivably, some hypotheses can be tested, only by data which are, in practice, impossible to collect or which would be destroyed by the collection process. For example, in practice, collecting data in order to confront hypotheses about unrecorded historical events or the transient internal state of an unavailable respondent would be impossible. In applied design situations, practical limitations on data collection include the amount of time and money available, interest among clients and research funders, and regulations that limit access. A hypothesis is necessarily untestable in a context that does not allow research.

In sum, testability is the possibility of improving a hypothesis by confronting it with empirical results and rival hypotheses. Testing either increases or decreases the tenability of a hypothesis. A hypothesis being tested must have a chance of being shown to be better or worse than another: the greater the chance of being worse, the more weight an investigator can give to the test.

CONTROLLED RESULTS

Whether the goal of a research project is improved theory or improved action, investigators want to apply findings—to describe concrete research situations in which they developed the data and use the findings in new situations. For example, did one "shared spaces" design in apartment buildings for older people actually make a difference to residents' use of them (Howell and Epp, 1976), and if other architects use this type of design, will it have the same effects? Did landscape design in Easter Hill Village actually lead to greater feelings of satisfaction among the residents Cooper interviewed (Cooper, 1975), and in what other situation will it have similar effects? *Specifiability* describes the degree to which research results can be used to control consequences of action in the testing situation studied; *generalizability* describes the degree to which results can be used to control action in new situations.

Specifiability

One improves the specifiability of results by controlling factors that might influence the observed changes in ways we do not see, making us credit an action or physical setting with effects it did not have. As the following hypothetical examples show, several factors can compound the interpretation of research results if investigators are not careful (Campbell & Stanley, 1966; Cook and Campbell, 1979).

1. History. Events outside an investigator's control occurring during the study can unwittingly cause observed results. An example would be if a "Plant a Tree" campaign started by neighborhood ecologists led to high resident satisfaction with landscaping in St. Francis Square (Cooper, 1971), and Cooper attributed this to the attractive initial planting.

2. Maturation. Natural growth taking place during a study can cause observed changes even though the growth is not causally related to the environment being evaluated. An example would be if Zeisel attributed reduced graffiti and property damage to school designs based on his research (1976a), when in fact the young people responsible had simply abandoned this activity because they grew up.

3. *Testing.* Research techniques early in a study can influence respondents so that later measures record changes resulting from the technique, not the environment. An example would be if Carp's (1966) move-in questions had sensitized residents so that a year later they showed more interest in the housing than they otherwise might have, and Carp attributed this to living in Victoria Plaza.

4. *Instrument Decay.* Measurement techniques themselves change during the research project and only appear to reflect change in the respondents. An example would be if observers of the buildings for older people studied by Howell and Epp (1976) grew used to their job and began to record briefer encounters as "social interaction," resulting in increases of reported interactions over time, although the number of actual interactions remained the same.

5. *Selection.* Selection procedures for respondents can bias some groups in a study. An example would be if Keller selected to interview only residents of Twin Rivers whose names appeared in the town newspaper and attributed a high level of environmental dissatisfaction to them, when they were actually acting dissatisfied to get their names in the paper again.

6. *Experimental Mortality.* Respondents drop out of studies in a way that systematically influences results. An example would be if antisocial residents in Westgate West moved out of apartment locations that forced them to meet other residents, and Festinger et al. (1950) attributed the mutual friendliness of present residents there to "functional distance" rather than tenant self-selection.

Factors of this sort also interact with each other to further confound the specifiability of a research project.

The hypothetical examples used to help define factors that can confound specifiability show that a careful researcher has many things to look out for merely to be able to interpret what she sees. Cooper's, Keller's, Howell's, and other environment-behavior studies referred to in the examples were well enough conceived and carried out that such confounding factors are either tested for or implausible. To increase the specifiability of a study, a researcher must consider and control outside influences on her data by using measures that include certain kinds of experimental designs, control groups, and multiple methods.

Generalizability

We also use research knowledge to control the effects of our actions in new situations. For example, knowledge that in 1966 at the University of California, Berkeley, students in dormitory rooms spent most of their time studying alone might be useful in designing a policy of primarily single-room dormitories for another campus (Van der Ryn and Silverstein, 1967). The more conclusions that were originally applicable in one setting or to one group that can be applied to others without unjustifiable side effects, the greater is their generalizability. Whenever we stretch the knowledge we have, we necessarily make errors; we use research to limit these errors.

There are several kinds of generalizability. One is generalizability to other, similar elements—whether those elements are settings, people, or events. For example, we can use what we know about property damage in a few Boston schools to plan social programs and redesign other schools (Zeisel, 1976a). Another type is generalizability to similar elements related in terms of time—in other words, to new situations. For example, studies of older suburbs (Gans, 1967) were applied five years later to plans for new towns throughout the United States. A third type is generalizability from one state of a developing organism to a new state. For example, small research projects to evaluate one housing-allowance experiment—providing poorer families with money to rent their own homes—were used in writing the final policy to be implemented nationally.

Procedures developed to increase the generalizability of information in these different senses so that we can improve our use of research include (1) reducing the degree to which research conditions influence the study topic—increasing validity; (2) increasing the similarity between elements being studied and other elements in the group; and (3) showing that results are replicable with representative groups of elements from different populations. Each of these measures, and others used to increase generalizability of findings, attempts to increase the likelihood that the particular research situation studied can be treated without uncertainty and risk, as if it represented other elements, new situations, and so on.

1. The less chance that the application of research methods unknowingly effected change in the sample of a population studied, the greater the chance that the sample behaved "as if" it were the rest of the group. For example, interviews with a group of residents before they move into a new building may unwittingly make them more aware of their environment than other tenants, leading them to make physical changes in their dwelling units they otherwise would not make. If investigators infer that other tenants in the building behave as this group does, they will be mistaken.

2. When it is impractical or impossible to observe everything or every person one wants to know about, investigators often sample part of the population to observe. For example, in E-B studies investigators have observed samples drawn from diverse populations of such things as hospital buildings, children playing, times of day, visitors to a world's fair, and social encounters. Various procedures may be used to choose the sample so that most of the variability of the total group is represented in the variability of the sample of elements observed so that, in turn, findings about the sample can be applied to describe the whole.

3. Investigators can define common problems and study them using essentially similar research designs in different populations. Such replications help us to apply more knowledgeably statements about one group to less restrictively defined groups. In E-B research, for example, one group of replications began with the neighborhood research of Whyte (1955), Fried and Gleicher (1961), Gans (1962), and Fried (1963) in Boston's Italian community, the North and

West End. Among the questions each of these investigators wanted to resolve was "Why are community members so strongly attached to their physically rundown, yet socially cohesive, setting?" These research projects all treated issues of territoriality, turf, environmental meaning, presentation of self, neighborhood symbolism, culture-bound user needs, and income-determined user needs. Replication studies in England (Young and Willmott, 1957) and India (Brolin, 1972), with African-Americans (Cooper, 1975) and Puerto Ricans (Zeisel, 1973a), in another low-income neighborhood near Boston (Zeisel and Griffin, 1975), and in still other settings dealt again and again with these topics and the basic question of attachment to a physical environment. As more opportunities for replications presented themselves, we increased our ability to apply relations between data originally applicable only to a small Italian community in Boston to other ethnic, income, and cultural groups.

The following case study of the Hypertherm Corporate Headquarters demonstrates how careful research applied in a dynamic interactive programming process can lead to creative design.

CASE STUDY 4

HYPERTHERM INC. CORPORATE HEADQUARTERS
Lebanon, New Hampshire

User participation in redesigning the space and the organization

Hypertherm is a successful manufacturing company located in Hanover, New Hampshire. In 1994 the company decided to plan a major facilities expansion in response to exceptional corporate growth and associated pressing problems of overcrowding and inefficient space-use. Hypertherm initially hired a Boston architecture firm that interviewed department leaders for information about adjacencies and square footage, and presented the Hypertherm management team with a "space program". While the "space program" provided a useful estimate of total square footage that could guide the town approvals process and cost estimating, it provided little useful information on what kind of space to design for the expanded organization. The architects used the "space program" to develop a concept drawing for the CEO, showing all the departments expanded to their projected future size, and where they would be located in the proposed expansion. The CEO, who was considering how to grow his organization, how to create a cross-functional team-based structure, and how to get all his people involved in change, was uninspired by this approach and asked the architects to stop work. Shortly thereafter, having read an article on workspace planning in MIT's *Sloan Management Review* (Vischer, 1995), the company interviewed and then hired as the project facilitator its author, Jacqueline C. Vischer Ph.D. and her firm Buildings-In-Use, a Boston and Montreal environment-behavior consulting firm specializing in managing workspace change.

Hypertherm main entrance.

The Planning, Programming, and Design Process

The workspace design process that the collaboration between Buildings-In-Use and Hypertherm established fell into the following stages:

1. Create a shared vision of the new space, set objectives, define the concept, and reach consensus around the decision to implement it
2. Set up a pilot study with an actual work team to test and evaluate the new workspace ideas within the Hypertherm organization
3. Communicate the concept to employees, work to get their buy-in, and identify spokespersons for the new cross-functional, team-based organization
4. Establish regular communication with the spokespersons, assign them tasks, and involve them in decision making during the design process
5. Hold a two-and-a-half-day work session at which each team carefully reviews then signs off on its new space, its location in the building, and the furniture it will be using
6. Collaborate with the contractor during construction
7. Plan and execute move-in
8. Manage the new space, gather feedback, fine-tune space needs, educate new hires who have not gone through the process, and publish a manual to guide users on how future space decisions will be made
9. Post-occupancy evaluation: survey users, comparing results to pre-move survey results; what have we learned?

The techniques and tools employed at each stage are presented below, with some description of how they worked. Pre- and post-change occupancy survey results are then compared.

The first step toward creating a shared vision was a *structured team walk-through* of the existing facility. The Hypertherm management team and consultants toured the facility as a group, discussing the tasks of each workgroup, pointing out difficulties and advantages with the present space, and commenting on each other's presentations. Recorded on cassette tape and transcribed, the tour commentary was presented back to the client along with a comprehensive set of photographs as a document of existing conditions. This activity effectively involved all the members of the team, efficiently gave the consultant a large amount of information, and began to build internal consensus on what needed to be done to solve the space problems.

Members of the five-person Hypertherm management team and the CEO met weekly thereafter for a series of two-hour *work sessions with the consultant*. The sessions were necessary for the leaders of the organization to define the organizational change they envisioned, to outline the main points of the physical environment they wanted to create to accommodate the new organization, and to set priorities that would enable them to communicate these decisions to their employees. The consultant acted largely as a facilitator during this stage in the process.

The meetings included goal and priority setting, documenting design criteria and guidelines for the new space, and even filling out questionnaires on individual decision-making styles to help the management team communicate and come to consensus. The consultant set the agenda and the tasks for each session. The consultant and her staff worked between sessions to organize and document the material they received and to produce sketches, drawings, and other illustrations that kept the process focused on design of the new building.

By the end of this stage, the management team had generated a set of goals and objectives for both their new space and their restructured organization. They had a set of design guidelines to be applied to the new design, and had established priorities ranking the relative importance of all they hoped to achieve. Most importantly for the future of the process, they had a consensus.

The three priorities for the new organization were team-based work, cross-functional communication, and a supportive and attractive work environment. The most important design guidelines were an open office environment with smaller workstations and lower partitions, collaborative spaces for group work, co-location of cross-functional team members, mutual inter-penetrability of office and manufacturing space, and convenient and accessible laboratories.

The next step required *involving the employees*, in order to assure acceptance of the new arrangement. A validated *questionnaire survey* about the physical conditions of work in the existing building started the process of employee involvement (Vischer, 1989). Every employee filled out the survey and was therefore alerted to the imminent new space-design process and to the importance of their role in it. The survey results, published in the company newsletter, also documented problems in the existing building.

The second stage of this phase was to *appoint one cross-functional team in the new organizational structure to test the new workspace concepts*. The team selected was an R&D group of mostly engineers that was beginning to work on a cross-functional basis, i.e. their administrative, marketing, and purchasing staff were co-located with the engineers and technicians. A room was set aside for this team, and all team members relocated there in an open plan layout with team worktables, shared file storage, and their research laboratory nearby. Six new workstations, representing different manufacturers' products, were located in this room for team members to test and evaluate. The consultants worked closely with team members, helping them understand the new cross-functional process, getting comments and feedback on the open plan, and encouraging management support of their initiative. In addition to providing feedback on the office layout and the new furniture, the presence of this group communicated the principles of the new space design to the rest of the organization, helping prevent gossip and speculation by openly showing management's thinking and what the other teams could expect. This group, in effect, piloted the process of managing change. Many team members were reluctant to part with a lifetime's accumulation of books and files—symbols of their history with the company—and others resisted the low partitions and shared workspace of the new concept. In the long run, this experience helped the pilot team adapt swiftly to the new teamwork environment after move-in. Their space in the new building has been one of the most effective and successful.

The *need for communication* was identified and respected throughout the process. The CEO and members of the management team spent generous amounts of time sharing design and planning decisions with team leaders and ensuring that these were in turn communicated to team members. The CEO spoke about the new space in a company-wide meeting, in team leaders' meetings, and in the Hypertherm newsletter. He also worked consistently with members of his own management team to ensure they stayed committed to and involved with the new organizational structure.

Once the new cross-functional work teams were formed, *representatives of each team—called "Space Planning Coordinators"—were selected to work with the design consultants*. These representatives were not the administrative assistants (who are often assigned tasks like space planning that no one else has time for, but do not have the authority to make necessary decisions) and they were not team leaders, who tend to be territorial. Those selected were experienced, responsible team members with a commitment to both the new organization and cross-functional teamwork, and with enough energy and determination to add space planning to their existing workloads.

The Space Planning Coordinators met regularly as a group with the consultants, who kept them apprised of design development decisions and assigned them specific tasks. These included providing detailed information about their team's equipment and storage needs, identifying adjacencies so that they could indicate where they would be located in the new building, working with their teams to identify where everyone would sit in the new layouts, and communicating the results of team decisions to the consultants. This process was not without friction: angry teams whose members did not welcome an open-plan concept raged at the consultants in space planning meetings, team members who disagreed about where they should sit in the new building confronted one another, some people could not give up their file storage cabinets, and some teams repeatedly sent their team seating layouts back into redesign because the Space Planning Coordinators could not get consensus from their teams (Vischer, 1999).

However, involving employees in the process was necessary in order for them to learn about the new, team-based organization and to prepare them for the new space. Identifying Space Planning Coordinators helped structure this involvement and make it real. The culture of Hypertherm is such that employee buy-in and ownership of change was needed in order for managers to move ahead with their vision. The space planning process became the mechanism for enabling this to occur successfully.

The design-participation process culminated in a two-and-a-half-day intensive work session the designers organized at the Hypertherm site. Drawings of the new buildings, showing team location and desk layouts, were produced as "final" versions and each team's Space Planning Coordinator was asked to sign off on the drawing as a contract agreement indicating that they accepted it and it would not be changed. The management team members and the CEO were present throughout the session to show support, out of interest, and to resolve any deeper conflicts confronting Space Planning Coordinators and environment-behavior design consultants. The process received considerable publicity at Hypertherm, with people coming in at scheduled times to have their say. Some simply signed, some required discussion and negotiation, and some ended in tears as employees gave up deeply held symbols of their history with the company (Vischer, 2005).

The Final Design

The resulting facility expansion consisted of a two-story office addition adjoining the much-enlarged manufacturing plant. The original building was retained and converted into expanded laboratories that communicate directly with the office space, an enlarged and updated main entrance, reception area, and an elegant client conference room where Hypertherm's tools and products are on display.

The new main entrance met management's goals of responding better to clients, suppliers, salespersons, and other visitors, demonstrating more of their product and how it was made, and providing associates with a separate entrance directly from the parking lot. Visitors arriving at the front move through a hallway connecting them to the plant and the offices, passing by viewing windows into the research labs to access the two-level main circulation walkway knitting together the manufacturing plant and the two-story office. The two-story walkway was designed in response to managers' and associates' concerns that the newer and larger office area might separate them from their colleagues operating the machinery. The walkway, open on both levels, pro-

Client conference room.

vides an impressive view of the manufacturing space from the second story, a particular advantage for Hypertherm's sales and marketing staff touring clients through the building.

In addition to the open-plan team space in the office building, the new two-story structure has a spacious cafeteria with double-height windows on two sides, a fitness room, and large men's and women's coatrooms and shower areas. The new associates' entrance, located adjacent to these amenities, offers direct access to the parking lot. Including a cafeteria of this caliber was a priority for management and staff, who previously had to eat in shifts in a small crowded room. Both plant workers and office staff value having access to showers.

Central to the design is an "agora"-type space at the juncture of the manufacturing plant, office building, and labs. Dubbed the "Town Square" by the CEO, this area is equipped with juice and snack machines, tables for people to place their coffee on while they talk, a large copy machine, employees' mailboxes, plants, and paper and electronic notice-boards. Successful collaboration between the contractor and the design consultants resulted in a large skylight being located directly over this space.

The main advantage of the employee participation process, and the one that paid off most for the company, was the understanding and acceptance of team workspace and how it should work. Everyone in the company has 48-sq.

Second-story walkway with views over manufacuring plant and stairway down to "Town Square."

Manufacturing plant as seen from walkway.

Associates' dining room with natural light.

Associates' entrance with convenient parking access.

ft. workstations with 52-inch partitions, including the CEO and the senior management team. Everyone has two pedestal filing cabinets, and each team has shared filing cabinets.

Each team also has a team worktable integrated into its team space, along with printers, fax machines, and other necessities. On each floor, a small number of enclosed workrooms are available on an as-needed basis for working alone, private meetings, and small group work sessions. Airy conference rooms were built throughout the facility for larger group meetings. While many of these decisions were controversial when they were made, all participants agreed that these design elements were necessary for effective teamwork. All these spaces

"Town Square" with stairs to second-story walkway.

Mailboxes and amenities in "Town Square."

were immediately used at move-in, saving the company time on revisions and redesign, and on responding to employee resistance and resentment. Information exchanges in the employee participation process also enabled the company to avoid major design mistakes that would have been costly to rectify.

The Evaluation

The survey results show employee assessment of the new space about one year after move-in compared to the results of the initial pre-design survey (Vischer, 1996). Not only were respondents pleased with their new space, but the process of buy-in and participation also helped them understand from day one how it would work. They accepted it without the period of discomfort and resistance often exhibited in new work environments because they knew exactly what to expect. They took ownership of it because they had been involved in decision making throughout.

For this environment-behavior approach to design to succeed, the consultants had to be skilled not only in research, office design, furniture layout, and space planning, but also in facilitating group processes and shared problem solving. Senior management's commitment to the process contributed to the project's success, as did the fact that the contractor was encouraged by the client to collaborate in the consultants' design process. The client's faith in the con-

Team work space.

Individual work space.

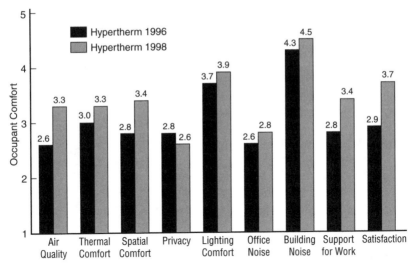

This figure shows that employee comfort has improved in all areas except Privacy, an expected result as the space was designed more for communication and collaboration than for isolation and solitary enclosure.

sultants' process has paid off in terms of improved employee morale, measurable improvement in team work processes, and a new and renewed organization in a building that everyone loves.

This case study is based on the work of Jacqueline C. Vischer, Ph.D., Professor in the Faculty of Environmental Design at the University of Montreal, and President of Buildings-in-Use, Montreal and Boston.

OVERVIEW

Useful research solves recognized problems and identifies new ones. Research methods that increase researchers' ability to do this improve the quality of research. If you use methods that allow other people to criticize your research, you can learn from them. If you can differentiate better research from worse research, you can improve your own. If you know when your research findings are applicable and when they are not, you can act on the world—you can use the results in planning and design—with greater control.

This chapter describes how seven quality criteria for research can be used to achieve these ends:

Intersubjectivity   Tenability   Specifiability
Reliability   Testability   Generalizability
Validity

The chapter proposes that continually asking oneself several questions helps to keep in view the meaning of these criteria. Have I carried out my research in such a way that it can be shared with others? Have I presented my research results in such a way that they can be tested in comparison with other researchers' results? Have I clearly identified what problems my research results can and cannot solve?

The next chapter presents an exploration of how greater understanding of the brain can provide ever more helpful approaches to environment-behavior research and design.

CHAPTER 7

THE BRAIN'S
ENVIRONMENT SYSTEM

The cerebral machine constructs mental representations because it contains, in its anatomical organization, in its neurons and synapses, representations of the world around us.

— JEAN PIERRE CHANGEUX
Neuronal Man

This chapter presents a brief overview of the brain, explores its environment system relating to memory, spatial orientation, and learning, and describes how the brain's fundamental creative process engendered the cognitive process of design.

The first section suggests that adding neuroscience concepts and tools to environment-behavior research can lead to a helpful approach and paradigm—Environment/Behavior/Neuroscience (E/B/N).

The next section describes in broad terms the brain's construction and why it is important for environmental designers to understand. The mind and brain are discussed, as is their relationship to environmental design.

The third section describes the brain's *environment system*—associated brain and mind functions that enable the external environment to play a role in other brain activities and systems such as memory, orientation, and learning.

The fourth section describes how the act of design—the image, present, and test spiral described in Chapter 2—emerged from our brain's basic creative process. Parallels among design, research, and the brain's creative process are discussed, as well as how each process aims to develop coherent perceptions and plans.

THE E/B/N PARADIGM

Wayfinding, perception and cognition, cognitive mapping, imaging, and designing are among the many ways people relate to their environment. Emerging neuroscience research shows that these environment-related activities are reflected both in our brains—their neuronal structure and electro-chemical processes—and in the way our minds manage environmental input and knowledge. The practice of designing the environments in which we live, work, and play has been carried out with little knowledge of these processes. Acknowledging this in his seminal book *Neuronal Man* (1986), neuro-pharmacologist Jean-Pierre Changeux poses a dramatic and challenging research and design question:

> [Do] the forms of architecture we enclose ourselves in, [and] the working conditions we endure . . . favor a balanced development and functioning of our brains? It is very doubtful (p. 283).

If Changeux is correct, E-B researchers not only have to do a better job applying our know-how; we must also embrace neuroscience tools as additions to our methodological arsenal.

The E/B/N Paradigm

- Changeux's challenge
- Neuroscience added to E-B

The Brain

- A physiological overview
- Debating the distinction between mind and brain
- Technological advances
- A note on interpreting laboratory experiments

The Brain's "Environment System"

- Environment and brain evolution
- Memory
- Orientation
- Learning

The Brain and The Design Process

- The Brain's Development Process
- Left Brain " Interpreter"
- Chameleon "Actor"
- Frontal Lobe "Comparator"
- The brain's search for coherence

The field of E-B studies has developed a user needs paradigm that might be characterized as follows: *Environment-Behavior (E-B) user needs paradigm*: If you study behavior, attitude, and opinion to determine how people in different organizations and cultures carry out particular tasks and actions in relation to their physical context, then physical settings that support tasks and actions and meet people's needs will contribute to the happiness, productivity, and stability of their users.

Changeux's challenge, as well as a great deal of previous E-B theory development and research, indicates that this approach solves some problems but not others. This is demonstrated in this chapter and Chapter 14, both of which include cases in which employing the E-B paradigm alone leads to faulty design.

Our minds and brains—their development, functioning, and creativity— are among the few truly renewable resources we have. If designed environments are to support this resource, we must better understand the brain. The more E-B researchers and designers grasp how our minds work, the more designers can improve their ability to program, design, use, manage, and study physical environments, and design new environments that better support our brains. An approach to environmental planning that takes into account neuroscience theory and research along with psychological and social science research may enable environment-behavior to contribute even more effectively to architecture, interior design, landscape design, and planning in the twenty-first century than it did in the twentieth. Thanks to advances in the neurosciences, an enriched way to conceive of the relationship between environment and people is now available. The following E/B/N paradigm adds a neuroscience dimension to the older paradigm and therefore is more effective for problems related to the design of environments such as neonatal intensive care units, hospital waiting and recovery rooms, therapeutic gardens, and housing for people living with Alzheimer's—all of which include a brain-related set of design criteria.

Environment/Behavior/Neuroscience (E/B/N) paradigm: If you understand how people's brains and minds develop and function in different situations, and how they have evolved over time to respond to physical environments, then environments designed to support these capabilities as well as tasks, activities, and user needs, will contribute to people's quality of life, creativity, and survival.

The E/B/N paradigm and the user-needs paradigm are complementary. Our understanding of brain capabilities employing a neuroscience approach reinforces and explains studies of users' needs, behavior, attitude, and opinion. The neuroscience E-B paradigm—E/B/N—adds understanding of neurological and biological function to traditional psychological, sociological, and anthropological environment-behavior knowledge. While the user-needs paradigm primarily rests on analytic interpretation of externalized data, the neuroscience paradigm rests on analysis of brain and mind backed up by observed behaviors. Employing the user-needs paradigm, environments meet essential needs; using the neuroscience paradigm, we can generate environmental designs that reflect how our brains have developed to produce experiences of environmental functions—ultimately to support brain development and functioning while meeting needs, and sometimes causing us to change how we interpret these needs. Applying the user-needs paradigm supports the status quo; applying the neuroscience paradigm supports the creativity necessary to survive and flourish.

Although environment-behavior research and design have clearly demonstrated that E-B perspectives and methods like those described in this book contribute usefully to design, practicing professionals employing the E-B paradigm have repeatedly had to justify their role in the design process by appealing to clients' social and humanitarian commitment. Employing an E/B/N paradigm, professionals can more precisely and more persuasively identify the improvements in functioning that a brain-responsive environment provides. As John Eberhard points out in the foreword to this volume, if we want to understand *how* people behave, the E-B paradigm is sufficient. If we want to understand *why* people behave in certain ways when they interact with their environment, E/B/N is useful (Eberhard, 2005).

Is This a Reductionist Exercise?

Engaging in neuroscience and design, some people say, is merely a reductionist exercise to analytically reduce how we think, feel, and behave to electro-chemical brain impulses. I think not. The debate over whether there is a difference between mind and brain, or whether they are just two words for the same thing, has been raging since the early seventeenth century when Descartes proclaimed, "I think, therefore I am." For spiritual and practical reasons, Descartes argued that spirit, mind, and consciousness were separate and distinct from the brain and body's physiology. He wanted to carry out autopsies without offending the church, and the church's acceptance of this argument was critical to his scientific freedom.

Two hundred years later physician and anatomist Franz Joseph Gall promoted "phrenology," a generally discredited theory that had sound foundations. Studying everyday language, the biographies of famous men, and mental disturbances, Gall developed a list of twenty-seven basic human intellectual capacities, sentiments, emotions, personality traits, feelings, and motor skills, two of which—sense of location and spatial relations—are environment-behavior capacities. Gall argued that mind and brain were not separate, that each capacity had its own particular location in the brain, and that the brain's size and shape reflected a person's character traits. Gall and his followers insisted that they could determine a person's character by feeling bumps on their skull, a practice that has been discredited.

A century after that, Freud, originally a biologist and pathologist, returning to a modified Cartesian view, asserted that "brain" represents the physical jellied mass in our skulls and "mind" represents its function. Now another hundred years have passed, and neuroscientists generally agree that specific parts of the brain are more closely associated than other parts with particular processes like long-term memory, cognitive mapping, visual thought, and speech, and that no single part of the brain alone controls any particular function. Rather several parts of the brain communicate to form *systems* that deal with these different mind functions (Damasio, 1994).

THE BRAIN

The average human brain weighs approximately three pounds, feels like jelly, and is about the size of two fists held knuckle-to-knuckle and palm-to-palm. The basic building block in the brain is the neuron—a cell that uses neurotransmitter chemicals like dopamine, norepinephrine, and choline to communicate with other cells. Carried along thousands of string-like threads called axons and dendrites that reach between cells, each neurotransmitter communicates different messages. Separating the dendrites of two cells is a small space called a synapse, which is bridged by neurotransmitters. Differing amounts of sodium and potassium ions on either side of a cell membrane generate the electric current required to send the neurotransmitters across this synaptic gap to complete interneural communication.

A relatively small organ, the brain performs extremely complex functions. Neurons, axons, dendrites, and synapses are also small. The number of neurons is staggering—100 billion (100,000,000,000) or 10^{11}—the same as the number of stars in our galaxy. With 10,000 dendrites associated with each neuron, the number of potential synaptic communication points is 10^{15}, or a million trillion (1,000,000,000,000,000)—the sheer number of parts to study is one reason that for the foreseeable future, discussions of how our minds work will not be reduced to mere physical examination.

There are right and left hemispheres in the brain. The right hemisphere tends to process information from and to the left side of the body and is generally associated with imagery and conceptual thought. The left hemisphere, thought to be stronger in linear thinking, processes information from and to the right side of the body, and is generally more closely associated with language than the right side. Mental activity often employs both sides of the brain, connected by millions of nerve fibers called the corpus collosum.

The brain has four lobes in each of its hemispheres. From back to front of the skull, the lobes are the occipital, temporal, parietal, and frontal, with the cerebral cortex covering all the lobes. In the center of the brain are several other smaller parts including the amygdala, the hippocampus, and the hypothalamus. All play unique roles in the brain's creative process and its *environment system*.

The environments we experience and the social events the environments enable spawn cell growth and learning. Based on the discovery of neurogenesis —the growth of brain cells that occurs throughout life—in the 1990s, researchers believe such environmental effects continue through old age (Eriksson et al., 1998).

Laboratory Experiments—A Two-way Street

Technological advances such as PET scans, which employ a sensitive radiation detector to measure gamma radiation from neurons using higher amounts of glucose as they work on problems, and fMRI scans, which employ magnetic forces to identify brain areas where working neurons are drawing more oxygen from the blood, enable neuroscientists to study neurons in people's brains when they are thinking, seeing, feeling, and otherwise using their brains. But even with such laboratory tools and techniques, the road between data and application remains rocky. Laboratory techniques yield laboratory-based data, which have both strengths and shortcomings. Interpreting laboratory experiments with human subjects in terms of likely real-world behavior is difficult. Interpreting laboratory data from rats and monkeys for their human meaning—which is often done—presents a still larger gap and runs the risk of gross interpretive blunders.

Our brains have evolved to help us negotiate natural environments, not artificial experimental ones. Our minds know when we are facing actual environmental problems that require our attention and when we are being tested in a laboratory. This may be why environment-behavior researchers often employ ethnographic, anthropological, and sociological methods that are designed to learn about people's natural behavior in real environments. Scientific advances from linking E-B with the neurosciences are likely to yield applicable results slowly because each discipline that E-B research and design draws on, while offering opportunities, also has limits. For the same reason, however, the linkage with field research is likely to bear fruit not only in environment-behavior studies, but in the neurosciences as well.

THE BRAIN'S ENVIRONMENT SYSTEM

In traditional environment-behavior studies, the physical environment is considered the context for and object of actions such as perception, memory, cognitive mapping, and use. The neurosciences tell us, however, that while environment is a contextual object for minds to relate to, it also plays a central role in basic mental functions such as learning, memory, orientation, and perception. Only by including neuroscience in environment-behavior studies can we understand the interaction between environmental stimulus and behavioral response in ways that inform and improve design. Neuroscientist Fred Gage describes the dynamics of this relationship:

> What this means in summary is that the brain controls our behavior and genes control the blueprint for the design and structure of the brain, but that the environment can modulate the function of genes and, ultimately, the structure of our brain. Changes in the environment change the brain, and therefore they change our behavior. Architectural design changes our brain and our behavior (AIA, 2003).

• *The role environment plays in memory.* Without memory—a fundamental brain activity—we are literally lost. Memory begins for a person when she has an experience and perceives what happens, where it happens, who is there, what her role is in the experience, and the feelings she has at the time. Her brain disaggregates elements of these perceptions, allocating each to a different part of the brain. The mood of the event goes one place, the colors of clothing another, and the size of the space a third. Faces of participants, action terms (verbs), nouns, and objects all go into different areas of the brain, and the way she traveled to or from the place (her cognitive map) into still another. A useful analogy for remembering this process is the science fiction "transporter" device the character Scotty uses in the TV series *Star Trek* to disintegrate people, beam their particles off the mother ship, and eventually reintegrate them on board. Our brains disaggregate experiences we have, storing their many parts in a myriad of neuronal pockets—called engrams—and reintegrate each experience in our minds when we remember it (Schacter, 1996).

Changeux describes the process of holding *mental objects* in the brain more precisely and poetically:

> the neuronal graph of a mental object is . . . both local and "delocalized." Neurons interact in a cooperative manner, as in a crystal, but are dispersed like vapors throughout multiple parts of the cortex, with no simple geometric relationship (pp. 141–142).

What our brains reconstitute as a memory is affected by the physical setting in which we experienced it, the situation and place in which we are trying to remember, the purpose to which we want to put the memory, and the length of time the memory has been stored in its disaggregated state. As a result, even if they agree on certain parts of a memory, different people naturally tend to "remember" the details of the same experience differently.

Awareness of "place" is critical to the definition of a memory. Physical environment is therefore essential to memory reconstitution. Schacter (1996) describes this well:

> In order to be experienced as a memory, the retrieved information must be recollected in the context of a particular time and place and with some reference to oneself as a participant in the episode (p. 17).

Schacter also describes how recall of visual information about the physical setting of an event is crucial to having a "remember" experience. *Remembering*—when we have a clear recollection of a person, an experience, or an idea—is different from *knowing*—the feeling that we have been someplace, heard something, or seen someone, but we don't "remember" the precise event (p. 23).

The where and when of each experience we have—*source memory*—is fundamental to remembering events accurately. Deformations in source memory due to stress or natural forgetfulness can lead to false eyewitness testimony about people and places. A person unequivocally swears he has seen someone at a crime scene, although that person is proved to be nowhere near the scene at the time. The eyewitness may in fact have seen the person, but not at the scene of the crime. Faulty source memory can lead to reconstituting a single event memory from two separate experiences. Accurate recollection, our ability to distinguish memories from fantasies and other products of our imagination, "often depends critically on our ability to recall precisely when and where an event occurred," according to Schacter (p. 114). When the mind is at work giving meaning to experience and remembered events, it needs mental images of environment to do so accurately. It needs to use the brain's *environment system*.

Another memory-related mental activity in which the brain's environment system plays a role is our use of fine-scale environmental memories to help reconstruct more complex ones—*scale effect*. We often use our memory of specific attributes of the physical context of an event in order to remember the time of day or season when it occurred. For example, if we remember attending a football game under artificial lighting, we assume it must have been nighttime. "People infer and reconstruct time of occurrence on the basis of other kinds of retrieval information, such as physical setting" (Schacter, p. 118).

• *The role of environment in spatial processing. Wayfinding* and *cognitive map* are terms environmental psychologists and other environment-behavior specialists employ for the memory people hold in their minds of spatial relations (Downs and Stea, 1973; de Jonge, 1962; Ladd, 1970; Lynch, 1960; Passini et al., 1999) If you close your eyes right now and think about going outside from the place you are now, you are likely to recall the pathways, signs, landmarks, and other environmental characteristics that you used to get to where you are and that can guide you back out of the place—a cognitive map.

The ability our minds have to create, hold, and reconstruct cognitive maps of the physical environments we encounter is essential to both our daily life and our very survival. In our daily life, cognitive mapping is necessary to carry out almost every task. In more extreme situations, effectively and efficiently creating and holding such cognitive maps enables us to remember how to find food sources, mates, our home, and how to avoid predators and dangerous locations.

Neurophysiologist and psychiatrist J. Allan Hobson calls the location of the brain's cognitive mapping facility "the map room of the brain" (1994, p. 88). According to Hobson, mental maps are connected to our emotional memories and central to how we experience the world.

> [Cognitive maps] . . . are stored in memory by a specialized brain region called the hippocampus. This map room is a specialized part of our memory bank whose contents are stored in intimate proximity to emotion central, located beside the hippocampus. The net result is that our sense of place is tied to our recollections of early experience and our sense of unease in the world (p. 88).

This dimension of spatial processing is a hard-wired part of our brain's environment system. O'Keefe and Nadel, neurophysiologists exploring this system in rats, located "place cells" in the hippocampus that signal most strongly when the rats move between spaces (1978, referred to by Hobson, 1994).

LeDoux (1996) also focuses on the hippocampus as the processor of spatial information based on experiments in which rats are immersed in a milky water bath and shown a platform where they can swim to safety and rest. When the platform is lowered into the water, healthy rats use contextual orientation cues to remember where it is. Those with lesions of the hippocampus have greater difficulty (p. 189).

Schacter points to a different brain location for this environment system attribute. "Patients with parietal damage," he writes, "forget once-familiar spatial layouts and have difficulty navigating routes that they used to travel with ease. Recent PET scanning studies have shown that parietal regions become especially active when people remember the location of objects" (p. 86).

The brain performs several different, connected actions in developing a cognitive map—which is not actually a complete "map" as we think of it, but rather a set of distinct and related spatial cues. Landmark objects contribute to cognitive maps, play a central role in spatial orientation, and are critical to the brain's environment system. The brain determines where the landmarks are and their context, and remembers the spatial relations among the objects.

As we learn more about how our brain's environment system structures our wayfinding ability, the wayfinding systems we design will be more effective.

• *The role of environment in learning. Contextual learning* is the term used to describe the influence that physical context, emotions, and state of mind have on our ability to recall subject matter that we learn. External physical environment—a contextual element whenever we learn—actively influences such recall just as place-memories in the brain's environment system play a role in the internal structure of general memory.

The contexts of learning—emotional, state of mind, and physical—are like learning glue. They influence how learning sticks in the mind. We learn history in classrooms, sports on playing fields, and bicycle riding on flat paved surfaces, and these places can help us learn. When people are shown an object or asked a question, they tend to remember it better—to have learned it more deeply—when it is put into a meaningful context connected to their experience (Schacter, pp. 45–56). When the places in which we learn a subject have more meaning to us, we are better able to recall the subject matter.

In a multi-year controlled natural experiment over sixty years ago, Abernathy (1940) tested this hypothesis. For five years she observed two classes of about one hundred students, each taught an identical curriculum in the same classroom. During a month of testing at the end of the study, two environmental conditions were varied: whether the students completed the test in the same room in which they learned the material initially, and whether the test monitor was the same person who had instructed them. Greatest recall occurred when the environment was entirely the same—both setting and teacher. Learning recall was least when the physical setting and test monitor were different. Most important, the physical environment and tester differences influenced results independently—a change in physical environment alone reduced performance on the tests. Over time the classroom and the teacher's presence there had developed meaning to the students that in turn contributed to their learning recall of the subject matter. This phenomenon is also likely to affect other forms of learning, such as recognition and reminiscence.

THE BRAIN'S DESIGN PROCESS

Early chapters of this book explore the similarities and differences between the ways researchers and designers process information. Imaging, presenting, and testing are identified as coordinated activities in the creative processes of both research and design. We saw that despite differences of emphasis in the way researchers work and the design process (researchers emphasizing *testing*;

designers emphasizing *presenting*), both processes aim at the same objective: coherence of conceptual or visual thought. Both creative processes—research and design—benefit from collaboration.

Neuroscience provides additional insight into both research and design, demonstrating the way our brains are physiologically constructed to engage in both activities. To understand who we are, our minds naturally create and hold images, present, and re-present those images both mentally as well as externally in words and drawings for others to see, review, and test. These design and research activities are fundamental to human thought. Their coordination is basic to humans' need for coherent visions, images, perceptions, and concepts. In fact, this three-part process appears to be critical to how our brains manage creativity.

Parallels Between Creativity, Design, and Research

Imaging, presenting, and testing constitute the creative process for everyone, not just great artists. Each brain possesses the three parts that aid creativity: an interpreter that helps us generate images, a set of actors that help us perceive and respond to the environment, and a comparator that helps us determine how valid our images are, given our experience.

• *Imaging.* The work of the brain's *left-brain interpreter* and one type of creativity—is the mental process of fabricating, fantasizing, and otherwise creating ideas and concepts. Generally people who image well see connections between elements that already exist in new ways. They also lead others by making creative leaps. Inventors, social visionaries, and artists who develop entirely new ways of seeing objects are people whose imaging ability is particularly creative.

The left-brain interpreter invents stories, myths, and concepts to explain experience, playing a major role in research and design imaging and in the greater creative process (Gazzaniga, 1998). It gives meaning to and makes sense of experience by creating explanatory models and concepts. The models always make sense to the person, although they are sometimes fanciful, like stories and myth, and other times are more descriptive, as in the case of research analysis and scientific theory. Changeux refers to early images as "pre-representations"—as if the mind actually sketches out images it is holding before making a final drawing.

• *Presenting*—the work of the brain's *chameleon-like actor* and a second type of creativity—is the outward expression of many creative acts. Creativity in presentation lies in the skill and refinement with which the person senses her world, perceives it, and communicates her art to others. Painters, sculptors, actors, and orators all express their creativity in performances or objects that others appreciate.

The brain's actor is essential to the second step in developing mental coherence, as is presenting in research and design. I call it chameleon-like because it employs several brain areas to confront the real world, and continually changes how it relates to the world, responding uniquely to the particular situation in which it finds itself (Ramachandran and Blakeslee, 1998). The actor starts as a *sensor* employing vision, touch, hearing, and the body's other senses to gather input from the environment. The mind then organizes these disparate sensations, giving meaning to and making sense of them. Much of this sensory activity takes place in the brain's occipital lobe.

As the brain explains sensory input to itself, the chameleon-like actor moves forward in the brain and turns into a *perceptor*, perceiving and identifying with increasing clarity the environmental stimulus to which the senses have reacted. At first, identification is fuzzy and questioning, but eventually there is recognition. The brain's parietal lobe is active during these activities.

The actor finally transforms into a *motor responder*. It has arrived at the front of the brain, in effect instructing the body to act on its environment in response to the sensory and perceptual interpretation it has developed. Motor responses link feelings and executive function in the brain, and are therefore called "emotional actions." As Damasio points out:

> Some regions of the prefrontal cortex are linked with the amygdala and together these regions, and possibly others, may play key roles in planning and executing emotional actions. . . . Another brain region that may be involved is the basal ganglia, a collection of areas in the subcortical forebrain. . . . long implicated in controlling movement . . . (p. 229).

• *Testing.* The work of the brain's *frontal lobe comparator* is the least understood of these three mental functions. How is reviewing and interpreting the work of others creative? This is the form of creativity that orchestra conductors, theatrical directors, and literary editors practice.

This third step in the brain's creative development cycle parallels the test phase in research and design, and is carried out in the brain's comparator, which maintains contact between the interpreter and the actor, helping the brain modify and improve the interpretation (Changeux, 1985, pp 161–162). The comparator contrasts the interpreter's hypotheses to the actor's perceptions and motor responses, identifying discontinuities that help further develop the emerging explanatory image. After the comparator modifies the holistic concept the interpreter has generated, a *re-entry* is made in the interpreter, and a new cycle of refinement and further interpretation begins. After sufficient cycles, consciousness and coherence are achieved, just like a design emerges after several design/research cycles.

In the brain, these cycles comprise three discrete steps, just as they do in research and design as described in Chapters 1 and 2. The following table presents the elements of each process—the brain's creative development cycle, design, and research—showing the parallels.

Table 7.1. Parallels between the brain's creative development cycle, design, and research

Domain	Brain	Design	Research
Step #1	Interpret	Image	Hypothesis
Step #2	Act	Present	Experiment
Step #3	Compare	Test	Critique
Result	Cohesive picture & valid action	Image & environments suited to needs	Holistic concepts reflecting data

THE BRAIN'S CREATIVE DEVELOPMENT SPIRAL

Blass (2005) suggests that designers and researchers should take advantage of the brain's natural creative process to achieve their ends and that understanding brain function can provide insight into the nature of research, design, and creativity. Therefore, exploring the brain even further must improve design and research in practice.

The brain creatively makes sense of its context just as designers create buildings, plans, gardens, and objects. Just as designers and researchers—both involved with forms of inquiry—have a natural urge to solve problems, the brain "has circuits that . . . want to work on problems" (Gazzaniga, p. 22), and a left-hemisphere interpreter that "insists on generating a theory, even though there is really nothing to generate one about" (p. 157). This drive for integration and coherence seems to represent a need fundamental to our well-being. It helps us make sense of who we are in relation to that context—to define our "self". Acting and reflecting so that we can see order in the world around us enables us to plan and make decisions—effectively to "design". The diagram below of The Brain's Creative Development Spiral illustrates that when we clar-

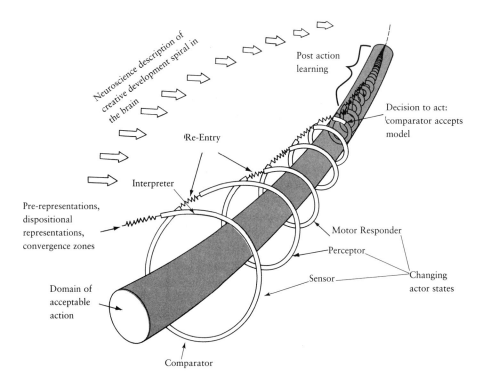

The brain's creative development spiral.

ify a perception, develop a plan, or react to our environments, the mind employs the same iterative process that designers use (see Chapter 1).

According to Damasio (1994) imaging is also universal—"the factual knowledge required for reasoning and decision making comes to the mind in the form of images." The first type of image our brains form is perceptual, images that represent the present. When you look at a building, read the words on this page, smell a candle, or touch an alpaca scarf you develop an image of what you sense. Our brains form recalled images that represent the past from interior thoughts and memories. "Shapes, colors, movements, tones, and spoken or unspoken words" (p. 96) in addition to visual experiences, make up recalled images.

Planning the future—what Damasio calls "memory of a possible future"—paradoxically, is the type of "imaging" that is closest to the term *image* as it is employed in this book to describe the design process:

> [An image is] formed when you planned something that has not yet happened but that you intend to have happen . . . As the planning process unfolded [in your brain], you were forming images of objects and movements, and consolidating a memory of that fiction in your mind. Images of something that has not yet happened and that may in fact never come to pass are no different in nature from the images you hold of something that already has happened. They constitute the memory of a possible future rather than of the past that was . . . [and] are concocted by a complex neural machinery of perception, memory, and reasoning (p. 97).

In this sense we are all designers. Imaging is a fundamental brain process by which we hold thoughts in our brains—perceptions, memories, and plans. Imaging is a process to which the brain is highly attuned; it is a process fundamental to thought; and it may even be an integral part of the self. Damasio points out: "You cannot have a self without wakefulness, arousal, and the formation of images" (p. 238).

Why the Brain's Actor Is Such an Important Player in Creativity

Just as designers must use a pen, pencil, or computer to draw their ideas if they want to develop them, only by acting on and trying out our mental images can our brains refine these images so that the actions they eventually drive are valid actions. (Chapter 4 describes valid actions as those that have the consequences we intend when we act.)

With each recollection, sensory response, perception, or action our brain presents images to itself. Damasio describes how these activities are not merely remembering, but acts of new construction and that "whenever we recall a given object, face, or scene, we do not get an exact reproduction but rather an interpretation, a newly reconstructed version of the original" (p. 100). This is also reflected in Changeux (1985) who asserts that before any external action takes place, "the brain spontaneously generates crude, transient representations with graphs that vary from one instant to the other. These particular mental objects, or pre-representations, exist before the interaction with the outside world. They arise from the recombination of preexisting sets of neurons or neuronal assemblies, and their diversity is thus great" (p. 139).

Re-presenting our research and design images in drafts of papers and sequential drawings without testing and critique merely repeats the same mistakes; it does not improve them. Only by critiquing and testing mental presentations do our brains truly refine knowledge and enable valid action to emerge. This is another way in which the brain's design cycle parallels design and research as described in earlier chapters.

The Brain's Critical Comparator

As described in Chapter 1, once a designer develops an initial image of the environment she wants to create, after she sees it in her "mind's eye" and sketches it on a piece of paper, she examines it critically—modifying her internal image and re-presenting it in an improved form. Knowledge develops from thought in the same way, with the brain employing the *comparator* to test its own image presentations. "The acquisition of new knowledge," according to Damasio, "is achieved by continuous modification of . . . dispositional representations" (p. 105).

Changeux identifies the brain's *comparator*—controlled by the frontal lobe and regulated by the dopamine A-10 nucleus in the brain stem (pp. 161–162)—as the locus of the mind's ability to compare and thus weed out internal images of the outside world that do not adequately reflect the lessons learned from failed actions. The brain generates many images, as do designers at the start of a design project and researchers as they start to analyze data, but only those images that successfully withstand mental testing are selected, retained, and stored (p. 139). Understanding this provides us with even more support for believing that testing our designs, attempting to falsify our research findings, and carrying out POEs of buildings and other environments in-use are critical to improving knowledge.

We know that people engage in research to learn more about the world and improve our ability to act on it with greater control over the side effects of our actions. We know that E-B-sensitive designers design environments to fit into their physical, social, and cultural contexts. But why do our minds and brains continue to engage in creative development? Does this complex evolved activity take place continually within us merely to study the environment with fewer side effects, or does it have a purpose—a function—of its own?

The Higher Purpose of the Brain's Environment System

Neuroscience literature seems to indicate that the higher purpose of the brain's environment system is to develop a clearer sense of who we are in relation to our environment. In this sense, the brain's environment system and creative development process contribute to what Damasio, Changeux, and Ramachandran respectively call the *self*, *consciousness*, and *truth*. If this is the case, the way we coherently manage our relationship to our environment contributes critically to how we define ourselves (and our *selves*.) The mental and physiological processes described above and their external manifestations in design and research play an even more fundamental role in our lives than previously thought.

In the face of what Hobson calls the continual internal "tug of war" (pp. 166–167) between obsession with particulars in the world around us and distraction by the general in that same context, our minds and brains need mechanisms to create a coherent worldview. Ramachandran and Blakeslee (1998) study the perceptions and misperceptions of people with phantom limbs. Although these people are missing an arm or a leg, their brains do not let them acknowledge this fact, and they see themselves and feel as if they are physically whole. Ramachandran identifies this behavior as a "need to create a sense of coherence and continuity" (p. 133) allowing "the emergence of a unified belief system . . . largely responsible for the integrity and stability of *self*" (p. 147).

In fact, particular groups of neurons implicated in "re-entry" testing of our contact with the environment enable the brain to develop integration and coherence through continual feedback. When Changeux describes how our brains confront resonance and dissonance between our external and internal images, allowing holistic integration between various brain centers, he says, "*consciousness* is born" (p. 158).

These neuroscientists each interpret differently the coherence making process that each describes as including images, re-presentations, and re-entry. For Ramachandran and Blakeslee, this process contributes to the stability of the *self*. For Changeux, it contributes to *consciousness*. For Damasio the coherence process makes up the *self* and *mind*. He writes: "the endless reactivation of updated images about our identity (a combination of memories of the past and of the planned future) constitutes a sizable part of the state of self as I understand it" (p. 239). Having a mind, to him, "means that an organism forms neural representations which can become images, be manipulated in a process called thought, and eventually influence behavior by helping predict the future, plan accordingly, and choose the next action" (p. 90). What better description of design could there be; or of research for that matter!

The creative design process that uses the brain's environment system is not a skill belonging only to a few gifted individuals. It is an act we all engage in daily. The mental process described here underlies all creative developmental processes—be they in our minds, in nature, or in our outward acts.

OVERVIEW

If we study people in environments strictly through disciplinary eyes—whether the social sciences, psychology, biology, physiology, or the design disciplines—we will always see only part of the picture. Each provides only partial solutions to environmental design problems. The twentieth century ended not only with many scientists and practitioners coming to a realization about the importance of the brain as the coordinator of human experience and action; but also with the realization that the distinctions drawn between the social, psychological, and physiological sciences may not be useful in certain situations.

This chapter proposes that to remain relevant in the twenty-first century, the field of environment-behavior studies needs to link social, psychological, and physiological research to the neurosciences. The chapter describes an *environment system* in the brain that relates integrally to memory, spatial processing, and learning. This chapter also describes how the brain has uniquely evolved to affect the physical environment through a structured creative design process. Like the design and research process described in Chapters 1 and 2, the brain uses an iterative process of repeated cycles of imaging, presenting, and testing to make sense of the world and ourselves in it.

RESEARCH METHODS

CHAPTER 8

OBSERVING PHYSICAL TRACES

Observing physical traces means systematically looking at physical surroundings to find reflections of previous activity that was not produced in order to be measured by researchers. Traces may have been unconsciously left behind (for example, paths across a field), or they may be conscious changes people have made in their surroundings (for example, a curtain hung over an open doorway or a new wall built). From such traces designers and environment-behavior researchers begin to infer how an environment got to be the way it is, what decisions its designers and builders made about the place, how people actually use it, how they feel about their surroundings, and generally how that particular environment meets the needs of its users. Observers of physical traces also begin to form an idea of what the people who use that place are like—their culture, their affiliations, and the way they present themselves.

Most people see only a small number of clues in their physical surroundings; they use only a few traces to read what the environment has to tell them. Observing physical traces systematically is a refreshing method because, through fine-tuning, it turns a natural skill into a useful research tool.

A simple yet striking example of the use of this method is Sommer's observation of furniture placement in a mental-hospital ward and corridor (1969). In the morning after custodians had straightened up and before visitors arrived, Sommer found chairs arranged side-by-side in rows against the walls. Each day, several hours later, he found that patients' relatives and friends had left the same chairs grouped face-to-face in smaller clusters. Among the inferences this set of physical-trace observations prompted Sommer to make was that custodians' attitudes toward neatness and their beliefs that furniture ought to be arranged for efficient cleaning and food service were incongruent with patients' behavior and needs.

To test these ideas, Sommer rearranged the furniture in the ward, expecting patients to take advantage of the increased opportunities for sociability. For the first few weeks, he was surprised to find, patients and nurses returned chairs to their against-the-wall positions; they asserted that the new way "wasn't the way things belonged." Eventually Sommer put the chairs around tables in the middle of the room, and on the tables he put flowers and magazines. When this threshold of environmental change was reached, changes in behavior took place as well: patients began to greet each other more, converse more, and read more, and staff members began a crafts program using the tables in the ward. And it all began when Sommer noticed a difference between how custodians left chairs in the morning and how patients and visitors left them at the end of the day.

The following discussion presents (1) significant qualities that observing physical traces has for use in E-B research, (2) types of devices for recording observed traces, and (3) a classification of trace types to make visible those relations between people and environment that are useful for designing.

QUALITIES OF THE METHOD

Observing traces is an exceptionally useful research tool that can produce valuable insights at the beginning of a design project, test hypotheses in the middle,

---

Observing Physical Traces

Qualities of the Method

>   Imageable
>   Unobtrusive
>   Durable
>   Easy

Recording Devices

>   Annotated diagrams
>   Drawings
>   Photographs
>   Counting

What to Look for

>   By-products of use
>   Adaptations for use
>   Displays of self
>   Public messages
>   Context

and be a source of ideas and new concepts throughout. If you take into account what the method can and cannot do, you can achieve the results you want; like any tool, if used inappropriately it can be destructive. The method can be a source of provocative images, is unobtrusive, easy to use, and deals with long-lasting phenomena. It provides opportunities for investigators but also sets up some traps.

Imageable

Observation of physical traces provides rich impressions and is highly illustrative. For example, walking through a home for older veterans in Oxford, New York, investigators saw wheelchairs in odd places, old furniture, new medical equipment, direction signs, people in uniforms, open cans of food on windowsills, and patients' get-well cards taped to walls in rooms (Snyder and Ostrander, 1974). The walk gave researchers an initial picture of what life in that home was like: its design successes, some problems, exceptional situations, and patterned wear and tear. At the beginning of a research project, such observations can prompt investigators to think about what the observed objects might mean. Skillful observers will notice even commonplace physical traces and figure out which of them will lead to fruitful inferences that can be pursued further. At Oxford, investigators focused their attention on cans of food on windowsills—developing from this information a central research hypothesis that residents lived a twenty-four-hour lifestyle that was out of phase with the institution's 6:00 A.M. to 7:00 P.M. schedule.

Once they observe a trace, investigators ask questions about what *caused* it, what the person who created the trace *intended*, and what *sequence* of events led up to the trace. The imageable quality of physical traces makes it easy to generate hypotheses about causes, intent, and sequence, but from the trace alone researchers cannot tell how tenable their hypotheses are; to do this, they need other methods. For example, in a brief evaluation of a somewhat run-down housing project in Roxbury, Massachusetts, Zeisel (1973b) found large, well-kept flowering shrubs in residents' backyards. At first he falsely assumed that residents beautified their small yards because they cared about the appearance of the project and wanted their own vistas to be more scenic. In later interviews with residents he found that shrubs had been planted years before in response to a management-sponsored competition for the best garden. A closer second look revealed that even good-looking plants in the backyards had been very much neglected.

The same potential pitfall can arise when investigators falsely infer intent. One morning a group of architects visiting a housing project for older people in a predominantly Italian section of Boston noticed a bocce-ball court surrounded by apartment windows. It looked as if it had never been used. They tentatively concluded that something was wrong with the facility, that residents did not like playing bocce ball, or that they did not like the location of the court. In fact, the court looked brand new because workmen had just completed it several days before. In addition, it was early morning, and anyone who might have used the court was still at home.

It is also difficult to infer process. In a suburban Boston prison, cell walls are papered from ceiling to floor with *Playboy*, *Penthouse*, and *Swank* centerfolds. At first glance it seems impressive that prisoners fix up their dwelling units so extensively—that they mark out and personalize territory so dramatically. But the impression the traces give is misleading. Most centerfolds have been glued to the cell wall by a series of previous inmates. Walls are not stripped when a new inmate moves in, every six to twelve months. The wallpapered surroundings that inmates move into offer them many diversions but little chance to personalize.

Visual trace records can be used as illustrations of research concepts. This can prove useful to investigators who want to follow up on trace observations with interviews to test their hypotheses. In studies of property damage in parks (Welch, Zeisel, and Ladd, 1978) and in schools (Zeisel, 1976a), for example, investigators showed slides of damaged property to groups of teenagers, park personnel, and persons living next to the property in order to focus discussion on what these people thought about property damage.

In lectures and reports, pictures of vivid traces can help viewers and readers understand physical settings in which projects were carried out. Lenihan (1966), in his report evaluating the VISTA program in the 1960s, wanted readers to understand the wide variety of volunteers' assignments: Appalachian mountain villages, Southwestern desert towns, and urban slums. He used photos of physical traces to augment the poetry of his writing.

The force of concrete visual impressions can be a pitfall for careless researchers. The visual impact of even low-frequency observations can be so great—flowering bushes, nearly new facilities, vandalized windows—that they dominate a researcher's mind. To a person walking through a well-kept housing development, the beauty of a few flowering bushes can give the impression that there are flowers in bloom everywhere, even though few residents have bushes and only some are flowering. When such traces are photographed and presented out of context, they can mislead—a problem of false emphasis the visual communications media face every day. It is important that observers also train themselves to see traces that do not stand out, such as the scarcity of certain expected objects or the absence of wear and tear. If you ask yourself "What traces are missing?" in addition to "What traces do I see?" you are more likely to avoid being seduced by visually impressive traces. You will begin to see what is not there.

Unobtrusive

Observing traces is an unobtrusive method (Webb et al., 1966). It does not influence the behavior that caused the trace.

Unobtrusiveness is particularly valuable when gathering data about situations that respondents find sensitive or when respondents have a stake in a certain answer. For example, an investigator who wants to know how strictly hospital attendants follow fire-safety rules will learn more from counting the fire exits blocked by stretchers than from interviewing attendants, who may want to paint a rosier picture than actually exists. School principals who want to avoid showing they are not doing a good job may report less damage to school property than a researcher might observe directly, while principals who want the school committee to increase the budget for maintenance may magnify the damage. If a respondent at home knows a researcher is coming, she may tidy up the house beforehand, putting away such physical traces as toys in the living room, which might indicate how different rooms are used.

Observing or measuring traces does not require being present when the traces are created. The method is therefore particularly useful to find out about rare events, hard-to-see events, private behaviors, and behavior of groups who cannot be interviewed. Zeisel's school study (1976a) provides an example of using physical traces to document private behavior that is hard to observe directly. During the day teenagers can be seen hanging out around schools, playing stickball against walls, and sometimes climbing onto rooftops. At night they sometimes find out-of-the-way places around back to sit together, drink, and smoke. Boston teenagers treat these half-hidden settings as clubhouses where outsiders are not allowed. The first hint of such nighttime clubhouse activity came from physical traces: empty beer cans, discarded playing cards, cigarette butts, graffiti, and broken lights.

Durable

Many traces have the advantage for researchers that they do not quickly disappear. Investigators can return to a research site for more observations or counting and can document traces with photographs or drawings. Of course, the more permanent a trace is, the greater its chance of being observed at all. For example, rock gardens and paving stones in someone's garden will be visible for years, long after grass and flowers have virtually disappeared.

There is, however, the problem of selective deposit. Some activities are more likely to leave traces than others. The extent of beer drinking that takes place behind a school can be detected by counting the number of cans the next day. Playing poker or smoking nonfilter cigarettes may leave no traces at all.

Another consequence of the durability of traces is their cumulative quality; earlier traces can encourage later ones. A large number of people may feel free to cross a lawn because people who did so before left a path, whereas fewer people would do so were there no path. This cumulative quality can cause problems for investigators who overlook it and think each act is independent of earlier ones. But if traces are not taken out of context, their cumulative character can provide insights for data gathering and analysis. The finding, for example, that litter tends to beget litter (Finnie, 1973) is particularly useful if you want to arrange maintenance schedules in parks and around schools.

Easy

Physical-trace observation is generally inexpensive and quick to yield interesting information. The inexpensiveness of a brief physical-trace survey makes it possible in most research projects not only to discover but also to explore in greater depth a host of initial hypotheses. Using more costly methods would mean discarding possibly fruitful but implausible hypotheses without looking at them closely. This same quality means, however, that researchers can waste their energy because time and money do not force them to think through each initial proposition rigorously before going into the field.

The speed and ease with which physical traces can be recorded—in photographs, sketches, and notations—make the method useful for collecting a great many data for speedy review. An initial site visit can yield enough recorded observations for weeks of review and analysis. This is helpful in generating a range of testable propositions and hypotheses. Yet the harvest can be so rich that it may entice a research team to stop looking: "We already have so much information. Why do we need more?"

In sum, observing physical traces is imageable and unobtrusive, deals with durable data, and is easy. The following sections of this chapter discuss ways to record trace observations and a classification of traces particularly relevant to questions of design.

RECORDING DEVICES

Investigators save energy and time by deciding before going into the field how and when they will record trace observations: annotated diagrams, drawings, photographs, pre-coded counting lists, or a combination of these. Digital photographs are the easiest to use because their cost is negligible and they are easy to file for later use as illustrations and for their analysis. Each decision about recording methods affects how trace observations can be analyzed, how they can be used in conjunction with other research methods, and how findings will be presented.

Observations should also be timed to avoid possible systematic effects of maintenance schedules or predictable activity cycles on the data—for instance, early morning cleanups that obliterate signs of teenagers' nightlife around schools.

Annotated Diagrams

Recording traces verbally and diagrammatically, as a rule, requires little preparation and no special skills. Except for a notepad, the recording method is unobtrusive; to make it even less obtrusive, trained observers may memorize major traces in a setting and record them later. This is possible when the setting is simple and the objective standardized, as when making diagrams of furniture layouts in people's living rooms for a study of what furniture people own and how they arrange it.

During a two-person interview one interviewer can inconspicuously draw a plan of the setting and note where objects are located and where there are physical traces. In settings where cameras are out of place or lighting is difficult and the researcher does not want the camera to flash, written trace notation is appropriate. Annotated diagrams are also suitable when traces can be recorded on two-dimensional plans and studied later. The arrangement of chairs Sommer (1969) observed in the patient dayroom could perhaps be represented in plan more effectively than in photographs.

When annotated diagrams are chosen as a recording device, several rules of thumb can be helpful. Agreement among researchers on a set of standard symbols increases comparability of the data within a project. For a residential floor plan, for example, a team might use traditional architectural symbols for furniture. When researchers on several projects use such standard and easily understood symbols, their data can be more easily compared and shared.

Outdoors and in special settings, investigators may have to be more inventive about the symbols they use. In their study of peddlers and pedestrians on Rome's Spanish Steps, Günter, Reinink, and Günter (1978) developed a set of symbols for recording how peddlers arranged their wares.

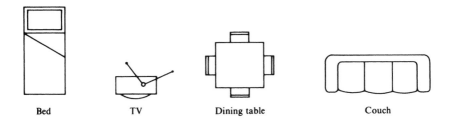

| Bed | TV | Dining table | Couch |

Architectural furniture symbols.

If you want to avoid confusion between your observation notes and your reactions to what you saw, you must not analyze them in the field. Provisions must be made to facilitate subsequent analysis.

A simple device can facilitate preliminary analysis of field notes with a minimum of fuss: Original notes and diagrams are made on the left half of the notepaper, leaving the right half open for recording hunches and preliminary hypotheses (see "Furniture Layout in El Barrio Apartment," p. 167). A wide margin can be made on any notepaper simply by creasing it.

If investigators know the floor plans of the places to be observed beforehand, and if more than one similar place is to be observed or the same place is to be looked at several times, their notepaper can have a floor plan printed on it. This facilitates making notes and ensures comparability of diagrams. This method can be used equally well for interiors, such as offices, waiting rooms, or dwelling units (Zeisel, 1973a) and for exteriors, such as playgrounds, street corners, or plazas (Günter et al., 1978).

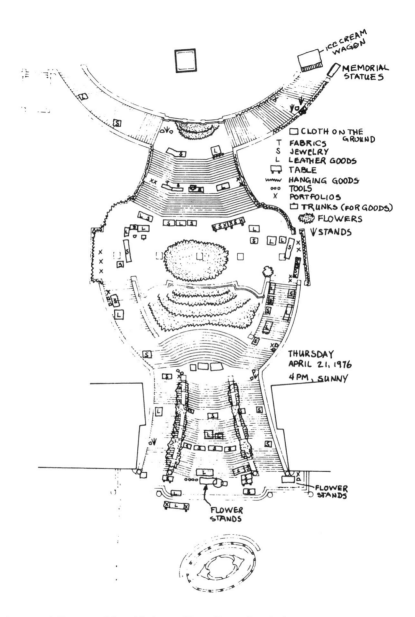

Annotated diagram of Spanish Steps. (From *Rome-Spanische Treppe*, by R. Günter, W. Reinink, and J. Günter. Copyright 1978 by VSA-Verlag, Hamburg. Reprinted by permission.)

OBSERVATIONS	COMMENTS
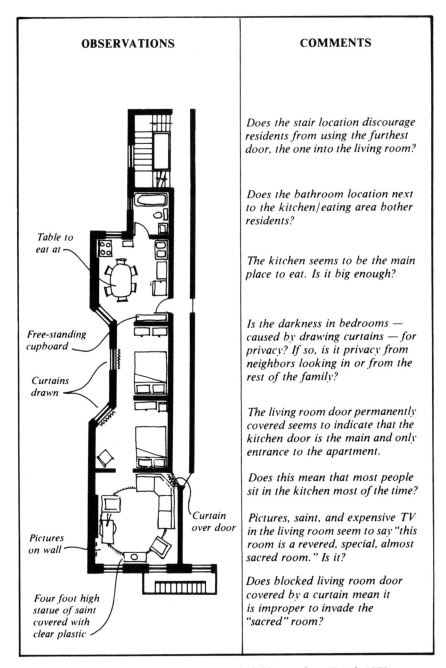	Does the stair location discourage residents from using the furthest door, the one into the living room?

Does the bathroom location next to the kitchen/eating area bother residents?

The kitchen seems to be the main place to eat. Is it big enough?

Is the darkness in bedrooms — caused by drawing curtains — for privacy? If so, is it privacy from neighbors looking in or from the rest of the family?

The living room door permanently covered seems to indicate that the kitchen door is the main and only entrance to the apartment.

Does this mean that most people sit in the kitchen most of the time?

Pictures, saint, and expensive TV in the living room seem to say "this room is a revered, special, almost sacred room." Is it?

Does blocked living room door covered by a curtain mean it is improper to invade the "sacred" room? |

Furniture layout in El Barrio apartment: Sample field notes from Zeisel, 1973a.

Drawings

If observers have the skill to make sketches of the traces they see, the time it takes may well be worthwhile. Drawings can be extremely useful in final reports because they are highly imageable and inexpensive to reproduce.

Photographs

Photographs of physical traces taken at the beginning of a research project can give all parties working on it an initial overview of the types of things they are likely to see in the field. Discussion among team members of photographs projected on a screen or wall can quickly generate hypotheses about issues that may be fruitful for further study. A group can leisurely discuss what behavior a trace might reflect and what intent might be behind it. For these reasons, it is generally valuable to document both easily photographed outdoor and indoor traces. Photographs are particularly valuable if the research site is not easily accessible because it is too far away, requires special permission to visit, or is altogether temporary (for example, a circus).

Investigators who expect to count traces—to use the method quantitatively—first analyze photographs of observations to decide on the categories in which to count. Photographs can be used as stimuli in focused interviews, to determine the categories respondents use when they see such things. At the end of a project, photographs are excellent to illustrate verbal presentations of findings. These qualities hold for photographs in any observation research, whether they are pictures of physical traces or behavior.

In the field several rules of thumb and a few tricks may save time, money, and embarrassment. Expensive cameras are seldom more useful as research tools than inexpensive ones. Researchers need to take some photographs themselves because they know what to record for analysis—what to include in the picture and what to leave out. For illustrative photographs, one can hire a professional photographer (or choose the most skilled researcher) to take photos. Even then the researcher will have to tell the professional precisely what to photograph. With digital photography, such problems are less critical because amateurs can often take good photos, especially if they take a large number and delete those that are badly exposed or have not captured the required data.

Digital photography offers great advantages. Photographs can be downloaded onto laptops in the field and immediately made available to all team members for analysis and discussion. Viewed in this way, photographs enable all members of a research group to participate in initial visits to the site. In addition to being convenient and captivating during oral presentations, digital photographs can be easily grouped and regrouped for analysis on the computer. By downloading on site, you can be sure that you have all the data you need before leaving a site. When you want to make a presentation shortly after making observations, such photographs are a lifesaver.

Counting

Certain traces yield their full value only when their quantity is taken into account. In such situations it will suffice to record one or two examples in detail and count the rest. For example, in a housing project where some families have fenced in their backyards and some have not, photographs of a few yards along with a careful count will do the job.

If you know what you want to count beforehand, pre-coded counting pads or checklists can be arranged—possibly linked to the site plan for accurate location data.

Equally important to choosing appropriate categories is intersubjectivity of the categories among observers. Each member of an observation team faced with the same physical trace ought to record it as a trace in the same category if data are to be comparable. To achieve a degree of intersubjectivity, observers in the U.S. housing census are shown photographs representing distinct levels—and therefore categories—of housing deterioration. On the basis of these "exemplars" this very large group is expected to develop a shared way of looking, at least to some extent.

Another practical way to develop intersubjectivity among investigators is to take them on a site visit to settings similar to those at the research site. Through group discussion they can learn from one another and arrive at a consensus of how items they see would be recorded.

Each method of recording traces catches another dimension of the trace and provides researchers with new data.

WHAT TO LOOK FOR

What an investigator chooses to observe depends on what he wants to do with the data he gathers. If I want to identify my wife in a crowd, I will notice only attractive women with short hair. If you want a police officer in New York City, you will look for and "see" only people in dark blue uniforms.

The following categories for looking at and gathering data about physical traces are organized to increase designers' control over the behavioral effects and side effects of their decisions and to increase people's own control over their relation to the environment. Both these purposes are means to another end: increasing everyone's ability to intervene through design and make settings better suited to what people actually do. These purposes translate into questions such as: How do environments create opportunities for people? Where do people and their surroundings impinge on each other? Where do they limit each other? How do people use the environment as means to an end? And to what ends? What design skills do people have? How do they manipulate their surroundings? How do people change environments to meet their needs? What takes place in particular settings? To answer these questions, the following organization for observing physical traces is useful.

Physical Traces to Look for

By-products of Use

    Erosions
    Leftovers
    Missing traces

Adaptations for Use

    Props
    Separations
    Connections

Displays of Self

    Personalization
    Identification
    Group membership

Public Messages

    Official
    Unofficial
    Illegitimate

By-products of use, the first category, reflect what people do *in* settings—such traces as litter or worn spots left behind by someone who used, misused, or failed to use a place. The other three categories represent things people do *to* settings. *Adaptations for use* changes that users make to an environment so it is better suited to something they want to do: building a fence, breaking down a wall , changing a lawn into a patio. *Displays of self* are changes people make to establish some place as their own, to make it express who they are personally: flags or religious symbols on front lawns; mementos of trips on windowsills. *Public messages* are changes such as wall posters and graffiti by which people use environments to communicate with a large public audience, sometimes anonymously.

What you look for depends on what you want to do with the data. Ruesch and Kees, in their perceptive book *Nonverbal Communication* (1970), describe using data on facial expressions, body movement, and physical traces to understand how people communicate without words. Their emphasis on communication leads them to underplay traces in the categories of adaptations for use and by-products of use but provide a more detailed analytic scheme for displays of self. Another important description of how to observe physical traces is included in *Unobtrusive Measures* (1966). In this work, Webb et al. describe the usefulness of a range of measures—for example, counting bottles in garbage cans to see how much people drink, observing litter in the park, and analyzing suicide notes. The categories they develop are not all equally suited to solving E-B questions. For example, they use the term *accretion* to describe any type of physical trace left behind, without specifying the manner in which it was left—the actor's environmental intent. All but one of the categories discussed in the following pages and several discussed in Chapter 14, on archival methods, are examples of accretion. For clarity I have avoided the use of this important but broad term.

By-products of Use

Fictional detectives like Sherlock Holmes, Miss Marple, Hercule Poirot, and Lord Peter Wimsey are masters at detecting and correctly interpreting side effects of behavior—worn-away stair treads, a smudge on a door, or a glass wiped suspiciously clean of fingerprints. These examples represent three types of by-products: erosions, leftovers, and missing traces.

• *Erosions.* Use can wear away parts of the environment, as when grass is trampled where people walk from a parking lot to a nearby building entrance or grooves are cut into the top of a butcher's block table. Some erosion traces, such as the scars in the butcher's table, indicate to the interested researcher that planned and predicted activities have taken place; others indicate that the environment is being used in a new way, such as the path across the lawn. Because most environments sustain some wear and tear, observers must be careful to distinguish between erosion traces that signify bad design, those that reflect uses designers planned for, and traces left when new and appropriate activities took place. Observing erosion traces and by-products of use can be the first step in finding out what those who use the setting feel about it.

 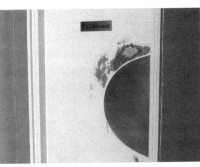

Erosions
Left: Shortcut path in the snow, New York, New York.
Right: Well-used bathroom door in architect's office, London, United Kingdom.

• *Leftovers.* As the result of some activities, physical objects get left behind: cigarettes in ashtrays after a party, dishtowels hung on kitchen-cabinet knobs next to a sink, open cans of food stored on windowsills in a veterans' residence. Like erosions, leftovers may indicate activities that have been planned for, such as parties, and unplanned for, such as residents eating soup in their rooms. Such leftovers as the dishtowel, however, tell you about planned-for

Leftovers
Left: Indicator of indoor smoking ban, New York, New York.
Right: Indicator of coffee with a view at Kahn's Salk Institute, La Jolla, California.

activities that have unplanned-for side effects—in this case the need for towel storage.

Leftovers help to locate (1) places that accommodate planned-for activities, (2) places that only partly accommodate expected activities, and (3) places that are used in unanticipated ways.

• *Missing traces.* Erosions and leftovers in settings tell us about what people do. When we see neither of these, or even very few such traces, it tells us about what people do *not* do. Apartment balconies with neither a chair to sit on nor a barbecue stored for the winter, and an office with nothing on the walls or table to betray the occupant's individuality demonstrate missing traces.

Inquiring about why traces are missing can uncover seemingly irrelevant physical design decisions that limit behavior. For example, some balconies have bars spaced so wide apart that families with small children are afraid to use them. Sometimes missing traces are explained when researchers probe rules about how a place may be used, for example, "No family photos allowed on office walls." Asking "why" may lead to answers that are not very useful: "The apartment is vacant because tenants just moved out." But it may also lead quickly to fruitful insights, because not using an available space is quite a strange thing to do.

Missing traces
Left: Is there something wrong with the balcony? London, United Kingdom.
Right: Is the teacher not there or is school not in session? Montreal, Quebec.

Adaptations for Use

When some people find that their physical environment does not accommodate something they want to do, they change it; they become designers. Some professional designers try to predetermine as little as they can in buildings and other facilities so that residents have the greatest opportunity to join in design by adapting the setting the way they want (Habraken, 1972; Turner, 1972; Wampler, 1968). At the other extreme are designers who try to plan for everything they think will occur—from built-in furniture to the color of curtains. The former is called "loose-fit" design, the latter "tight-fit." But no matter what the original designer wants or expects, people who use environments redesign them. Researchers and professional designers can learn a great deal from this adaptive redesigning.

Adaptive traces are significant for designers because they are direct manifestations of design by users. They take place in the fuzzy area between what professional and lay designers do. Such traces are difficult to interpret, but one does not have to estimate whether they will lead to action, as one does with attitudes.

People change settings to better support activities: to facilitate and sustain them. They may remove inappropriate props, such as built-in lights that are not adjustable, or add new ones, such as a backyard barbecue pit to make eating outdoors easier. For the same ends, they can alter the relations among settings—creating both new connections and separations, such as windows and walls.

• *Props.* When users add objects to or remove objects from a setting, they create new opportunities for activity. Inasmuch as the objects support activities, we can think of them as staging props purposefully arranged by users, such as a wood-burning stove installed in someone's apartment living room or play equipment added to an empty lot to change it into a playground.

New props may have been added because users or uses have changed or because certain activities were overlooked or considered unaffordable in original designs. Props added for either reason may reflect a particular user's idiosyncratic wants, such as the living-room stove, or they may reflect more normative behavior common to a larger group.

Props
Left: Bike rack supports riding to work at Natural Resources Defense Council, New York, New York.
Right: Added garden trellis extends planting options, Montreal, Quebec.

Separation
Left: Added privacy for ground-floor garden, Sydney, Australia.
Right: Barriers keep cars off park steps but let people in, Sydney, Australia.

• *Separations.* Changes may separate spaces that formerly existed together, increasing such qualities as privacy, control, and darkness or more sharply dividing territories; examples are ground-floor apartments with covered windows, stones along a property line, and "Keep Out" signs on back doors of buildings.

Separations can be particularly informative about side effects of design decisions. The parking areas in the interior of Castle Square, a housing project in Boston's South End, were officially deeded to the city so that it would maintain them, plow them, and pick up garbage on them. But as an unanticipated side effect, people who work in the surrounding neighborhood park there during the day and sometimes all weekend. Residents feel that this infringes on their informal right to park their cars just in front of their houses, so they place wooden sawhorses across the parking places in front of their doors to stop other people from parking there.

Separations do not necessarily block physical movement or all the senses at once. They may, for example, be only visual (an opaque cardboard wall around a work area), auditory (a blaring radio in an office so nobody can overhear a conversation), olfactory (a fan to keep kitchen smells out of the living room), or symbolic (a three-inch-high brick border around a front yard).

• *Connections.* Physical adaptations for use may connect two places, enabling people to interact in new ways: holes that teenagers strategically cut in a playground fence so they can enter without walking to a distant gate; or pass-throughs cut in walls between living rooms and windowless kitchens to provide a view out when residents eat in the kitchen. Buildings converted to restaurants often have windows cut into swinging kitchen doors so that servers can avoid bumping into each other when coming from opposite directions.

Connections that users of a facility make can indicate that the original designer overlooked a common behavior that requires being able to move, see, hear, or talk between spaces or that such activity has developed since the place was designed (as with the window in a swinging restaurant door). Of course, sometimes users may want a connection that setting managers do

Connections
Left: Construction ramp connects street and sidewalk, Edinburgh, Scotland.
Right: Kitchen-to-dining-room pass-through connects rooms, Montreal, Canada.

not. An example would be hack-sawed bars on a prison-cell window after a jailbreak.

Displays of Self

Residents change environments to put their stamp on them—to say "This is mine and it says something about me." Displays of self may be directed toward other people, but just as often the changes mean something mainly to the person who makes them: mementos of trips, family portraits, doll collections. Displays may help others identify a person's environment such as name plaques on the front door, or may tell people about the person by announcing her group memberships.

 • *Personalization.* People use environments to express their uniqueness and individuality by using a certain style of furniture in the living room, placing trinkets on the windowsill, or, in the case of office workers, placing silly signs on their desks. Each such use shows how someone is different from his neighbor—in taste, in personality, and in habits.

Personalization
Left: Desk clutter and photos are uniquely this author's, Lexington, Massachusetts.
Right: PEZ dispenser collection is uniquely this architect's, Venice, California.

To show off personalization traces and other displays of self, people find and make such display cases as windows, walls, doorways, car bumpers, shelves, and window ledges in almost any kind of setting, from offices to homes, from hospitals to schools. By observing how parts of the environment are useful as display cases, one can improve his ability to design environments that provide opportunities for displays of self.

• *Identification.* People use their environments to enable others to identify them more easily, like schools putting students' names on lockers, or homeowners putting their initials on commercially bought awnings. Such markings are people's individual street signs, even if they are just numbers: house numbers, office numbers, cell numbers.

Identification
Left: Numbers on the stairs identify the houses, Woburn, Massachusetts.
Right: Photo and memento magnets identify this assisted-living resident, Palisades, New York.

Who leaves a trace can be significant. If a student writes his name with felt-tip pen on a school locker, the locker might mean something to him. How important is a home territory like this to him? Felt-tip ink is difficult to remove. Did he do this on purpose to leave his mark for the next student? Would he use a nametag provided by the administration? If so, what would he feel about it? More important, what would this indicate about the relationship between students and administrators?

The permanence of a trace may also be significant. Does the name of a family etched into the wood of their front door mean they hold different attitudes toward the neighborhood than their neighbors whose name is spelled out with store-bought plastic letters on the lawn? The family with plastic letters may feel no less permanent, but have greater respect for wooden doors.

• *Group membership.* In addition to displaying their individuality, people also display their membership in formal religious, academic, fraternal, political, ethnic, cultural, and professional groups and organizations. The presence of religious statues on front lawns, professional diplomas on living-room walls, ethnic dolls in windows, pictures of President Clinton or President Bush in someone's home, or awards for reaching a sales quota in someone's office all tell you about the groups with which an individual identifies. Group-member-

Group membership
Left: Virgin Mary shrine in bedroom indicates religious membership, Vancouver, Canada.
Right: An enthusiastic group—Boston Red Sox baseball fans, Woburn, Massachusetts.

ship signs are often carried around on more mobile display cases such as car bumpers, high school jackets with emblems, and T-shirts.

Observers can easily overlook group-membership traces of unfamiliar groups. For example, hot-rod owners identify themselves by extra-wide wheels on their cars featuring the manufacturer's name in large, raised, white letters. This practice is derived from actual racecar drivers, who are paid to advertise brand names on their cars and hence have wheels like this. Such signs of group identifi¬cation can be meant mainly for other group members. To attune yourself to see traces like these with in-group meanings, you can assume that displayed objects you see have such meanings and then ask about them.

Public Messages

Physical environments can be used to communicate to the public at large. Most, but not all, public messages appear in public places.

• *Official.* Probably the most frequently seen public messages are official ones erected by institutions, which may even pay for the right to do so. These include advertising signs, the names of commercial establishments, and street signs. They reflect official uses of settings—the behavior of paying clients.

Official public messages
Left: "Mind the Gap" warning in a London tube station, Barons Court, London.
Right: Multiple signs minimize clutter, Sydney, Australia.

Official public messages usually appear in environments designed for a specific purpose. The private right to display official public messages is increasingly being challenged by the public asserting its right not to see them.

• *Unofficial.* Individuals and groups also communicate publicly by means of settings not designed specifically for communication. Unofficial messages usually announce short-term events and are often accepted and even expected on surfaces in public places; they include items like theater placards on wooden walls surrounding construction sites, political posters stapled to telephone poles, and "Lost Cat" announcements taped to Laundromat windows.

Unofficial public messages
Left: Notices posted on a bike rack, Montreal, Canada.
Right: "No Dumping" message seems to have little effect, Chinatown, Toronto, Canada.

Informal public messages tell investigators about such things as cultural events taking place in an area, the proportion of students living there, and political activity. Some bookstores and supermarkets establish bulletin boards for such messages. But the usual traces left from unofficial public communications are shreds of paper stuck to lampposts, brick walls, and newspaper stands.

• *Illegitimate.* Unplanned messages to the general public, for which environmental adaptive changes are not made, are seldom if ever approved of, and are considered by many to be illegitimate uses of public environments. The most

Illegitimate public messages:
Left: Decorative graffiti are not allowed yet are universally tolerated, Sydney, Australia.
Right: Initials scrawled on a wall establish territory, Montreal, Canada.

frequent example of illegitimate public messages is graffiti. Political graffiti with antiauthority slogans often appears in prominent public places. Members of teenage gangs in large cities stake out their turf by writing their names and street numbers on walls.

The term *illegitimate* as I am using it here does not imply a value judgment. It merely refers to official disapproval of the activity. Those who engage in the activity may find it completely legitimate. For example, students almost everywhere paint hockey goals and strike zones on school walls to enable themselves to play games. They consider such lines as legitimate as the neatly painted official lines on the basketball court (Zeisel, 1976a). Others may consider the lines attacks on society.

Such "illegitimate" expression may have useful social side effects. Gang graffiti, by establishing territorial boundaries, may reduce gang conflict; and political slogans give minority political groups visibility.

Context

Traces clarify their context and are clarified by them. A square painted on a wall may mean nothing, but near a school it is a stickball strike zone and signifies that the area is used for street games. When looking at physical traces, researchers must keep in mind that they are trying to look beyond the trace itself to understand a larger picture. That larger picture can emerge only if one sees the context of what is observed.

PHYSICAL TRACES UPDATE

Environment-behavior studies have tended to employ physical trace observation to gain unobtrusive insight into the meaning or use of environments so that quantitative methods could later be used to measure the frequency of traces and related attitudes. Recently, researchers employ physical trace observation to collect data that are useful in their own right and equal in analytic weight and importance to other, more traditional quantitative methods like questionnaires. Brown et al. (2003) and Saegert et al. (2002), which are discussed below, illustrate this.

Physical trace observations are being made with greater assurance. Early E-B studies described physical traces observation with tentative phrases such as: "This observation seems to indicate that the user may have used the environment in such and such a way." Today's author writes with greater assurance: "In support of [interview data that show wheelchair-bound patients and staff have no problems with wheelchair access] behavior trace analysis performed after a wet morning showed wheelchair tracks going all around the garden over both concrete and decomposed granite surfaces" (Whitehouse et al., 2001). This post-occupancy evaluation (POE) of a children's garden environment at San Diego's Children's Hospital and Health Center, employed observation of physical traces as well as interviews, questionnaires, and behavioral observations—both tracking and mapping.

Physical trace observations are also being linked to large-scale established theory. Banning (1993), for example, analyzes physical traces in terms of Brand's (1994) concept of the building as a learning organism. College Union buildings, according to Banning, represent the heart of a campus community and therefore are particularly important to campus life. He urges administrators to observe physical traces to learn the lessons buildings have to teach about "how to manage the building for users," and change it to respond to users needs (p. 17). He points out the importance of studying wear and tear on floors that indicates traffic patterns, trash, litter, leftover food, and even "furniture migration." The chair that ends up in front of the pay phone is a message from the learning building, he suggests.

> If management can decipher what lessons the building is teaching, then decisions regarding whether they are lessons that should be taught can be evaluated. But if the lessons the building is teaching remain unknown, then the shaping cycle of building learning and teaching continues without management participation or intervention (p. 18).

Banning also observed signs, symbols, and artwork in terms of their social meaning. For example, he points out that "an important message about gender awareness is sent by unions in which the male restrooms are marked 'Men' and the female restrooms are marked 'Ladies'" (p. 19). In a similar vein, he observes that "several union buildings struggle with the social messages being sent or taught by murals in the building in reference to race relations, tolerance and celebration" (p. 19). The way such observations are linked with Brand's approach and so assertively proposed could only occur in an evolved disciplinary atmosphere.

Brown, Perkins, and Brown's (2003) study of neighborhood attachment establishes physical trace observation as a major method in its own right. Pairs of trained raters systematically collected detailed observational data of "physical incivilities, such as graffiti or litter, poor roofs and crumbling sidewalks . . . that signal financial disinvestments" in a neighborhood (p. 260), and "the opposite of incivilities—home personalization and maintenance" that relate to strong personal neighborhood attachment bonds (p. 261).

> A total of 55 sample blocks were chosen with a probability proportionate to size procedure that enumerated households from the 1990 census, followed by random selection of a household, which then determined the chosen face block. . . . The physical conditions of between 9 and 19 properties were studied per block, yielding 849 property assessments (p. 261).

Combining these observations with 619 interviews, Brown and her colleagues determined that those living in places with greater "objectively observed physical incivilities and decay on their property had lower place attachment," defined as the average attachment to both house and block/neighborhood. The inverse was also true—the fewer incivilities, the greater the place attachment. The researchers found that although this relationship holds for attachment to the individual dwelling it does not hold for place attachment to the block or neighborhood, indicating an interesting future direction for such research—

namely, the implicit cognitive definition of home and home territory among groups like those studied.

Analyzing the combined physical trace and interview data, Brown et al. suggest that "housing repair, maintenance, or rehabilitation programs may enable residents to convert place attachment to housing improvement" (p. 269). They recommend that future policies focus on programs that can translate residents' positive bonds of place attachment into place improvements (p. 269). On a theoretical and model-development level, their findings "suggest [that] researchers can incorporate collective efficacy, perceived incivilities, and observed incivilities into residential attachment models" (p. 270).

• *Geographic Information Systems (GIS) analysis technique.* One of the most interesting additions to the study of physical traces and the relationship of physical environment to behavioral and social constructs in general, is the use of Geographic Information Systems (GIS) analytic tools to compare findings from more than one data set arrayed on the same map. Originally developed to array geographic data from satellite images of the earth, this tool has been creatively incorporated into environment-behavior analysis. One such application is Saegert, Winkel, and Swartz's study of the relationship between "social capital" and crime in New York City's low-income housing (2002).

GIS is a difficult "method" to place because it is not strictly a data-gathering method; it is a method that can be used to analyze direct physical environment data from satellite or other "physical trace" observation methods, and to analyze archival data from governmental or other data bases—including housing data, data on financing programs, and police statistics. It is most closely linked to physical trace observation—and therefore included here—because its origins lie in dealing with data from direct observation of the physical environment—housing census data, satellite geographic data, and crime scene investigation data.

Saegert and her colleagues explored the relationship between resident organization and ownership policies and the incidence of crimes against people in low-income housing. Pointing out that previous studies tended to focus on the neighborhood scale with little success in finding connections, these researchers decided to focus on the "multi-family residential building" as their unit of analysis. "Unlike the ambiguous concept of the 'neighborhood,'" they write, "buildings define boundaries and inhabitants by their physical form" (p. 195). Selecting buildings as the analysis unit enabled them to link into all the other building-level data available in a major city, as well as organize and then correlate by building their questionnaire data on resident participation in formal and informal groups, home ownership, and perception and experience with criminal acts. The use of GIS analysis techniques enabled the researchers to define the buildings in which people live as the organizing principle for the entire study.

Data on the following independent variables were organized by building and mapped with GIS: participation in formal resident organizations, legal structures that define ownership, and "social capital." The study defines social capital as a construct of four factors:

- Basic participation in tenant association activities
- Informal social relationships with other building residents
- Formal participation in building leadership, management, and maintenance
- Pro-social norms in which other residents are reported to contribute to the well being of the building and its residents

They mined two databases, one that covered Brooklyn, New York, and included data on building conditions (an observed physical trace assessment) and tenant organizations (an indicator of social context). The other was an NYPD database of reported crimes—including their location. A two-page face-to-face interview was administered to residents in a sample of buildings the city had taken over and each interview was "geocoded" by address so it could be correlated to the other data sets via the GIS building-level analysis. A critical decision the team had to make before correlating the GIS data was what "bandwidth" to use—the size of the GIS physical unit of analysis. Bandwidth can be adjusted to be as large as the entire map—the borough of Brooklyn in this case—or as small as 100 feet. The team decided to set the bandwidth for this study at 2,000 feet (the size of two city blocks) for assaults, burglaries, and robberies, the crimes they were studying.

What did they find and what are the policy implications of these findings? Broadly expressed, they found that when participation in tenant organizations and strong pro-social norms are linked to a strong home ownership program in a building, criminal activity against persons in low-income neighborhood buildings was definitely reduced.

This research combined interview results with data on crime, physical building conditions, and home ownership—mapped and manipulated through GIS analysis. The researchers found that:

- The more female-headed households in a building, the lower the within-building crime
- The more formerly homeless people living in a building, the higher the within-building crime
- In tenant-owned and -managed buildings and in buildings owned by community-based groups, within-building crime was less than in buildings still owned by the city
- There was less crime in buildings with more residents receiving Social Security
- There was higher within-building crime in neighborhoods with a higher crime rate
- With greater ethnic diversity, within-building crime is less
- Buildings with greater resident participation in tenant organizations have less within-building crime.

The following design case study for an Urban Wildlife Preserve demonstrates how a multi-method research approach including physical trace observation can be used not only in research for design but also in evaluating a project's use. The methods have been employed together to successfully merge ecological support and human use in the same outdoor place.

View of Urban Wildlife Preserve.

CASE STUDY

URBAN WILDLIFE PRESERVE

A university medical center located in Sacramento, California, developed a 4.3-acre Urban Wildlife Preserve in the mid 1990s as a healing garden. The Center for Design Research (CDR) at the University of California, Davis conducted a five-year research, design, construction, and post-occupancy evaluation (POE) of the Preserve. The research informed both the master plan for the entire Preserve and the programming and design of its first phase, a 1.8-acre park completed in 1996 for $385,000.

Research

People involved in the various phases of the design process included the design team (CDR, HLA Group, and UCDMC Engineers and Architects); medical center staff; schoolteachers, staff, and eleven classes from the neighboring Marion Anderson School; and community residents. Ideas generated in participatory workshops and surveys used to gain child and adult input were summarized in a design program for the Preserve.

Research methods employed to program, design, build, and then evaluate the Urban Wildlife Preserve included physical trace analysis, behavior mapping, biological assessment, site analysis, behavioral analysis, and interviews. Observational site surveys recorded types and numbers of human and animal

Research workshop
with children.

users and their behavioral traces in the Preserve. After construction was completed, a yearlong post-occupancy evaluation of the project was conducted and the results summarized in a POE report (Bowns and Francis, 1998).

The participatory planning process employed to inform design included children at a nearby elementary school, and focused on students' existing perceptions of the site and ideal images of what an urban wildlife preserve could be. This resulted in identifying a number of unique program elements. One was to provide an outdoor classroom in the Preserve with "loose parts" such as fallen logs and boulders children could interact with and use to manipulate the environment.

A water feature was another surprising and unusual element that would not have been incorporated without the research. Among elementary school children, water emerged as the most desired element for the Preserve, appearing repeatedly in the students' drawings and stressed by them in site visits and tours. Yet the design team and administrators had rated water as one of their least desired elements due to concerns over maintenance and safety. The workshop results convinced the team that these issues could be successfully addressed and a major water feature was included in the first phase of construction. The post-construction POE identified water as one of the most popular elements among users.

Design

The resulting Urban Wildlife Preserve balanced creating a habitat for birds and animals with designing a place for schoolchildren, hospital staff, and patients. The Preserve was originally planned as a habitat providing shelter and forage for animals, birds, and insects found on and around the medical center campus and in similar urban areas of the Sacramento region. It consists of a plant community representing the ecological niche in which small animal species can generally live and thrive that in turn is the framework for built elements, like seating and a fountain, that serve specific human purposes. Seasonal wetlands were created as an open-channel drainage on the Preserve to provide a temporary stop/resting place for migrating birds. The Preserve functions as a relaxing, educational, and recreational environment.

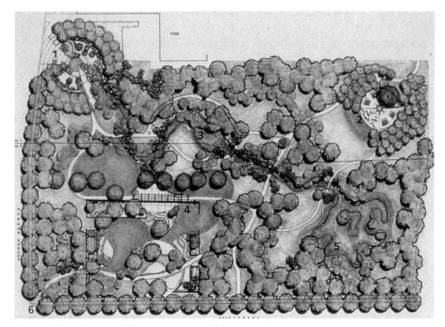

Research-based master plan.

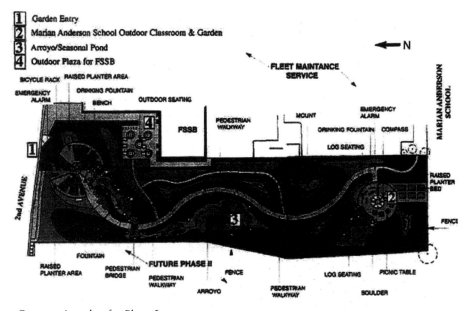

1 Garden Entry
2 Marian Anderson School Outdoor Classroom & Garden
3 Arroyo/Seasonal Pond
4 Outdoor Plaza for FSSB

Construction plan for Phase I.

The final master plan divides the site into four quadrants: an entry garden, a cultural "ruin" area, a habitat pond, and an outdoor education area for the adjacent school. The Preserve's main entry garden, located at the north end of the site, has formal landscaping that transitions from the adjacent buildings to a meditative garden space centered on a fountain. Future plans include a "ruin" area featuring the arch colonnade of the former California State Fairgrounds stable building, honoring the site's cultural history. Lawns and gardens surrounding the arches serve as a ceremonial gathering place for staff, patients, community members, and schoolchildren, and a habitat pond is a permanent water source for seasonal wildlife. An arroyo of rocks and gravel connect the pond to the main entry and accommodate storm water runoff in the winter months.

An outdoor educational area in the Preserve is located immediately adjacent to a local schoolyard, a gate in the school's fence providing access for students and teachers. Envisioned as an outdoor classroom and gathering place for formal and informal activities, it is the core of this open-air room. Surrounded by orchard trees and school garden plots and dominated by an existing Deodora cedar, the plan reflects requests the students expressed in the workshop for an edible landscape and retention of existing trees. The outdoor classroom serves as the base from which groups of children can spread out to interact, explore, and engage in educational opportunities of the Preserve. The whole Preserve is designed for explorative and educational interactions.

Outdoor classroom.

Child in outdoor classroom
discovers bugs.

Natural elements in preserve.

In E-B literature there has been a marked increase in empirical studies and design guidelines for healing gardens and landscapes (Gerlach-Spriggs et. al., 1998; Cooper, Marcus and Barnes, 1999; Tyson, 1998; Francis et. al. 1994). The Urban Wildlife Preserve demonstrates clearly how research can be used successfully to inform design of an urban landscape. Without the research that informed the participatory process for the project, a much more formal and less user-friendly design would have developed. The participatory process served to educate both designers and clients to a holistic and naturalistic approach to design.

Evaluation

To guarantee even greater success in the final design, the client supported a yearlong post-occupancy evaluation after construction of Phase I. POE methods employed included behavior mapping of the site's uses, recording of behavior traces, a questionnaire mailed to 500 individuals in the community surrounding the Medical Center, in-depth interviews with six teachers and staff and with eight local school students, on-site interviews of users, as well as biological inventories of the site. In-depth interviews were carried out with client and design team members to assess their perception of the project in use.

The POE identified successes and problems with the first phase of the design and areas for potential redesign or improved management of the Preserve. For example, the POE documented that the site worked well as natu-

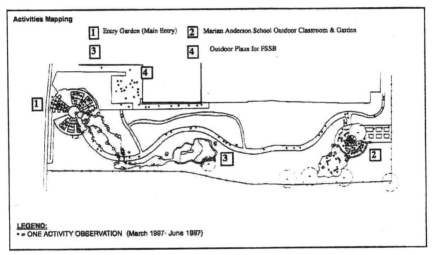

Behavior map.

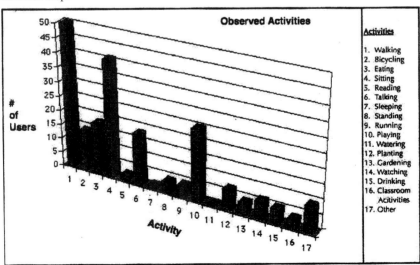

POE observed user activities graph.

Wildflower meadow.

ral habitat, is well used and loved by the local school children and teachers, but is under-utilized by hospital staff. Increased outreach and information dissemination to the larger Medical Center community resulted. The POE data employed in Phase II provides information useful for others designing natural landscapes as healing environments.

In sum, the Urban Wildlife Preserve robustly balances human and animal use with plant ecology in a single area. Without the time spent and money invested in design research, participation, and evaluation, the project would not have achieved these goals so successfully. The Urban Wildlife Preserve Project is open to the public seven days a week and is located on Second Avenue, east of Stockton Boulevard in Sacramento, California.

This case study was drawn from the work of Mark Francis, Professor of Landscape Architecture, University of California, Davis and Caru Bowns, Department of Landscape Architecture, Penn State University. In 1999 the project was awarded a National Merit Award for Research from the American Society of Landscape Architects.

OVERVIEW

A good way to begin almost any E-B research project is to walk around the research site looking for physical traces of behavior. It is easy to do, can be done unobtrusively, and provides investigators with rich imagery to build on in solving their problem. Trace observation can be carried out both qualitatively and quantitatively, and can also be employed as a major research tool.

This chapter has discussed categories of traces particularly appropriate for E-B observations: by-products of use, adaptations for use, displays of self, and public messages. The first category represents remnants of what people do *in* an environment, the others of what people do *to* it. This way of looking is aimed at increasing our ability to intervene through design and make settings better suited to what people actually do.

The next chapter discusses how to observe the other half of the E-B equation: behavior.

CHAPTER 9

OBSERVING ENVIRONMENTAL BEHAVIOR

Observing behavior means systematically watching people use their environments: individuals, pairs of people, small groups, and large groups. What do they do? How do activities relate to one another spatially? And how do spatial relations affect participants? At the same time, observers of environmental behavior look at how a physical environment supports or interferes with behaviors taking place within it, especially the side effects the setting has on relationships between individuals or groups. In a park, for example, an observer sees a child playing, watched over by her father, who anxiously jumps up every time the child moves out of his sight. The child being hidden from view triggers a reaction by her father. The event tells an observer something about the child's activity and the importance for the relationship of maintaining a visual link between father and child.

Observing behavior in physical settings generates data about people's activities and the relationships needed to sustain them; about regularities of behavior; about expected uses, new uses, and misuses of a place; and about behavioral opportunities and constraints that environments provide.

You do not have to be an expert to observe behavior. Before entering a party or a restaurant, you may survey the scene to see what behavior is appropriate there. An alert new student in a school watches who plays where in the gymnasium, who sits where in class, and who sits with whom in the cafeteria. Designers and environment-behavior researchers systematically make the same types of observations with different ends in mind.

Hall's classic description of how people behave in and use space, *The Hidden Dimension* (1966), draws heavily on behavior observation in natural settings. Sensitive behavior observation led Hall to discover the important spatial dimension to human communication. He observed, for example, that how far or how close people stand reflects their social relationship—distance generally meaning coldness and closeness generally meaning friendliness. Further behavior observation turned this rather simple conclusion into an exciting insight: The way people from different cultures interpret spatial distances can lead to misunderstanding, even insult. For instance, a westerner might feel he is being friendly by standing several feet from an Arab friend during a casual conversation. The Arab, attributing meaning to space, feels the westerner is cold and distant and moves closer. The westerner takes this move to be aggressive. He steps back. To the Arab, this is clearly an attempt to be unfriendly—an insult.

This chapter presents qualities of the research method for E-B studies, some practical steps observers can take to prepare for observing environmental behavior, and how to organize observations to learn the most about the relationship between settings and what people do in them.

Observing Environmental Behavior

Qualities of the Method

    Empathetic
    Direct
    Dynamic
    Variably intrusive

Observers' Vantage Points

    Secret outsider
    Recognized outsider
    Marginal participant
    Full participant

Recording Devices

    Notation
    Precoded checklists
    Maps
    Photographs
    Videotapes and movies

What to Observe

    Who: actor
    Doing what: act
    With whom: significant others
    Relationships
    Context
    Setting

QUALITIES OF THE METHOD

Observing behavior is empathetic and direct, deals with dynamic phenomena, and allows researchers to vary their intrusiveness in a research setting.

Empathetic

Researchers observing people soon get a feeling for the character of a situation. Observation, especially participant observation, allows researchers to "get into" a setting: to understand nuances that users of that setting feel. When personal quirks of observers influence the recording of observations, their reliability can be questioned. Yet personal feelings may provide essential initial research insights that a study can revise and elaborate.

Jane Jacobs' *Death and Life of Great American Cities* (1961) is based largely on behavior observations that she made while a resident in New York's Greenwich Village. Her perspective enabled her to describe empathetically what it is like to live on a street where people look out their windows at passersby, children play on the sidewalk in view of neighbors and parents, and shopkeepers serve as news outlets and street guardians.

That observing behavior seems so easy and obvious can present problems. It is common for observers to report observations in seductively authentic descriptions that, unfortunately, omit details and transfer untested feelings. Missing are standardized procedures for observing and a theoretical framework for interpreting observations. Having explicit procedures and theory increases the likelihood that different observers' descriptions are comparable, enabling readers of observation reports to interpret and evaluate them more easily.

Empathy can be taken too far: Observers may assume that the way they personally feel in a situation is the way everyone else feels. For example, an observer who dislikes being with many people might assume that the high level of contact on Jacobs' close-knit urban street makes most people anxious and uncomfortable.

Observers also run the risk of overlooking differences between people, unless they formulate their feelings into testable hypotheses. On Greenwich Village streets, how many people choose to look out their windows to participate in a neighborhood life important to them, and how many do so because they have nothing else to do? How many parents talk to other parents while watching children play because it is what is expected of them, and how many do so because they are lonely and want the contact?

Direct

Respondents often hesitate to report that they break formal rules by smoking in school hallways near "No Smoking" signs; or having two families living in an apartment designated for one family. Yet they do not care if they are seen doing such things, because they and their friends or neighbors find such behavior acceptable.

The same can be true for behavior that, although acceptable to a particular group, breaks the informal rules of a larger one. A cross-cultural example of the need for direct observation is evident in Chandigarh, Le Corbusier's modern capital of India's Punjab province. Many residents of this administrative center are aspiring middle-class civil servants who live in buildings that reflect modern norms that some of the more traditional Indians do not follow. For example, some residents reported that they used the kitchen counters to prepare meals, but when Brolin (1972) looked more closely, he found that they followed the traditional Indian practice of cooking on portable stoves on the floor. One resident assured Brolin that, caste distinctions being obsolete, everyone including servants used the front door. Brolin was surprised to observe household servants using the back door. Had Brolin used only interviewing techniques, he might never have observed such rule-breaking activity.

People also tend not to report to interviewers activity they think is trivial and therefore not worth reporting. Nonetheless, a seemingly trivial datum may be central to an environmental research question. For example, if someone asked you now to describe what you had been doing for the last two minutes, you would probably say that you had been reading. You might also describe the position you are in—sitting, or lying down. You probably would not say that you were leaning forward or backward and that you had just turned the page, although to design a comfortable library these details may be important.

Because observing behavior can be intensely personal, trained and sensitive researchers who are able to perceive relevant nuances can use the method more fruitfully. Being on the spot allows researchers to adjust their observations to a particular setting and to a refined understanding of the situation. Whyte's personal research capabilities are evident in his participant-observation study *Street Corner Society* (1955). His day-to-day involvement with a street gang enabled him to uncover more than ordinary evidence. Whyte noticed, for example, that one gang member, Alec, regularly bowled higher scores than gang leaders when bowling alone during the week. But when the whole gang bowled together on Saturday nights, their scores paralleled the gang's hierarchy. The leaders bowled the highest scores, while Alec came in last.

When a "follower" was bowling too well, his companions would heckle him, saying such things as "You're just lucky!" and "You're bowling over your head!" When Doc, the leader, bowled poorly, they would shout encouragement, telling him he could do better. Whyte noticed that gang members exerted subtle—and not so subtle—social pressures on one another to conform to the hierarchy. He was able to make this insightful observation on what sociologists call *social control* because he had many opportunities to observe general and specific gang behavior and could adjust his observations to each situation.

Dynamic

As you look at people doing things, what you see changes: activities affect other activities; episodes take place. You get a glimpse of the role of time in the life of an environment: a mother leaning from her window calling her child to supper, the child coming. More complex chains of events are exemplified by a hospital emergency room when an ambulance arrives. As the weekly television drama *ER* shows, an ambulance arrival can have simultaneous effects on nurses, doctors, other patients, nearby staff members, police officers, and many others who participate both actively and passively.

In complex situations observers of behavior get a sense of chain reactions: the effects of effects. No other method gives a researcher such a rich idea of how people bring places to life. Ellis' (1974) explanation of "occasioning" among poorer African Americans shows how they manipulate both behavior and time to cope with limited space. For example, although kitchens are predominantly associated with cooking and eating, residents might regularly use them for other occasions such as card parties, sewing bees, or visiting with friends. Although "occasioning," according to Ellis, is a strategy used by poorer African Americans in the United States, observing behavior among other groups of people could test the hypothesis that they use the strategy as well.

When you observe behavior, you soon become aware of repetitive activities in identifiable places—what Barker calls "standing patterns of behavior" (1968). Place-specific activities within such a pattern are more closely related to one another than to patterns of activities in other places. The set of activities in an old-fashioned drugstore connected to ordering, making, drinking, and paying for an ice cream soda are more closely related to one another than to those activities which constitute getting a prescription filled—although there may be no precise boundary defined between the two places where they occur. Training helps observers identify sets of activities that are closely related to one another, to define significant patterns, and distinguish significant patterns from unimportant ones.

In conducting research on bank design, for example, an observer might watch customers make bank transactions, from filling out slips at the desk to getting or depositing money at the window. It is easy to overlook parts of the sequence that occur before clients enter the bank or after they leave the teller's cage, which includes seeing that documents are in their pockets and that money is safely put away into a purse. Does the security guard standing watch consider himself to be part of every transaction? To look carefully at events, observers continually question whether they see the whole event, whether they see all the participants, and whether something significant has been missed.

Observers in dynamic research situations can test their hunches on the spot. An observer who believes she has detected a regularity can try to predict what the next few individuals will do and can revise or refine the hunch right away, depending on how these people act. Instant feedback like this enables researchers in the beginning of a study to test many hunches, quickly identifying the more fruitful research ideas.

The more explicit predictions and tests are made in notes and reports, the more you can use team members to check your interpretation. Writing down predictions and tests also helps observers avoid the trap of thinking that false starts have really been well tested and enables them to review their own work later with a clearer mind.

Variably Intrusive

Researchers have to decide how far they will intrude and from what social and physical vantage point they want to participate in observed events. At one extreme they can choose to record and observe behavior unobtrusively from a distance—for example, with a telephoto lens. In addition to possibly creating ethical problems, observing in this way removes the observer from the scene of action, depriving the method of a large part of its research potential. However, close participation increases the chance of unwittingly affecting the observed situation. Choice of vantage point depends on such things as research problem, available time, and investigator skills.

To offset research bias resulting from their presence, participant observers adopt social positions with which people are familiar. In a hospital, this could mean sitting in the waiting room like a patient; in a restaurant, it could mean working as a waitress or being a customer. In order to take account in data analysis of changes they themselves induce, observers record any incident in which people may be reacting differently because the observers are present in their adopted position. For example, patients in a waiting room may be whispering because another patient (the observer) is waiting too. The more crowded a setting—for example, a rush-hour subway platform—the less the observers' actions affect the situation.

Of course, intrusion may be part of the research project's design. For example, the observer has the ability to change situations and watch results, as Lefkowitz et al. (1955) did in their natural experiment, mentioned earlier, on pedestrians' reactions to differently dressed jaywalkers. Felipe and Sommer (1966) used themselves as both observers and stimuli to test a personal-space hypothesis that people get uncomfortable enough to leave if their personal-space norms are invaded. Observers sat very close to students in a library and compared the time before the students left with the time before another student across the room moved, whose space was not invaded. The same natural-experiment approach to observing behavior can be taken by moving furniture, erecting signs, or changing an environment in some other way. Natural experiments are an example of artificial intervention made possible because observing behavior is such a variably intrusive research method. (The students next to whom Felipe and Sommer sat regularly moved away first.)

In sum, observing behavior is both empathetic and direct, deals with a dynamic subject, and allows observers to be variably intrusive. These qualities make the method useful at the beginning of research to generate hunches, in the middle to document regularities, and late in a research project to locate key explanatory information.

OBSERVERS' VANTAGE POINTS

Observers can choose to be outsiders or participants in any situation. As outsiders, they may be secret or recognized observers; as participants, they may be either marginal or full.

Secret Outsider

The distant observer unobserved by participants in a natural setting is a secret outsider. Moore (1973) initially chose this vantage point for a study of children's play at an elementary school in Berkeley, California. School officials replaced half an acre of blacktop with dirt that children could dig in and objects to play with, such as timber, aluminum pipe, and tree stumps. For five months, every week at the same time, before, during, and after the change, Moore climbed to the roof of the school and recorded what the kids did, using time-lapse photography. He chose this vantage point so he would not alter their behavior with his recording equipment until he showed them the film and because he thought this would later enable him to analyze patterns of use. He found, however, that by choosing to record only an overview of the playground, he missed what individual children and adults did over time and any indications of depth of personal involvement in what they did. To catch some of these dynamic attributes of his topic, he took the camera down to the ground, becoming a recognized outside observer.

Recognized Outsider

When Blau (1963, 1964) compared two job-placement offices, he introduced himself as a researcher to those who were to be observed, explained his study, and was given a desk by the department head to work at and observe from.

A pitfall of such a recognized-outsider position is what is known as the Hawthorne effect—that subjects who know they are being observed as part of an experiment often change the way they act. The Hawthorne effect derived its name from the now-classic environmental experiments at the Western Electric Company's Hawthorne Plant in Chicago, where Roethlisberger and Dixon (1939) wanted to determine, among other things, how lighting levels affected workers' productivity. They carried out their studies as recognized observers. When they raised light levels, production increased. When they lowered light levels, production also increased. They concluded that consciously being under a microscope changes workers' behavior.

You can try to minimize the Hawthorne effect by spending enough time at your research site that people there get used to you and take you more for granted. Observers can develop tasks to do while observing so that they can blend into the setting more easily. Whatever observers do, there will always be the danger of some Hawthorne effect, which must be recognized and considered during data analysis.

Another problem for recognized observers is that no matter how honestly and convincingly they present themselves, their study, and their ethical commitment to respect privacy, someone may not believe them. Observers can exacerbate this problem by oversight. Blau obtained permission to study the placement offices from the department head. The staff members therefore assumed that Blau would report everything he saw to their boss. This was a mistaken, but not surprising, interpretation. Observers need to avoid giving off clues that they are partisan watchdogs. They must remain as unaffiliated as possible by being careful about who introduces them, where they sit, whom they have lunch with, whose office they use to make phone calls, and generally from whom they accept favors.

Sometimes you cannot help being a victim of natural institutional mistrust, particularly when you are interested in informal uses of physical settings. Recipients of public assistance with relatives staying over in the living room, students smoking in the school bathroom, teachers making private calls from an office phone, and patrolmen resting in coffee shops between emergencies are worried about being caught by an authority figure. In such situations, subjects tend to fear that researchers are spies—perhaps tax inspectors or school administrators. Subjects normally play along with the "spy," feeding him harmless information but not admitting the mistrust they feel. The more researchers explain their harmlessness, the guiltier they seem. To reduce the effects of mistrust on the validity of the research, observers must sensitively record situations in which mistrust is likely to have changed behavior. They can also make a special point not to ask questions about rule-breaking activities that are clearly irrelevant to the study problem.

Secret- and recognized-outsider vantage points both have disadvantages along with their advantages. Secret observers are by definition distant and removed from the action, and their position raises ethical questions. Recognized observers may affect action in unknown ways.

Marginal Participant

Researchers who adopt the vantage point of a commonly accepted and unimportant participant want to be seen by actual participants as just another patient in a hospital waiting room, another subway rider, or another art student drawing in a park. A marginal-participant vantage point is a comfortable one for E-B researchers to adopt because observant professionals and laypersons adopt it naturally in daily situations.

Marginal positions that observers choose are likely to be somewhat familiar. We have all been bus passengers, members of the audience at a street concert, restaurant patrons, and tourists at a national monument. Familiarity, however, can prevent observers from looking carefully at what is actually going on. It is tempting to assume that a quick glance will tell you everything because, after all, you have seen it all before. Such an attitude dulls the observer's ability to be surprised by what she sees—a crucial ability if research is not merely to record the obvious.

An observer who is familiar with her vantage point can also be misled into assuming that she knows how others in a setting feel about *being watched*. For example, the marginal observer assumes when watching an informal football game in the park that he is taken to be a casual spectator. Meanwhile, the football players may think he is a park attendant about to tell them to stop playing on the grass. To increase the validity of their research, observers must test their assumptions about how they are perceived by others. For example, observers can slightly change their natural behavior to see how people in the situation respond.

Ways to control unwanted side effects include deliberate choice of clothing, physical posture, and objects one is carrying. Researchers observing in Harvard Yard will be seen very differently if they carry green book bags than if they carry leather attaché cases. One useful trick is to use one's behavior-recording device as a prop to indicate a familiar, yet inconsequential, participant position: a camera for tourist, a notebook for student, or a sketchbook for an amateur artist.

In general, being a marginal participant observer requires the least amount of research preparation time. But precisely for this reason it requires that observers be introspective and self-aware.

Full Participant

To observe behavior, researchers can use positions they are already in and positions they adopt central to the situation they are studying. Full participants in a study of housing design might be residents of a neighborhood. A study to plan an office might be helped by researchers taking jobs as office clerks and typists.

Participant observation by a waitress would have been appropriate in an E-B situation described by Whyte (1949). In twelve restaurants where tension was high between dining-room and kitchen staff members, he observed that when waitresses gave orders to the cooks in the kitchen, the cooks resented it. They were higher-paid and resented taking orders from less-skilled waitresses. Although they could not avoid communication flow in this direction, they could avoid taking orders directly. Tension was reduced in some restaurants when a clipboard was installed on the counter between the dining room and kitchen. Waitresses put order slips on the clipboard, and whenever a cook decided to take the next order, he went to the board and picked up a slip. He put the plate back on the separating counter. He no longer took orders directly; the environmental change gave him control over his own actions.

In some cases researchers may not be able to choose full participation, as when all participants are highly skilled professionals (doctors in a hospital) or when membership in the setting being studied is restricted (men's athletic clubs). Gaining full participant-observer status by taking up residence, taking a job, or joining an organization usually means making a long-term commitment. Return on such an investment potentially comes in the form of an insightful and empathetic position from which to gather behavioral data.

RECORDING DEVICES

Devices suited to recording behavior observations include verbal descriptions and diagrams, pre-coded checklists or handheld PDA computers for counting, floor plans or maps, still photographs, and videotape. What devices to choose depends mainly on how much detailed information the problem demands and how much the observer already knows about the behaviors to be observed.

Notation

Recording behavior in verbal and diagrammatic notes demands that observers decide what to describe and what to overlook on the spot. For example, in describing how people use a hotel lounge, the observer must decide whether to record how people meet each other and move around, how people sit and watch others, how they hold their newspapers and shift their weight, or how they move their eyes and twitch their noses. Each level of analysis is useful to design researchers for solving different problems. Each individual observer decides on and then isolates the level of analysis that is particularly relevant to his or her own study or design project. If multiple observers work on the same research project, they must be trained and sensitized together, comparing their observations so that each knows what types of behaviors to note. That well-trained observers make decisions about levels of analysis can be an opportunity to see richness in a situation and catch that richness in discrete notes.

Procedures for descriptive behavioral notation are relatively simple. Notes are recorded by researchers working alone or by one team member when the other member is conducting an interview. As with notes of physical traces, it is useful to crease a note page, creating a wide right-hand margin. When observations are written in the left-hand column, the right side is open for individual or group analysis. Table 9-1 shows a sample of field notes.

Several small tricks help avoid embarrassing mistakes in descriptive behavior notes: always include yourself in observations to avoid finding out that a crucial observed behavior was actually a response to your presence; when sitting and taking notes in public, make a drawing on the top page of the notepad so that anyone who looks over your shoulder will find an acceptable sketch; never leave notes around. What are harmless descriptions of the obvious to a researcher can be highly insulting snooping to participants.

Table 9-1. **Sample field notes from site visit to hospital emergency room.** (Observations made from nurse's station at 1:00 p.m.)

Observation	*Comment*
Woman waiting in wheelchair has been waiting in corridor between nurse and row of examining rooms since at least 10:30. She is watching all the activity.	*Does watching emergency activity make waiting easier?*

Table 9-1. (continued)

Police arrive with stretcher. Announce in loud voices that they have a woman who fell down and passed out. She is lying still on stretcher with eyes closed, covered.	*Why do they announce it? For nurses to clear a path?*
All other patients sitting in corridor lean forward in chairs to look. The stretcher will not fit through corridor where patients are sitting.	*Patients looking again! Is it just something to do?*
Police struggle to maneuver stretcher through the crowd of nurses and doctors in the nursing station to get to uncrowded corridor on other side. Patient is put in examining room. Curtain pulled part-way closed by last policeman to leave. Patients waiting in corridor have full view of patient in exam room.	*Hallway waiting causes traffic problems for stretcher cases.* *This probably bothers patients being examined.*
A policeman wheels stretcher out back door into middle of waiting area, while another tells a nurse the details about the woman they brought in, leaning over counter at nurse's station.	*This public discussion surely seems like an invasion of privacy.*
Nurse leaves nurse's station, walks around counter into corridor, scans all patients waiting there. She walks up to one man who is seated, stands three feet away and tells him the results of lab tests and what they mean. Doctor walks over and asks same patient to go into exam room with him.	*Nurse in her "station" cannot see the informal or overflow waiting area in corridor. What are the design implications? Behavior of nurse in telling lab results is another type of invasion of privacy.*
Doctor's voice, shouting angrily, comes from an exam room.	*What acoustical control is needed in exam rooms?*
Doctor leaves nurse's station, approaches woman waiting in wheelchair, pulls up a chair, sits down beside her, and talks in low tones. Other patients sitting nearby watch and occasionally speak to each other.	*Consultation in waiting areas may be standard emergency-room procedure? Is there a way to allow this to take place but provide more privacy?*
Sound of friendly chatter, laughing from one exam room.	*Does this perhaps relax people in waiting area?*

Field notes by architect/researcher Polly Welch for "Hospital Emergency Facilities: Translating Behavioral Issues into Design," by P. Welch. (Graham Foundation Fellowship Report) Cambridge, Mass.: Architecture Research Office, Harvard Graduate School of Design, 1977.

Pre-coded Checklists

Descriptive notes provide a qualitative understanding of what is going on: what types of behavior patterns exist, what characteristics of participants are salient, and what level of descriptive abstraction is appropriate to solve a problem. If researchers want to know in greater detail how often an activity takes place, they can use qualitative observation data to develop a pre-coded checklist for counting. Pre-coded checklists can either be used in a paper-and-pencil format or data can be input directly to a handheld personal digital assistant (PDA) computer. The qualitative approach serves in such situations as the diagnostic phase of the research project.

In their study of behavior on a psychiatric ward, Ittelson, Rivlin, and Proshansky (1970) recorded over 300 descriptions of behaviors during extended periods of time. For example: "patient reclines on bench, hand over face, but not asleep; patient cleans table with sponge; patient plays soccer in corridor; patient sits on cans in hall watching people go by." For counting purposes, they coded the descriptions into categories representing types of activities observed, such as lying awake, housekeeping, games, and watching an activity.

For each activity on a checklist, observers record characteristics of participants (alone or in groups), place, time, and other relevant conditions, such as the weather. When a PDA (personal digital assistant) is used, time can be noted automatically by programming a time function into the data collection program. Perhaps the most significant task in developing a checklist is specifying the descriptive level of abstraction to record. Ittelson et al. decided, for example, that activity types (housekeeping, personal hygiene) were more relevant to their problem than activities (cleaning a table with a sponge, setting one's hair). Rather than describe subjects in terms of approximate age, sex, weight, and height, which might be relevant to a study of children's play equipment, observers in the psychiatric ward coded the gender of the subject, whether he or she was acting alone or in a group, and, if in a group, the group size and mix of genders.

To set up a checklist demands previous diagnostic observation, a thorough understanding of how the data will be used, and an understanding of how to develop coding categories. Once a pre-coded checklist is set up, it provides relatively comparable quantifiable data with only a moderate amount of training for observers.

Maps and Plans

Recording activities on floor plans, diagrams, or maps is particularly convenient if researchers want to observe and analyze several people in one general area at the same time, such as groups at a cocktail party, patients in a waiting room, or office workers eating in an open-air plaza. Looking at behavior recorded on a plan gives investigators a better sense of how a whole place is used at once than they would get looking at statistical tables.

Maps are also useful to record sequences of behavior in settings where people have a choice of several paths: from home to bus stop, or from desk to desk in an open-plan office. Analyzing map records in the light of an actual setting can give an idea of the characteristics of popular paths.

If investigators want precise physical-location data, they can construct base plans with grids corresponding to regular elements in the actual setting, such as floor tiles or columns. These can be used in paper and pencil format or entered into a PDA with a program that identifies patterns in the data in real time.

Photographs

Still photographs can capture subtleties that other methods may not record, such as the way someone sits on a chair or leans against a column; or the way two people avoid looking at each other by adjusting their body postures. In addition, as presented in Chapter 9, photographs are useful throughout a research project because of their illustrative quality. The same procedures hold for deciding on photographs to record behavior as were described for using photographs to record physical traces.

Videotapes and Movies

Whenever time is a significant element in an E-B problem, videotape should be considered as a data-recording tool. For example, universal urban design of streets for people with disabilities and older people, among others, demands understanding the pace of these special users: How fast do they move? How long can they move before resting? How fast can they move out of other people's way? To design a safe escalator, it is essential to know how different types of people approach it, prepare to get onto it, and embark (Davis and Ayers, 1975).

WHAT TO OBSERVE

Observing behavior looks like a simple E-B research technique. Everyone watches people every day. Doesn't everyone know how to do it? In a way, yes; but few know what to look for and how to analyze what they see so that it is useful to design.

Designers make places for people to do things in—either alone or with other people. A structure for looking at environmental behavior that is useful to designers results in data that help them make decisions that improve places for people. The better information designers have about how the people they design for behave in physical settings and how those people relate to or exclude other people, the better they can control the behavioral side effects of the design decisions they make.

But that is not enough. Designers must also know how the contexts of observed activities affect those activities, because in different socio-cultural and physical settings the same behavior can have different design implications. For example, children may do homework at the kitchen table for different reasons in a house with several available rooms to study than in a one-bedroom apartment shared by four people. In some groups people react to neighbors sitting on the front stoop with disdain, while for others the front is where everyone sits.

When you structure the way you look at something, you replace complex reality with a simpler version to guide your reactions and action. To increase our control over the behavioral side effects of design decisions, we can describe behavior in terms of actor, act, significant others, relationships, context, and setting.

Elements in Environmental Behavior Observation

Who is	*Actor*
doing *what*	*Act*
with *whom?*	*Significant Others*
In what *relationship*,	*Relationships*
	aural, visual, tactile, olfactory, symbolic
in what *context*,	*Sociocultural Context*
	situation culture
and *where?*	*Physical Setting*
	props spatial relations

The following illustrations are verbally annotated to show how you can use these observation categories to describe environmental behavior in actual situations.

Each observation comprises a relationship between an actor and a significant other to which the physical setting contributes in some way.

Who: Actor

The subject of a behavioral observation, the "actor," may be described in numerous ways, depending on the purpose of the description. Designers use research in large projects to better understand similarities and variations among types of people. For example, instead of designing a school for 273 unique individuals, designers use research to differentiate the needs of students, teachers,

With whom?

Setting?

Who?   Doing what?   Relationship?

Swimming pool and sitting area on roof of LeCorbusier's
Marseille Block Housing, Marseille, France.

Who?   Doing what?

Relationship?

Setting?

With whom?

Children watching girl play ball on roof of LeCorbusier's
Marseille Block Housing, Marseille, France.

principals, and maintenance workers. Assisted living residences are planned for residents, resident assistants, administrators, nurses, doctors, maintenance crews, and visitors; furniture and space are planned for the range of people who work in offices. In a sense, individuals in observations are treated as representatives of a social group.

We can use individuals as representatives by describing a person's social position or status: age status, marital status, educational status, professional status, and so on. It helps to be complete in observations if we describe both a person's ascribed statuses (the characteristics that a person has automatically, such as gender and age) and his or her achieved statuses (those that the person had to do something to get, such as finding a job, graduating from college, getting married, or inviting people to a party). Many positions are defined as part of a relationship to others: party hostess (guests), wife (husband), teacher (student), nurse (patient), salesperson (customer).

An observer unable to describe statuses accurately in field notes can describe clues from which he and other researchers reading the notes may be able to infer status. For example, when Snyder and Ostrander (1974), observed patients, family members, visitors, and staff members in their Oxford nursing-home study, they knew most individuals personally after a few days or could infer their status from such things as dress (uniform means nurse; street clothes mean visitor) and tools (stethoscope means doctor; sitting in a wheelchair means patient). But when they were not sure, they described in their field notes whatever clues they had and whether they were guessing about the person's status. It is better to record "It could be a nurse's aide resting in the wheelchair" than to write "It is a patient asleep in the corner," so that other researchers can help evaluate the data.

Sometimes relevant descriptions of actors in behavioral observations are names of groups—teens, teachers, and girls—not individuals. In Zeisel's property-damage study (1976a) researchers observed groups of boys playing street hockey and stickball in open spaces around schools. It was not important for their research and design problem to identify each street-hockey participant as an actor in a separate act. Researchers treated the group as the actor, describing the group's size and composition. Groups can be described in the same status terms as individuals. For example, the psychiatric ward study by Ittelson et al. (1970) identified groups by the number of male and female patients, doctors, and visitors they contained.

One pitfall for observers to avoid is subsuming significant individuals under general group descriptions. If four teenagers are shooting a hockey puck at the front doors of a school while five others look on from a bench nearby and one gets ready under a tree to play, it would be misleading to write in one's field notes: "A group of ten boys are playing street hockey at the school entrance." To design a place to play street hockey, the relationship among players, spectators, and reserve players is relevant.

A group of two also raises problems for observers: are they a group acting together with common significant others, or do they themselves represent actor and significant other for each other? If they are very similar and are doing the same thing, it may be appropriate to describe them together as two boys playing street hockey with each other, two elderly men playing chess, or two women walking down the street together. However, when the couple is made up of two different types of individuals interacting, it may be useful to describe them separately, seeing one of the two as the actor in the observation, for example a parent and child in the park, or a nurse and patient in a hospital. But even here, as with all descriptive observation techniques, the researcher's judgment is the most significant determinant of what is important to describe.

Doing What: Act

The people you observe will be doing something. An observer needs to decide the level of abstraction he will use to describe behavior and how he will distinguish individual acts from a connected sequence of acts.

Table 9-2. Behavior descriptions and corresponding questions for a shopping-center design, by level of detail

	Behavior Observation	*Design Question*
General Description	"Shopping" as opposed to "hanging around"	In a shopping-center plan, how many places are needed for people to hang around, and how can they be designed to augment rather than interfere with shopping?
	Shoppers browsing as opposed to buying something	How should items be displayed so that browsers and buyers can see them but buyers have greater access to them?
	Where and how often shoppers stop in supermarket aisles	How can flooring materials, lighting, and aisle length be designed for maximum convenience to customers, maximum exposure of sales items, and minimum maintenance?
	How high patrons will reach and how low they will stoop	What shelf design and what product placement (what size container on what shelf) will ensure that customers have the easiest time reaching items?
Detailed Description	Where customers' eyes focus while moving down an aisle	Where should standard signs be placed to convey the most information, and where ought sale signs be located to catch customers' glances?

The level of description observers choose depends mainly on the design and research problem facing them. Let us take as an example an observational study to write a design program for a supermarket. Observers could describe very generally that some people there are "shopping" and others are just hanging around. More precisely, they can describe that some shoppers browse, while others buy something. Or observers might record where and count how often a supermarket patron stops in the aisles. They might record how high patrons reach and how low they stoop when getting items off the shelves. Or observers might go to the trouble to observe and record in what direction patrons turn their heads and focus their eyes while walking down the aisle. Each observation is either interesting or useless, depending on the problem researchers are trying to solve. The series of design questions in Table 9-2 shows how each level of described activity might be useful.

Along with deciding on appropriate levels of analysis, researchers must explain how the acts they describe relate to one another. In the sequence of acts called "shopping," a person prepares a shopping list, leaves home, goes to the store, looks at items in the store, reaches for them, examines them, places them in the cart, walks down the aisle, pays at the cash register, returns home, and unpacks. Each of these can be seen as a discrete act linked to the others as part of a larger "shopping" sequence. If researchers observing behavior maintain clarity of descriptive level and completeness in describing related acts, they will be able to analyze their data more easily.

Even more critical than having the skill to decide how and what to describe, is describing what you see with minimum interpretation. If observers try to interpret what they see before writing it down, they run the risk of recording interpretations rather than description, losing the data for good. The data cannot be retrieved for analysis by others or later review. Well-recorded observations leave ample time and space for analysis after data have been collected. If data on behavior are to be sharable, it is vital that observers record "a smiling person," not "a happy person," because a smile can mean many things.

With Whom: Significant Others

Acts people engage in are partly defined by how other people are or are not included. Other people whose presence or absence is significant in this way can be seen as participants in the act itself. Girls for whom boys playing street hockey show off make the activity what it is. If the girls were not present, the situation would be different. The same is true in reverse for studying alone in the library. Those who are not there—friends, roommates, and strangers—contribute to the situation by their absence. To understand and present what is going on, descriptions of girls watching the boys and of absent roommates must be included in research observations of behavior. The latter requires the skill to see who is not there.

"Significant others" are especially important in environmental design research because so many design decisions about adjacencies, connections, and separations have side effects for relationships. To continue one of our earlier examples, boys playing street hockey need a hard, flat surface to play on. If this surface is provided for them in the middle of a deserted field far from other activity, it is unlikely to be used because the "significant others," the girls and passersby, have not been taken into account. A tot lot without places for parents to sit and watch may go unused in favor of a more convenient one or may be used in a different way than the designer had hoped.

The positions or statuses by which actors are described often have standard role relationships associated with them. In a family, for example, one finds role relationships between parent and child, sister and brother, husband and wife, and grandparent and grandchild. In hospitals there are role relationships between doctor and patient, doctor and nurse, patient and nurse, patient and visitor, nurse and visitor, and between patients. A sensitive researcher observing a doctor making notes in a hospital will use the concept of significant other to direct attention to the relationship the doctor making notes has set up between herself and the patients, nurses, and other doctors. Does she sit among patients in the waiting room, or does she retire to a private lounge? Does she discuss notes with nurses or just hand them in? To design appropriately for medical note taking in hospitals, the answers to these relational questions can be important.

Relationships

Between actors and significant others in a situation there will be specific relationships for observers to describe. In extreme cases relationships can be described simply: "together" (two lovers on a park bench at night) or "apart" (a person in isolation after a bone marrow transplant).

Most E-B relationships, however, are not so simple. Are two people talking to each other through a fence together or apart? What about two people sit-

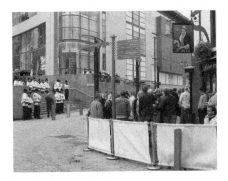

Simultaneous connections and separations
Left: Urinal dividers separate visually, and that's about all,
Liberty International Airport, Newark, New Jersey.
Right: Manchester United football fans isolated in a pub before a match,
Manchester, United Kingdom.

ting back-to-back in adjacent restaurant booths? The problem researchers face is to describe relationships like these systematically so that differences and similarities between two situations are clear. Researchers and designers can then use the information to develop broader strategies for design rather than continually approaching each situation as totally new. To gather such information, researchers need to agree on a set of categories to describe connections and separations between people, and they must understand how the effects of relationships on activities differ in different behavior settings.

Hall (1966) shows us that behavioral connections and separations between people in environments can be conveniently and efficiently described in terms of seeing (visual), hearing (aural), touching (tactile), smelling (olfactory), and perceiving (symbolic).

Describing two people as completely together, or "co-present" (Goffman, 1963, p. 17), means that, like two children in the bathtub, they can see, hear, touch, and smell each other and they feel that they are "in the same place."

When we move away from extreme relationships, the sensory terms we have for describing relationships enable us to discriminate among and compare various types and to begin to identify the role that the physical environment plays in relationships between people. A mother on the third floor calling to her child playing on the street is connected visually and aurally but is separated in terms of touch, smell, and perception. Two students studying at opposite ends of a long library table are separated symbolically and in terms of smell and touch but are connected visually and aurally. Persons in an L-shaped living room, around the corner from someone cooking in the kitchen, are separated by sight, touch, and perception but are connected in terms of food smells and sound.

Once observers see and describe relationships like these, they try to find out what the relationships mean to participants. Although they must also use other research methods to determine meaning, behavior observation provides clues to meaning. The clues are the ways people react when other people talk to them, touch them, and so on.

Context

People react to others differently in one situation than in another and in one culture than in another. It is as if they filter what they see through a series of screens—situational and cultural. The screens are usually used unconsciously, as Sommer (1969) and Hall (1966) have pointed out. People assume that other people see things the same way they do. It is the observer's job to identify how people's situational and cultural screens are constructed—how they interpret their own and others' behavior.

This is particularly important in environmental design research because the meanings people attribute to relationships determine how they react to environmental features, such as walls, doors, and lights, that affect those relationships.

• *Situations.* A person sitting alone and apart from others, or facing a wall in a library probably indicates that she wants to be left alone to read or study. In a bar, this same physical behavior can be interpreted as an invitation for conversation (Sommer, 1969). The person might still reject any advances, but she is unlikely to be distressed and insulted, as the person disturbed in the library may be.

An extreme example of how a situation can influence the meaning people attribute to behavioral relationships can be seen if you watch people's shocked reactions when you talk in a normal voice to a friend over the hush in a crowded elevator. In a department store, a market, or a crowd viewing a parade, your voice would not even be noticed. In an elevator, however, the definition of personal space is different, as are the definitions of unacceptable behaviors. An observer must try to understand the situational rules being applied by participants to interpret the meaning they attribute to even a simple observation such as "Two persons stood next to each other talking."

• *Culture.* Cultural context also influences how people interpret and react to behavioral relationships. For example, Hall (1966) reports that in England, sitting alone reading in a room at home with the door open means, "Do not disturb; do not even knock." In the United States you would close you're the door to indicate you wanted to be alone; an open door means you are available. It would not be inappropriate for people to knock on an open door and ask whether they might come in. A designer laying out open-plan offices in these two cultures needs to be aware of these differences if she wants to control the behavioral side effects of his physical design decisions.

It is particularly important to record cultural contexts for behavior when carrying out observational studies in another country or in parts of your own country with strong regional differences. Otherwise, designers using the data will be making decisions that are irrelevant to users. As in Le Corbusier's Chandigarh, people may end up cooking on stoves on the floor in efficiency kitchens and establishing illegal street markets in the plazas in front of modern government buildings (Brolin, 1972). To see behavior from a cultural perspective other than one's own requires general observation and study of another culture, awareness of one's own cultural biases, and at times requesting the help of members of or experts on another culture in interpreting behavioral data once they are collected. As the basis for this interpretation, it is necessary to describe as fully as possible people's reactions to relationships in which they find themselves.

Setting

The meaning of behavior in a particular setting depends on the potential of the setting for use—the options it provides (Gans, 1968). If people in an airport lounge are sitting on the floor surrounded by empty seats, their behavior may have a different meaning than if no seats are available. Understanding participants' choices and possibilities to act helps you interpret what they finally choose to do.

• *Behavior potentials of settings.* *Objects* imply obvious options for use: Seats in telephone booths are for sitting down when calling; bathroom sinks are for washing hands. At the same time they have a host of less obvious latent implications limited only by users' physical capabilities, daring, and imagination. The telephone seat provides tired noncallers a place to rest. Sinks in school bathrooms may fall off the wall when teenagers sit on them during cigarette breaks between classes. On a hot summer day urban fountains turn into swimming pools. These objects can be seen as *props* for behavior.

Elements that divide and connect places organize potentials for behavioral relationships. The glass divider, acoustic paneling, and corner placement of a phone booth provide users with the option for limited acoustical privacy but neither physical nor visual privacy. The visual privacy school bathrooms provide enhances their suitability for taking cigarette breaks.

• *Relational design decisions. Barriers* clearly determine potentials for relationships between people in settings. Barriers include walls of various materials and consistencies, screens in different sizes and materials, objects used to mark the edges of places, and symbols ranging from color changes to verbal signs. Design decisions defining *fields* in space influence behavior relationships less obviously. Field definitions include such characteristics of places as shape, orientation, size, and environmental conditions—sound, light, and air.

To define the ways these physical characteristics affect relationships between people, we can use the simple relational scheme developed earlier: seeing, hearing, touching, smelling, and perceiving.

• *Barriers.* Barriers are physical elements that keep people apart or join them together on one or more of the five dimensions—seeing, hearing, and so on. As one progresses from walls to symbols, barriers become more permeable.

• *Walls* separate people in places. The absence of walls allows people to be connected. The thickness, consistency, and materials of walls influence the quality of separation. For example, walls with no soundproofing between bedrooms provide neighbors with aural opportunities (and inhibitions) that denser walls do not.

• *Screens.* Glass panels, garden hedges, shower curtains, doors, counters, and windows—separate and connect people more selectively than complete

Screens
Left: Architect buys a burrito through a glass screen, Venice, California.
Right: Glass blocks visually screen showering partner from bathing partner; but they can still talk, Santa Barbara, California.

walls. Glass enables visual connection but tactile separation; a shower curtain does the opposite. Materials can be combined to provide different degrees of connection and separation along any mix of dimensions. Screens can also be designed to give selective control over the screen to users. For example, the lock and doorbell on a glass-paneled house door provide a range of permeability options for family members, friends, and thieves (Hoogdalem, 1977).

• *Objects* form another class of barriers. Things placed in space may be perceived as space dividers or connectors: a piece of sculpture on a public plaza may be a separator or a place to meet; a couch in a living room is either a place for two people to sit or an object separating two areas; a tree in a garden can separate two garden areas or provide a place for two people to chat together in the shade.

An object, here a column in a shared interior porch, can help people divide space perceptually. (Congregate House for Older People. Design-research team: Barry Korobkin, John Zeisel, and Eric Jahan. Donham & Sweeney, associated architects.)

Finally, *symbols* can be barriers. Color changes in the rug around a public telephone and change in ceiling height in a room signal that someone considers this space to be two separate places, perceptually.

Depending how people interpret spatial symbols, they may change their behavior by not walking too close to the phone caller because of the floor color, or calling one part of a room by another name because of the shift in ceiling height.

Symbols that separate and connect include overt signs such as, "Do Not Walk on the Grass" potentially keeping people off; or "Open for Business" potentially bringing people in. Sitting on the grass near a "Keep Off" sign conveys another impression to observers than if there is no such separator.

• *Fields*. Field characteristics of an entire place can alter people's ability to be together or apart. Field characteristics do this not by standing between people, like barriers, but by altering the physical context within which visual, aural, tactile, olfactory, and perceptual relationships take place. Field characteristics of places include their shape, orientation, size, and environmental condition.

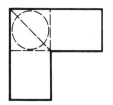 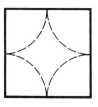 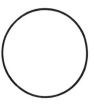

L-shape separates space visually and symbolically

Shape suggests perceptual separations

Corners suggest potential symbolic separators

Round shape connects parts

Effects of shapes.

• The *shape* of a setting affects primarily visual and perceptual relationships. If people want to, they can use the cues that shapes provide to consider areas within one space as separate places. Corners in a square area, for example, can be more easily seen as separate from one another than parts of a round place can. In a study of children playing in different rooms, groups of children quickly claimed as distinct territories the places in the leaves of clover-shaped rooms (Hutt, 1969).

• *Orientation* of one place to another influences the behavioral relationship between people in them. Two places oriented so that people using them have a higher chance of casually seeing or meeting one another may be considered "functionally" closer than two equidistant places oriented to minimize chance encounters (Festinger et al., 1950).

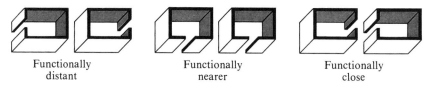

Functionally distant

Functionally nearer

Functionally close

Effects of functional distance.

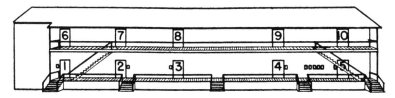

Schematic diagram of a building in Festinger's dormitory study. (Reprinted from *Social Pressures in Informal Groups*, by Leon Festinger, Stanley Schachter, and Kurt Back, with the permission of the publishers, Stanford University Press. Copyright 1950, renewed 1978 by the Board of Trustees of the Leland Stanford Junior University.)

Festinger et al. found that this concept helped explain why certain pairs of neighbors regularly liked each other better than other pairs, although the two sets of apartments studied were the same distance apart. Apartments 1 and 6 and apartments 2 and 7 (see diagram facing page) are exactly 53 feet apart. The location of the left-hand stairway forces residents of apartment 6 to pass apartment 1 whenever they come or go. But people living in apartments 2 and 7 can leave home and return without ever running into one another. As the hypothesis of Festinger et al. leads us to expect, residents in the functionally closer pair, 1 and 6, selected one another more often as friends than did residents in apartments 2 and 7.

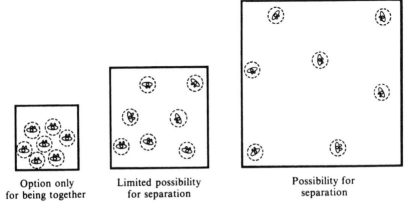

| Option only for being together | Limited possibility for separation | Possibility for separation |

Degrees of setting size.

Possible distance between people is a major determinant of potential behavior relationships. The *size* of a setting offers opportunities for people to put distance between themselves or limits their options. A 4-meter-square conference room does not offer any of seven participants at a meeting the option to separate from the rest of the group. In the main hall of Washington D.C.'s Union Station, the same people could easily be dispersed.

Loudness, light intensity, and air flow are *environmental conditions* that directly affect possibilities for behavior relationships by limiting and augmenting people's ability to hear, see, and smell other people and activities. For example, light turned low in a restaurant effectively separates people at different tables as if there were a physical screen between them. A single worker in an open-plan office listening to a radio at high volume acoustically invades the space of other workers and separates himself from them aurally. Machines that emit high-pitched sound and mask background noise without participants' awareness protect acoustical privacy as a closed door might. An exhaust hood and fan over a kitchen stove keep kitchen smells out of adjacent rooms—olfactorily separating people cooking in the kitchen from others.

OBSERVING BEHAVIOR UPDATE

Given the fact that observing behavior is such a basic E-B research method, it is not surprising that many researchers and designers have refined and expanded the method. Among these changes are the use of behavioral observation as a fine-scale precise method (Moser and Corroyer, 2001; Passini et al., 1999), recording behaviors in situ with tape recorded commentaries (Naser and Jones, 1997; Passini et al., 1999), handheld pre-coded PDAs (Olsen et al., 2000), or computers (Devlin and Bernstein, 1997), and applying behavior observation in commercial settings (Underhill, 2000).

• *Fine-scale observation.* Moser and Corroyer's analysis of door opening behavior as an indicator of politeness in Paris and Nantes provides an excellent example of a fine-tuned behavioral observation method. These French researchers precisely define the behavior they are studying and then carefully use observation data gathering techniques in three parallel real-world settings—two sets of doors in Paris, one at the BHV department store near the Place de Beaubourg a second at a Galleries Lafayette department store in Montparnasse, and a third at a Galleries Lafayette in the provincial city of Nantes. After recording descriptive demographics of each subject, the researchers observed whether the previous person within a precise time span held open the door for the next person (the situational context), and then whether or not the actual subject held open the door for the next person entering the store. When the initial politeness led to a second similar polite act, they considered politeness to be contagious, like a virus.

Moser and Corroyer's precise observation protocol began with the observer standing in front of the entrance to the store and selecting distance and ideal angle to ensure that nothing would be missed in observing the target behavior. Each time a participant corresponding to a pre-set operational definition approached the door, his or her behavior with respect to the person following was noted if at least one other person was four to six steps behind.

The research team recorded 880 observations in this careful and precise way, 480 in Paris—an urban setting—and 400 in provincial Nantes. In Paris they found that if the person before you holds the door open for you—is polite—you tend more often to do the same thing for the person following you whether that person is a man or a woman. Politeness may be contagious in the city. On the other hand, in the provincial town, people are more polite in general—holding the door open whether or not the person preceding them did so. Not surprisingly, when the density of shoppers rises, everyone is less polite and the contagious nature of civility breaks down in both Paris and Nantes.

On-the-spot tape recording during behavioral observation was employed by both Naser and Jones in their study of landscapes of fear and stress on the Ohio State University campus (1997) and Passini in his study of people living with Alzheimer's finding their way in a Montreal Hospital (1999). Both studies focus on subjects' reactions to moving through a planned sequence of spaces—a campus walk in one case and a series of hospital wayfinding tasks in the other.

The recordings made by an accompanying observer recorded subjects' momentary feelings and thoughts.

Because the validity of an entire research effort is only as strong as the study's weakest link, care and precision in defining and implementing every research step is as important as which specific method is employed. After recruiting female students by letter for a study about fear of crime, Naser and Jones (1997) asked volunteers to take a fifteen-minute walk along a potentially frightening path between 8:15 and 10:00 P.M. Each volunteer was given a handheld tape recorder to "record what it is about the landscape and surrounding environment that makes you feel safe and unsafe, and indicate any emotional reactions and feelings generated as a result of particular elements or as a result of the situation in general." On the basis of content analysis of the 591 comments transcribed onto a written log, the following categories emerged to code settings that feel unsafe: blocked prospect, concealment, entrapment, and generally fearsome settings. The inverse—extensive view, exposure, access, and other safety settings—were classifications for places that felt safe. Each female volunteer was assured in advance that a researcher and a member of the campus security police would follow at a distance during the walk to ensure that she was "never out of sight."

> The most frequently mentioned features associated with fear included darkness (35%), trees and bushes (18.7%), parked cars (11.2%), building enclosure (8.4%), strangers (7.9%), and being alone (6.1%). The most frequently mentioned features associated with safety included lights (40.6%), large numbers of other people (32.7%), seeing across an open area (14.7%), and trees and shrubs not obstructing the view (5.9%). All relate to reducing concealment (improving surveillance) and entrapment (p. 316).

It is important that the authors do not use these data to suggest that all fear of the night be "designed out." In a creative turnabout they urge respect for both deflected vistas and mystery in park design—essential elements for appreciating the outdoors in daytime. "Although eliminating all such features may create places feeling safer after dark," the authors write, "it may deaden places during the day" (p. 319). They do suggest, however, "designing out concealment" by providing diffuse and uniform lighting behind shrubs on a curved path, lighting on the path itself, and developing daytime activity-generators to bring people into the park to reduce fear and increase safety.

Passini et al. (1999) employed a similar recording methodology in their study of "residual wayfinding abilities" of people living through the early and middle stages of Alzheimer's disease, aimed at developing a hospital and wayfinding design that diminishes "the extraneous weight on cognitive functioning while still providing an acceptable level of stimulation" (p. 175). The team pre-coded wayfinding decisions into *lower order* ones that lead directly to a behavioral action such as passing through a door opening, and *higher order* decisions that require further choices in order to be executed, such as locating a specific wing within a hospital. The accompanying researcher in this study served a different purpose than in the park safety study:

> [Subjects, after being given a card with the name of the destination in the hospi-
> tal,] were asked to express verbally and aloud everything that went through their
> mind while reaching the destination. In order to assure full verbalization, an
> observer accompanied the subject. If the verbalization was not forthcoming, the
> observer inquired what the subject was doing (to identify decisions) and why the
> subject was taking a given action (to identify the underlying information). The
> conversation was taped and then transcribed (wayfinding protocol) (p. 180).

The observer's intervention was included in the wayfinding performance
classification scheme. Subjects who found their way with no backtracking or
observer intervention were classified as high performers, those that made errors
but then corrected themselves were classified as moderate performers, and subjects who needed one or more observer interventions to complete the task were
classified as low performers. The observer's intervention or non-intervention
became part of the experimental condition.

The finding that most subjects, even those with advanced dementia,
respond correctly to *lower order* environmental decisions supports Donald
Norman's concept of "naturally mapped" environments—designs in which all the
information you need to use the environment is embedded in the environment
itself (1990). Another finding, that people living with dementia have particular
difficulty distinguishing between relevant and irrelevant information on the same
sign, highlights that "extra" information on a directional sign (e.g. the luncheon
specials written on the direction sign to the cafeteria) can thoroughly devalue the
directional information of the sign for this group (p. 192). A resulting study recommendation: "Clean up cluttering information on circulation routes" if you
want to help people with dementia use signs to find their way (p. 196).

PDAs are also emerging as useful behavior-observation recorders. Olsen,
Hutchings, and Ehrenkrantz (2000) developed a "Media Memory Lane"
machine to provide residents in Alzheimer's long-term care units access to music
(Musical Memory Lane) and clips from old movies and television shows (Video
Memory Lane). They placed Memory Lane consoles in the hallway of a social
day center for seniors, 75 percent of whom had some form of dementia. The
researchers then observed clients as they participated in various planned activities—physical games, bingo, arts and crafts, live musical entertainment—and
later when they could choose their own activity among those that included
using the Memory Lane console.

To record their observations during either forty-five- or ninety-minute
continuous observation periods:

> Data were collected on handheld computers and tabulated with a custom designed
> software program that converted the continuous observational data into discreet,
> one-minute observation segments. Each segment contained an engagement score
> and the frequencies of specific behaviors observed during that minute. . . . The
> computers beeped softly every 15 seconds to remind observers to record any con-
> tinuous or ongoing behavior (p. 165).

Data from the handheld PDA computers were downloaded during the
study onto larger computers for analysis focused on choices clients made and

specific behaviors such as smiling, laughing, talking, fidgeting, and complaining. One test was carried out during "free time" when clients themselves chose what they wanted to do—use the Memory Lane console, engage in physical activity, work on puzzles, or read magazines. Clients chose the Memory Lane significantly more frequently and engaged with the music and videos significantly longer than the other activities. An unintended finding the observational data reveal is that activities in general dampen negative behaviors, such as agitation, wandering, complaining and exhibiting negative affect, underscoring the importance of keeping people with dementia as engaged and active as possible (p. 174).

In Devlin and Bernstein's study for design of computer-based maps to help people find their way in new environments (1997), the team installed a Map Kiosk with a continuously running "attract loop" inviting passersby to test their wayfinding skills. Passersby thought they were testing themselves, but were actually testing different map formats. The study aimed to determine differential impacts of color vs. black and white maps, maps that had more or less detail, and maps in which labels were either placed on the side of the map or in the map itself near the object being labeled. The computer program contained instructions related to the maps shown and a timer to determine whether participants actually found their way on a map, and how fast.

Map labeling made a large difference in wayfinding performance, while neither color nor detail in the map had any effect. With labels located off the map and keyed by number to landmarks, the average length of time to find the way to a particular building on the computer was 50 percent longer than when the labels were immediately adjacent to the landmarks on the map itself. Called an "intact map," this latter type of labeling means fewer cognitive steps must be taken when using the map. Devlin and Bernstein link their findings to Schwartz and Kulhavy (1981) and Kulhavy et al.'s (1989) "conjoint retention hypothesis," an extension of Paivio's neuroscience dual coding theory (1986) that holds:

> Spatial/perceptual information and linguistic/verbal information are coded separately but that the codes lead to connected representations that can be used simultaneously when retrieval cues are provided for each (p. 101).

These studies demonstrate not only two innovative ways to capture behavioral observation data, but also how such data can build on others' theories and inform practical applications.

Underhill describes a commercial application of behavior observation to help stores, banks, restaurants and other retail environments better serve their clients (2000). Underhill finds that paper-and-pencil "track sheets" work best to record observations in these settings because the sheets combine observation, recording, counting, and analysis in a single tool. Underhill starts each observational sequence:

> with a detailed map depicting the premises we're about to study, whether it's a store, a bank branch, a parking lot (for a drive-thru project) or just a single section or even just one aisle of a store. The map shows every doorway and aisle, every display, every shelf and rack and table and counter (p. 15).

"Trackers" who follow selected shoppers from the moment they enter an establishment until they leave, have identified nearly 900 different dimensions of "shopper-store interaction," among them the "butt-brush effect" and the "dog treat" misplacement problem. At the large New York department store Bloomingdale's, video recordings revealed many shoppers looking at neckties hanging on a rack at the side of the main aisle leading into and out of the store—a favorite location among display designers for such impulse purchases. Standing in a busy aisle, shoppers looking at ties were often bumped by passers-by, and after a few such jostlings, both genders, but more women than men, abandoned their necktie shopping at this particular location. When store designers moved the tie rack away from the aisle, sales increased substantially.

The research team also studied placement and purchase of dog treats, such as liver-flavored biscuits, with surprising results in a study for a dog food manufacturer. Older shoppers who spoil their pets—as they probably also spoil their grandchildren—and young children who beg their parents for such pet treats buy treats more often than adults who buy regular dog food. Dog treats are not a supermarket staple and are therefore often stocked on the top shelf of the pet food aisle—out of the reach of their most frequent purchasers, elders and children. Placing the dog treats within reach led quickly to increased sales. While this applied finding may be trivial, and the observation obvious after the fact, the structure of the method is critical, as is the fact that decisions were based on repeated systematic observation, not off-the-cuff suggestions.

Underhill initially hired "graduate environmental psychology students" as behavior trackers but found they often observed through the lens of theories that obscured the simple behaviors they were meant to observe and record. Most effective were artists, actors, writers, and even a puppeteer, who could be totally empirical—recording what they saw without the burden of theory.

In sum, the observation of external behavior has evolved into a subtle, sophisticated, and complex environment-behavior method. Observing and measuring internal behavioral states is the topic of the next section.

The research and design case study that follows was carried out for the United States Postal Service. The multi-method iterative research and design project draws heavily on behavioral observation employing a PDA as well as photos and video recording, and integrates these data with individual and group focused interviews.

DESIGN CASE STUDY

POST-OCCUPANCY EVALUATION OF INNOVATIVE RETAIL SPACE DESIGN FOR THE UNITED STATES POSTAL SERVICE
Albuquerque, New Mexico

With about 35,000 post offices in the United States and a $1 billion annual building and renovation budget, the United States Postal Service (USPS) is one of the largest organizations in the world with a long-term commitment to

Exterior signage promotes Post Office visibility.

design research. Since 1985, the environment-behavior team of architect Jay Farbstein and psychologist Min Kantrowitz has conducted a series of design research projects for the USPS. The research results applied and leveraged over this large a building program have had significant impacts on successive generations of design and management (Farbstein and Kantrowitz, 1992).

Small-scale design research studies the team carried out include assessing prototype automated postal teller machines and testing durability of alternative counter top materials. Large-scale studies have evaluated mail-processing plants of up to a million square feet and assessed the USPS design image nationally. At a mid-scale, the E-B consultants examined system-wide design issues such as image policy and maintenance procedures, very small post offices, standard plan post office design, a so-called "kit of parts" computer-based modular design system, vehicle maintenance facilities, bulk/business mail centers, and several generations of "retail" post office designs.

As the USPS has become increasingly customer service oriented, retail space design in post offices has changed significantly. This case study describes research carried out to test new retail design concepts.

Introduction

In 1995 and 1996, the USPS renovated customer lobbies in seventeen Albuquerque-area post offices to develop and test new design concepts supporting a retail and customer-oriented approach to providing postal products and services. To learn from the test and improve the design and operation of future post offices, the USPS commissioned a comparative post-occupancy evaluation (POE) of ten renovated post offices. While the individual post offices selected had many similarities, they presented systematic variations on design approaches to addressing customer service issues. These included: how queuing is handled, the presence of a "take-a-number" system, whether customers are offered the opportunity to select their own merchandise—including stamps—from open displays, several types of self-service arrangements, new site and interior signage, and alternative color schemes. Two of the post offices represented a new prototype "Post Office Express"—a smaller post office retail space located in supermarkets.

The study's goals were to learn how customers and employees used the new design features; to determine which features worked well and which did not; and to suggest design modifications for future facilities and improvements in the evaluated facilities.

To decide which data were needed, the team conducted telephone interviews, analyzed plans, and examined post office policies. Each data gathering team of architects and researchers spent approximately 60 person hours per post office employing a wide range of data gathering techniques to collect the following data:

- Approximately 30 customer interviews (for a total of nearly 300 at the ten post offices)
- Focus group interviews with about 10 customers recruited by an independent market research firm (for a total of about 100 individuals at the ten post offices)
- Structured interviews with facility managers and postal clerks
- "Tracking" five to seven hours of customer activities and behaviors using a PDA with a customized program (for a total of over 60 hours of tracking, with over 600 customers tracked at the ten post offices)
- "Snapshot observations" recording the number and location of customers and staff on a plan of the post office at 10-minute intervals
- Inspecting and documenting the physical conditions in the facilities (such as materials, equipment, lighting, and temperature)
- Photographic documentation of the alternative designs in-use
- Video-recording customer activities and behaviors (to illustrate findings)

Customer interview and tracking study data were analyzed quantitatively. Other data, such as clerk interviews and focus groups, were systematically reviewed using qualitative data analysis techniques. Overall, this excellent data set—both sample sizes and variety of sources—allowed the research team to draw sound conclusions about each post office as well as make comparisons among them.

Data were analyzed and reported separately for issues such as image, circulation, and wayfinding that are general to post office facilities and for issues such as site, self-service area, full service area, and post office box area that are specific to Full Service Lobby Design.

POE General Design Findings

Customers were generally positive about the changes at all ten post offices, reporting that the changes in layout, color, and other design features made visiting the post office more agreeable experience. One said "I think it's nice because they obviously care about us, that we have a pleasant place." Many customers reported that their overall image of the USPS was more positive because of facility and service improvements.

Most important for customers in facility identification is exterior signage. While many customers liked the exterior signage, they complained that signs identifying the post office often were not clearly visible from main vehicular and pedestrian approaches. However, once in the post office parking area the main entrance of most facilities is highly visible.

Interior signage, the research found, was generally well coordinated and well executed, but not always well placed or appropriately sized. Customers as a whole reported that the signs and notices effectively conveyed information, but some described the interior image as "cluttered" with too many signs and "confusing." Raspberry, gray, and white, and white, blue, and red color schemes were tested at the ten post offices. Most customers liked both, generally preferring the scheme at the post office they frequented. Customers were enthusiastic about post offices located inside a supermarket or other large store.

Retail Service Lobby POE Findings

Almost all the lobbies gave customers the opportunity to select merchandise, including prepackaged stamps from an open display—and often to pay for such merchandise at a centrally located cashier, rather than at a full service clerk counter where they might stand behind another customer for some time. Most customers embraced this concept enthusiastically. However, in lobbies with

Research-based retail service lobby.

Naturally mapped queuing system.

open displays that were difficult to see or get to, researchers recorded fewer customers making use of them. Merchandise displays that are easily seen on the customer's way into the facility are most likely to be noticed and used, much like any retail store.

The tracking study determined actual waiting times, enabling the team to compare these times to customer perceptions. Overall, customers were very satisfied with waiting times, being more satisfied at post offices with the shortest actual waiting times—a mean of forty seconds versus about two minutes at the rest. Customers in post offices where take-a-number systems were added—where customers are served according to a paper number they receive from a dispenser—tended to believe that the wait had become shorter even though tracking data revealed that average wait times were significantly longer than at facilities without them.

The take-a-number system was intended to make shopping easier for customers in store-like post offices where browsing and self-service are encouraged. With customers' numbers being called out when it was their turn, the system was intended to liberate customers from having to stand in a queue. However, some customers took a number and then stood in a queue, reluctant to leave it to shop, lest they lose their place. A strong link was found between the layout of furnishings and the success of the take-a-number system. In particular, the presence of visual queuing devices such as cordons or a "parcel slide" are confusing for many customers who, seeing them, assume they are supposed to form a line. Facilities without such devices did not experience this problem. The four diagrammatic plans show queuing patterns in post offices with a variety of queuing devices.

In these visually complex environments, when the take-a-number system dispenser was not readily visible, a great deal of confusion ensued. Many customers joined the queue only to find they lacked a number, occasionally leading to conflict among customers about who had been waiting longer.

Recommendations and Results

The study yielded recommendations for keeping, improving, and eliminating various lobby design and operational features.

- Carefully size and place exterior signage for maximum visibility by passing traffic
- Study color schemes further because results comparing the two present color schemes were mixed and decisions relating to color can have major implications for the overall USPS corporate image
- Make more evident and visible on signage critical information such as hours of operation
- Coordinate interior graphics and signage to emphasize critical information and to avoid distracting customers with unnecessary or low-priority messages
- Fully implement the take-a-number system within a coordinated design program to successfully free customers from the queue
- Create clear graphics for the take-a-number dispenser indicating that numbers are to be taken only for clerk service and that there is no need to wait in line and make these graphics prominent and bold and locate them where customers cannot miss them upon entering the service lobby
- Redesign or remove queuing devices such as parcel slides to avoid giving customers a "cue to queue"
- Make open merchandise displays highly visible and accessible

Service counter.

These key recommendations from the multi-site POE were combined in a single Full Service Lobby test site that was evaluated prior to being "rolled out" nationwide. Features include:

- Newly designed graphics, information, and casework for the take-a-number dispenser and system.
- Elimination of the parcel slide, with the addition of sufficient surfaces for writing and resting packages.
- Redesigned cashier station with adequate workspace, a location that reinforces visibility, and sufficient queuing space in front of it.
- Improved relationship between layout, circulation, and function by locating primary merchandise display sections (especially stamps) where they are easily seen and accessed by customers and ensuring clear view and circulation throughout the area so customers can see and reach all key elements.

This case study is based on the work of research architect Jay Farbstein, Ph.D., FAIA, of Jay Farbstein Associates, Inc., Los Angeles and San Luis Obispo, CA. and Min Kantrowitz, psychologist, architect, and planning and design consultant, School of Architecture and Planning at the University of New Mexico.

OVERVIEW

To design environments suited to what people do in them, we must understand environmental behavior: *Who* does *what* with *whom*? In what *relationship*, sociocultural *context*, and physical *setting*? This chapter proposes that by looking at how environments affect people's ability to see, hear, touch, smell, and perceive each other, we can begin to understand how environments impinge on social behavior.

Environmental elements that affect relationships include barriers such as walls, screens, objects, and symbols; and fields, such as shape, orientation, size, and environmental conditions. Design decisions about these elements have identifiable side effects for social behavior.

Environmental-behavior descriptions that can enable designers to improve control over behavioral side effects of their decisions include six elements: actor, act, significant others, relationships, context, and setting.

The next three chapters discuss how to find out about people's feelings, attitudes, perceptions, and knowledge—namely, by asking questions.

CHAPTER 10

FOCUSED INTERVIEWS

Asking questions in interviews and questionnaires means posing questions systematically to find out what people think, feel, do, know, believe, and expect. When we think of a focused interview we generally have in mind the type of group questioning used in market research and when we think of a questionnaire, we think of the yes/no or multiple-choice questions of most public opinion polls. The term "interview," meaning any form of face-to-face questioning is so broad it can lose its meaning in a sentence describing a research project, such as "We interviewed the building manager." In almost all cases of E-B research, interviewers ask questions to learn how an individual feels about, perceives, or otherwise reacts to a particular environment or situation. For this purpose, the mix of structure and open-endedness that the focused interview technique provides is helpful. The popular form of group interview discussed at the end of this chapter is a variation of this basic method. In most cases, when E-B researchers say they are carrying out interviews, they are actually using a form of focused interview.

You can use focused interviews with individuals to find out in depth how people define a concrete situation, what they consider important about it, what effects they intended their actions to have in the situation, and how they feel about it. Originally formulated to tap reactions to films of military instruction and propaganda, radio broadcasts, and other mass communication devices, focused interviews are particularly suited to the needs of environment-behavior researchers interested in reactions to particular environments. Many of the concepts this chapter explains and the way it explains them are based on Merton, Fiske, and Kendall's insightful and inventive book *The Focused Interview* (1956).

PRE-INTERVIEW ANALYSIS AND INTERVIEW GUIDE

To understand thoroughly how someone reacts to a situation, an interviewer cannot just start asking haphazard questions. She must first analyze the structure of that situation, always using observational research methods and sometimes theory in doing this. This analysis can then be used as the framework for discussing the situation in detail with the respondent. Such a situational analysis guides the discussion; the interviewee's responses are used to test, refine, and modify the analysis. A skilled focused interviewer negotiates with a respondent to find correspondence between his own analytic structure and the respondent's mental picture of the situation. By structuring the information themselves, focused-interview respondents become participants in the research.

The *interview guide* is a loose conceptual map, such as a family might draw up before taking a cross-country camping trip. It lays out major sights to see, places to stay, and so on. After the trip begins, the family members find some of the sights closed, others uninteresting, and others so arresting that they stay longer than expected. They also find that they do not drive as many miles as planned each day and that the children like to stop to eat more often than originally planned. Every day they adjust their plans, and end up having a fine trip that mixes the plans they made on the basis of advance analysis with reactions to events as encountered. Skilled focused interviewers similarly modify their original plans to correspond to the conceptual map reflected in the respondent's answers. That conceptual map is the respondent's definition of the situation for which the interviewer is searching.

In the focused-interview guide, the map is a set of topics, elements, patterns, and relationships that the interviewer tentatively intends to cover. Adjustments to the guide during the interview are carried out by skillful use of the major focused-interview tool, the *probe*: the interviewer's prompting for further elaboration of an answer. An interviewer probes to find out how a respondent's definition of the situation differs from the hypothesized one; this information allows the interviewer to adjust and refine the guide. The researcher's goal is to determine which of the many hypothesized elements are important to the respondent and then to understand as thoroughly as possible what these elements mean in the respondent's definition of the situation.

To avoid misunderstandings, one should know that for surveys in which questions are posed with prescribed rigidity, a "good interviewer" is one who adheres to the text and never develops his own initiative. In a focused interview, the opposite is true.

OBJECTIVES OF FOCUSED INTERVIEWS

Definition of the Situation

An individual's *definition of a situation* is the way she sees and interprets it— the personal light in which a particular event is cast. This definition influences the way she responds to that event.

For example, during focused interviews custodians, school administrators, and neighboring residents reported that children ruined public lawns by playing ball on them and broke public street furniture by jumping on it (Zeisel, 1976a). Teenagers involved in these activities described them differently. They played ball in open fields to avoid the danger of traffic and the bother of people walking by. They hung around benches and play equipment in tot lots because the equipment was convenient for sitting, climbing, and jumping. In the beginning of this school property-damage study, the research team heard repeated reports from administrators of costly "vandalism" at the schools. The investigators assumed, along with the respondents, that the property damage was indeed "vandalism"—maliciously carried out—until, of course, they got the teenagers' definition of the situation.

Knowing how participants define a situation helps to interpret data gathered through other methods, no matter how unreasonable the respondent's definition sounds. To keep an open mind and see situations as others see them, one must be prepared to find as many definitions as there are participants.

Strength of Respondents' Feelings

Throughout any design project, decisions about priorities are made. In housing, is it more important to plan direct access to cars from apartments or to keep cars parked far from the front door? Is it more important for patients in a cancer-treatment center to wait with relatives, or is modesty more important for them, which is maintained by waiting alone? Designers making such tradeoffs can better control the side effects of their decisions if they know the strength of respondents' feelings about convenient access, a view free of automobiles, relatives' support, and modesty.

Intentions

Observing behavior and physical traces tells investigators about the unintended consequences of activities. In Boston's West End "urban village," men spent a lot of time on the street washing and polishing their cars. Observations showed that the men polished their cars next to one another and talked to passersby as well, creating a close-knit network of neighborhood friends. This social contact is another consequence of car washing in this neighborhood. Both consequences could be observed in the situation, but only by asking the actors what their intentions are can researchers distinguish conscious intent from unintentional side effects. Did the men, in fact, wash their cars to keep them clean or expressly to maintain social contacts?

BASIC CHARACTERISTICS OF FOCUSED INTERVIEWING

Focused interviewing has the following characteristics:

1. Persons interviewed are known to have been involved in a particular concrete situation: they have worked in the same office building, lived in the

same neighborhood, or taken part in an uncontrolled but observed social situation, such as a tenants' meeting, a street demonstration, or a design review session.

2. An E-B researcher has carried out a situational analysis to identify provisionally any hypothetically significant elements, patterns, and processes of the situation. The researcher has arrived at a set of hypotheses about what aspects of the situation are important for those involved in it, what meaning these aspects have, and what effects they have on participants.

3. On the basis of this analysis, the investigator develops an interview guide, setting forth major areas of inquiry and hypotheses.

4. The interview about subjective experiences of persons exposed to the already-analyzed situation is an effort to ascertain their definitions of the situation.

5. The basic interview tool is the probe.

PROBES

Probes are primarily questions that interviewers interpose to get a respondent to clarify a point, to explain further what she meant, to continue talking, or to shift the topic. The probe is the systematic development of an everyday device used in conversation when one person is actually interested in what another has to say.

- *Addition probes* encourage respondents to keep talking—to keep the flow of the interview moving.
- *Reflecting probes* determine in a non-directed way which of the analyzed topics in the interview guide are significant to the respondent and which new ones should be added because they were overlooked.
- *Transitional probes* ensure that the respondent discusses a broad range of salient topics.
- *Situational probes* stimulate the respondent to specify which parts of a situation prompted the responses.
- *Emotion probes* encourage in depth discussion of how the respondent feels about each specified part of the situation.
- *Personal probes* get respondents to describe how the context of their lives influenced their reactions.

This chapter will discuss each type of probe, showing with examples how each can be used to enrich an interview.

Addition Probes to Promote Flow

Addition probes urge respondents to continue talking by conveying the researcher's interest in what is being said. Skillful interviewers use addition probes to get respondents to express themselves more fully and to keep the overall flow of the interview moving. They are so simple and natural that interviewers sometimes use them inadvertently.

Addition probes may be *encouragements* such as "Uh-huh," "I see," "Yes," "Good," "That's interesting," or "I understand," interjected during and after answers. Encouragements can be combined with *body movement* probes, such as nodding your head, leaning forward, looking directly at the respondent, and putting your hand to your chin thoughtfully. Skillful interviewers invent a number of such probes. If it seems inappropriate to make utterances, interviewers can combine attentive body movements with one of the most difficult types of probes—*attentive silences*. This probe, during which an interviewer patiently waits for the respondent to begin or to continue speaking, requires much tact

Focused-Interview Probes and Their Purposes	
Probe	*Purpose*
Addition	*Flow*
Encouragement	
Body movement	
Attentive silence	
Reflecting	*Nondirection*
Echo	
Question-to-question	
Attentive listening	
Transition	*Range*
Cued	
Reversion	
Mutation	
Situation	*Specificity*
Re-presentation	
Environmental walk-through	
Reconstruction	
Emotion	*Depth*
Feeling	
Projection	
Attentive listening	
Personal	*Context*
Self-description	
Parallel	

and skill because the lack of conversation between two persons alone in a room is uncomfortable. This silence is socially unacceptable in many Western cultures, and as a result, inexperienced interviewers often fill up a silence by asking another question or by changing the topic.

They may be unwittingly stopping the respondent from finishing a difficult answer that he would just as soon avoid because it may be a particularly weighty topic for him and is likely significant for the interviewer.

Reflecting Probes to Achieve Non-direction

Non-direction pervades the focused interview. Respondents, rather than interviewers, decide what issues and elements are salient to them and will be discussed and which are irrelevant. Interviews that include non-direction are often mistakenly lumped into the term *qualitative interview* because researchers using this method seldom count answers. This technique often deludes inexperienced interviewers into believing they can carry out interviews with little or no preparation. The ideal focus interview would be one in which the interviewer analyzes a situation—its parts, patterns, relationships, and overall structure—and then asks one general, unstructured question. The ideal respondent then launches into a monologue in which he describes his feelings about each topic, pointing out in detail which are and are not relevant to him and adding new topics that the interviewer has overlooked.

Ideal interviews do not occur. Respondents mention important issues but seldom raise and then discard unimportant ones. The interviewer must bring up various topics in order to find out whether a particular topic was not raised because the respondent thought it was obvious or because he thought it irrelevant. Few respondents are specific enough about issues or explain their responses in sufficient depth. The interviewer's job is to test and modify the interview guide by inferring from the discussion how well the respondent's definition of the situation meets the guide's hypothetical one. To do this, the interviewer uses probes to ensure that the discussion covers all the hypothesized topics, leaving room for the respondent to raise additional ones. The interviewer also makes sure that each topic is discussed in enough detail and depth.

The focused interviewer's success is closely linked to her skill in using addition and reflecting probes to encourage complete reporting from respondents without telling them directly what to talk about. Beginning the interview with general, unstructured questions, the interviewer urges the respondent to express which topics are important and which are unimportant, and what types of answers are relevant for the different questions. As the interview continues and topics are discussed at length, the interviewer divides and focuses general questions into more specific ones, sometimes even suggesting the types of possible answers. These more structured questions are based on the sometimes-implicit leads that respondents provide when they answer general, unstructured questions.

Example	Comment
Int: What is your general feeling about this hospital?	General unstructured question
Resp: I really like it.	Respondent expresses a general feeling
Int: What do you particularly like about it?	Focus on aspect of environment that generated expressed feeling
Resp: Well, I don't know.	Stalling tactic to think
Int: (Nods head and listens silently)	Body movement and silence probes
Resp: I suppose the thing I like best is the waiting areas; a real person has taken the time to put personal things on the walls and tables.	Focused answer explaining with greater specificity what it is about hospital environment respondent likes
Int: What do you mean when you say you like that best?	Question probing depth of feeling
Resp: I mean it makes me feel comfortable, like I don't mind being here.	Focused answer beginning to explain feeling more completely
Int: Is there anything else here that makes you feel that way?	Question structuring response category but keeping stimulus unstructured

While the interviewer probes and focuses, the respondent sets the stage, directing the conversation into areas she feels are important. This procedure enables interviewers to find out two things at the same time: which topics respondents think are relevant and how they feel about these topics.

To avoid directing the focused interview, a useful position for an interviewer to take is that of a *potential convert* to the respondent's point of view. The crucial word here is *potential*, because interviewers who voice strong agreement or disagreement may inhibit further explanation of a topic. Respondents may not go on if they feel they have convinced the interviewer or feel they have come up against a brick wall. The trick is to use probes to show the respondent that by continuing her report, she may indeed make a convert of the mildly skeptical interviewer.

Direction can also be avoided by reflecting the respondent's own words back at them. One reflecting probe is the *echo probe* (Richardson, Dohrenwend, and Klein, 1965), in which the interviewer literally repeats the respondent's last phrase in the form of a question:

Example	Comment
Resp: The thing I like best about this place is its location.	General response
Int: Its location?	Echo probe
Resp: Yes, you know, the fact that it is right near two bus stops and a store.	Focused response specifying stimulus

An equally simple reflective probe is the *question-to-question probe*. The interviewer employs this probe by answering a respondent's question with a question, to avoid stating an opinion:

Example	*Comment*
Resp: What did the architect think when she put these windows next to the playing field?	Respondent's question to interviewer, apparently for clarification
Int: You mean it is not clear what the architect had in mind when she did this?	Question-to-question probe
Resp: No. She obviously didn't think about the fact that kids on the playing field are always being rough and showing off to other kids by breaking everything in sight that's breakable.	Focused response explaining situation from respondent's point of view

A third reflective probe, the *attentive-listening probe,* demands more interviewer participation. The interviewer listens for the implied meaning of the respondent's remarks, repeating back to the respondent as a question what the interviewer believes is meant:

Example	*Comment*
Int: Is there anything you do regularly on a daily basis in the building?	General question about routines
Resp: I always go down to get my mail late in the morning, at least half an hour after the mail arrives. This way I don't meet anyone and no one knows if I get mail or not.	Descriptive response about personal routine
Int: You mean it bothers you if there are other people there who see that you might not receive any mail for a day or two?	Attentive-listening probe
Resp: Yes, it's none of their business. I like to meet my friends when I want to, but I don't like to be forced to see them when I am doing chores around the building.	Focused response explaining resident's avoidance behavior in terms of forced meetings

Transition Probes to Extend Range

The *range* of an interview is the number of topics it covers that are relevant to the respondent and to the situation or environment that is the interview's focus. Extensive range is often a measure of the quality of an interview. Probes can extend range by making certain that the discussion covers the topics listed in the interview guide, any, unanticipated topics the respondent brings up, and topics that suggest interrelations between the focused interview and data from other research projects. In maintaining sufficient range in an interview, it is difficult to move from one topic to another without giving the respondent the impression that the interviewer is running the show. The major danger is that respondents may become passive and wait for the interviewer to ask a series of structured questions, thereby destroying the purpose of the interview.

In easy interviews respondents demonstrate their involvement with each topic by giving short shrift to irrelevant items and discussing in depth topics that hold meaning for them. When this occurs, a skilled interviewer stays out of the picture, yet listens closely to the order in which topics are covered as an indication of their importance within the respondent's definition of the situation.

When such ideal conditions do not occur, the interviewer uses *transition probes* to facilitate movement from topic to topic with a minimum of overt direction. In focused interviews several situations requiring transition probes arise regularly. For example, respondents may continue to discuss a topic the interviewer feels has been covered with sufficient specificity, depth, and context at detailed levels of abstraction. The interviewer can then use a *cued transition probe*, in which "the interviewer so adapts a remark or an allusion by an interviewee as to ease him into consideration of a new topic" (Merton et al., 1956, p. 58). Cued probes use analogy, association of ideas, or shifts in emphasis to effect smooth transitions.

Example	*Comment*
Resp: (School maintenance worker discussing maintainability in various areas of the school) . . . another thing particularly convenient about cleaning the bathroom is the special water faucets there, although the outlets might be a bit larger to allow water to get out faster.	Final remarks of a sufficiently detailed explanation
Int: Another place with readily available water must be the school swimming pool. How is that as far as maintenance is concerned?	Cued probe using the topic of water to move from a discussion of lavatories to one of play facilities
Resp: In the swimming pool, water is not the main maintenance problem. There it is the type of tile; it is difficult to clean . . .	Response related to new interview topic

When a respondent finds herself discussing a topic with intense personal meaning, her answers become highly charged. She may try to change the subject either because of unpleasant associations or because she does not feel at ease talking about important things with a stranger. Since such topics may be particu¬larly relevant to the study, an interviewer tries to keep respondents on the topic by showing how interested he is using silence and body probes.

If a respondent nevertheless moves on to a new topic, the interviewer is better off dropping the topic and picking it up later in a new context or when rapport with the respondent has improved. A mental or written note to use such a *reversion probe* will help. Reversion probes take advantage of a connection that is at least superficial to bring up a topic insufficiently covered earlier:

Int: That reminds me of something we spoke about earlier.

or

> *Int:* Isn't this a continuation of the
> point you made before?

A reversion probe is particularly useful when a respondent becomes distracted from an interesting topic to focus on one that interests her still more. The interviewer knows there will be no difficulty returning to the first topic but hesitates to do so quickly for fear of interrupting the respondent's train of thought.

Another common situation is one in which the respondent, happy to have an audience, warms up to a topic that has nothing to do with the subject of the interview. A lonely hospital patient who is asked to discuss a hospital setting, for example, may show the interviewer pictures of his grandchildren and discuss them in detail—their ages, education, and exploits. The interviewer should be grateful for such excursions because they strengthen rapport with the respondent. Nevertheless, cued transitions help to bring the conversation on track:

Example	*Comment*
Resp: . . . and my fourth grandchild just started nursery school . . .	Irrelevant discussion
Int: That raises the issue of families visiting patients in the hospital. Where do you entertain your family?	Cued probe
Resp: Usually my family sits in the bedroom with me, but when the grandchildren come we sit in the dayroom.	Response moved back to interview topic: the hospital setting

With garrulous respondents, however, an interviewer may need to resort to *mutation probes* that blatantly change the subject. Mutation probes are generally unstructured questions, and raise questions out of context, with no reference to previous discussions. Interviewers must use mutation probes sparingly. Otherwise they can cut off discussion of relevant topics because they are too tired to listen carefully or because the topic is mistakenly not on their interview guide. Potentially informative leads are easily lost this way. The temptation to use mutation probes unwisely is particularly great at the end of an interview when some topics have not been covered. The interviewer wants to translate his guide topics into specific questions and ask these in rapid succession. As a rule, if an interviewer does not have the time to follow up on a topic, it is inefficient to raise it using mutation probes, in fact, it is better to skip the topic altogether.

Situation Probes to Encourage Specificity

Specificity in the focused interview is a respondent's ability to state with precision which elements in a situation she reacted to and in what way, rather than just saying that the situation as a whole had an effect on her. Specificity is vital if you want to understand respondents' reactions to such complex environments as housing projects. Merton et al. (1956) point out that the importance of specificity was evident in Chapin's early research on public housing: Chapin (1940) studied the gains in social participation that can be attributed "to the effects of living in the [public] housing project." As he recognized, "improved housing" is an unanalyzed "experimental" situation: managerial policies, increased leisure, architectural provision for group meetings, and a host of other items are varying elements of the program of "improved housing" (p. 7).

Chapin used focused interviews to find out what specifically about the housing project influenced people's social participation. Researchers interested in influencing design decisions need to know which decision in a complex set of decisions has had what effects.

Interviewers who want respondents to specify further a particular stimulus situation can ask them to do so directly:

Int: What in particular did you like about the building?

or

Int: What part of the schoolyard do you play in most?

The more an interviewer repeats references to the stimulus situation, especially in a series of progressively detailed questions, the more likely the respondent is to make reference to specific parts of the environment.

Researchers can either initially request that respondents specify aspects of the environment and then discuss their reactions to each aspect or ask respondents to describe a reaction, and follow up by asking for further specification of what is being reacted to. Merton et al. (1956, pp. 71–72) surprisingly found the latter sequence of questions more effective in achieving specificity—namely, first eliciting a description of reactions, then asking respondents to specify just what was being reacted to.

Example	*Comment*
Int: How do you feel about the office you work in?	General question requesting reaction to environment
Resp: I feel that if I don't always stay aware of where I am, I'll get lost.	General response describing reaction to environment
Int: What is it about your office that makes you feel that way?	Probe requesting specification of environmental stimulus
Resp: The windows. I can't see any windows from where I work, so I never know what time it is or which direction I'm facing.	Focused specification of environmental stimulus

When interviewers repeatedly request specification of an environmental stimulus, respondents may revert to mere description of the environment. Interpreting a request for specification as a request for information, they may try to remember as many details about the environment as they can—even irrelevant ones. To avoid this pitfall and to elicit sufficiently specifying responses, interviewers can use probes aimed at helping respondents clearly remember the settings they are asked to specify.

Using *re-presentation probes*, interviewers present respondents with a photograph or drawing of some part of the setting being discussed—a doorway, an area, a piece of hardware. This active probe is least directive when the picture is presented *after* the respondent has verbally identified an element or place as relevant to him.

Example	*Comment*
Int: What in the school causes the most maintenance problems?	Request for general information about problems
Resp: Well, we have the most trouble keeping the thermostats in order.	Mention of an object
Int: (Presenting photograph of thermostat to respondent) Here is a photograph of the type of thermostat you use throughout the building. What is there about it that gives you the most trouble?	Re-presentation probe, combining photograph of object with request for specification
Resp: If you look closely, you can see how flimsy the adjustment switch is. When kids fool with the switch or even when faculty members try to adjust the temperature, the switch often breaks off. This means we have to replace the whole unit at cost . . .	Focused response specifying aspect of object that causes reaction

Graphic re-presentations can be used together with cued transition probes or with mutation probes if interviewers want to discover respondents' reactions to a broad range of environments. Re-presentations then take on the added directive nature of these other probes.

A special case of re-presentation, the *environmental walk-through probe*, can be used if the focused interview takes place in the environment that is the topic of the interview. During a walk-through the interviewer asks the respondent to point out and describe places and objects that are important to him. For particularly salient items the interviewer and respondent can stop to specify more precisely what about the item is relevant.

A walk-through is not just a guided tour. To get the most out of an environmental walk-through, interviewers first question the respondent in one place, asking him to describe the environment they will walk through, and his general reactions to it. As places and objects are mentioned, the interviewer discusses them up to the point of requesting detailed specification, noting these items for later reference during the walk-through. In this way, the interviewer uses the respondent's personal definition of the situation to define important elements and the walk-through to elicit further specification.

Reconstruction probes may be used when respondents have trouble remembering the setting they are asked about or when they remember it only in

general terms. Reconstruction probes ask respondents to think back to particular events in a place in order to recall their reactions to it *at the time* the event
took place.

> *Int*: When you first entered the hospital
> three weeks ago, which entrance
> did you use?

or

> *Int*: What do you remember about
> the last time you sat at your old desk,
> before moving to this office?

When the respondent refers to a complex set of phenomena that she
remembers only as a whole or when she replies "I don't know" or "I can't
remember" after being asked to specify her answers, reconstruction probes
often help switch her attention to specifics.

Example	*Comment*
Int: How do you feel about the park?	General request for information on feelings
Resp: I think it is a particularly good place to come with my children.	General report of feelings
Int: What makes it a good place for children?	Specifying probe
Resp: I don't know, it's just the way it's planned.	"I don't know" meaning "I can't verbalize it."
Int: Well, do you remember the last time you went to the park with your kids?	Reconstruction probe
Resp: Yes, we played hide-and-seek on the curved pathways, and . . .	Response beginning to reconstruct specific situations

Reconstruction probes help respondents to look retrospectively at the situation they are commenting on—to bring themselves back in time and re-expe-
rience the setting. In general, specifying probes do more than isolate specific
parts of a whole situation for analysis. By linking specific parts to specific
respondent reactions, they set up the interview so that each reaction can be
explored in depth.

Emotion Probes to Increase Depth

Depth in a focused interview is the degree to which the respondent's feelings
about a situation are explored. Reports that a respondent "likes" or "dislikes"
a place, that it is "very satisfying," or that it is a "frightening" place can signify a variety of things. For example, someone can dislike her workplace but
choose to work there because it is better than any other place she has found. Or
a street can be frightening to someone, but the fear can be such a peripheral
concern that it does not hinder his walking there.

Interviewers use *emotion probes* to determine how strongly a person feels about a response he has given. The probes encourage respondents to explore and explain in depth the meaning and richness of general expressions of feelings. Emotion probes keep respondents from merely describing a setting by directing them to explain their feelings about it as well.

Feeling probes continually use the term *feel* or *feeling* in questions or repeatedly ask respondents to explain what they mean by a given, generally expressed feeling.

Example	*Comment*
Resp: I am frightened by the teenagers who walk through the project.	General reaction
Int: What do you mean, "I am frightened"?	Feeling probe
Resp: The teenagers are rough and could hurt us. We are old.	Descriptive response
Int: Are you actually afraid they will harm you?	Feeling probe
Resp: No. In fact, they are actually well-behaved if you talk to them. They just walk across the lawn where there is no path and sometimes throw rocks at the lights.	Specifying response
Int: What do you feel about this?	Feeling probe
Resp: I am very angry that they do not obey the rules, but I am glad that the kids respect our being old and that they stay out of our front yards.	Depth response

A series of feeling probes can bring to the surface strongly felt sentiments that initially appear to be peripheral, and can show seemingly deeply felt sentiments to be no more than offhand remarks. As a rule, no briefly expressed sentiment ought to be taken at face value until it has been probed in depth.

Another probe for depth of emotion is the *projection probe*, in which interviewers ask respondents to project their feelings about a situation onto another, hypothetical person. This is useful when discussing sensitive emotions that the respondent himself might not admit having but would be at ease admitting that "others" or "someone else" might have.

Example	*Comment*
Int: How do you feel about playing at the central basketball court with the older kids?	General request for feeling
Resp: I don't mind. I'll play anywhere. I play there sometimes, and sometimes I play on the smaller court down the block.	Neutral feeling response
Int: Why do you use the smaller court?	Feeling probe
Resp: Because I just don't feel like	Response indicating avoidance

hassling with the older kids.

Int: Does anybody avoid the central courts because they're afraid?

reaction
Projection probe

Resp: Sure, some kids are really afraid of getting picked on by the older kids. Some even avoid walking down the block if they know that someone playing on the central court is after them.

Projective response describing feelings of "some kids" in depth

When respondents seem to avoid answering a feeling question, this is a clue to interviewers that they should try a projection probe—particularly when respondents deny that they personally have a certain feeling. At the same time, interviewers must be careful not to think that every response referring to "a friend" or "someone else" actually describes respondents' unexpressed feelings. The ability to make such distinctions increases with interviewing experience.

A final emotion probe is the *attentive-listening probe*, in which interviewers listen for the meaning implied in the respondent's answer and make this meaning explicit in a follow-up probe:

Example

Comment

Int: How do you feel about the rules that the school principal makes about what you can and cannot do on school grounds?

General request for feelings about a specific subject

Resp: He has a right to make any rules he wants. But they should apply equally to all grades, not just to us seventh- and eighth-graders.

Response obliquely describing reactions and feelings

Int: You mean you feel you are being treated unfairly?

Attentive-listening probe

Resp: Yes, it really makes me angry that they can . . .

In-depth feeling response

Sometimes stating implied feelings in terms of limits to action—or extremes—allows respondents to reject the extreme statement and clarify what they were trying to say.

Example

Comment

Resp: I can't think of any place I'd rather live.

Seemingly extreme statement of feeling

Int: Does that mean you like it here so much you wouldn't move for anything?

Extreme attentive-listening probe

Resp: Not exactly. If my best friend bought a house where it is warmer, I'd consider moving.

Rejection of extreme restatement and clarification of attachment to residence

Interviewers should be careful not to put words in a respondent's mouth by restating implied feelings approximately and using a feeling probe too forcefully: "You did mean this, didn't you?"

Attentive-listening probes, like many others, have side effects as significant as their direct effect. Respondents who see that interviewers are interested and listening tend to relax, be more talkative, and feel greater rapport.

Personal Probes to Tie-In Context

Reactions to environments have, as a rule, a dual chain of causes: the environment and characteristics of the reacting person. One such characteristic is his or her position in the environment as nurse, doctor, patient, or visitor; teacher, student, principal, or parent; tenant, janitor, landlord, or delivery person. More general characteristics, such as age, sex, and family status, can also heavily influence a respondent's reactions. The most important factors, however, may derive from the respondent's biography, history, personal background, experiences, or idiosyncrasies that influence his or her feelings about things. For example, one high-rise urban tenant may have lived most of his life on a farm, while another was brought up in high-rise city buildings. One doctor may be particularly sensitive to problems of cancer patients because she had a parent who suffered from the disease. If a researcher wants to understand a respondent's answers throughout a focused interview and to generalize data to any larger group of people, the researcher must know the personal context within which a respondent is answering questions: position in the system, personal characteristics, background, and personal idiosyncrasies. Biography is a dimension that can provide useful insights, but it requires particular tact from the interviewer.

Self-description probes directly request respondents to describe themselves and why they react to situations the way they do. This achieves results when respondents are self-analytic and conscious of underlying reasons for their actions.

Example	*Comment*
Resp: I hate people talking in the library.	General statement on depth of feeling
Int: Is there anything particular about you that makes you feel so strongly?	Self-description probe
Resp: Yes, my mother was a librarian, and . . .	Context response explaining personal background

When self-descriptive answers result from non-personal probes, they are also significant.

Example	*Comment*
Resp: I am afraid to live in that area.	Response stating general feeling
Int: Why are you afraid?	General probe
Resp: My age means that my legs are not so strong, so I am afraid of falling down when I walk. And in that area the kids play ball and ride bicycles on the sidewalk.	Contextual response explaining reactions in terms of personal characteristics

Parallel probes help respondents talk about themselves in one setting by requesting that they find parallel situations in their own lives. This often has the effect of getting respondents to explicate the parallel by talking about personal contexts.

Example	Comment
Resp: I find this office extremely inefficient and wasteful.	General response
Int: In what way?	General probe
Resp: I don't know, just "inefficient."	Difficulty expressing self
Int: Is there any setting you can think of which is inefficient like this office or which explains what you mean by "inefficient"?	Parallel probe
Resp: A submarine is efficient. When I was a sailor, we learned that . . .	Response explaining personal context

GROUP FOCUSED INTERVIEWS

Focus interviewing is associated in most people's minds with the well-established market research tool called *focus groups*. While many of Merton et al.'s initial experiences with focused interviews took place with groups, not individuals (1956), the principles were established with individuals and the method is most powerful when used with an individual. Carrying out interviews in groups is a good idea if you want to identify the range of definitions of a situation that interviewees hold, find out whether a particular opinion is held at all, and save time. In a study to design social-service offices for a staff of forty, researchers can carry out interviews with four groups of ten respondents much more easily than with forty individuals. Farbstein and Kantrowitz, in the case study of post office design that ended the last chapter were able to interview 100 post-office patrons in the time it took for only ten group sessions. Group interviewing works out best if the size of the group is kept under fifteen people, if the interview is held informally around a table or in a circle in a small enough room that respondents feel they are all part of one event, and if respondents in the group have something in common.

The same probes used in successful focus group interviews are used for individuals because interviewers in a group face many of the same problems as they do with individuals. You have to keep the flow of discussion moving, remind people of specific details you are interested in, and maintain sufficient range. Sometimes the fact that others are present in the room makes an interviewer's job easier—when, for example, an emotional statement by one person incites others to express their feelings more openly.

A group also presents special problems, most stemming from the "leader effect" (Merton et al., 1956, p. 148)—namely, that in most groups of people one or two persons inevitably emerge as louder, more dominant, or more opinionated. Such a person can easily take over an interview, divert it from its focus, and inhibit others from talking. In addition to employing the basic probe techniques described earlier, what else can be done to prevent this without damaging an interviewer's rapport with the group or interrupting the flow of the meeting?

Appeals for Equal Time

When one person takes over an interview, that person and others usually know it. Sometimes people even do so as a subtle challenge to the interviewer. It is your task to appeal to the person's sense of fair play in order to give others a chance to talk:

Int: Good point. Perhaps we should hear some other opinions now.
Int: To get a broad enough picture, it might be good to see what other people think about this as well.

Attention to Body Language

Reticent respondents in a group often remain quiet, leaving the floor to the self-chosen leader. This does not, however, mean that quieter interviewees have nothing to say; they just do not create their own openings in the conversation. So you must to create openings for them when you notice they want to say something. Cues that they have an opinion to express include:

- A respondent sitting forward on his chair, looking at you intensely
- A respondent raising her hand as in a classroom
- Two respondents chatting quietly—probably expressing minority opinions to each other

Asking for a Vote

When discussion has been limited to several respondents, or when more respondents have contributed but it is unclear who holds what opinion, you can ask for a vote on an issue. But you must first show that you have been listening attentively by clearly stating the opinion or alternative opinions the respondents are to vote on:

Int: Charley has stated that the most important thing about an office is that it has a window, and that this is more important than privacy or anything else. Who agrees with this and who disagrees? (This type of question in part challenges respondents to contribute.)

Int: Some of you say that you dislike moving from desk to desk when more people are hired; others seem to be saying they don't mind. Could I see a show of hands: How many of you dislike moving? And how many don't mind it?

Group focused interviewing can be disappointing and exhilarating, and insightful and frustrating because the range of participants you find can lead to infinitely varied interactions between and among interviewers and respondents. As with every research tool, to use group focused interviewing successfully you need to know more than you can read about in books. This is particularly true for the skills necessary to carry out a group focused interview.

FOCUSED INTERVIEW UPDATE

The design and research case studies that conclude each chapter of this book include interviewing—often focused interviewing. Vischer (Chapter 6) carried out focused walk-through interviews with managers to discover attitudes toward office planning; Preiser (Chapter 13) interviewed administrators to understand the needs of visually impaired students; Farbstein and Kantrowitz (Chapter 9) conducted group interviews focused on customers' experience with post-office design; Zeisel (Chapter 5) conducted group focused interviews with news teams in the *Star Tribune* newsroom employing photos by participants and 3-D models as probes. He also used focused interviews with HEB managers (Chapter 4) to find out how a grocery chain works. This method is so pervasive that researchers tend to report their use of focused interviews in an off-hand manner. "We also carried out several interviews," they might write as an aside. Interviewing—and most interviews are closely related to the focused interview—is widespread not because it is a useful extra, but because it is such a basic tool, almost seamlessly integrated with other methods in E-B studies.

Interviewing techniques have been refined and elaborated, rather than fundamentally altered. Interviews are being employed not only to explore a respondent's definition of a situation directly but to do so indirectly using informants who can expose a third party's view of the environment. For example, Michael and colleagues inventively conducted interviews with detectives to understand how auto burglars relate to the environment in which they carry out their crimes (2001). The process of developing interview schedules is becoming more sophisticated with the systematic use of multiple methods to determine topics and questions, and in their analysis with the use of established content-analysis software programs to help interpret and quantify open-ended data. Finally, visual aids are increasingly being used as probes to explore psychological dimensions of environments. Despite this, one challenge that remains for the field of environment-behavior is developing standardized interview procedures, such as those outlined in this chapter, that will enable researchers to compare and build on interview data across studies and between researchers.

With remarkable effectiveness, Michael, Hull, and Zahm (2001), employ the focused interview as their only method to explore the role environmental factors play in public park car burglaries—thefts from inside parked cars. The project's goal was to assess whether typical anti-crime environmental changes, such as removing vegetation where criminals can hide was effective in reducing crime of this sort and if so, why. If it was effective, was it because it reduced the number of places to hide as intended, because such actions indicated that attention was now being paid to the site, or because there was a concomitant surge in police presence? The team wanted to broaden its understanding of this type of crime in order to identify other contributing environmental features that might be manipulated.

The team started with phone interviews of park managers and police personnel in thirty-five U.S. cities with populations over 200,000, determining that Washington, D.C. was the city with the most to teach them. Washington has many visiting tourists who are targets, an extensive park network with parking areas in which such burglaries take place, a high rate of this particular crime, and a highly skilled law-enforcement agency, the U.S. Park Police. The Monumental Core, including the National Mall, the Washington Monument grounds, and West Potomac Park, is the site of just over 25 percent of all such crimes in Washington.

In Washington, the team carried out an audio- and videotaped group focus interview with uniformed and plainclothes police, park maintenance crewmembers, and park management personnel. Focusing on a large wall-mounted map, group members identified and described "bad spots" most frequented by such criminals and "good spots" they avoided. The team then carried out a focused walk-through interview at the "bad spots" with a plainclothes police officer from the focus group. Both the informant subject and the interviewer were fitted with mobile lapel microphones and the informant used a video camera to illustrate the points he made during the interview. Police officers described how specific criminal behavior unfolded and what environmental characteristics contributed to each crime—the "script" of auto burglaries and a clear direction for the most effective environmental manipulations to reduce such crimes.

Car Burglary Script

• *Select a target vehicle.* Choose a car or van to burgle by physically concealing yourself behind some shrubs or a tree. If there is no place to hide, you need to conceal your purpose by blending into the social landscape. Getting a snack at the food wagon and lounging on the grass to eat it conceals purpose. Nearby public toilets are good for concealing purpose as well. They provide an excuse for hanging around, and relief for the burglar who has been waiting a long time.

• *Approach the target vehicle.* Get close to the car while concealing your purpose by dropping a newspaper or other object to see unobtrusively if a car is locked.

• *Perpetrate the burglary.* Carry out the burglary so fast that it would be difficult for the police to catch you in the act. To overcome this tactic, police must identify and react immediately to behaviors that telegraph the shift from approach to perpetrating, "such as donning gloves, leaning against a vehicle (to surreptitiously check the lock), reaching for an object on the ground (e.g., a rock), pulling out a tool from under a coat, or looking around to detect police before gaining entry" (p. 378).

• *Escape.* Quickly get to a place with enough physical concealment to examine what was stolen, or into a large enough crowd to meld away. If a burglar is not apprehended in the act, he is usually caught during the escape. After the escape it is too late.

• *Examine the loot.* Look through the stolen goods and discard the less-valuable material to reduce the risk of being caught with evidence. The research team identified as the primary escape and examination places a group of holly trees near a statue of Einstein, the Ninth Street tunnel, and the bathroom in the National Sculpture Garden and Ice Rink.

• *Discard evidence.* During the day, the examination place serves as a discard location, while at night, evidence can be discarded on the run. A nearby river also serves this purpose. Some auto burglars leave discarded items in public to help their victims.

• *Cache the valuables.* Store bulky stolen items such as camcorders and larger cameras for later retrieval. If you drove yourself to the site, your car or mini-van is a good place for caching. If you don't have a car, coin-operated lockers are used frequently for valuable storage, such as the ones in the National Sculpture Garden and Ice Rink.

Informant focus-interview techniques enabled the researchers to identify a well-worn auto burglary script with a single two-part goal: minimize effort and risk while maximizing reward. What does all this imply for environmental design? The study found that the most effective environmental interventions for reducing auto burglaries are those that disrupt the routine and increase effort and risk. Because so much of the setup rests on concealing purpose, disrupting that act has a major impact. The study suggests simple but effective strategies, for example, moving food wagons to where cars are less easily observed and converting public toilets to coin operated facilities. Changing toilet access also disrupts routines for examining loot and discarding valuable items. Locating parking further from easy escape routes also has a major impact. Traditional anti-crime environmental actions such as removing vegetation, adding lighting, and improving litter control and site aesthetics are less likely to reduce auto burglaries because they disrupt neither the criminal's nor the tourist target's routines.

Interview techniques are also integrally combined with other methods. For example, in her extensive analysis of strategies employed to reduce rapes and sexual assaults on U.S. college campuses, Day (1995) employs interviews with administrators and students as her major data collection method, backed up with archival research. She successfully determines "the definition of the situation" of both groups, finding that both define the problem of campus rape as one of attacks by strangers—even though incident data show that acquaintance and date rape are much more prevalent.

Day's interviews with administrators focus on how they define this particular behavior, how data on assaults are gathered, analyzed and disseminated; what strategies are implemented and what actions taken to prevent such crimes; and how the physical environment is modified to reduce opportunities for rape. Student interviews focused on students' awareness of their own and the university's preventive strategies and actions; their feelings of fear and safety; and the intended and unintended consequences of actions taken to reduce sexual assaults.

Following the trend of evolved multi-method environment-behavior research, *interviews* are seamlessly interwoven with several other methods, starting with two *archival methods—existing statistical data* on actual reported crimes and *extensive literature searches* on the topic of sexual assault design strategies.

Day not only employs literature as "background" to the problem statement, but also weaves literature references into the entire data analysis phase. As she describes it, "literature review continued throughout data collection and analysis, in a 'back and forth' process that confirmed, questioned and qualified emerging findings" (p. 287). Literature employed in this way became central to Day's "testing" of hypotheses as they developed through continuing data analysis iterations.

Day exploits the iterative research approach in the way she uses three data analysis methods in combination. First is explicit *coding* of the verbatim interview transcriptions employing two developed coding approaches—Patton's *detailed coding* (1988) and Strauss and Corbin's *memoing* (1990). Second is the use of "experts" as an analysis panel. Developing content codes and linking these to specific hypotheses,

> coding was interspersed with increasingly sophisticated and substantiated memos. Early memos posted hypotheses developed during data collection. Hypotheses were then iteratively refined, verified and discarded against coded data. Increasingly sophisticated memos were written to detail and support explanations as they emerge (p. 266).

As part of this memoing approach to data analysis, Day used expert environment-behavior colleagues as "peer debriefers." While informally sharing analysis memos with colleagues may not seem to be a "method," using an *expert panel* in this way definitely is. Two final methods are woven into this methodological story. Day labels the first method *participant photography*, the photographs students were asked to take of "feared and safe places on and near campus" that they brought to the interview for discussion. Second are the brief *questionnaires* students filled out after their interview describing themselves and their use of the campus.

This rich interview-based multi-method research study sheds light on a disturbing set of paradoxes. Prevention strategies that focus on out of door attacks by strangers promote the idea that women need to change their behavior—how they dress, where they walk and when, if they walk alone—and that the changes will prevent such attacks. Since the behavior that needs to be prevented is acquaintance and date rape rather than stranger attacks, this approach focuses on the wrong set of behaviors, implicitly blames women for sexual assaults by strangers that happen outdoors at night, (although this is not the case) and results in what Day calls the "gendering" of public spaces.

Day's research highlights the irony and side effects of a policy that targets the wrong phenomenon. Women dress conservatively, even though revealing dress has been shown not to increase the likelihood of victimization (Gordon and Riger, 1985). Women curtail their outdoor activities out of fear, which may actually increase the danger outdoors by reducing activity there at night. The approaches even convince victims to misperceive the situation they face: "even women victimized by their partners report greater fear associated with strangers" (Gruebbels et al., 1987, in Valentine, 1992).

Day also discovers that although students do notice that places with views out to surrounding areas, that are well lit, and that have trimmed hedges are safer, the only design elements recognized as consciously planned to reduce crime are those whose "sole or primary purpose" is "safety (e.g., alarms, locks) and those that required action by students as potential victims (e.g., emergency phones, badge access card readers)" (p. 277).

Kupritz uses a similarly thorough multi-method interview approach in her privacy study at the Gulfstream Aerospace Corporation headquarters in Savannah, Georgia (1998). Employing a careful review of the literature as the basis for her research and analysis, Kupritz identifies three operational definitions of privacy.

- Retreat from people
- Control over information
- Regulation of interaction

To identify physical characteristics of offices that most influence "privacy," she carefully develops a linked interview/questionnaire approach to uncover office workers' *definition of the situation* in two open-office environments in the same company. Like Day, Kupritz employs formal content-analysis techniques and triangulates on her subject matter with each of the six methods described in this book. Her goal is to uncover more individual workspace characteristics of privacy than height, type, and number of partitions enclosing the workspace, and whether or not there is a door. She adds to this list "what Zeisel (1984) labels as field characteristics . . . physical elements that perceptually alter physical context through shape, orientation, size and environmental condition" (p. 350). She found that:

> Field characteristics associated with privacy regulation are considered more important to Gulfstream engineers than barriers associated with privacy regulation. The two field characteristics, having minimal traffic routed through the workers area and the workspace located away from the main traffic flow, are ranked as more important than barriers. Each of these characteristics deals with orientation of the workspace, and stresses the importance of "functional distance" (see Festinger et al., 1950; Zeisel, 1984) (p. 352).

She also found that for the engineers she studied, privacy did not seem to be the most important item in their workspace:

> Those design items that are necessary to perform basic job functions are considered more important: having an adequate work surface to spread out drawings; adequate storage; easy access to reference materials; and [having] groups that work together located close together (p. 352).

What methodology did Kupritz use to uncover these findings? Her main method was a particular type of focused interview, called the Heuristic

Elicitation methodology (Harding, 1974; Harding and Livesay, 1984). This anthropological interview technique begins with eliciting subjects' definition of the situation and then carrying out a content analysis—which Kupritz did by employing "domain, taxonomic and componential analysis procedures" (Spradley, 1979). To construct her interview schedule, Kupritz conducted a document search, reviewed floor plans of work areas, and studied background information on Gulfstream. After the interview, she carried out behavioral observation, physical trace observation, and photo documentation to construct a structured questionnaire asking subjects to link specific environmental characteristics they identified in the interview to their work and privacy needs.

Her behavioral observations at Gulfstream supported this analysis that being near traffic paths contributed to loss of production time. She counted "the number of times five engineers [sitting near pathways] glanced up as people walked by their desks . . . in 15- and 30-minute intervals," and found that one engineer, the worst case, glanced up twenty-two of fifty-seven times someone passed by his desk in a fifteen-minute period.

This multi-method triangulation approach gives her a particularly complete picture of a study phenomenon and the focused interview as a critical probing tool.

The following case study describing a highly specialized individual focused-interview technique to help people make better-informed housing decisions for themselves demonstrates that with ingenuity and insight, the focused interview can be a powerful research instrument.

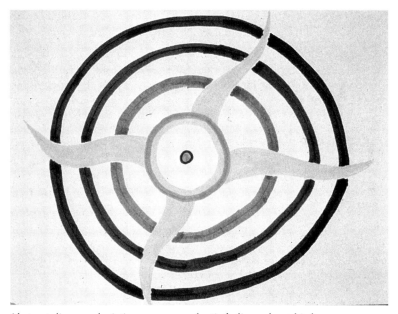

Abstract diagram depicting one respondent's feelings about his home.

CASE STUDY

HOUSE COUNSELING
Practical Application of the House-and-Home Dialogue Interview

Trained designers do not make most design decisions that affect our daily lives. In creating a home, the inhabitant makes almost all the decisions relating to design—where to live (site selection), whether to buy or rent (tenure), how to decorate (interior design), and how to present a "face" to the neighborhood (garden design and personalization).

Environment-behavior researcher and consultant Clare Cooper Marcus employed a specially developed research tool—the house-and-home interview—in "House Counseling" sessions to help people with house problems make more informed design decisions. Participants included people torn between living in an urban area and living in the country; people who had lost their homes in a fire and could not decide whether to rebuild or move somewhere else; and couples who had different images of their "ideal home."

The house-and-home dialogue interview, as this creative method is called, is aimed at sensitively exposing a basic problem many people face when making decisions about their own housing choices: the often strong and confusing feelings they have about the place where they live, have lived, or aspire to live. These positive, negative, and sometimes painfully ambivalent feelings often interfere with their decision-making. While it is common knowledge that peo-

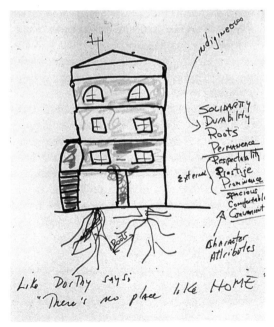

"There's no place like home."

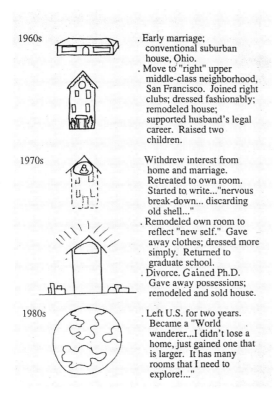

1960s	. Early marriage; conventional suburban house, Ohio.
	. Move to "right" upper middle-class neighborhood, San Francisco. Joined right clubs; dressed fashionably; remodeled house; supported husband's legal career. Raised two children.
1970s	Withdrew interest from home and marriage. Retreated to own room. Started to write..."nervous break-down... discarding old shell..."
	. Remodeled own room to reflect "new self." Gave away clothes; dressed more simply. Returned to graduate school.
	. Divorce. Gained Ph.D. Gave away possessions; remodeled and sold house.
1980s	. Left U.S. for two years. Became a "World wanderer...I didn't lose a home, just gained one that is larger. It has many rooms that I need to explore!..."

Dwellings in Sara's life.

ple hold strong feelings about where they live, until Cooper Marcus innovated her special form of focused interview, which facilitates access to these deeply held emotions, there was no clearly defined way to elicit, analyze, and understand this phenomenon. Questionnaire surveys and traditional interviews tap only the surface reasons for making such decisions: they do not get to the heart of the emotions involved.

Employing the house-and-home approach, Cooper Marcus probed long-held feelings about people's past and present living environments. As subjects gained new awareness of their feelings, they were able to make better design decisions. A young woman living in an isolated, lonely environment was able to decide to move into an urban apartment that better suited her psychological needs. An artist whose home was cluttered to the point of paralysis was able to understand the basis for this compulsive behavior. A woman who had tried unsuccessfully to locate a house to buy came to understand why she was emotionally blocked, found a house, and moved. A retired man living in a house much too large for his needs realized the roots of the emotional attachment he felt, and concluded that he could never move away. A wife whose husband had made all the decisions about the location and design of their "trophy" house understood her dislike for their current living situation. She eventually divorced her husband and moved to a setting that better supported her emotional and lifestyle needs.

"How I feel
about my home."

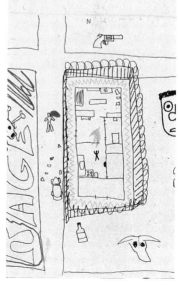

"House, the way I feel about you is . . . "

The house replies: "The way I feel is . . . "

This innovative focus interview approach was originally developed as a research tool to better understand the emotional links between person and dwelling place (Cooper Marcus, 1995). Sixty randomly selected subjects were interviewed, and all interviews took place in the person's home so that they would be on "home turf." To begin the process, after being supplied with a large pad, crayons, and markers, the person was asked to put down in some graphic or pictorial form their feelings about their house.

The images people drew ranged from representational house layouts to abstract diagrams color-coded for emotion. Representing their feelings graphically allowed each person to focus on their emotions and express them non-verbally before the start of the interview. Not having to put feelings into words immediately often released profound emotions. While the respondents were drawing, Cooper Marcus left the room and—with their permission—looked around the houses, making note of her own feelings about each place she was about to discuss with the person living there, which became topics for an interview schedule in focused-interview terminology.

The verbal interview starts with the picture the person drew being placed on a chair or cushion to represent the house, while the interviewee sits facing it a few feet away. The person is asked to explain what she or he thinks the picture depicts. A second question asks the person to speak to the house as if it were animate, directing his or her remarks to the house-picture and starting with the words: "House—the way I feel about you is . . . ." After the interviewer feels sufficient depth and breadth of answer has been reached, the interviewer asks the person to switch places and "become" the house speaking back to them. Thus, a dialogue ensues between the person and the house in the form of role-playing. Sometimes other "characters" enter the conversation such as an influential grandfather, a deceased mother, or an estranged husband. The interviewer stays in the background, closely follows the material being revealed through the dialogue, and prompts the person to change roles when the interviewer feels a particular topic or "conversation" is completed. The drawing and other interview prompts are focused interview probes designed to move the interviewee seamlessly through the topics and allow him to express himself fully. Cooper Marcus tape-recorded the interviews for later analysis.

The house-and-home interview method has its roots in the way role-playing is employed in Gestalt therapy. In order to learn how to adapt this method as a research tool and to use it responsibly, Cooper Marcus trained with a Gestalt therapist. Since the method frequently evokes strong emotions, it should not be employed without some psychological training. However, without such training it is possible to use the general principle of role-playing to access the essence of environments that are less emotionally "loaded" than a person's home. For example, in post-occupancy evaluations of neighborhood parks in Berkeley, California, before conducting in-person interviews with park users and behavior mapping of activities in the park, landscape architecture students were asked to imagine that each park could speak and communicate the pros and cons of its current situation. Many of their one-paragraph statements were remarkably accurate in capturing the essence of the situation, which was later confirmed by the data they generated on how the parks were actually used, misused, and could be improved. Role-playing interviews appear to access a deeper knowing than is reachable using other methods, suggesting that a student looking carefully at a park or a person considering their home knows more than they think.

In the house-and-home interviews described here, when people spoke as the house, they often spoke more openly and deeply about issues than when they spoke as themselves—leading to a gasp of recognition or even tears. Speaking as a significant house or dwelling place allowed unconscious material to come into consciousness, as in a dream.

As practical applications of environment-behavior methods increasingly present themselves, and as probing methods like the house-and-home interview are developed, they must be approached with care. In this case, it is critical that only someone with psychological training employ this interview technique. In general, however, this case study demonstrates how creativity and methodological exploration can lead to both new research and new applied research opportunities.

This case study is based on the work of Clare Cooper Marcus, Professor Emeritus, University of California, Berkeley, and Principal, Healing Landscapes, Berkeley, California.

OVERVIEW

You cannot find out how people see the world and feel about it unless you ask them. The focused interview is uniquely suited to discovering a respondent's personal definition of complex E-B situations. Skilled interviewers analyze situations to develop a guide of interview topics. The purpose of the guide is limited to reminding the interviewer of topics and issues to cover. The skilled interviewer then enables the respondent to approach and discuss these topics in her own special way.

To achieve full coverage and depth of insights, the interviewer's main tool is the probe: an indication by the interviewer to the respondent to provide more information about depth of feelings, other topics, the respondent's personal context, or details of a situation. Interviewers use probes to keep an interview flowing without directing it.

Focused-interviewing techniques are as useful with groups as with individual respondents if the interviewer knows how to keep one member of the group from dominating and can encourage diversity of opinion rather than forced consensus. Focused interviews, however, are not suited to gathering large amounts of easily comparable and quantifiable data. For this, researchers can use standardized questionnaires—the topic of the next chapter.

CHAPTER 11

STANDARDIZED QUESTIONNAIRES

Standardized questionnaires are used to discover regularities among groups of people by comparing answers to the same set of questions asked of a large number of people. Questionnaires can be delivered by mail or administered over the phone or in person by interviewers trained to ask the questions in the same way. Questionnaires administered in person are also called *scheduled interviews* when interviewers are instructed to follow up certain questions with structured probes for depth or specificity.

Questionnaires provide useful quantitative data when investigators begin with a very well-defined problem, knowing what major concepts and dimensions they want to deal with. Observations, archival data analysis, and focus interviews are generally used to define such issues for questionnaire construction. Analysis of questionnaire responses can provide precise numbers to measure, for example, the degree of satisfaction with thermal comfort among employees in an open-plan office or the percentage of residents who participate in apartment house self-management committees.

Skilled researchers begin the process of using standardized questionnaires to test and refine their ideas by creating hypotheses about which attributes relate to each other. What they do not know is which hypotheses are going to stand up best to empirical study and how, precisely, the concepts will relate. For example, a research team may hypothesize that type of previous dwelling influences satisfaction with apartment living. Using questionnaires, they might find that residents moving from single-family houses are more satisfied with high-rise living than previous apartment dwellers because they expected to have drastically less space than before (Merton et al., 1960).

Fried (1963, 1972) demonstrates insightful use of questionnaires to show how reactions among residents of a neighborhood to being forced out in the wake of urban renewal were related to their "sense of spatial identity" with the neighborhood, "based on spatial memories, spatial imagery, the spatial framework of current activities, and the implicitly spatial components of ideals and aspirations" (1972, p. 234). Fried's quantitative analysis of responses from 259 relocated female residents before and after moving showed that the more they liked living in the West End and the more they viewed the West End as "home," the more they reported severe grief reactions after moving (see Tables 11-1 and 11-2).

This chapter discusses some of the qualities of questionnaires, how to organize a questionnaire, and ways to code and formulate categories.

The next chapter will show how asking questions in both questionnaires and interviews is suited to such environment-behavior topics as perception, aspirations, knowledge, attitudes, and intentions. That chapter also discusses how to formulate questions in order to find out what you want to about these topics.

Table 11-1. **Post-relocation "grief" by pre-relocation "liking"**

	Percent Severe Grief Reactions
Among those who said they *liked living in the West End:*	
"very much"	73%
"positive but less than very much"	53%
"ambivalent or negative"	34%
n = (259)	

Table 11-2. **Post-relocation "grief" by pre-relocation "feeling like home"**

	Percent Severe Grief Reactions
Among those who said their *real home* was:	
"the West End"	68%
"in some other area"	34%
"they had no real home"	20%
n = (259)	

Standardized Questionnaires

Qualities

  Control
  Intrusiveness
  Convincing rigor

Organization

  Rapport
  Conditioning
  Fatigue

Coding Open-Ended Responses

  Mutual exclusiveness
  Exhaustiveness
  Single abstraction level

Precoding Responses

  Nominal
  Ordinal

Visual Responses

  Maps
  Drawings
  Photographs
  Games

QUALITIES

By organizing questionnaires and their administration, investigators can learn a great deal in a short time. But this takes preparation. The quality of questionnaire data depends on the thoroughness that E-B researchers apply to defining the problems they are studying. This is a significant burden because resulting quantitative data often unreasonably convince other people of arguments that qualitative data do not—even when the conceptual basis of the numbers is weak.

Control

Interviewers structure questionnaires and control their administration. There is an implicit contract between researcher and respondent that the researcher defines what happens during the interview: how it begins, the ordering of questions and answers, and how it ends. Control has positive side effects, not the least of which is efficiency—large amounts of specific and comparable data can be gathered at minimum cost. Some control over the situation is surrendered when questionnaires are delivered by mail; accordingly, to increase control, mail questionnaires are usually shorter and more tightly organized.

Repeating standardized questions the same way to many respondents enables researchers to easily compare answers from different respondents. When individual questionnaire items are repeated in separate and similar studies, answers can be shared and compared to build a cumulative body of data.

Intrusiveness

Control in administering questionnaires acknowledges that respondents can change and distort answers either for some reason of their own or in response to the methods themselves. For example, respondents can be directed by the questions themselves to treat some issues in greater depth than others, define things in certain ways, or respond in provided categories. This is not a problem if questions and response categories correspond to respondents' definitions of the situation. However, when they do not correspond, respondents sometimes feel that the implicit contract to answer questions means they should not correct obvious mistakes because the researcher surely knows what she is after.

Before going into the field researchers using standardized questionnaires must determine the level of refinement they want answers to achieve to solve their problem. There is little room for adjustment once data gathering begins. One of the most frustrating things that can happen to researchers employing structured interviews and questionnaires is to find that they have spent a great deal of time and energy learning about everything except one item that is essential to explaining relations between crucial variables.

To avoid some of the side effects of control in any method and in any type of interview (not only questionnaires), researchers carry out thorough preliminary diagnostic research. Focused interviews may be used when preparing a questionnaire to determine how people similar to intended questionnaire respondents define a situation: what is important; the names they use for places or things; and the types of answers they give. Observation methods can also be used during diagnostic studies. Using diagnostic data, investigators structure standardized questionnaires. But the process does not end there.

After the questionnaire is written, investigators *pretest* it with more people who resemble the expected respondents. Pretesting a questionnaire means administering it to self-conscious respondents while asking them to comment on points such as: What do they understand each question to mean? Is it clear or confusing? What do they think is its intent? Do response categories give them ample opportunity to express themselves? Is the introduction to the questionnaire clear? Does the sequence of questions make sense? Pretests are invaluable aids not only in questionnaire construction but also in designing any research instrument to fit the needs of a particular situation, group of respondents or elements to observe, or research problem.

Pretests carried out skillfully also alert investigators to unforeseen problems in other dimensions of the research approach: problem definition, research design, methodological mix, observer training, and interviewers' skills, "even of the first steps of analysis." A pretest is a small, self-conscious pilot study, a microcosm of the actual project carried out to identify, if possible, unintended side effects (Galtung, 1967, p. 138).

Convincing Rigor

Quantitative analysis of questionnaire data not only contributes precision to knowledge, it can also make research data convincing to others. The apparent exactness and rigorousness of statistical analysis is a useful device to win arguments with people who do not understand the value of and rigor involved in achieving *qualitative knowing* in scientific research. This is an important characteristic of the method when research results are to be used in a court of law, in a political setting, in applied design, or in any competitive decision-making situation. Such situations are increasing as citizens' groups and environmental legislation bring E-B research issues into the public eye.

Naive researchers are themselves sometimes convinced by the numbers they can obtain using questionnaires. They think they can learn something significant by asking a lot of questions and running answers through a computer. Something can, of course, be learned in this way but it has a low probability of solving the researcher's, the client's, or the respondents' problems.

Quantitative questionnaire data that are not augmented by researchers' qualitative insight or by qualitative data from other methods can provide a hollow and unscientific understanding of important problems (Campbell, 1975). Statistically significant data are not necessarily meaningful data.

ORGANIZATION

If you are not careful, the way your questionnaire is structured can antagonize, bore, confuse, or tire respondents. If it does, you might as well not ask any questions.

Rapport

Questionnaire respondents participate in a research project as informants about themselves. Research results are only as valid as the relationship between interviewer and respondent is open and non-defensive. Introducing oneself and the purpose of the interview can establish rapport clearly, honestly, realistically, and without threatening the respondent. Environment-behavior research projects may be introduced to respondents as attempts to ask their *advice*—how to make future similar environments better, what could have been improved in a setting, or just what people like and think. Respondents like to see themselves as advice givers rather than guinea pigs.

Questions requesting positive responses ("What do you like best about working in this building?") can start an interview on a friendly note. Later, requests can be made for suggestions on improvements. Initial questions can ask for general impressions; simple demographic information, such as previous residence; or, especially, address interesting topics to elicit respondents' attention. For every situation and problem each investigator must determine the most appropriate way to begin.

Conditioning

Early questions can influence the way respondents will answer later ones. For example, if early questions give respondents the feeling that interviewers really want to find out what is wrong with a place, they may criticize the place more than they praise it in later questions. When information is presented in the wording of an early question, knowledge of that information cannot be tested later. A good rule to follow is to go from general to specific questions so that questions asked later in the interview require greater specificity of information, intent, and purpose.

Fatigue

In the half hour or so during which a questionnaire is administered, interviewers often have to choose between gathering a great deal of information and not tiring out the respondent. To maximize information gathering and minimize fatigue, you can group questions that relate to a single topic, such as a neighborhood, an event, or a set of activities in one place. For clarity each group can be introduced with a unifying sentence: "I would like to ask you some questions about . . . ."

Interviewers can also group questions that have similar types of response categories, like those discussed in the next section, for example a series of preference questions, followed by semantic differential questions and attitude questions. Grouping questions can unwittingly lead to "response sets" among answers—namely, respondents' natural tendency to answer questions in a way that seems logically consistent. For example, respondents may tend not to admit to criticism of one part of a setting while praising another. It is therefore necessary to mix up questions about different dimensions of the same topic and to limit the length of any one set of questions with identical response categories.

Another way to use the time respondents give you wisely is to avoid asking them questions that do not apply to them. *Filtering questions* help you avoid inapplicable questions by, for example, finding out who drives to work before asking how long it takes by car, how many people are in the car, and what parking conditions are like. When *follow-up questions* are used for explanation ("Why?"), specification ("What precisely?"), or clarification of intensity ("How much?"), it saves time to target them only to respondents to whom they apply.

All this can be achieved with clear layout and written interviewer instructions to keep the interview flowing and to avoid confusing respondents with irrelevant questions. Saile et al. (1972) faced many of the problems discussed here, and their questionnaire helped resolve many of them.

OMIT QUESTION #s 127-135 for SCATTERED SITES:

"Now, we have just a few more questions to go, and we'd like to get your views on the Housing Authority..."

127. In general, would you say that the management here does a good job, a fair job, or a poor job in running the project?

> Good job.................1
> Fair job.................2
> Poor job.................3

128. Do they repair things fairly quickly   YES   NO
when something goes wrong?...................1⌐   2
                       GO TO
                       # 130

129. What problems have you had? (Record exact answer)

130. Do you think the rules and regulations   YES   NO
about living here are fair?.................1⌐   2
                       GO TO
                       # 132

131. Why not? (Record exact answer)

132. When you first moved here did you go through a training program to learn how to look after   YES   NO
this house?.................................   1   2

133. Would you recommend a training program like   YES   NO
that for other people moving in here?........   1   2

134. Would you like to have a booklet explaining   YES   NO
how to look after this house?................   1   2

135. Do you think it would be helpful to have a handbook to explain the rules and regulations   YES   NO
about living here?...........................   1   2

136. Do you think you'll stay in this house or do you expect to move sometime?.......STAY   MOVE SOMETIME
                     1⌐   2
                   GO TO
                   # 138

(From *Families in Public Housing: An Evaluation of Three Residential Environments in Rockford, Illinois*, by D. Saile, J. R. Anderson, R. Borooah, A. Ray, K. Rohling, C. Simpson, A. Sutton, and M. Williams. University of Illinois at Urbana-Champaign Committee on Housing Research and Development, 1972. Reprinted by permission.)

CODING OPEN-ENDED RESPONSES

No matter how researchers pose questions in a structured interview or questionnaire, they must record the answers and prepare them for counting and analysis. By grouping similar responses together, they make responses comparable to one another. For example, four respondents who are asked a free-response question about why they like a room might give four answers: "I like it because it is big," "I like it because sound travels well there," "I like it because of its size," and "I like the way many people can fit into it." The researcher must decide whether each response is unique, whether the responses can be partitioned into categories of answers (two mention largeness, one notes good acoustics, and one mentions accommodating many people), or whether they can be partitioned into two categories (large size and acoustics). His decision will be based on how the different groupings, or partitions, help him solve his research problem.

This process of deciding how to partition responses into groups is called *coding* because researchers use a few responses to develop a category *code*, which is then applied to the rest of the responses in a study. Three characteristics are essential for coding categories—partitions—if they are to be helpful rather than confusing. They must be mutually exclusive, exhaust all the possible types of responses, and all be at the same conceptual level. These characteristics also define the difference between a system and a list. The following examples explain these three essential characteristics.

Mutual Exclusiveness

Mutual exclusiveness means that responses clearly fall into either one category or another. There can be no overlapping, either numerically or conceptually.

The age categories "under 11, 11–20, 21–40, 41 or over" are mutually exclusive; the categories "under 10, 10–20, 20–40, 40 or over" are not. Examples of mutually exclusive categories for residential location are "in this neighborhood," "in this city but outside this neighborhood," "outside this city but in this state," "within any other state in the country," and "in another country."

Exhaustiveness

Exhaustiveness means that any possible response fits into some category. Researchers can include an "other" category to achieve exhaustiveness in complex questions.

Qu: How did you travel to the supermarket the last time you went?

Categories that are not exhaustive:	car, bus, on foot, other
Exhaustive categories:	Own car, other's car, taxi, bicycle, public bus, special shopping bus, subway, on foot, combination of two or more modes (please specify): (a) (b) (c) other (please specify): (a) (b) (c)

Single Abstraction Level

Single abstraction level means that response categories are conceptually parallel. They do not partition responses into, for example, apples, pears, oranges, and fruit.

Qu: What do you feel is the nicest part of a house?

Multi-level abstraction code:	bedrooms, shared rooms, aesthetics, windows, hardware
Single-level abstraction code:	bedrooms, private workrooms, other rooms, passageways, outside grounds

PRECODING RESPONSES

In a standardized questionnaire, if there are open-ended questions that need coding, analysis of the survey can be time-consuming and costly. Computer programs that analyze textual information can help speed up this process, but the time must be planned for. In addition, a great number of free-response questions reflects a lack of researcher preparation and wastes the potential benefits of using a standardized questionnaire. In some cases, what the researcher wants to find out cannot be rigidly structured—for example, when the subject of the study is how respondents mentally picture their surroundings or how they react in complex decision-making situations. In these studies, as discussed at the end of this chapter, special methods of recording and coding information may be developed.

In some situations, it is possible to *pre-code* responses to questionnaires: to partition possible response alternatives into sets of categories for respondents to choose from that are exhaustive, mutually exclusive, and have a single level of abstraction. This means asking questions of the form "Are you very tired, somewhat tired, or not tired at all?" (pre-coded) rather than "How tired are you?" (open-ended). Codes may organize things parallel to one another or in rank order. The first type is nominal and the latter ordinal categories.

Nominal

Things such as building types or types of research methods may be partitioned for certain purposes into separate and parallel categories. Chapters 9, 10, 11, and 14 of this book represent a nominal code of methods. A simple, nominally pre-coded response asks respondents to reply yes or no to a question such as, "Do you have a driver's license?" or offers a binary choice: "Sex? male _____ female _____ ." Usually, however, nominal codes classify more than two alternatives, for example, "What is your religion? Protestant _____, Muslim _____, Catholic _____ Jewish _____, Hindu _____, agnostic _____, atheist _____, other _____, none_____" or "Do you find it difficult to climb the stairs? Yes; no; don't know, no opinion; does not apply, never climb stairs."

Nominal codes are most useful to collect information, to offer non-ranked choices to respondents, and to obtain attitudinal data useful in a binary "yes" or "no" form.

Ordinal

To analyze intensity, direction, and quality of such variables as verbally expressed attitudes and perceptions, it may be helpful to arrange responses in a rank order representing different degrees or magnitudes.

When each category is separated from others by what seems to be an equal magnitude, ordinal categories are called *intervals*. There are some problems with this idea. For example, a uniform difference in temperature—say, 2° F— may be experienced differently if it represents a rise from 6° F to 8° F than a rise from 65° F to 67° F. The same problem holds for age differences. A year has a different quantity and quality at ages five, thirty, and eighty. Therefore, interval categories are not presented in the following discussion as distinct from ordinal ones.

•. *Information.* Ordinal pre-coding can be used for questions gathering *information* that are reasonably seen as "how much" or "how many" questions regarding age, income, size of household, or the number of clubs a respondent belongs to.

> Age: Under 11 ❏, 11–20 ❏, 21–30 ❏, 31–40 ❏, 41–50 ❏, 51–60 ❏, 61 or over ❏.
> Club membership: None ❏, 1 or 2 ❏, 3 to 6 ❏, 7 or more ❏.

• *Attitudes.* Ordinal coding may also be useful for response categories following questions that ask respondents to judge the intensity of an *attitude* about a situation, person, object, or setting.

> Would you say the rules in this factory are very fair ❏, fair ❏, unfair ❏, very unfair ❏, or do you have no opinion ❏ about this?

> Would you say the work areas you have are very supportive ❏, supportive ❏, unsupportive ❏, very unsupportive ❏, or are you uncertain about this ❏?

When a questionnaire is administered orally, the "no opinion" or "uncertain" category is sometimes not read to respondents, encouraging them to make some kind of choice—no matter how weakly felt. If they still have no opinion, interviewers check the box.

Some coding categories are associated with both a format for responses and quantitative procedures for analyzing responses. One of these is the *Likert attitude scale*, in which groups of statements are presented to respondents for them to indicate the intensity of their agreement or disagreement. If standard scores are assigned to responses in such a way that high agreement with positive statements is equivalent to high disagreement with negative statements, and if several questions tap dimensions of the same general attitude ("feelings about company management"), then cumulative scores on these statements can be used to indicate a respondent's position on that attitude.

Example of Likert Attitude Scale

Please check the appropriate box:

	Strongly Agree	Agree	Uncertain	Disagree	Strongly Disagree
The rules in this factory are unfair	1	2	3	4	5
Management is very helpful in job training	5	4	3	2	1
The work areas we have could easily be much better	1	2	3	4	5

(Number scores in the boxes are not presented on the questionnaire.)

When Likert-scaled questions are used, they can be grouped together in a questionnaire so that once respondents understand how to use this system of recording responses, they can use it for several questions. When this is done, however, the list must be short enough and must mix positive and negative statements to avoid respondents' going down a long list checking only one column and not thinking about their responses.

If researchers feel that using Likert-scale items on a questionnaire can help them solve their problems, they should carefully study the assumptions underlying this type of attitude quantification. If they decide they can make these assumptions, they carry out careful empirical procedures to choose and score groups of statements that actually do relate to one another (as explained, for example, in Shaw and Wright, 1967).

The same caveat holds for the use of every empirically developed measurement scale, including the *semantic differential scale*, which is discussed below.

• *Meaning.* When you look at the Eiffel Tower, Mount Fuji, or the chair you are sitting in, you react to it in part on the basis of what it "means" to you. You may, for example, feel uncomfortable and tense in the chair because it is an antique that you see as dainty, weak, and silly, but tasteful. Most people find it difficult to express verbally the range of meaning things have to them. For example, in a taste test of different ice creams, few tasters could spontaneously manage to say anything but "creamy" or "tasty" when trying to differentiate brands. But when presented with lists of appropriate descriptive terms to choose from, they could easily indicate what the different tastes meant to them (Osgood, Suci, and Tannenbaum, 1957).

The principle that people express the meaning things hold for them more completely when presented with a set of appropriate alternatives underlies another analytic coding technique—the *semantic differential scale*. Like the Likert and other scales, this one must entail careful procedures for determining what alternatives are "appropriate" for particular respondents and situations. It also entails important and often questionable assumptions about quantification and the ensuing analysis of data (Osgood et al., 1957).

If the scaling technique is critically examined, it can be selectively used to identify the *quality* and *intensity* of meaning that E-B topics such as environments, persons, places, and situations hold for people. The format for semantic differentiation presents respondents with the name or picture of an object (place, concept, and so on) or with the object itself, followed by a series of polar opposite terms: good/bad, happy/sad, big/little. For each pair of terms, respondents are asked to indicate how the terms apply to the object on the basis of what the object means to them. They do this in the following format:

Your Chair

Wide — / — / — /— /— / — /— / Narrow
(1)   (2)   (3)   (4)   (3)   (2)   (1)
Contemporary — / — / — / — / — / — / — / Traditional
Functional — / — / — / — / — / — / — / Nonfunctional
Tasteful — / — / — / — / — / — / — / Tasteless
Cheerful — / — / — / — / — / — / — / Dreary
Orderly — / — / — / — / — / — / — / Chaotic
Private — / — / — / — / — / — / — / Public
Sparkling — / — / — / — / — / — / — / Dingy

Respondents are instructed that marking the line above a response of 1 means the object is extremely wide, contemporary, etc.; 2, quite wide; 3, slightly wide; 4, neutral, equally wide and narrow, or width is unrelated to the object.

Choice and interpretation of scale items are difficult. Osgood et al. carried out several studies and much computer analysis to develop a scale of fifty paired items particularly relevant to general concepts. They found that the descriptive terms fell mainly into categories of evaluation, potency, and activity. A great deal more work is necessary to adapt this scaling technique to E-B studies.

Using semantic differential scales to elicit and code responses is not merely a matter of listing a set of opposites the investigator feels is appropriate to the subject matter, and separating items with a seven-point pre-coded checklist. When semantic differential scales are used, it is essential to later data analysis to choose categories that are appropriate to the particular research situation and the respondents' definition of the situation. Not doing so is a common mistake among inexperienced researchers. As an example of a well-executed study, Howell and Epp (1976) pretested the following semantic differential question in their study of housing for older persons:

How would you describe the way the building looks from the outside?
Like a private — / — / — / — / — / — / — / Like a public
home   (1)   (2)   (3)   (4)   (3)   (2)   (1) building

Hard — / — / — / — / — / — / — / Soft
Simple — / — / — / — / — / — / — / Complex

Older respondents were able to choose between the attributes in the first pair, but could not understand what the other two pairs had to do with the way their building looked.

Question construction has developed into a complex skill—perhaps too complex. The semantic differential scale exhibits a problem many such techniques face: They may cause more damage than they are worth. It is unclear, for example, that seven-point polar-opposite judgment tests yield more information than a three- or five-point agree/disagree rating scale. If respondents feel that the adjectives they are asked to rate are nonsensical (*cheerful* and *dreary* applied to a chair, for example), the loss of rapport with the interviewer may invalidate other parts of the interview. Careful pretesting is one way to avoid such mistakes. Another is to include on the team constructing questions some people who are similar to potential respondents. This is good advice no matter what type of question you are constructing. In sum, rating scales of any sort must be used only after careful examination of their wording and the operational assumptions they embody.

• *Rank-ordering of items.* It may be useful to pre-code responses to questions asking respondents to rank a group of items relative to one another on a single attribute such as importance, beauty, usefulness, or worthwhileness. For example:

Which of the spaces on the following list do you feel it is most important to include in a house? (Please circle "1" for the most important, "2" for the second most important, "3" for the next, and so on until you have ranked all places in terms of their importance to you.)

	1	2	3	4	5	6	7	8	9	10	11	12
bathroom	1	2	3	4	5	6	7	8	9	10	11	12
kitchen	1	2	3	4	5	6	7	8	9	10	11	12
laundry room	1	2	3	4	5	6	7	8	9	10	11	12
living room	1	2	3	4	5	6	7	8	9	10	11	12
bedrooms	1	2	3	4	5	6	7	8	9	10	11	12
den or rec. room	1	2	3	4	5	6	7	8	9	10	11	12
study	1	2	3	4	5	6	7	8	9	10	11	12
storage attic	1	2	3	4	5	6	7	8	9	10	11	12
vestibule	1	2	3	4	5	6	7	8	9	10	11	12
dining room	1	2	3	4	5	6	7	8	9	10	11	12
Other: specify _____	1	2	3	4	5	6	7	8	9	10	11	12
Other: specify _____	1	2	3	4	5	6	7	8	9	10	11	12
Other: specify _____	1	2	3	4	5	6	7	8	9	10	11	12

When items in the group are unduly complex—alternative lifestyles, for example—it is easier to present them in pairs for sequential comparison rather than in a simultaneous list.

Each technique for pre-coding responses creates opportunities for researchers, but also limits what researchers can do with the data. Only experience with using classification and scaling methods—asking the questions, recording answers, tabulating responses, and analyzing data—will give researchers the knowledge and self-confidence needed to choose a form for pre-coded responses.

VISUAL RESPONSES

Some cognitive, expressive, and perceptual information about respondents' physical surroundings may be better expressed visually rather than verbally, through non–pre-coded techniques, such as freehand area maps, base-map additions, drawings, photographs taken by respondents, and games.

This is especially true for people's *cognitive maps*, the mental pictures of their surroundings that are used to structure the way they look at, react to, and act in their environment (Downs and Stea, 1973; de Jonge, 1962; Ladd, 1970; Lynch, 1960). Although the neurosciences have given us insight into the nature of cognitive mapping, and we know the major role that landmarks play in this cognitive process, one can still envision this continually changing picture as a two-dimensional map or drawing, a three-dimensional model, a hologram, or a file of pictures kept in one's mind. "A cognitive map is not necessarily a 'map'" seen as a flat piece of paper (Downs and Stea, 1973, p. 11). It is more of an ongoing "process . . . by which an individual acquires, codes, stores, recalls, and decodes information about the relative locations and attributes of . . . his every-day spatial environment" (Downs and Stea, 1973, p. 9).

You refer to your cognitive map whenever you deal with an environment. Your map tells you, for example, that if you find yourself in the dining room of a modern, middle-class Western home you have not visited before, one of the doors around you probably leads to the kitchen. You will be surprised if this is not so—if, for example, you find that the kitchen is on the third floor.

It is interesting enough that we can use the idea of implicit mental maps to help design places to be more comprehensible to people. Still more interesting is that cognitive maps only partly correspond to the measurable attributes of environments that might be represented by a street map drawn to scale or an aerial photograph. People's cognitive maps are influenced and distorted by their background, their experience, their purposes, and so on. For example, in a hospital, workers estimated a path outside the building to be twice as long as a path inside the building, although the two were the same distance (Stea, 1974).

If designers know how people who use their environments see these environments, they can better control the side effects of design decisions. In the hospital mentioned above, for example, if the designer knows that outside paths are seen as longer than inside ones, he might make different decisions about enclosing paths so that they are actually seen as alternative routes around the hospital.

There is no one way to study the complex set of perceptions and attitudes that make up a person's cognitive map. Lynch (1960) carried out a ninety-minute focused interview with respondents, one part of which requested them to draw freehand maps of the city. Some of Lynch's respondents were shown a series of photographs of downtown areas and asked to choose those they felt were most typical of the way they saw the city. The volunteers in this group were also interviewed with a walk-through probe (see Chapter 10) of the downtown area. During the trip, interviewers asked respondents why they took a particular path, what they saw, and when they felt confident or lost (Lynch, 1960, pp. 140–142).

The visual-response techniques discussed in this section are essential—used together with verbal responses and observational methods—to study people's attitudes, perceptions, and knowledge concerning physical environments. Broadly defined, people's "cognitive maps" comprise all these mental processes—requiring for their study the same array of methods and techniques.

Freehand Area Maps

Lynch's instructions to respondents were to draw "a quick map of ____. Make it just as if you were making a rapid description of the city to a stranger, covering all the main features. We don't expect an accurate drawing—just a rough sketch" (Lynch, 1960, p. 141). Lynch analyzed the resulting maps for such things as omissions, precision, distortions, and differential knowledge of areas.

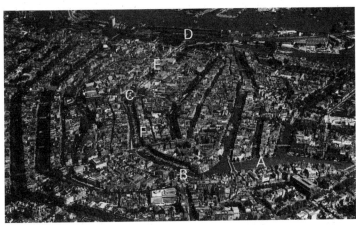

A. Amstel River
B. Mint Square
C. Dam
D. Central Station
E. Damrak
F. Rokin

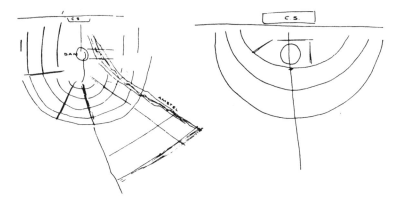

Standardized and freehand area maps of central Amsterdam. (Freehand map from "Images of Urban Areas, Their Structure and Psychological Foundations," by D. de Jonge, *Journal* of the *American Institute of Planners*, 1962, 28, 266–276. Used by permission of the *Journal of the American Planning Association*.)

He also established what is now an extremely useful and influential coding scheme for map responses, which he called "city image elements": paths, edges, districts, nodes, landmarks, and element interrelations.

Lynch's study began a tradition of freehand area-map drawing in interviews, both to develop the method (de Jonge, 1962) and to look at cross-cultural and group differences in maps.

Interpreting area maps has shown that people with limited movement—often poorer people—have detailed knowledge of their immediate neighborhood but only an ill-formed image of the city they live in as a whole (Orleans, 1973) and that children see things differently from adults, and women see things differently from men. For designers, this means that if they want to control the behavioral side effects of places they design, they must understand the ways different groups see them.

Area maps can be used to find out where respondents feel at home, where they are afraid, and where they spend time. Limits on topics are imposed only by investigators' imagination. However, there are unresolved difficulties of interpretation. Some people draw particularly well, while others refuse to draw. Some people can easily draw landmarks only when starting with a base map with major streets already indicated; others do so just as easily on a blank piece of paper. As with all methods, the more area maps are used and the more people that use them, the more we learn about how to turn the data they provide into useful information.

Additions to Base Maps

Providing respondents with simple base maps to fill in answers can be an efficient way to find out how they use or feel about a place: paths they take, things they do in settings, names they use for places. If one wanted to find out, for example, the terms used for rooms in a house, one could give respondents an unlabeled floor plan and ask them to name each space

In their housing-evaluation study, Zeisel and Griffin (1975), wanted to find out how residents moved through the project, particularly how often they passed through a central space planned by the architects to be an active social area. In interviews, the research team presented a completed scale map to respondents and asked them to draw or point out the paths they took on the way to their cars, to the shops, and to the bus stop. These pathway maps were requested instead of verbal descriptions because they seemed more reliable, more accurate, and more expressive of the process of taking a trip.

Maps like these may be quantitatively coded, and they lend themselves particularly well to comparison and visual analysis on composite data maps.

Drawings

Sometimes people's mental images of the future can actually be expressed in a picture. Sanoff and Barbour (1974) worked with an architect commissioned to design a grade school. They were interested in finding out what a "dream

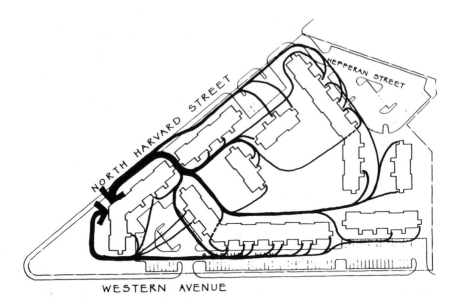

Composite path-map of respondents' trips from home to local store. (From *Charlesview Housing: A Diagnostic Evaluation*, by J. Zeisel and M. Griffin. Cambridge, MA.: Harvard Graduate School of Design, Architecture Research Office, 1975.)

school" was like for students. One approach they used was to ask students involved in the programming research to draw typical African, Japanese, and American schools and their dream school. They found particular contrast between the factory-like drawings of typical American schools and the multi-level, almost "treelike" dream schools. Although this type of response is more abstract and difficult to interpret quantitatively than maps, it can provide investigators with important qualitative insights.

Photographs

Lynch asked respondents to choose typical views of a city from a stack of photographs. This approach can easily be extended to asking respondents to take photographs themselves. An instruction might be to take pictures of "the things you like best in your neighborhood" or of "the things that mean the most to you." Zeisel and Eisenman used this technique in programming and space planning for the *Star Tribune* newsroom, the subject of the case study in Chapter 5.

As with the focused verbal interview, respondents using photographs to answer questions can decide for themselves what is important and what is not. However, this method is not one that can simply be used as one question in an otherwise fully pre-coded questionnaire; it is a separate method in itself.

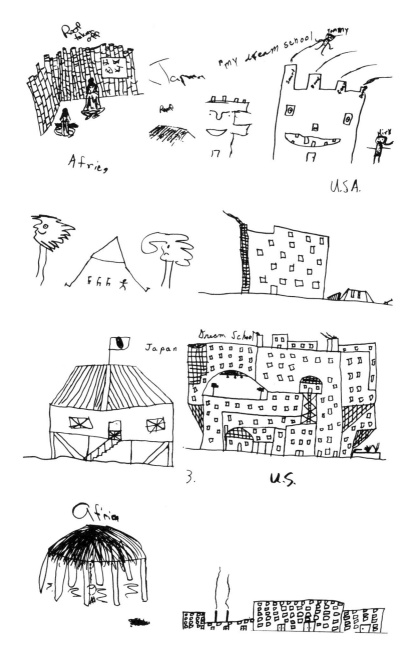

Drawings by children participating in the design charrette for the Wallace O'Neill Alternative School, Pinehurst, North Carolina. (From "An Alternative Strategy for Planning an Alternative School," by H. Sanoff and G. Barbour. In G. T. Coates (Ed.), *Alternative Learning Environments*. Copyright 1974 by Dowden, Hutchinson & Ross, Inc. Used by permission.)

Games

Another way E-B researchers have recorded respondents' ideas has been to develop games through which respondents express themselves by making a series of linked choices (Robinson et al., 1975). One of the oldest such games is Wilson's neighborhood game (1962), in which alternative degrees of attributes such as neighborhood physical quality and sanitation services each have a price tag attached. Respondents are given a set of chips representing the total amount of money they can spend to "buy" the amenities on the game board. With the amount of play money they have, they are forced to choose among attractive alternatives, not all of which they can afford. Their final judgments express not a linear series of individual choices, but a balanced set of simultaneous ones.

Zeisel, in his design programming and evaluation studies of a low-income housing project in South Carolina (1971), and Zeisel and Griffin, in their housing evaluation (1975), developed a Dwelling Unit Floor Plan Game to present respondents with a series of simple design decisions: in which rooms entrances ought to be; how the kitchen should to relate to where you eat; how the kitchen should relate to the living room; how the living room should relate to eating; and balcony location (Zeisel, 1971). Each decision, a choice of three alternatives for separation and connection, is presented in the context of earlier choices. Together they result in an entire floor plan from which respondents' preferences can be interpreted. In addition to composite results, interviewers use the opportunity the game provides to ask respondents why they made each choice, probing to find out what behavioral or cognitive side effects respondents were trying to achieve by making the choice.

Development of Visual-Response Techniques

A catalog of all the non–pre-coded visual-response recording techniques developed and used in E-B interviewing would be very lengthy. To improve the quality and comparability of such techniques, investigators beginning a new project can review relevant literature to identify response, recording, and coding categories useful to their project; test each technique in practice to improve its quality; and report to the larger E-B research community when experiments with new uses of old techniques or entirely new techniques are carried out, to help improve the overall quality of E-B research.

QUESTIONNAIRES UPDATE

Questionnaires, which were traditionally distributed in paper format to individual respondents by mail or in person, are now more frequently distributed through computer networks or on the World Wide Web. In environment-behavior studies, questions in questionnaires have become more sophisticated, analytic techniques more complex, and the use of computers to disseminate questionnaires more pervasive.

Pretty, Chipuer, and Bramston's study in rural Australia (2003) exemplifies how a thoroughly organized research project relying on a well-constructed theory-based questionnaire can result in practical policy information and shed light on theory development and concept construction. Part of a national study of rural life in Australia, Pretty and her colleagues focused on how a person's identification with the place they live affects their decision to stay or move in hard economic times, and how place identity, place attachment, sense of community, and place dependence interrelate.

The research sites were two small towns of under 2,500 residents in the largely uninhabited Outback of southwest Queensland, six hours by car from the nearest city and eight hours from each other. The study sample comprised over 350 adolescents and 250 adults from the two towns. The questionnaire was handed out in schools, community centers, door to door to a selected sample, and by enthusiastic respondents to friends who otherwise would not have been included in the sampling frame.

Agreement or disagreement with a single statement—"I would rather live in a different town. This is not the place for me."—represented the one indicator of the dependent variable *place identity*. Five levels of agreement and disagreement were offered in the closed-ended response. This question and indicators for the other three study concepts were all standardized subscales from the Neighborhood Cohesion Instrument (Buckner, 1988) and the Neighborhood Youth Inventory (Chipuer et al., 1999). A single well-selected and well-constructed question or a short, precise questionnaire has a great deal of data-generating power when used judiciously.

• *Place attachment*, comprising *behavioral commitment* and *emotional bonding*, is measured with two multi-item scales. Behavioral commitment is measured using an eighteen-item multidimensional scale that taps perceptions of sense of community, attraction to neighborhood, and neighboring. The team measured emotional bonding with a twenty-two-item scale "developed from interviews with young people, specifically, to assess adolescents' perceptions of their neighborhood (that has also) been found to have similar psychometric properties for adults" (p. 278).

• *Sense of community* was measured with a ten-item scale indicating a respondent's sense of belonging to the group of people and neighbors in her community. A four-item scale and a single question indicated the last major concept, *place dependence*, comprising the *quality of the community itself as a resource for goal-directed behavior* and the perceptions of that quality *compared* to alternative communities.

Careful construction of each indicator for these concepts, along with thorough planning of sample selection, questionnaire distribution, and analytic techniques provided the researchers the opportunity to state their findings with a high degree of certainty. What were the findings?

> • Adults reported significantly higher levels of sense of community, friends, activity, quality, and quality comparison than young people. There was no difference between adolescents and adults on perceptions of neighboring behavior (p. 279).

- The best predictors for distinguishing those preferring to stay and those wanting to leave are, firstly, the quality aspect of place dependence, secondly the sense of community, and thirdly, the comparative quality aspect of place dependence (p. 281).
- . . . for the adolescents from these rural communities, the overall quality of resources for living in the community, and their sense of belonging to the community have greater potential to protect identity and willingness to stay than indicators of attachment that is emotional bonding the behavioral commitment and activity.
- Focus group participants recruited to interpret and analyze the data with the investigators felt that those who described the quality of community resources as interesting and diverse were mostly men referring to the natural environment and opportunities to fish, hunt, ride, and walk. "Those less satisfied with the community tended to be adolescent girls and female adults" (p. 283).
- The investigators point out that a high degree of place identity among residents is not necessarily positive from a policy point of view.
- From our focus group data the negative consequences of strong community identity are also evident. Several middle-aged residents made the comment that they wished they could leave to enjoy retirement by the sea and younger adult residents preferred to sell the farm and move to more promising jobs elsewhere, but because of elderly family and their own roots, both groups felt they had to stay (p. 285).

Altogether, this study and the one that follows demonstrate how deeply an environment-behavior phenomenon can be understood employing a questionnaire.

Kuo and colleagues carried out two questionnaire-based studies that link green environments to health outcomes (Kuo and Sullivan, 2001; Kuo and Faber Taylor, 2004). Each study delivered the questionnaires in ways that were suited to the particular needs and abilities of their subjects.

Kuo and Sullivan gathered data from a sample of African-American families, mostly women, to determine the relationship between green plantings around public housing buildings, ability to focus, and spousal abuse at Chicago's infamous inner-city Robert Taylor Homes complex. To assure the highest "return rate" the team recruited a group of poor African-American women to administer the questionnaires verbally and in person to a carefully selected sample of the project's residents. After extensive training, the "interviewers" knocked on doors of a random sample of residents living on floors 2, 3, and 4—those who would be closest to the trees around the building. The rate of completion of the questionnaire related to the selected sample was 92 percent. Each respondent received $10 when they answered all the questions.

Because the instrument was administered in person, it could include a standardized neurocognitive interactive memory/stress question and scale. In the Digit Span Backwards test as administered by Cimprich (1993), the administrator reads aloud a series of numbers—"6, 8, 4, 9"—and the respondent repeats them backwards. The length of the longest string correctly repeated after two attempts is considered a measure of capacity for direct attention. Kuo and colleagues found that residents living in buildings with more adjacent green planting exhibited less aggression toward their spouses.

In the other study, comparing the effects of outdoor and indoor activities on Attention Deficit/Hyperactivity Disorder (AD/HD) symptoms among young children, Kuo and Faber Taylor posted their questionnaire on the Internet. The research team directed parents and legal guardians of children with AD/HD to the website through print advertisements in major newspapers across the United States, and through a link to the study placed on the website of the largest interest group of children and adults with Attention Deficit/Hyperactivity Disorder. In order to avoid letting people know that the research was examining outdoor versus indoor activity, the link pointed to "The National Coping with AD/HD Project." Incentives offered to those who responded included a list of recommendations for coping with AD/HD, and for the first 200 participants, a gift certificate to either Amazon.com or Pizza Hut.

During the seven weeks the questionnaire was available on the Internet, 1053 people "hit" the site. After weeding out those who did not fill out the questionnaire (210) and those whose child had not been "professionally diagnosed," 452 completed questionnaires were available for analysis. The final sample represented mostly people with annual incomes over $25,000, covered much of the country, and mostly suburban respondents although larger cities and small rural areas were also represented. In discussion of the study, Kuo points out,

> The Internet enabled us to accumulate a substantial national sample in less than 7 weeks of automated data collection . . . (making it possible) to enable a wide variety of subsample analyses. (p. 96)

This distribution method makes it more difficult to gather data from people who do not have access to Internet connections, such as those "who are poor, the elderly, and recent immigrants." However as major computer and software companies make their products more universally accessible and spread their message more broadly to these groups, limitations to this questionnaire distribution method will be less prevalent. Among respondents to the Internet questionnaire, activities carried out outdoors in green areas with children living with AD/HD were found to have greater therapeutic effects than the same activities in outdoor urban areas, or indoors.

The following case study of the DEGW offices in London represents the elaboration of the questionnaire approach in design, and demonstrates how sophisticated questionnaire data analysis can lead to innovative design responses.

CASE STUDY

REFURBISHMENT AND POST-OCCUPANCY EVALUATION OF DEGW OFFICES
London, U.K.

DEGW, a large London-based architecture, planning, and interiors firm occupies a large part of the old Porters North industrial building on the side of

Battlebridge Basin, part of the Grand Canal system that was used to transport goods and produce to and from the north of England. Before Porters North became an office building it was a beer bottling plant consisting of three linked warehouse-type buildings, each approximately 33 meters deep. The main floor DEGW occupies is just over 1,000 square meters in area with additional space on the ground floor containing shared meeting rooms, a staff canteen and 200 square meters of overflow space.

Founded in 1975 by environment-behavior designer and researcher Frank Duffy and three partners, DEGW occupied the building in 1989, employing the space in a conventional way for design studios, with trestle desks, drawing boards and large-plan chests laid out across the office area. Originally, each "unit" of DEGW had its own space, with filing cabinets and other items of furniture serving as boundaries. Although hierarchy has never been a major issue at DEGW and no one has ever had an enclosed office of their own, at some point the senior directors of the company were moved into a side area of the building behind one of the building cores, effectively creating an "executive area" that limited communication with the rest of the office.

Eight years later, DEGW began to rethink how it was using its space. Like many of its clients, DEGW was concerned that its existing office layout was limiting teamwork and interaction and reinforcing dysfunctional boundaries between groups within the company. In addition, many of the consultants and designers were often absent from the building and it was felt that giving everyone a dedicated desk that would stand empty for a large part of the time was not an effective use of space. DEGW felt it could not responsibly advise clients on how to deal with such problems if they did not themselves solve them.

To identify the key work styles to be accommodated in DEGW's new environment, the company used two analytic tools it also employed with its clients, the Time Utilisation Survey and the Workplace Performance Survey.

• The *Time Utilisation Survey*™ is a method for quickly and cost-effectively obtaining quantitative information about how an office is used. Trained observers using hand-held computers closely monitor specific locations in the building. The data on the number of people and their activities at each location provide an unbiased picture of how the building is used throughout the working day and week.

• The *Workplace Performance Survey*™ questionnaire asks staff for their perceptions of the importance and effectiveness of their office space—how well it supports the work they are doing. Bar charts broken down by group show the average importance and performance of each aspect of the office environment, providing information on the best- and worst-performing items and, in particular, highlighting the performance of those aspects that are most important to each group.

The work styles that resulted at DEGW varied in terms of technology and work setting requirements. Each was given a unique and expressive name:

- Nomad
- Independent
- Manager of Multiple Teams
- Team Resident
- Support

WORK STYLES FOR
NOMADIC WORKERS AT DEGW

The design for the office that resulted from this process included fixed work areas for support staff, long-term assigned spaces for team residents, and a range of bookable and non-bookable spaces for nomads, independents, and the managers of multiple teams; these included a club area, quiet booths, and an Information Technology quiet room for data processing and report writing. Mobile telephones and laptops were provided for all mobile staff and connection points in all work locations allow easy access to the DEGW network.

A year after the refurbishment of the offices was completed, a post-occupancy evaluation (POE) of the new office environment was carried out to determine whether any further improvements were needed. An added practical motive for this review was to inform and improve the change-management strategies DEGW was developing for its clients by reassessing and learning from the experience of introducing new working environments into its own organization (Duffy, 1997; Liang et al., 1998; Myerson, 1998).

The POE project was also seen as an opportunity to review the effectiveness of DEGW's standard POE methodologies: the Time Utilization Study and the Workplace Performance Study. In parallel with the use of these tools,

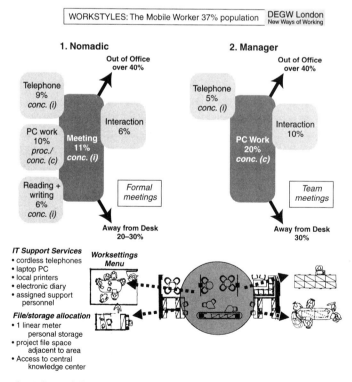

Work styles: The mobile worker.

Left: The club.
Right: Hub—touch-down zone.

DEGW commissioned its sister company, Marketing Improvements plc, to carry out an independent assessment of the office using its own methodologies. The objectives for the POE study were to:

- Assess the new workplace together with business systems and processes
- Identify staff perceptions of the strengths and benefits of the new workplace as well as any weaknesses or problem areas
- Determine any areas that needed improvement
- Clarify staff attitudes, perceptions, and values regarding the workplace

An additional objective was to determine whether Marketing Improvements' POE methodology could be developed as a standard POE "product" to be used on other projects with DEGW clients. This alternative POE methodology consisted of individual staff interviews (eleven were carried out, covering most types of staff), structured walks around the office taking photographs, and a three-hour focus-group interview with each of the following groups of employees:

- Nomads and managers of teams
- Independents
- Support/administrative staff
- Team residents

The POE study conclusions indicated further problems to solve, the mixed impact of refurbishment, and the intended success of the project:

- Employees experienced the refurbishment process as very disruptive and there was a perception among staff of not being consulted or listened to adequately. This was partly because the refurbishment was carried out in phases, with staff having to move repeatedly as the construction progressed.
- Since the refurbishment, patterns of work have changed throughout the office, and some people felt that the changes suited DEGW's consultants more than its designers.
- The new office layout complemented and reinforced the organizational changes that were occurring simultaneously—the abandonment DEGW's "unit"-based structure.

- The office very clearly achieved its image objectives in terms of exemplifying DEGW's beliefs about the work environment.
- Most staff felt more motivated, inspired, and comfortable in the new office layout than they had before the refurbishment.
- The new layout did not provide designers with all the tools and equipment they need: drawing boards, CAD computers, space for samples, and layout/pin-up space for large drawings.
- Support staff sometimes found it difficult to locate employees they needed to contact, as they could be sitting anywhere in the building. The initial overuse of voicemail made this situation worse as it meant people were often not even contactable by telephone.
- Overall communication in the office had improved, with nomads and independents in particular using the central club area for informal communication.

The POE identified that many of the early post-refurbishment dissatisfactions with the office layout appeared to be directly related to technology issues. During the refurbishment mobile phones were introduced into the office, computers were switched from Macintoshes to PCs, a new networking system was installed, and automatic voicemail answering of unanswered calls was added. As technology skills increased among employees, many of these problems resolved themselves naturally. But a change in policy on voicemail was needed to respond to client concerns that senior staff, in particular, were becoming increasingly difficult to contact directly. Partners telephones were reprogrammed so that during the day, unanswered calls were transferred to support staff rather than voicemail. Support staff also worked as a team to answer telephone queries, using voicemail only outside of office hours.

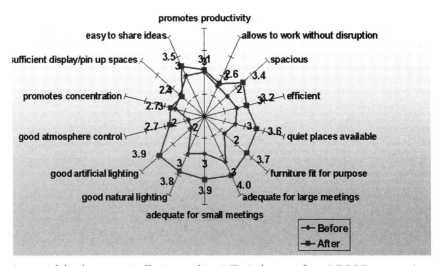

Impact of the changes on "effective working." Typical output from MI POE presentation.

One of the most interesting findings of the POE project was that space was generally used differently from how it was planned. Plans were made assuming that mobile staff would move from work area to work area during the day as their work tasks changed. However the POE showed that most employees set up a "home base" when they first arrive in the office and connect their computers to the network there. From their new "home base," they move to other work locations for ad hoc meetings or leave the office for other meetings, returning periodically to check e-mail and pick up papers. While a number of "touchdown" spaces were provided for this type of usage, the pattern of space use has proven more common than expected.

Unanticipated growth in the number of DEGW staff was responsible for some problems with the new layout which was designed to cope with growth from seventy-five to a maximum of ninety-five staff in the London office. By the time the POE was undertaken, there were more than 120 staff based in the office, and by 2000 there were 135 staff. As a result, expanded project teams "invaded" team layout areas and bookable work areas for "independents." This in turn has put pressure on non-bookable spaces such as the club, quiet booths, and the knowledge center. The increased number of staff has also been a problem for housekeeping; a number of office-wide cleanups were necessary to reduce the amount of unofficial storage in work areas.

One of the impressive qualities of the new office is the way it has accommodated such an unanticipated increase in staff without seriously reducing productivity and quality of work. Nevertheless, the problems the POE uncovered could only be solved by adding new space in the building, allowing the reintroduction of bookable areas for "independents" and providing additional "touchdown" spaces.

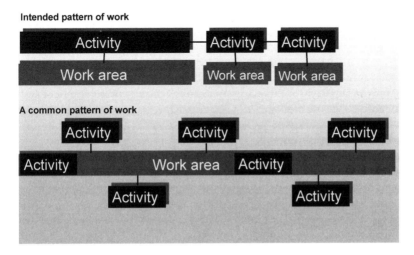

Planned and actual work patterns.

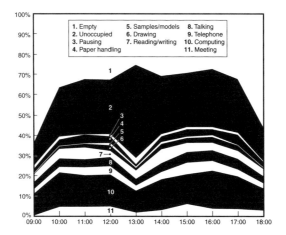

1999 Daily Activity Plan for DEGW First-floor Spaces.

The DEGW post-occupancy evaluation presented the design firm with new challenges in the development of its own study methodologies. While the Time Utilization Survey demonstrated itself as a valuable tool to identify how different types of spaces in the office are used over the working day, in the new type of working environment DEGW has created, it cannot identify the work styles (daily working patterns) of different employee groups. Moreover, mobile furniture and flexible workspaces cause recording difficulties for the observers, who rely on fixed space and objects for repeated observation. While in more conventional offices the norm is for a single activity to be carried out in a single space, now a single space often accommodates a variety of independent and group activities. DEGW used this experience to investigate and develop new means of assessing work styles, for example, using radio transmitters to track movement between work settings.

The Workplace Performance Survey captured the key dimensions of change and staff attitudes and, as already mentioned, similar results were obtained by Marketing Improvements' focus-group based POE methodology. The comparison demonstrated one advantage of the Workplace Performance Survey to DEGW, namely that it is less time-consuming for individuals (twenty minutes to complete the questionnaire compared with three hours for a workshop). On the other hand, the graphic display of the results of the Marketing Improvements' study had more visual impact and appeal. DEGW's

Methodology Group used this finding to develop better ways to display the complex Workplace Performance Survey data.

The POE process clearly identified both the successes and shortcomings of the current office layout, and the shortcomings have been rectified where possible. For example, pin-up boards have been installed in project areas and more display space was provided in other areas as well. Guidelines for the use of "touchdown" spaces and quiet booths were developed to encourage people to use only one space at a time. However, many of the more serious problems relating to the overcrowding could only be resolved by taking on additional space in the building.

By employing an evidence-based research approach to its planning process, DEGW determined that without doubt, the new office layout has changed the way it works. More importantly, research enabled planners to understand the effects and side effects of their decisions: team working has increased, communication within the office has improved, and project groups were able to form, evolve, and disband much more easily as the projects in the office changed. All office environments are dynamic and DEGW evolved the design of its own office to better meet the changing needs of its organization. The refurbishment process and the introduction of New Ways of Working has also been an invaluable experience for DEGW, helping it to understand the complexities of the organizational change process that must accompany changes to the physical work environment and work processes if they are to be effective.

This case study is based on the work of DEGW plc, London, U.K. with Francis Duffy, RIBA.

OVERVIEW

Standardized questionnaires are useful if you know what you want to learn from people, if you want to discover regularities among groups of people with particular characteristics, and if you want to be able to quantify your data.

After discussing how to organize questions in a questionnaire so that it establishes a non-defensive, open interview situation, this chapter presents ways to record responses to standardized questions. Open-ended responses can be coded for analysis into mutually exclusive, exhaustive categories at a single level of abstraction. The same criteria for coding categories may be used to pre-code response categories if the investigator has developed the categories empirically to be sure they fit respondents' definitions of the situation and enable respondents to express themselves adequately on the topic. Otherwise, the control exerted by using an intrusive method, such as a questionnaire, distorts data and makes them worthless.

Visual data are difficult to pre-code. Response categories for such data include visual presentations by respondents of freehand maps, additions to base maps, drawings, photographs, and games. The visual character of such data makes them available for both quantitative analysis and qualitative visual presentation on composite maps or charts.

Used together with observation methods and focused interviewing, standardized questionnaires are particularly useful to gather information about topics such as people's perceptions, their attitudes, their values, and the meaning the environment holds for them.

The next chapter presents E-B topics that are particularly suited to questionnaire and interview investigation and discusses some rules of thumb for asking questions.

CHAPTER 12

ASKING QUESTIONS: TOPICS AND FORMAT

The quality of interview and questionnaire data rests heavily on whether questions address topics that are salient to respondents and to the researchers' purpose and whether questions are asked so that answers may be understood clearly. This chapter first analyzes topics listed below, which are particularly relevant in environment-behavior research.

Topics
Actual and Abstract Environments
Physical
Administrative
Behavioral
People's Responses
Seeing
Feeling
Doing in
Doing to
Knowing
Linking and Using the Categories
The question matrix

Format
Simplicity
Can respondents understand questions?
Precision
Can we assume that respondents understand questions in similar ways?
Neutrality
Do questions avoid implicitly influencing the direction of respondents' answers?

Then the chapter describes how using several straightforward rules of thumb for asking questions (listed below) can improve a researcher's ability to compare answers.

TOPICS

Whether E-B researchers use interviews focused on an individual's definition of the situation or questionnaires that standardize an inquiry over people, they want to know how people respond to environments. Questions are asked to find out what people can verbalize and otherwise express about themselves in their surroundings.

One way to approach the question of what to ask is to consider what we might want to do with the data. We may, for example, want to effect changes in environments. We may also want to increase the visibility of possible side effects such changes have on people. Environment-behavior research illuminates both these purposes simultaneously, showing the interrelationship between environment and people. Table 12-1 gives an overview of the complex relationships between various types of environments and people's responses to them.

Actual and Abstract Environments

Environments to which people react include those they actually experience daily—places of work, homes, transportation, open spaces for play. Their reactions to these settings affect their behavior not only in those particular settings but in others as well, as when a train ride to work makes riders tense, which in turn affects their performance at work. Past experience in environments also affects behavior—for example, the place where you were brought up or a street you used to know. Even if memories of past settings are gilded or perceptions of present ones distorted, the environments themselves are or were actual ones.

People also change the way they behave in the light of their mental images of future environments that they plan to be in and ideal ones they dream about.

To understand how people relate to environments and be able to make design decisions about those settings while controlling behavioral side effects, we want to know how people respond to both abstract and actual environments.

Physical, Administrative, and Behavioral Environments

To make decisions about a setting and improve our understanding of side effects decisions have on people, we must speak of environments as more than physical settings. We must also take into account the behavioral and administrative contexts that surround people in a setting.

Environments

Physical

Objects
Places
Relations between places
Qualities

Administrative

Formal rules
Informal rules

Behavioral

Characteristics of people
Activities
Relationships between people

A corner delicatessen, for example, is a physical setting in which there may be such things as a sandwich counter with two sides, several small tables and chairs, a checkout counter where money is exchanged, a magazine rack, shelves of canned goods and toiletries, and a glass storefront with a sign over it. A delicatessen also comprises an administrative environment: There are rules about who may go behind the counter or take things off shelves, whether people handling food must wear plastic gloves, and whether local schoolchildren are allowed into the store during school hours. Changes in either of these environments will necessarily have side effects on the other.

Of course, both physical and administrative environments are related to the behavioral environment, which is defined by the types of people who frequent the delicatessen, their familiarity with salespersons, whether kids and adults can comfortably hang around to read comic books and magazines and whether teenagers hang around outside the front entrance.

To be able to act on environments with greater awareness and control of side effects, it is useful to distinguish among elements of physical, administrative, and behavioral environments. Understanding each separately improves our knowledge of how they relate to one another in an E-B system.

- *Physical environments* include objects in a setting; *places*, such as street corners, tot lots, rooms, and stairwells; *relations between places* created by such things as walls, distance, windows, barriers, adjacencies; and *qualities* of the setting, such as light and sound.
- *Administrative environments* include *formal* rules governing such things as use of a setting, contractual arrangements for use, and required entry procedures. Also included are *informal* rules about, for instance, what it is appropriate or inappropriate to do there and when it is all right to break rules.
- *Behavioral environments* include *characteristics of people* there (both individuals and groups), their *activities* there, and *relationships* between people.

People's Responses to Environments

Environments and changes to environments affect what people do. How people see and interpret their surroundings mediates environmental effects. Effects also are tempered by experiences people have had with past surroundings and their intentions for future ones. Hence, the more you know about how people see environments and what they know about environments, the more you will

---

People's Responses to Environments

What They See in Environments

    Perception
    Meaning

What They Feel about Environments

    Opinion
    Value

What They Do in Environments

    Place
    Path
    Relation

What They Do to Environments

    Adaptations
    Displays
    Messages

What They Know about Environments

    Knowledge
    Data

understand their behavioral, emotional, and cognitive reactions to them.

• *What people see in environments.* People make sense of their surroundings by observing them with all their senses and then organizing, interpreting, and giving meaning to what they observe. This interpretation in turn has consequences for what people do in an environment and what they do to it. The better designers understand this process, the better they are able to understand the side effects of environmental design decisions they make. The better E-B researchers understand what sense people make of their surroundings and how they do so, the better researchers can interpret other people's behavior.

Making sense of environment is a process of *perception*: the way people select and organize what they are aware of in a situation through all their senses (Goodey, 1971, pp. 2–3; Theodorson and Theodorson, 1970, p. 295). People's interpretation of what they perceive is its meaning to them. The ascribed meaning of things that often holds unforeseen consequences for people making decisions about environments is what linguists call *connotative meaning.* Connotative meanings reflect the personal associations things call up, and the emotionally toned inferences that are drawn (Manis, 1966; Theodorson and Theodorson, 1970). The connotative meaning of an object can be distinguished from the explicit, "dictionary" *denotative meaning.*

The meanings of and difference between perception and meaning are apparent in the following statements:

> *Perception:* "Streets in European cities appear to be cleaner than streets in U.S. cities."

> *Meaning:* "When people sit on the front steps of their house, it means they are lower-class."

• *What people feel about environments.* The attitudes people hold toward an object, person, situation, or environment—the way they evaluate it—influence how they respond to it. Environment-behavior researchers therefore ask questions to discover people's *opinions* about things: conscious verbal expressions of their feelings about particular places, objects, persons, or events. Underlying opinions about things are people's *values*: commitments to larger, abstract ideals (Theodorson and Theodorson, 1970).

> *Opinion:* "The rules in this factory about work assignments are unfair."

> *Value:* "It is a bad thing to have too many rules for children in a kindergarten."

• *What people do in environments.* Observing behavior tells you about what you see people doing—externalized activities and their externalized consequences. Asking people questions about their environmental behavior tells you other essential things, such as what effects they expect their actions to have, what they intended to do but never did, and what they still intend to do. Asking people questions about what they do may be useful to augment direct observation of behavior, especially when the activities studied are infrequent ones, when investigators only want to know about certain activities of

Table 12-1. **E-B questions: Illustrative examples**

		Present and Past Actual Environments	
	Physical	*Administrative*	*Behavioral*
		SEES	
Meaning — Perception	Streets in European cities seem cleaner than streets in U.S. cities.	Around here, everyone is really free to do as he or she likes.	Most people who use this park seem to take care of it.
Meaning — Meaning	The glass and steel in this building make it seem like a factory.	The many signs in this park make it seem like a prison yard.	When my neighbors sit on their front stoop, they make the neighborhood lower-class.
		FEELS	
Value — Opinion	I like the colonial-style house we have.	The rules in this factory are unfair.	The new residents here are making a mess of the place.
Value — Value	*Does Not Apply:* Values applied to actual environments are opinions		
		DOES IN	
People's Responses — Place	My family usually eats dinner at the kitchen table.	No one in this office obeys the rule about no smoking at one's desk.	The secretaries all take a coffee break at 10 o'clock.
People's Responses — Path	Going to the store, I jump over the fence and run down an alley.	Residents in this home for retarded adults aren't allowed to go to their bedrooms during days.	Visitors tend to get lost when they first come to this building.
People's Responses — Relation	I sit on the front porch so I can watch people go by and can say hello.	People here are expected not to bother each other when they're working.	My neighbor drops by to chat at least once a day.
		DOES TO	
Adaptation	I cannot finish my basement as a playroom because it costs too much.	If you change your apartment at all, you have to return it to the original condition when you move.	Nobody can look into my living room now that I've planted bushes in the yard.
Display	I put all my diplomas on the wall only because there was no room in the closet.	You are not allowed to pin up or tape posters to the wall in this dorm room.	All anyone has to do is look at our souvenirs to know we travel a lot.
Message	When my cat ran away, I pasted reward posters on lampposts all over the neighborhood.	The police don't mind if you put posters up on windows of vacant stores.	While people wait for their Xeroxing, they usually read messages on the wall.
		KNOWS	
Knowledge	I think this park was designed by Frederick Law Olmsted.	I think people are not allowed to bring dogs into this building.	Approximately 300 people work in this hospital, I think.
Data	There are 3 rooms and a bath in this house.	There is a 24-hour doorman in this building.	I am 33 years old and have one child.

Table 12-1.(cont.)

Ideal and Future Abstract Environments

	Physical	Administrative	Behavioral
		SEES	
Meaning — Perception	*Does Not Apply:* Perception of abstract environments does not occur		
Meaning	If a house is made of brick, it means it is well built.	Strict teachers teach well.	Men who hang around street corners are just there to bother others.
		FEELS	
People's Responses — Opinion	The new sports facility will be really comfortable.	Adventure playgrounds probably stimulate children's imagination more than regular ones.	It's nice when people from different backgrounds live together.
Value	Buildings are better if designed to fit visually into their context.	Too many rules for schoolchildren is a bad thing.	People living in single-family houses are better than apartment-dwellers.
		DOES IN	
Place	My ideal house would have a special room for smoking cigars.	In good playgrounds there are no rules about what kids can and cannot do.	In progressive schools, dormitory bathrooms are all coeducational.
Path	At a well planned university campus people in wheelchairs can get into every building and room.	Ideally, street signs keep tourists from driving through residential areas.	Crowds in hallways can be a hazard to getting out if there is a fire.
Relation	In modern jury rooms everyone can see and hear each other easily.	In high-income areas people frown on too much dropping in.	I would choose to live in a place where people look after each other's unoccupied houses.
		DOES TO	
Adaptation	In any new house I would want to build a pigeon coop.	I hope they won't enact any laws against keeping pigeons in your home.	People generally don't have the skill to make their own home improvements.
Display	It is hard to put up pictures on walls in houses with concrete walls.	If I painted my name on the door, I'd probably be fined by my boss.	When I buy a new car, I want everyone to see it in my driveway.
Message	In elevator buildings you usually have a ready-made place to leave notices—the elevator.	I wish the city would make a law against people who write political graffiti on public walls.	People get to know about their neighbors when they read "lost dog" and "for sale" notices.
		KNOWS	
Knowledge	It is impossible to build a house out of concrete.	Next year's tax bill will allow deductions for energy-saving insulation.	The new subway stop should be completed in two years.
Data	The next house I buy will have wall-to-wall carpets.	Next year I am going to develop a tight budget for running this household.	My mother will be coming to visit over Christmas.

a great number of people, and when the activities of interest are non-illicit behaviors in private settings that are inaccessible to investigators. Comparing observational data with interview data about the same activity provides investigators with information that is unavailable when using only one method: the relation between a person's conscious perception of himself and its external expression.

To make informed design decisions that separate and connect a set of places, it is useful to distinguish *place* activities, which are situated in one bounded physical setting, from *path* activity, that is aimed at getting from one place to another and finding one's way. For the same design purpose it is useful to ask people about their *relations* to others when they do something.

> *Place:* "When friends drop by in the evening, we usually sit around the kitchen table."

> *Path:* "Visitors tend to get lost when they first try to find their way around this building."

> *Relation:* "Whenever my daughter wants privacy on the telephone, she takes the phone into the bathroom and closes the door."

• *What people do to environments.* Observing physical traces tells you something about actual changes people have made to their surroundings. Asking questions about the same topic tells you about unfulfilled desires to make changes; while you see a solid wall, you find out that someone would like to build a pass-through between the kitchen and living room but does not because the separating wall contains the plumbing or because the project seems too expensive. Questions tell you about the intended effects someone had in mind when making adaptations. Questions tell you about expectations for future adaptations and the conscious reasoning behind past displays of self.

In the same way that reports of behavior in environments can be usefully compared with observations, reports about what a person does to his surroundings may be usefully compared with observations of physical traces. Questions about environmental change can be grouped into the same categories as observation of changes: adaptations, displays of self, and public messages. The same subsections for each of these categories also hold (see Chapter 10).

> *Adaptations:* "If the room were bigger, I would build a wall between the living room and dining area."

> *Displays:* "I put that bronze American eagle over my front door because it lets other people know I love this country."

> *Messages*: "If I wanted to buy a used sofa, I would look first at the notices on the window at the corner Laundromat."

• *What people know about environments.* One reason to ask someone questions about her surroundings and herself is to assess what she knows—to assess her *knowledge.* Knowledge questions inquire how much respondents know about a situation, how they found out about an event, what they think occurred. To interpret the answers—to assess someone's knowledge—it is helpful to have used other methods to observe and find out about what happened.

Another reason to ask such questions is to ascertain which *data* the respondent has and which are more efficient to ask about rather than using other methods to learn—for example, the availability of different types of public transportation. This topic area also includes what are generally called *demographic data*, such as a respondent's residential history, marital status, family size, age, and other personal characteristics.

Knowledge: "I think that they close the gates to the park at sunset."

Data: "My parents were brought up on a farm in Kentucky."

Linking and Using the Categories

The matrix of topics in Table 12-1 shows how environmental concerns can be linked by questions to people's responses. Each box in the matrix represents a potential link between environment and behavior. For each link an illustrative statement is presented to convey concisely what is meant by the intersection of categories.

You can use this list of topics as part of a focused interview guide to probe respondents' definition of a situation. You could use this system of categories like scissors to help cut out the picture of what people have in mind. If your goal is to find out about groups or types of people without focusing on individuals, you might use the categories outlined here to suggest possible questions. You would generate those questions you thought would be most useful in solving your particular problem.

FORMAT

If you want to compare answers to the same questions from different respondents, respondents must understand the questions, they must understand them in the same way, and questions must not unwittingly influence the direction of respondents' answers (Payne, 1951). Simple, precise, and neutral questions achieve these ends. The nine pitfalls listed in Table 12-2 frequently stand in the way of simplicity, precision, and neutrality.

In writing and asking interview questions these rules of thumb can help both experienced and inexperienced researchers avoid invalid or unreliable questions. But, like many such rules, they cannot ensure that all questions will cut through irrelevant concerns to focus on important concepts. This ability lies with researchers' skill and with their having enough personal insight to apply the rules strictly where necessary and to bend them when useful.

Be Simple

Avoid double-barreled questions. Frequently researchers think they are offering respondents alternative response categories when they are actually combining two questions into one. An example is this discarded question from the Howell and Epp survey (1976):

> *Qu*: Do you ever see people on your floor whom you don't recognize or who don't seem to live here?
>
> Yes ❑   No ❑

A respondent might answer yes because he sees people all the time whom he does not recognize due to poor vision and has lived in the building only a short time. Another respondent might answer yes referring only to the second part of the question, meaning that she sees people on her floor whom she recognizes as children from the surrounding neighborhood (who come into the building through the unlocked fire-exit door). These two "yes" answers would actually be answers to two separate questions.

Table 12-2. **Rules of thumb for asking questions**

Purpose	*Pitfalls to Avoid*
So that respondents understand questions	Overcomplexity: • Double-barreled questions • Words and phrases outside respondents' experience • Questions assuming knowledge respondents might not have
So that different respondents understand questions in the same way	Imprecision: • Complicated words with multiple meanings • Simple words with implicit double meanings • Questions about general times and places rather than specific ones
So that questions do not unwittingly influence the direction of respondents' answers	Loading: • One-sided alternatives • Emotionally charged words • Embarrassing answers

There are several strategies to correct double-barreled questions. First, you can simply ask two single-barreled questions:

> *Qu*: Do you ever see people on your floor whom you don't recognize?
>
> Yes ❑   No ❑
>
> *Qu*: Do you ever see people on your floor who don't seem to live here?
>
> Yes ❑   No ❑

Second, you can separate the double-barreled question into one question with follow-up questions:

Qu: Do you ever see people on your floor whom you don't recognize?

Yes ❑   No ❑

(If "yes," ask:)

Qu: Why is this? Is it because
1 — They do not seem to live here?
2 — You know only a few people in the building?
3 — The light on the floor is not strong enough?
4 — ....
5 — ....

Data obtained using double-barreled questions are worthless because they are virtually impossible to analyze.

• *Use words and phrases within respondents' experience.* First, this means that researchers must not use jargon. Professionals in environmental design and research often use terms that have little or no meaning to most people, such as *layout*, *ambiance*, *facade*, and *cluster*. Questions including these words or concepts may elicit misleading responses:

Qu: If you could suggest to the designer changes in the layout of apartments like this, what would you suggest?

None, I like it just as it is —— 1

Suggestions to be coded —— 2

Probing respondents in a pretest will likely show that many of those who say, "I like it just as it is" are actually saying that they do not know what the word *layout* means. Sometimes the word can be replaced by an explanatory phrase: "*Layout* means the way the rooms are arranged" or "*Ambiance* means

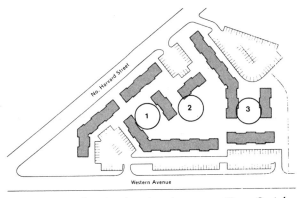

Site plan of Charlesview, showing three interior courts. (From *Sociology* and *Architectural Design*, by John Zeisel. © 1975 by the Russell Sage Foundation, New York. Reprinted by permission.)

the way the place feels to you." But as often as not such phrases will be as confusing to respondents as the original terms, not because they do not understand the words but because the sentiment expressed by the phrase is outside the respondents' cognitive experience.

Two blatant examples will be instructive. In a study of family housing (Zeisel and Griffin, 1975), researchers tried to find out whether residents noticed or could identify that the architect had planned the buildings to create three interior courts in the project, as illustrated below. They asked the following question:

> *Qu*: Do you think the buildings in Charlesview are grouped together in any way?

Most respondents registered confusion to this question, answering, "I don't know." One interpretation of this result is that the architect's intention of clustering was not achieved, but an equally valid interpretation is that the phrase "buildings grouped together in any way" was beyond residents' conscious experience and that they did not understand what was being asked of them.

In this case the researchers might have been better able to clarify what they wanted by asking an open-ended question and recording whether residents spontaneously mentioned the planned space:

> *Qu*: How would you describe to a friend the arrangement of buildings in Charlesview?

Researchers might also have explained the architect's intent to residents using drawings, and asked for their reaction.

Another question in the Howell and Epp study (1976), which was pretested and later dropped, aimed to find out whether older residents felt disoriented if they had no view of the outside when they stepped off the elevator onto their floor. The question included phrases asking respondents to think in unfamiliar ways :

> *Qu*: When you get out of the elevator on your floor, do you ever feel as if you are closed up inside the building or don't know where the front is?

This example also shows that it is not easy to ask questions about complex environmental design phenomena.

- *Do not assume respondents have much information.* If a question requires information available only to some respondents, the answers will not reflect informed opinions. Answers will reflect an indistinguishable mixture of opinion and amount of knowledge. For example, researchers might ask housing residents:

> *Qu*: Do you feel that the amount of money being spent on grounds maintenance ought to
>
> be increased? ☐ be decreased? ☐ remain the same? ☐

This is a fair question if it reflects resident attitudes toward quality of maintenance. If, however, an increase in the maintenance budget would require an increase in rents, then the question has an altogether different meaning. Confusion occurs if only a portion of the respondents know the connection between rents and maintenance costs.

Sometimes researchers try to overcome this difficulty by using a short introduction to provide an informational frame of reference for respondents:

> *Qu*: Management says that if grounds maintenance costs increase, they will have to raise rents. Given this possibility, do you feel . . .

Although such introductions begin to resolve the confusion, researchers must avoid creating additional confusion by providing only a partial frame of reference that does not fully close the knowledge gap between respondents. For example, if some informed residents know that the rent increase would be on the order of 50 cents a month, their answers to the question will not be comparable to those of residents who think the researchers' introduction means larger rent increases.

Be Precise

• *Avoid complicated words with multiple meanings.* We often use words that can be understood in various ways. Words such as *territory, privacy, satisfaction*, and *bother* mean different things to different people. To some, *privacy* means being able to be alone if one wishes. To others, it means not being overheard or seen by others—even by neighbors through thin walls. To still others, it means avoiding being the topic of neighborhood gossip. Because of these differences, researchers will have difficulty analyzing answers to the following question:

> *Qu*: Do you have enough privacy in your backyard?

The main point to remember in using this rule of thumb is that one can best compare answers to questions if respondents have generally understood the questions in the same way. This problem does not occur only with complicated words; seemingly simple words can have multiple meanings as well.

• *Explicitly define even simple terms.* Older residents were asked the following question in a pretest:

> *Qu*: Do you find the trip from the building's front door to your apartment to be too long a trip?

The question was discarded because although many residents answered yes, they showed by their verbal elaboration that they interpreted the term *too long* in two ways: (1) too far to carry groceries and heavy objects and (2) too long for people in wheelchairs and walkers because the ramp in the lobby is too difficult.

In reformulating this question, the researchers might have explained:

> *Qu*: Do you ever get tired going from the building's front door to your apartment because one is so far from the other, just in terms of distance?

One could then follow up with specific questions on whether barriers present special difficulties and whether there are special conditions, such as carrying groceries, which make a trip strenuous that is otherwise not tiring.

In E-B research there are some typical terms that seem precise but often prove to be more complicated. *Eating* may mean eating breakfast, lunch, dinner, or snacks; or eating alone, with family members, or with friends. *Talking* may mean chatting, having a deep private conversation, or just hanging out. *Food shopping* may mean going to the store daily for a loaf of bread and quart of milk or doing weekly grocery shopping. *Children's safety* may mean safety from car traffic, from bigger children, from dangerous play equipment, or from child molesters. This list could go on and on, but the point is made. Even simple concepts have several dimensions, and researchers must use phrases that describe most precisely which phenomenon they are interested in.

• *Be specific about time and place.* If researchers want to find out how often or where respondents do something, there are several types of questions they can ask. As a rule, the more specific are the response categories and the event being queried, the more likely respondents will be able to answer the questions and the more likely are the answers to be comparable. A common type of question asks:

Qu: How many machine loads do you wash each month at the Laundromat?

Such questions often elicit a high proportion of "don't know" responses, not because respondents have no idea of the answer but because they do not know how to figure out the answer precisely. They do not usually think about Laundromat use in terms of months. In such cases researchers can help them by asking two separate and more precise questions, each of which takes the pressure of precision off the respondent by asking only for an approximation.

Qu: About how often do you use the Laundromat?

❑ More than once a day
❑ Once a day
❑ About every other day
❑ Once a week
❑ Less than once a week

Qu: When you use the Laundromat, generally how many loads of laundry do you wash each time?

❑ One   ❑ Three
❑ Two   ❑ Four or more

This series of questions helps respondents calculate monthly loads and provides researchers with additional information about frequency of use. Introducing such questions with words like *about* allays respondents' fears about not having precisely the right answer and thereby reduces the number of "don't know" answers. Another way to make such questions more precise is to ask about specific recent events at specific times.

Qu: Yesterday, did you pass by or go into the following rooms:

	Pass by	Go into
Recreation room	❏ Yes ❏ No	❏ Yes ❏ No
Pool room	❏ Yes ❏ No	❏ Yes ❏ No
Sitting room	❏ Yes ❏ No	❏ Yes ❏ No

Questions put this way are more likely to be understood than those asking respondents to report whether they frequently, sometimes, or seldom use a place. More important, responses will be more comparable because it is not up to respondents to interpret "frequently, sometimes, or seldom."

The same rules of thumb about specificity apply to questions about place. To avoid misunderstandings in analysis, it is always more fruitful to ask about specific rooms, street corners, or events than to construct a general question.

Be Neutral

• *Avoid one-sided questions.* It is essential that researchers not "lead" respondents, as television lawyers sometimes do, by asking respondents to agree or disagree with only one side of an issue:

Qu: Do you think this place is a good place to raise children?

Yes ❏   No ❏

Qu: In the project at night, is the outside lighting too low?

Yes ❏   No ❏

Such questions tend to pressure respondents to answer in the affirmative because it is the easiest answer to give. They choose the most convenient alternative explicitly offered them, rather than choosing one of several implied alternatives that would put them in the position of contradicting the questioner. Researchers analyzing answers to such questions would have difficulty distinguishing between "yes" answers from people who felt strongly that the environment was a good place to raise children or that the lighting was too low and "yes" answers from respondents who merely felt this was the "correct" response.

In the actual survey (Saile et al., 1972), researchers avoided one-sided questions by making alternatives explicit:

Qu: Do you think this place is *better* than most places to raise children, is it *worse*, or is it *about the same* as anyplace else?

Qu: In the project at night, is the outside lighting *too bright, about right*, or *not bright enough*?

•. *Avoid emotionally charged words.* Blatant stereotypes implied in questions obviously sway respondents in their answers. Asking school principals about "vandals" or nurses about "chronic complainers" arouses emotions that almost certainly take respondents outside the frame of reference of the question. Cautious researchers can avoid this pitfall by describing people, situations, and places in simple, less inflammatory words: "people who knowingly damage property," "patients who complain a lot."

This pitfall can subtly trap even cautious researchers when they are interviewing people for whom quite normal, seemingly neutral terms are loaded with meaning. This usually happens, for example, when asking questions about "teenagers," unless the respondents happen to be teenagers. Researchers Howell and Epp (1976) found a similar situation in their study on older tenants' use of certain shared spaces in buildings. They wanted to find out whether residents knew that these common areas were sometimes used for activities in which both the building residents and older residents of nearby buildings participated, such as Bingo, federally financed meal programs, or meetings of neighborhood senior citizens' clubs. The researchers asked:

> *Qu*: Are there ever activities in the community room to which people from the neighborhood are invited along with the people who live here?

Although the investigators knew such programs were carried out there, they found that over 50 percent of residents in all four buildings studied reported no such shared programs. On further probing in the pretest, the researchers found that there had been several disputes over who controlled the shared spaces—residents or the public housing authority. To residents, the term *people from the neighborhood* raised the specter of "public events" attended by strangers of all ages at the invitation of management. When such hidden stereotypes are not discovered through either pretests or thoughtful analysis of questions, they can invalidate crucial questions during later analysis.

• *Avoid embarrassing answers.* Respondents tend to avoid giving answers that they feel put them in a bad light, especially in face-to-face interviews. As with emotionally charged words, it is particularly difficult to avoid this problem in its subtle forms. People are embarrassed by the strangest things!

The best-known example of this problem comes from political polling. After an election, when pollsters ask a random cross-section of the population who they voted for for president, a higher percentage always say they voted for the winner than actually did (H. Zeisel, 1968, p. 202). The difference comprises people who are embarrassed to admit they voted for the loser and those who want to be seen as winners. There are many possibilities for such problems to arise in E-B research. Researchers trying to find out whether color-coded walls on different floors help older residents find their way asked:

> *Qu*: Have you ever gotten off the elevator on the wrong floor?

Although many residents admitted having done so, there is no way to tell how many said they had not because they felt it would be admitting absent-mindedness or the onset of Alzheimer's.

The same is true for persons who are embarrassed to admit that they usually use the back (kitchen) door instead of the formal front door, which they know a professional architect planned for them to use. Well-to-do respondents may have the same reaction to questions about income because they are embarrassed that they make so much money.

When researchers realize they might run into such problems, they can provide a face-saving way out within the question itself:

> *Qu*: In many buildings it is difficult for people of all ages to find their way and even to recognize the floor they want. Have you ever gotten off the elevator on the wrong floor of this building?

> *Qu*: Many people living in apartments tend to use the back door most often, while others use the front door. Which door do you tend to use most often when you are going out to the store?

Interviewers may also reduce embarrassment by handing respondents a card on which answers are labeled with letters. Interviewers can then ask respondents to say which group describes them best, "a, b, or c." This is often done with categories of income to make it easier for both high- and low-income respondents to tell interviewers what their income is.

The following multi-year case study for design of the Minnesota Center for Arts Education could not have been carried out successfully if the researchers and designers had not posed their questions carefully and integrated interviewing and asking questions into a long-term participatory design project.

CASE STUDY 11

MINNESOTA CENTER FOR ARTS EDUCATION: PARTICIPATORY RESEARCH-BASED DESIGN AND PLANNING

In planning for the new design of the Minnesota Center for Arts Education, researchers employed rigorous on-site data collection to define justifiable emerging educational needs and their corresponding costs. The intensive process began with interviews focused on the environment that took place during a walk-through evaluation of the existing facility. Recorded assessments of each space systematically determined the adequacy of space, lighting, acoustics, temperature, flexibility of use, aesthetic appeal, functional requirements, and floor area. An analysis of these data formed the basis for a report on the spatial requirements needed for subsequent stages of the process. Student/faculty teams working in small groups also employed these data to develop proposals for their new facility using a site plan of the campus, a floor plan of each building, a listing of required areas for each space, and corresponding graphic symbols. Proposals included changes in present use, expansion of existing buildings, addition of floors, and the creation of new buildings. Results of the walk-throughs, interviews, and recommenda-

Minnesota Center for Arts Education.

tions generated by the participating teams influenced the development of three design proposals, one of which received unanimous support from students and faculty.

In 1990, the state of Minnesota purchased the thirty-three-acre campus of the former Golden Valley Lutheran College for use by the Minnesota Center for Arts Education (MCAE). On the campus were a main administrative classroom building, a secondary classroom building, and three dormitories surrounding an existing pond. Some remodeling was done to convert the junior college campus to an arts high school and outreach educational resource center, but for years the facilities remained inadequate.

In 1994, an accreditation committee visiting the school reported that physical constraints and the forced sharing of space for incompatible functions restricted curricular focus and potential, displaced students from the classroom, required all major performances to be conducted off-site which was expensive and logistically difficult, created safety hazards, and exacerbated conflict. The physical plant, they concluded, was inadequate.

In response to this report, in the spring of 1995 the Minnesota Center for Arts Education selected The Adams Group architects and environment-behavior design research consultant Henry Sanoff to carry out a participatory design effort (Sanoff, 2000). This process began with a three-day planning charrette during which Center staff, students, some parents from the parent advisory committee, and clients of the resource programs division articulated deficiencies, needs, and dreams, designing what they considered to be "ideal" spaces.

In order to determine how the existing buildings on campus met the needs of the new Center and where renovations were necessary, the team evaluated all campus buildings. This exercise was also useful in justifying the cost of the project, particularly when many state agencies were competing for the same resources. The initial evaluation provided data on the client-user—including functional requirements for the physical setting and user satisfaction with existing settings—the immediate environmental context, and the social/historical context of the campus. Focused interviews during walk-through evaluations provided a building performance audit and a summary of indicators of successful and unsuccessful building features. Prior to the site visit, drawings of the campus were obtained, as were documentation of curriculum goals and factors affecting the demand for new and improved facilities. The team developed a Spatial Data Inventory Form to record these data, including locational requirements, functional requirements, and a floor plan and area of each existing space.

Two research and design teams were given specific assignments regarding the parts of the campus they would assess, and the focused interviews about spatial adequacy they would carry out with staff, faculty, and students. The walk-through assessment process lasted four and one-half hours on the first day, and resulted in a review of all campus buildings, revealing problems with the current buildings such as:

- Overcrowding in the main building and the general computer lab
- Classes being held in the cafeteria and in administrative conference rooms
- Music space with no rehearsal area, an inadequate number of practice rooms, a shortage of instructional space, and no acoustical treatment

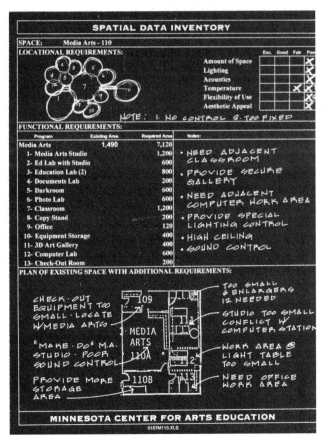

Spatial Data Inventory Form.

Left: Visual props and team communication.
Right: Programmer-Architect team.

- Painting and construction of sets occurring within the theater itself, so that dust and debris caused damage to lighting and sound equipment
- Students eating in and otherwise using the existing art gallery area as a spillover lounge, which jeopardized the integrity of the exhibited artwork
- A general lack of meeting space leading to higher expenses for programs that had to be held off campus

After the environment-behavior evaluation of present conditions, the team carried out a day-long space planning exercise involving 200 students and 40 faculty members who worked collaboratively on a vision for their new campus. Participants assembled in the performing arts area where they received instructions about the planning process and the procedures to be followed. The architects prepared a site plan in advance, locating all existing buildings and including a floor plan of each building. Lists of required areas developed from the interviews and walk-through evaluations provided additional data for the participants to discuss.

In groups of five to eight people, team members analyzed the uses of existing buildings and proposed new functions where appropriate. They used sets of graphic symbols the research design team had prepared that corresponded to each of the activity areas. These graphic props allowed participants to reconfigure the existing spaces. Teams selected themselves, with music students tending to group together, visual arts students tending to group together, and so on.

Each group's bias was apparent in its solution, reflecting the fact that everyone experienced some difficulties and inadequacies in their present working environment. The student-faculty teams devoted three hours to this phase of the planning process and developed thirty-nine proposals.

This space- and site-planning exercise allowed participants to consider redistributing all existing functions on the campus and to propose appropriate locations for new uses. Considering that future ideal space needs totaled twice the available space in existing facilities, participants were forced to reconsider the flow of movement on campus in order to arrive at suitable locations for all functions. Results of the space- and site-planning exercise revealed considerable insight among students and faculty about future campus development.

Content analysis of the site drawings the thirty-nine teams prepared indicated that 38 percent included proposals to expand the existing administration/classroom building, with several proposing that a new addition be wrapped around the building. A majority of teams proposed additional classrooms, dance, media, and performance space around the dorms. Although theater and dance have similar performance requirements, responses made evident that their present location was inadequate for both to function simultaneously. Music students who voiced a concern about being isolated from other arts activities attempted to relocate themselves centrally. The severe cold climate in Minneapolis emerged as critical factor in a site plan that connected all buildings so that students changing classes could remain indoors.

This analysis led to the environment-behavior design team's developing three design alternatives, each embodying the ideas expressed in the student/faculty space-planning exercise. One scheme located a new theater arts building to the west of the existing administration building, another positioned a new arts complex to the east of the administration building, and both schemes maintained the campus character of disconnected buildings. A third proposal wrapped the existing building with new functions to alter the building's image while using a classroom wing to connect an adjacent dorm to the expansion of the main building, thus changing the overall character of the campus.

Plans and models for each design alternative were presented to faculty and students, allowing them to compare and evaluate the schemes. The experience of manipulating buildings on the site had prepared faculty and student participants to comprehend the technical site drawings, enabling them to arrive quickly at consensus on the wrap-around proposal.

The final master plan proposal accommodated the Center's strategic goals while allowing for expansion in later phases. Key strategic goals included alleviating overcrowded conditions, increasing enrollment, expanding and improving class offerings in functionally appropriate spaces, accommodating students' informal social needs, preserving Center assets and resources, meeting the needs of teachers statewide, encouraging community access, and providing safe and secure buildings that comply with all applicable codes.

New development proposed in the master plan included a performing arts theater, dance studios, music rehearsal, and technical support area. New science classrooms, laboratory areas, and classrooms for literary arts, social studies, and communications were proposed adjacent to the northwest corner of the existing facility. The final report summarizing the planning process included an evaluation of the existing facilities, a comprehensive architectural program, a phased capital budget plan, and estimated construction costs.

For legislative review and funding, a separate programming document presented the participatory process and the justification for capital requests. The legislature awarded $7 million to the Center for the first phase of construction: a new building adjacent to the administration/classroom building with space for music, literary arts, science, social studies, and communications. The architects who took part were awarded the contract to design the new performing arts building.

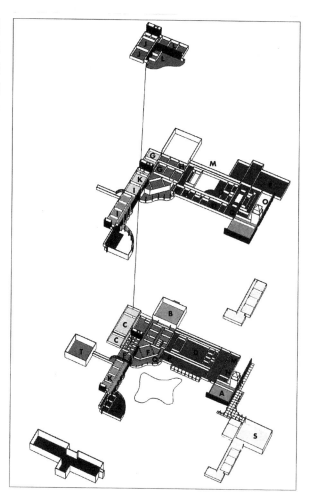

Building Key

Media Arts — A

Theater — B

Dance — C

Visual Arts — D

L.R.C. — E

Music — F

Science — G

Communications — H

World Languages — I

Social Studies — J

Math — K

Literary Arts — L

Faculty Offices — M

Student Services — N

Administration — O

Dining/Kitchen — P

Gallery — Q

Student Areas — R

Teacher Education Center — S

Final building proposal.

The participatory process, however, did not end here. To facilitate the decision-making process for implementing the first phase of construction, an advisory committee was established consisting of faculty, staff, students, and parents. During the two years that elapsed between phases one and two, the students who participated in the first phase of the project graduated. While it was expected that new members of the student body would be asked to participate fully in this phase of the project, it was equally important not to revisit and revise the issues that were agreed upon in phase one.

Students, faculty, and staff therefore participated in a more focused workshop to initiate the building design phase. The alternative design solutions were presented along with specific criteria established by a newly formed Building Advisory Committee. A single seven-part question constituted the evaluation

Building Advisory
Committee members
reviewing proposals.

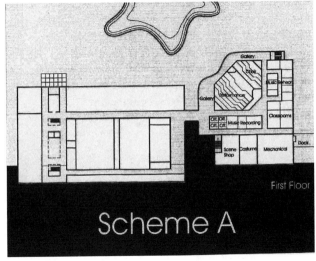

Final building
proposal.

criteria that each participant was asked to use in selecting one design alternative. The question was:

"Which plan . . .

- Has the best location for the entrance?
- Has the best circulation connecting the old and new buildings?
- Provides the best security for people and property?
- Creates the best informal gathering spaces for students and faculty?
- Has the best arrangement for classrooms?
- Has the best location for the music performance hall?
- Do you like best?

More than 80 percent of the new respondents selected a design similar to the proposal that previous participants had selected during the earlier master-planning phase (p. 308), with the location of the performance hall opening to the pond cited as the most important planning feature. The final building proposal therefore included two critical entrances and facades—a visitor entrance facing north and a student entrance facing south. With substantial agreement on the plan for the buildings from students, staff, and parents, space programming and design was carried out. Architects and the teaching staff developed detailed space requirements that met specific teaching and learning needs, and the building was completed and in use in 1999.

This case study was based on the work and writing of Henry Sanoff, Distinguished Professor of Architecture, College of Design, North Carolina State University, Raleigh, North Carolina.

OVERVIEW

If asking questions is to help you solve a problem, you must focus accurately on the topics you are interested in and formulate questions so that answers can be usefully interpreted. This chapter suggests that to achieve these ends in E-B inquiry, you should ask yourself quality-control questions as you construct interviews.

To improve the topical relevance for your E-B problem, ask yourself:

- Have I generated questions about behavioral and administrative environments as well as physical ones?
- Have I asked about both actual past and present environments and abstract environments pictured in respondents' minds?
- Have I asked about respondents' reactions to an environment in breadth—what they see in it, feel about it, do in it, do to it, and know about it?
- Have I linked people's environmental responses to the various types of environments and environmental elements I need to know about to solve my particular problem?

To remind yourself of significant rules of thumb for formulating usable questions, ask yourself:

- Are my questions simple enough for respondents to understand?
- Are my questions precise enough so that respondents will generally understand them the same way?
- Are my questions neutral enough so that they do not influence the direction of respondents' answers?

Sometimes, however, we face E-B problems for which there are no respondents to interview, no people to observe, and no physical traces to record. When this is so, we may approach our problem by analyzing documents and data that others have compiled in the past—archives. We may also turn to archives to augment results from other methods. This is the topic of the next chapter.

CHAPTER 13

ARCHIVES

If you borrow a friend's country house for a winter weekend and find that the front door does not close, you might look in the basement for a screwdriver and machine oil. If these were not available and nearby stores were closed, you would find another way to close the door: fixing it with an old knife and cooking oil from the kitchen, tying it shut with picture wire, or using a large nail to replace the hinge bolt. What you uncover through improvisation may serve your purposes better than the tools you originally thought you needed.

Environment-behavior researchers are often caught in old, cold houses without a screwdriver—as when they study historical problems or past events about which they can neither interview participants nor observe behavior. For example, when Goffman (1963) wanted to see how ideas of "public" places and "public order" developed during the past several centuries, he turned to histories of medieval England, nineteenth-century etiquette books, and published historical letters. Interestingly, he found many parallels: today's laws "that a householder is obliged to maintain his walks and roads in good repair and to keep his town land free of noxious refuse" (p. 9) are presaged by medieval ones to "keep one's pigs out of the streets, even though there was much available there for the pigs to eat" (pp. 8–9).

Researchers who want to find out what decisions designers made and when they made them during a particular design project might turn to archives of drawings for data. In her study of Twin Rivers (1976), Keller analyzed architects' plans in the project files of three design offices that had worked on this large project before its final stage. From the plans she gleaned what the designers' original intentions had been and when design changes had been made—

essentially, how the final design had emerged. For example, planners originally wanted the community to be primarily pedestrian. They planned footpaths connecting such places as home and school and did not provide car drop-off or pickup areas around the school. When other planning teams eventually acknowledged that cars were inevitable, they made some changes but did not redesign the schoolyard; "the ensuing chaos culminated in one child being knocked down in 1975 and stringent restrictions being put on cars in those areas" (1976, p. 43).

Institutional records also serve as sources of data. Snyder and Ostrander (1974) wanted to find out what kinds of people lived in the existing nursing home they were studying, to augment their observation and interview research. When they analyzed files that the institution had collected for administrative purposes, they found a much higher proportion of physically impaired residents recorded than they observed personally. They looked for an explanation. Were patients recorded as more severely ill than they actually were? Were physically impaired residents prevented from moving around the building? Or did investigators not know how to recognize the severity of residents' impairments?

Each of these researchers turned to archival data sources to solve his or her problem. In archival research investigators turn data someone else has gathered for one purpose into information useful for another. In some research situations—for example, Goffman's and Keller's—archives may be the only source

---

Archives

Qualities

    Pragmatic
    Imaginative
    Historical

Using Archives

Document Files

    Differential accessibility
    Deposit and survival
    Definition of the situation

Types of Data

    Words
    Numbers
    Nonverbal representations

Behavioral Plan Analysis

of data. Other investigators—for example, Snyder and Ostrander—choose to use archives because it is more efficient than collecting new data.

This chapter presents some characteristics of archival methods, approaches to identifying useful document files, and operations that researchers may find helpful in analyzing contents of documents—words, numbers, and especially nonverbal representations such as architectural plans.

QUALITIES

In reusing data designed or recorded for other purposes, investigators *pragmatically* and *imaginatively* mix and match available data. For *historical* topics that cannot be studied through methods such as direct observation and interviews, archives may be the only available source of data. Because archival methods are one remove from the people, activities, and settings a researcher is studying, using such methods requires that investigators take into account the potential bias introduced by those who originally collected the data.

Pragmatic

Researchers approach archives much as architects approach an old building on a site where they have chosen to build. If the old building is totally incompatible with the intended use of the new one, it might be razed. If the building or any of its parts can be reused, the designer might do so; or the designer might make major changes to adapt the existing building creatively to new uses.

The designer's approach is pragmatic. Can he use what is already there to meet his needs, or is it more efficient to tear it down? If a regulation prohibits his razing a building—as historical topics might prohibit researchers from carrying out basic data gathering—the designer asks only how he can use what is there.

Archives present researchers the opportunity to reuse data adaptively—to make it do double duty. Less adaptation is needed when a researcher wants to analyze data as they were originally meant to be analyzed. For example, if researchers want to study problems related to population shifts, changes in the quality of housing stock, or types of family organization, they can select and analyze census data collected by others for this purpose.

More adaptation is necessary when the original data were meant to be analyzed for purposes different from those of the researcher. This often occurs when investigators use data from records that institutions or public agencies keep for housekeeping purposes. For example, when Wilner et al. (1954) used public school and housing authority records to find out how children from new and old public housing projects performed in school, they first had to sample existing archives to find out what data they contained, analyze the coding categories used to organize those data, and create new records tailored to their own research purposes. When reusing institutional records, investigators have to make sure they understand how the institution defines the recorded events (Kitsuse and Cicourel, 1963). For example, does an industrial plant include workers' suggestions for environmental improvements under "complaints"? If an investigator still finds the records useful, part of her data collection has already been carried out for her. She is then like the designer who finds that the heating system and floors of an old building can be reused as part of a new one.

Imaginative

If you decide to draw information from archives not meant to be analyzed as part of a systematic research project, you must approach your problem *imaginatively*. You must reimage the data and their source; you cannot simply reanalyze them. For example, Günter et al. (1978) carried out a behavioral study of a large open space in Rome called the Spanish Steps—a cascading series of steps and landings built between 1721 and 1726. The steps are used much the way streets and plazas in Rome and other cities are used: by craftspeople and painters selling their goods; by people promenading to see other people and be seen; by families; by lovers; by guitar players and singing groups. Günter et al. combined a behavior study with a historical perspective to show "that architectural science is a specific type of social science . . . [and] that use is an essential part of architecture" (1978, p. 2; my translation).

To show how the Spanish Steps were used during the past three centuries, these E-B researchers analyzed the behavior of people depicted in paintings and prints of the area. The authors proposed that the paintings from 1730 to the early 1800s indicate the historical use of the steps. They analyzed an 1835 painting by Moscheti of the steps and the plaza at their foot as follows (1978, p. 80; my translation):

- No one stands alone—rather, people are always together in groups.
- There are many large groups (over four persons).
- There is some interaction between groups.
- The groups appear to move along invisible parallel lines. (We can draw no conclusions about movement from this observation. It appears, rather, to reflect one of the artist's presentation principles.)
- Most people are walking.
- Some people are riding horses.
- Some people are being drawn in a carriage.

Imagination is required to redefine data sources in this way.

In their classic *Unobtrusive Measures* (1966), Webb et al. present a host of archival studies that "reveal the power of insightful minds to see appropriate data where associates only see someone else's records" (p. 86). Such an approach means being able to see maintenance reports in a hospital as indicators of which places are most used and what materials were least well specified for the use they get. Union grievances recorded at a state labor relations board about the discomfort caused by poor air conditioning and heating systems might indicate that this is a major concern among service workers. An E-B researcher could use suggestion-box submissions as a substitute for survey information. The examples presented in the archival methods update later in this chapter all successfully build on creative and imaginative data mining.

To the *records* category one can add paintings, correspondence, news reports, and other archival files. Keller turned newspaper reports of a garden competition into surprisingly appropriate information. As part of her multi-method study of the Twin Rivers planned unit development (1976), she wanted to find out what residents "who had a special esthetic sense" felt about their surroundings. Because it would have been difficult and expensive to identify such people through interviews, Keller would have had to abandon this part of the study had she not found a news article reporting on winners of a local garden contest—including names and addresses. Assuming these gardeners to be particularly interested in how their physical environment looked, she focused her environmental-aesthetics interviews on them and other people they identified as having similar aesthetic attitudes.

These examples do not merely demonstrate good intuition, they reflect minds trained to see similarities in seemingly disparate events, minds that can identify qualities of useful information implicit in other people's data, and practical minds willing and able to transform what is at hand into something useful.

Historical

Past use and perception of environments can be essential *contexts* for understanding present use and perception. Goffman (1963) studied hundred-year-old etiquette books to get a sense of middle-class norms about what was appropriate public and private behavior at that time. He used these historical documents to describe the background of present-day behavior. Commonly accepted past definitions of situations provide clues to how present-day definitions have evolved.

When investigators are able to interview past participants to uncover historical data, they must take into account the gilding of events that takes place over time. Records kept of daily events at the time of those events may be written with an eye to establishing history in a certain way, but they are not rewritten or changed with hindsight. The recent past is sometimes most validly studied through archival methods, as is shown by recorded election results that post-election voter interviews cannot reconstruct because more respondents say they voted for the winner than actually *did*.

To establish what appeals the developer and residents made to each other as the Twin Rivers community was being debated years before, Keller used verbatim public records of planning-board hearings. She found that when the builder had requested zoning revisions, he talked about providing low-income housing, building an impressive community center, and other community facilities he would develop simultaneously with the housing. The planning-board records show that local community residents did not expect these promises to be fulfilled. When Keller's data from news analysis and interviews later revealed the complaints Twin Rivers residents had about these issues, Keller could demonstrate the way such potential problems were dealt with during the adversary planning process. As an added and unexpected benefit, the hearing records provided Keller and her team with names and addresses of professional consultants called in at the time by both builder and residents: physical planners, tax experts, and lawyers. They were not mentioned in other documents because their part in the project was temporary. Keller later carried out focused interviews with these persons to fill in details about Twin Rivers' evolution.

Archives resulting from records kept over time—for a society, an institution, or a project—enable investigators to study *patterns of activity* and *change*. Visual records can show how uses of a building, street, or plaza evolve slowly over centuries (Günter et al., 1978); news articles can reflect how complaints grow from isolated incidents to public issues in a new town (Keller, 1976); and two-dimensional plans can reflect how a design emerges through several phases of planning, each developed by a different planning firm (Keller, 1976).

In sum, investigators with the imagination to see opportunities where others see waste can use archival methods to adapt other people's data to new E-B purposes. Such methods are particularly well suited for studying past E-B events and things that change. The opportunity of using archival methods is often worth the risk that results from using data gathered by someone else with different ends.

USING ARCHIVES

The key to using archives is locating and gaining access to *document files*: the groupings into which other people have deposited documents. A file of paintings may be a museum room; files of school-attendance records may be computer files; files of *documents* relating to a particular design project may be file cabinet drawers or CAD files. Once you have access to a file that you think meets your research needs, you will want to look more closely at the kinds of documents it contains, such as letters and plans, text and data reports, accountings, and pictures. To plan a strategy for analyzing the documents, you must determine what *type of data* you have to analyze—words, numbers, or nonverbal representations—because each type requires different handling operations and analytic procedures. Within each type you can choose the *analytic unit* most appropriate for your research purposes. For example, analysis of a newspaper might focus on headlines, articles, letters to the editor, or announcements; within any one of these categories—articles, for instance—a researcher might decide to record the theme of the article, the structure of every sentence, or the number of times a certain word appears. If the documents are design plans for a building, a researcher who wants to see how spaces were pared down to reduce costs might record square-footage changes for a particular room in successive plans. But if she is interested in the designer's behavioral intentions, she might analyze the possibilities the plan provides for relationships among people who might eventually use the building. All such choices depend on what a researcher wants to find out—his or her purpose.

DOCUMENT FILES

Someone puts documents into archival files, and someone keeps the files: a census organizer, an editor, or an office administrator. Although this fact can provide efficiencies for an investigator, it also presents problems of data accessibility, completeness, and relevance.

Differential Accessibility

The more public a file is, the more likely it is to be available for research. Public archives include, for example, census data, published research and other books, newspapers, public announcements and records, and records of publicly sponsored competitions.

Some public files, although accessible, still need to be ferreted out by investigators. For example, Zeisel et al. (1978) used published research documents as data to generate research-based performance criteria about older people. To demonstrate how designers meet the needs of older people in their designs, the research team located and analyzed microfilms of submissions to a statewide architectural competition.

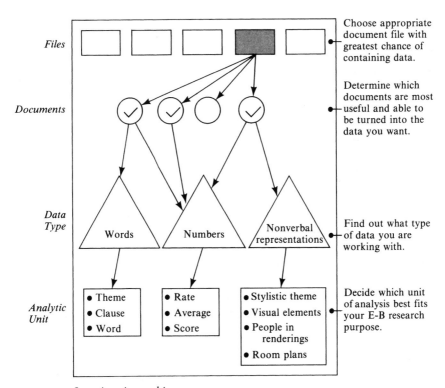

Steps in using archives.

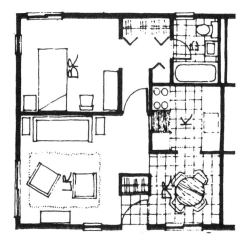

+ bedroom is not visible from public areas in the apartment

+ kitchen is visually separate from
the living room

+ bedroom door location allows
private access between bedroom
and bath

− there is a partial view into the
bedroom from the hallway

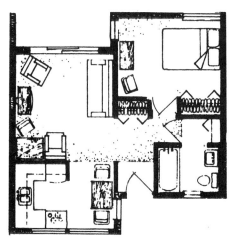

+ bathroom is accessible without
going through the bedroom

+ kitchen has visual privacy from
living room and entry

+ location of linen closet adds to
visual privacy in the bathroom

+ bedroom door swings against
wall and in direction of travel

− there is a partial view into the
bedroom from the entrance
hallway

Annotated plan from design competition showing comments on control of background areas. (From J. Zeisel, G. Epp, and S. Demos, *Low-Rise Housing for Older People: Behavioral Criteria for Design*. Washington, D.C.: U.S. Government Printing Office, 1978.)

From published research they generated—and had a panel of experts review—performance criteria, such as the following one for the degree of control that residents need over "backstage" areas. With increasing problems of agility and balance, easy accessibility between different areas in the apartment becomes more important for older persons. Areas difficult to reach not only create inconveniences but can also be hazardous to residents' safety and well-being. However, easy physical access must not be achieved at the expense of visual privacy in "backstage" areas such as bedrooms, bathrooms, and kitchens. To maintain their dignity with visitors, residents need to control visual access to these "backstage" areas where the more private activities such as personal hygiene, sleeping, and cooking take place. As a result, careful consideration must be given to minimizing physical distance and barriers between public and private areas in the unit while maximizing visual privacy (Zeisel et al., 1978, p. 30).

They accompanied this guideline with annotated examples from the competition. Institutional records may be accessible only to researchers who can show that their purposes are scientific or benign and that anonymity is ensured for people the data represent. Such records may be regulated by public bodies protecting patients' rights, or closed by officials of an organization who feel that merely identifying the organization is an invasion of their clients' privacy. Clearly, when the institution is itself a client for the research, as was the Oxford nursing home for Snyder and Ostrander (1974), records that are cleansed of data that might identify specific residents may be easier to acquire.

Private files such as personal letters and diaries are the least accessible unless they have somehow been made public by being donated to a library or by being published. Private files in the public realm often represent historical figures and times past.

Deposit and Survival

Once an investigator gains access to a digital or paper file, she must determine which out of all possible documents are included in the file. Are all significant documents there? Have some been excluded or suppressed? Have some been deleted or weeded out? Selective deposit, self-selective deposit, and selective survival are processes influencing what is deposited into document files and what survives over time. Each reflects the fact that any available file is in some way an edited sample of actual documents. To use a file for her purposes, each investigator must be able to assess how that particular file has been edited.

Selective deposit (Webb et al., 1966) refers to the fact that what is put into files depends not only on what documents are generated but also on which documents an archivist decides to keep. In a single complex office transaction like a meeting between architect and client, participants might generate a host of documents (Zinnes, 1963):

- A meeting report (which may be deleted after it is printed out for that meeting)
- Annotations in the margins of the paper report by participants (which may be left on the table to be thrown out)
- Preliminary and follow-up phone conversations (which may or may not be documented and saved in the file)
- Internal office memoranda (which may be deleted either carelessly or by design)
- Casual conferences among participants (which may or may not be confirmed by e-mail)
- Secret or embarrassing letters (which are purposely deleted)
- Preliminary drafts of reports or plans (which are deleted as a matter of course after the final draft is accepted)

An editor, archivist, or clerk might delete documents before archiving files to limit data storage needs. An investigator who overlooks such a systematic bias can easily carry out an unbiased analysis of thoroughly biased archival data. In her newspaper analysis for Twin Rivers, Keller (1976) was able to put this realization to use. In initial interviews, she found that when Twin Rivers residents first moved to the area, they were dissatisfied because the reality of a suburban planned community was not like the suburban dream they held. Although residents told Keller that they complained vociferously to officials, the editor of Twin Rivers' newspaper did not report all their outbursts: He felt that publishing short-lived complaints would merely fan flames of discontent. Sometimes, however, the editor reported problems the community faced as a whole although individual respondents did not mention them spontaneously to interviewers. For example, the paper reported dangerous problems of access to the public school by children and cars. The editor tried to make issues visible to his readers when, in his view, they had reached the scale of a community-wide problem.

Keller incorporated this insight about the editor's point of view into her understanding of the role a small newspaper plays in the development of a new community. Discovering how such a community grows was one of her goals. Keller also used the discrepancy between individual reports and news articles to distinguish problems that developed slowly over time, eventually becoming grist for the editor, and transitory problems that the editor never advertised. Keller honored the difference between the data she gathered from the two methods, using their difference as a resource rather than making an inappropriate amalgam of the two sorts of data. They reflected a legitimate discrepancy of perspective, which Keller felt to be a significant part of community life that her multiple-method approach was able to catch.

In *self-selective deposit* no intermediary editor or archivist is involved. For example, an investigator of high school life who turns to the yearbook for information about individuals or cliques is likely to find descriptions of students written by themselves. The same self-reporting of information also occurs in biographies in professional directories, public-relations releases, and other personal announcements.

Self-selective deposit is sometimes determined not by individual volition but by structural constraints in a setting or organization. In a design office, for example, partners and job captains may be the only ones allowed to correspond with clients, consultants, and suppliers; client e-mail communications files therefore will not directly include the ideas of draftsmen and other members of the design team.

A significant influence on self-selective deposit is the degree to which archives are meant to be evaluated by supervisors. For example, in the study of school property damage (1976a), Zeisel was interested to know how much money was spent on various types of damage, what types of damage were most prevalent, and what proportion of all damage could be called malicious damage versus wear-and-tear damage. Naturally, he looked for this information in "vandalism reports," which custodians requesting repair funds turned over to their superiors. Unfortunately, the reports reflected the custodians' selective presentation of the situation. The custodians knew that their supervisors would come to inspect the damage and would then judge the custodian as well: Did he report minor damage that he could repair himself? Did he report wear-and-tear on which he should have done preventive maintenance? Did he report only "vandalism," as he was expected to do, or did he report other damage as well? The custodians, knowing they themselves were "on the record," modified their reports accordingly.

Blau faced the same problem in his study of worker behavior (1963). He wanted to compare the performance of workers in competitive and cooperative offices. To measure placement officers' performance, he decided to use the record the office supervisor kept of how many job placements each officer made. At the same time, Blau observed placement officers' behavior. When calls with job offers came into the office, the officer receiving the call was expected to write down the offer on a phone message pad and put it in a basket from which all officers chose jobs for clients. Blau noticed, however, that officers "hoarded" job offers that could be easily filled by putting the paper phone slips under their desk blotters rather than in the communal basket. In this way, they raised their own placement rate and biased Blau's archives. Like Keller, Blau turned this problem into an opportunity and used the observation to give him further insight into the informal organization of the office. Today, such recoding devices are computerized, so this particular type of job sabotage would be more difficult to engage in.

Document files are also subject to editing that purges certain documents from the file as time passes: *selective survival*. Housekeeping documents such as memos may be routinely, systematically, or casually deleted when the file is archived for long-term storage or when an office consolidates files. Digital records of sensitive transactions and controversial planning proposals may be systematically deleted and paper files of such transactions shredded. As the authors of *Unobtrusive Measures* (1966) point out, "Using archival records frequently means substituting someone else's selective filter for your own" (p. 111).

Environment-behavior researchers who use archival materials face the same dilemmas historians face. You have to figure out what you can do with the available material, and you must determine what the material you have represents. How authentic is it? What part of the actual universe of documents do you have? What types of documents are missing? Are key documents represented, or have they been lost? Can you carry out any internal checks to identify missing documents—for example, seeing whether change orders issued during construction refer to working drawings that are no longer on file?

Definition of the Situation

The most elusive problem that document files pose for researchers is that the way an editor defines the situation he records may result in identically named records that containing counts of phenomena different from what the investigator wants (Kitsuse and Cicourel, 1963). When, for example, the official statistical rates are labeled "acts of vandalism" or "substandard housing" and an investigator wants to study these phenomena, can he assume that the rates reflect what he defines to be the problem? Kitsuse and Cicourel argue convinc-

2. Perspective through Interior Street

OBSERVATIONS AND REQUIREMENTS

12 OBS: After they are ten years old, boys are generally unsupervised while outside, and enjoy the freedom to roam the neighborhood.
REQ: Many places for pedestrian movement.

13 OBS: Groups of teen-agers of different sexes spend a lot of time "hanging around" or looking for something to do. Often they do this with adults or teen-agers of the opposite sex.
REQ: (A) Connection between boys' group and peer groups of other statuses.
(B) Connection between boys' and girls' outside areas and apartments.

14 OBS: Teen-agers gather on corners near small stores.
REQ: Areas for informal congregating outside and around commercial areas.

15 OBS: Although boys meet with boys, and girls with girls, the girls meet near the corners where the boys hang out.
REQ: Adolescent girls' areas visible to boys' areas.

16 OBS: Young teen-age girls take care of younger children on the streets.
REQ: Adolescent girls' areas near children's play areas.

17 OBS: Both men and women use dress as a means of self expression, spending much money on clothes.
REQ: General visibility among pedestrian, apartment, commercial, and recreational areas.

18 OBS: Men wash their cars on the streets as often as once a week. For men, the car is important as a means of expressing their identity.
REQ: Visibility for areas related to automobiles.

19 OBS: Bars and luncheonettes are places to exchange news and gossip, as well as message centers for regular customers.
REQ: (A) Commercial area connected to living areas.
(B) Commercial area visible from street and other commercial areas.

20 OBS: Women socialize while shopping.
REQ: Commercial areas visible to and from streets.

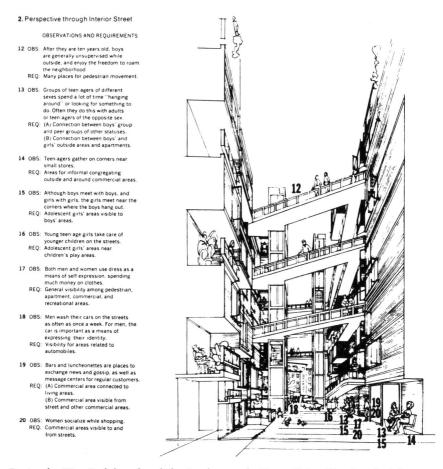

Design for West End, based on behavioral research. (From "Mass Housing: Social Research and Design," by B. Brolin and J. Zeisel. *The Architectural Forum*, July/August 1968, 71. Reprinted by permission.)

ingly that such rates reflect the rate keeper's definition of the situation and the institutional process of keeping rates as much as the number of actual occurrences of events. This is not to say that rate keepers lie by recording less or more substandard housing in a neighborhood than they observe. Rather, what they see and count is largely determined by the way they look at the world.

This was brought home forcefully to planners when Jacobs' *Death and Life of Great American Cities* (1961) showed that what mortgage banks and municipalities saw as slums, were viewed by residents as healthy social neighborhoods. The banks called housing in Boston's West End "substandard" because building exteriors were not kept up and plumbing was bad; yet residents kept up the interior of their apartments with their own money. Had Jacobs used only official statistics to assess the degree of "substandard" housing, she would have developed a one-sided picture.

In Zeisel's study of school vandalism, the same situation almost arose. As mentioned earlier, custodians reported only certain acts of property damage because they knew their supervisors would review the reports. These reports had another bias as well: Custodians defined all damage as vandalism if it was not obviously wear and tear from normal use. For their purposes, they merely needed to isolate special damage to buildings. If a child's swing was broken because a teenager was swinging on it in the evening, this was "vandalism," not "unintended damage" or "damage from misuse." If windows behind a basketball backboard were broken during a rough game, this was "vandalism," not "incidental breakage." If a door was damaged during the theft of a typewriter, this was "vandalism," not a "professional crime." Custodians who filed reports did not distinguish between different types of damage; to them breakage meant vandalism. Had the E-B research team not seen the difference between its definition of vandalism and the custodians' definition, their findings would have been very different.

The definition of the situation held by a once-removed recorder can also present opportunities. Brolin and Zeisel (1968) found that Gans' *Urban Villagers* (1962) described life in Boston's West End with a participant-observation perspective they shared. They used this insightful social-planning book as a document in which to locate data about how the predominantly Italian-American residents used their physical surroundings: rooms, streets and street corners, grocery stores, bars. Brolin and Zeisel used these data as the behavioral research basis for a hypothetical building designed to meet some specific needs of these residents (see figure).

TYPES OF DATA

Documents comprise numbers, words, nonverbal representations, or combinations of these. Newspapers are clearly combinations; paintings are not. Each of these types of data found in documents requires different kinds of procedures to solve E-B problems. You need different analytic skills to analyze an architectural plan than to analyze a newspaper article.

Types of Data

Words: Content analysis
Numbers: Secondary analysis
Nonverbal Representations: Behavioral analysis

Words

What Webb et al. (1966) call "running records"—records kept over time—can be used to find out about such things as changing patterns, past conditions, and particular past events. For example, verbatim transcripts of a public speech provide clues to the speaker's state of mind, intentions, goals, and perceptions at the time she gave the speech. Heimessen and de Jonge, in another example, used verbal content analysis of poems to find out how teenage students felt about high-rise housing in the Netherlands (1967). Their source for data was the countrywide high school graduation examination given one year. As one of ten questions to choose from that year, students were asked to write an essay commenting on a modern poem about high-rise housing. The investigators found that 76 percent of students answering this question were against such buildings, 24 percent for them. Positive attributes the students suggested dealt mainly with green space and play areas; negative attributes mainly addressed the social and psychological climate in high-rise buildings. Among Heimessen and de Jonge's most interesting findings is that a large majority of the students, both for and against high-rise housing, perceived such housing as inevitable. According to the students, only this efficient building type could meet the housing needs of the rapidly increasing Dutch population. The authors point out that this is a misperception: among 6,487 housing units completed in one month in 1967, only 1,599 employed labor-intensive industrial building systems.

• *Subjectivity and context.* In interpreting verbal data—especially to determine the writer's or speaker's intentions and perceptions—it is difficult to avoid reading your own subjective meaning into the material. For example, when a student writes that a building is "large and imposing," does she mean it positively or negatively? If a designer writes to a community client that she feels "social concerns are vital to the success of the project," is she catering to the client's desires, or does she mean what she writes?

To avoid subjective ratings and to increase the reliability of such analysis, you can analyze documents in several ways and compare results; you may have several raters analyze the same documents, or develop a definition of a situation by analyzing one sample of documents and develop another one by analyzing a second sample chosen from the same file.

Another way to interpret what someone means is to know the context of his expressions (George, 1959). This includes *situational* attributes: What is a writer's position? What is the intended reader's position? What events surround the communication? Situational attributes may be summarized by the question "Who is writing to whom under what circumstances?" The answers to these questions may be found in the document file itself, or the investigator may have to find them by other research means. The same is true for *behavioral* attributes of a writer's context—namely, "the purpose or objective which the specific communication is designed to achieve" (George, 1959, p. 27). The meaning of the phrase "social concerns are vital" in a letter to a client might be explained by another document in the file—a message to the writer from her boss telling her to assure the client that everything is all right. Clues to the behavioral context of a phrase may be found in another part of the same e-mail. In either case, developing a contextual overview of files before analyzing partial units, such as phrases or words, helps to identify data useful in interpreting those partial units.

• *Frequency and non-frequency coding.* For some research purposes, it can be useful to record how often a theme or a word appears in written documents. For example, Keller (1976) analyzed every article in the sixty issues the

Twin Rivers newspaper had published. She counted the mentions of problems (from design defects and controversial management policies to poor police protection), broken promises (a youth and community center that was never built), and the growth of communitywide organizations. Counting such items alerted Keller to the magnitude and salience of each issue. For example, the lack of promised storm windows turned out to be a much more significant community problem than the research team had expected. There are several readily available software programs to digitally code, count, and analyze such textual data.

Frequency content counts might be irrelevant or even misleading for other research purposes. If, for example, a researcher is interested in the types rather than the magnitude of topics covered in a set of e-mails, counting themes may cause infrequent yet important topics to be disregarded. When a problem mentioned once is as important to an investigator's purpose as a problem mentioned many times, coding frequency does not help. Brolin and Zeisel (1968) used a non-frequency approach when they translated portions of Gans' *Urban Villagers* into hypothetical housing designs for the Italian-American families Gans described. To develop a culturally responsive behavioral design program, they excerpted from the book each quotation that "described an activity taking place in a physical setting" (Brolin and Zeisel, 1968, p. 68). Carrying out this analysis separately and then comparing results, the two investigators generated over 200 quotations. Brolin, an architect, began to design buildings using the quotations as data. He did not know before he began which quotations would be more valuable and which less. He did not know precisely what it meant to "use" such data. But during the months it took to design the hypothetical buildings, he and Zeisel realized that only 20 of the 200 original quotations were "useful." Those describing relationships between people proved most helpful to Brolin in making design decisions about objects, places, and how places were to relate to one another. Frequency counts would have been irrelevant for this content analysis. Qualitative analysis and quantitative measurement are both appropriate techniques to use with each research method discussed in Part Two, depending on the purpose of the particular project.

• *Coding unit.* What word or set of words in an e-mail or an article should you count or record? Perhaps you should not record words, but rather the theme of the whole document. There is no rule to use in deciding what to record. The best you can do is choose a coding unit that is neither too broad to be irrelevant nor too narrow to make the writer's strategy invisible. For different purposes such a coding unit may be a word, a clause or thought unit, a sentence, a configuration, or the composite theme of the entire document.

Numbers

Much information is stored in archives in the form of numerical records: crime rates and turnover rates; student grades and patient illnesses; production figures. Records provide indicators of such things as the amount and quality of output, characteristics of a group of people or places, and occurrences of a type of event or action.

A major source of easily accessible numerical archives is the Bureau of the Census, which publishes online and bound reports containing data from the Decennial Census of Population and Housing collected every ten years. The Bureau of the Census also makes available files with more detailed summary statistics such as the number of units in particular types of buildings in a geographical area. The ten-year time span is a barrier to studying shorter-span trends with this data, but smaller sample surveys are carried out and reported yearly and even monthly on particular problems.

• *Institutional and organizational records* present investigators with the task of tailoring existing numbers to achieve new ends. Wilner et al., in their 1950s housing experiment (1954), used housing-authority files to determine that their test and control groups of housing residents were comparable on date of birth, length of residence in Baltimore, degree of overcrowding in their former dwellings, and whether their dwellings had hot water and indoor toilet facilities. Similarly, the researchers used public school records to show that children earned higher grades if they lived in newer housing. Geographic Information Systems (GIS) data management programs make such analysis even easier.

However, before Wilner et al. could make these judgments, they had to tailor the data to their own needs—translate them into information for their own purposes. They sampled records to determine the type and format of data they contained as well as their completeness. When did the records begin? What characteristics were left out? How was *overcrowding* defined? Once the researchers determined that these data were suitable for their purposes, they devised forms on which to record precisely those items of data relevant to the study they were engaged in. Only after pretesting and revising these forms did they transfer the data so that they could analyze them appropriately.

When archives offer only composite rates—of vandalism or felonies, for example—investigators may not be able to determine whether the events the rates comprise are the ones they want to know about. The easier it is to disaggregate rates back to an original reporting unit, the more easily the data can be evaluated and—if acceptable—reorganized to fit a researcher's needs. For example, when Zeisel was studying school vandalism in Boston, he was able to analyze individual custodian reports in addition to overall rates. The reports mentioned broken equipment but failed to differentiate between damage from normal use and damage from malicious acts. They mentioned broken glass but did not differentiate between windows located on highly visible streets and windows in out-of-the-way hangouts. Zeisel wanted to find out whether the location of damage, intent of the "vandals," and breakage costs were related. The way rate keepers defined vandalism made these records inappropriate for his purposes.

In sum, organized numerical files may reduce the need to collect raw data, but they may still require analysis to determine their appropriateness for a researcher's purpose and reorganization to make them useful for this purpose.

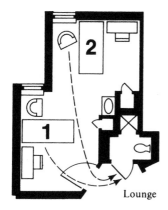
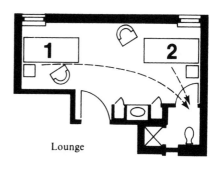

Alternative plans for hospital rooms. In the first scheme, patient 2 has his own bed area. When either patient wants to use the toilet, he must walk out of the common room into the shared lounge. In the second scheme, the toilet room is near the bed of patient 2. When patient 1 uses the toilet, he must go by the bed of patient 2.

Nonverbal Representations

Because behavioral scientists seldom analyze diagrams, photographs, and plans, they usually do so on an ad hoc and common sense basis. Environment-behavior researchers, in contrast, often find that to understand places and buildings the way they want, a major source of data is the analysis of behavioral implications of nonverbal and non-numerical representations. Analyzing how people and environments are presented in paintings, housing advertisements, and designers' renderings are still exceptional E-B research techniques, but analyzing the behavioral content of plans of physical settings is now common.

• *Behaviorally analyzing plans* means using them to develop tentative predictions, or hypotheses, about what might take place in an environment if it were built. For example, in planning two sets of hospital rooms, Good provided several bedroom and bathroom arrangements, which are illustrated in the figure below (Good and Hurtig, 1978).

Analyzing plan A might raise such questions as these: Does Patient 2 develop a sense of territory about his part of the room because only he has access to it? Will both patients feel that using the toilet requires making themselves presentable because they have to go through a public place (the lounge)? You can raise related behavioral questions for plan B: Does Patient 1's going to the toilet near Patient 2 prevent Patient 2 from developing a sense of territory in the room? Does Patient 1 feel like an intruder?

There is obviously no limit to the diversity of behavioral questions that researchers and designers can ask of plans. People must decide what type of behavioral plan analysis is best suited to solving their particular problem. For example, for her study of Twin Rivers, Keller (1976) analyzed sets of plans that were designed and redesigned over a period of years during several phases of planning—each in a different designer's office. The final set of plans was used for construction; the earlier ones were never built. Keller wanted to trace the design process over time by identifying design elements that were planned and later changed, then finding out why the designers made these changes. Keller used behavioral plan analysis as the basis for focused-interview questions with designers about their design intentions.

In their housing evaluation at Charlesview, Zeisel and Griffin (1975) not only used behavioral plan analysis to formulate questions for the architect about his intentions; they also developed behavioral hypotheses from the plan to direct later observational research at the site. For example, the plans showed parking areas located on the street side of most buildings (see figure). Entrances to these buildings are on the same side. At the "backs" of these buildings there are pathways and open grassy areas apparently intended for play. Zeisel and Griffin presented their analysis of these relationships as hypotheses to be tested:

- Tenants will consider the car location to be extremely convenient.
- Tenants will use the front entrances to the buildings when traveling to and from work, shopping, and other activities.
- Side effects will include use of the "front," parking-area side of buildings as play areas by children and observation areas by older residents—both of whom like to be "where the action is."
- Residents will use the shared "back" open spaces only infrequently because there is nothing to do there and because the doors near parking areas will draw any interesting "people watching" activity to the front of buildings.
- Area 1, where front doors are located on the interior of the housing complex, will be used more frequently.

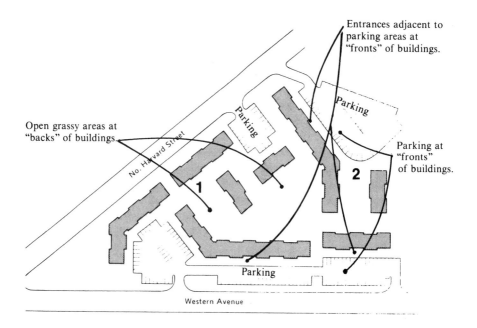

Site plan of Charlesview, showing parking areas and grassy areas.

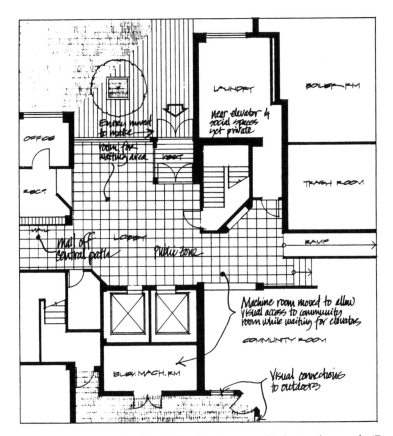

Annotated plan of housing for the elderly, showing uses of behavioral research. (From "Monitoring Environment-Behavior Research," by G. Epp, D. Georgopulos, and S. Howell. *Journal of Architectural Research*, March 1979, 7(1), 12–21. Reprinted by permission of the American Institute of Architects.)

Such hypotheses served as the basis for an evaluation study using behavior observation, trace observation, and structured questionnaires. This research helped to identify another part of the site where parking and entries behaviorally reinforce each other: area 2, at the right of the diagram.

The contradiction at Charlesview between activity generated by entries on the outside of the complex and the architect's apparent desire for activity to take place in the interior of the complex makes visible a significant type of design condition you can look for when analyzing plans: *apparent behavioral inconsistencies and contradictions* in the arrangement of design components (Jones, 1970). If you can identify unintended behavioral inconsistencies in the design of a project, you can improve your understanding of and control over the behavior consequences of design decisions and avoid contradicting yourself in design.

Epp et al. (1979) used behavioral plan analysis to still another end: tracing the way designers of housing for older persons used E-B research information about older people in their designs. Firms using an early version of Howell and Epp's research report, *Shared Spaces* (1976), were asked to analyze their own plans and record as annotations on the designs "what they perceived to be important design decisions with an explanation of why each decision was made and the projected impact they expected that decision to have on future elderly residents" (p. 15). Epp et al. (1979) used the designers' annotations to trace which data from the book designers included and how they did so. For example, in one project, responding to what they felt the research implied, designers relocated a main entry door to provide a place for residents to wait and watch for taxicabs or friends picking them up. They also relocated a machine room to enable residents waiting for the elevator to "preview" the community room—to see what is going on there without having to walk into it. The designers themselves behaviorally analyzed the resulting design of the entry and annotated their plans, enabling the research team to review the predictions from their point of view (see figure).

PLAN ANNOTATION

Annotating plans is a useful communication method in collaborative and group design projects to identify neuroscience and behavioral issues in plans—to point out which are significant to the use and impact of the eventual environment, to identify which have been addressed or not, to indicate which have been adequately responded to in design or not, and so on. Annotation simply means writing observations, comments, and hypotheses directly on architectural plans to make issues explicit and to share them easily with others. What is difficult and requires time and skill is to do this without obscuring the message the plans themselves are intended to impart.

Plan annotation can be useful in both practice and research, and is particularly useful in linking the two.

• *Issue identification annotations:* At the start of design, plans can be annotated with questions to be addressed in the next phase of design such as: "Wayfinding: Will this entry location contribute the most to building users being able to find their way easily?" and "Privacy: Will the windows between the corridor and the offices provide enough privacy for employees to concentrate adequately?"

• *Critique annotations:* In design reviews during design development, plan annotation can be employed when research data and evidence are being brought to bear on design decisions. Design review critique annotations identify where behavioral and neuroscience design performance criteria are or are not well met. For example, "Wandering or walking: Is the hearth destination at the end of the hallway path for Alzheimer's residents in an assisted living residence large enough and clearly identified to make sense to them?"

• *Presentation annotations:* When designs are being shared with clients, presentation annotations can focus the group's attention on the neuroscience and behavioral intentions and goals of the design. For example,

"Territory: Laboratory work areas are clearly separated from all circulation to provide scientific teams with a sense of territory and cohesion necessary for creative work."

• *Hypothesis annotations:* Plans can also be annotated as part of ongoing design research. In preparation for a POE study it is useful to draw out and indicate on the plans those elements that represent hypotheses that future research can test. These often are restatements of presentation annotations in language that makes explicit how the design intention might be tested. For example, "Stress recovery: The employee cafeteria has been located on an exterior wall with access to a garden to reduce work-related stress (cortisol levels) as quickly as possible (time) when breaks are taken."

To be internalized by designers, *critique annotations* must describe positive as well as negative elements in the design; otherwise, authors of the plans are likely to react by either disregarding the annotations entirely (if too negative), or focusing on improving problem areas while unwittingly making successful areas worse.

When presenting designs to clients, *presentation annotations* can be organized on plans to highlight selected attributes that respond well to E/B/N evidence. For example, a presentation annotation for a hospital with an accessible therapeutic garden could point out how the garden is located and designed to improve patients' recovery time after surgery. In a plan for a commercial setting, an annotation might describe how the location of a display near the entrance but off the main pathway is likely to improve sales of the item displayed, and why. Notice that these presentation annotation examples include a variable such as recovery or increased sales that a POE could eventually measure.

Annotations help the design process move forward. Presentation annotations at the end of a design cycle can alternatively be treated as hypothesis annotations at the beginning of a subsequent cycle identifying testable hypotheses that serve as the basis for a future POE.

BEHAVIORAL PLAN ANALYSIS

When you watch people analyze, or "read" plans, it can seem like an esoteric skill developed through mystical ritual. Reading behavioral implications of plans is a skill that can be developed by everyone who can (1) imagine things from perspectives that research shows other people have, rather than imagining that other people share one's own perspective, and (2) imagine in three dimensions things drawn in two—including objects and relations between places.

Other People's Perspectives

• *Generic E-B issues.* Environment-behavior research has developed a host of research-based theoretical issues that can help describe how people relate to their physical surroundings. These include:

```
┌─────────────────────────────────────┐
│  ┌───────────────────────────────┐  │
│  │ Behavioral Plan Analysis      │  │
│  ├───────────────────────────────┤  │
│  │ Other People's Perspectives   │  │
│  │                               │  │
│  │   Generic E-B issues          │  │
│  │   Generic issues: specific users │
│  │   Unique user-group needs     │  │
│  │                               │  │
│  │ Reading People into Plans     │  │
│  │                               │  │
│  │   Research-based scenarios    │  │
│  │   Behavioral side effects     │  │
│  │   Physical elements           │  │
│  └───────────────────────────────┘  │
└─────────────────────────────────────┘
```

- Degree of privacy: The degree to which people control the access of others to where they are
- Territoriality: The feeling individuals or groups have that they control what happens in a place—that they can use it as they like and can change it physically to reflect their personalities
- Personalization: The ways people change their physical surroundings—display, paint, furniture shifts—in order to have those places reflect their personalities, tastes, and identities
- Backstage behavior: The activities people engage in before and after presenting themselves to others: nurses present themselves to patients and doctors; job applicants to their potential employers; a host and hostess to their guests.
- Backstage behavior includes both "getting made up" and "letting down your hair"
- Wayfinding: How people find their way through new, and sometimes familiar, surroundings; the things that help people orient themselves and those that disorient and confuse them

These concepts do not tell you how each individual will react to a setting or how groups of people tend to react. However, if you keep these E-B issues in mind when you look at a plan, your looking is likely to raise questions that existing knowledge or further research may be able to answer. For example, in Good's hospital-room arrangement, potential problems for patients related to territoriality and privacy were identified. To answer questions about these problems, we need further knowledge of how hospital patients adapt to their surroundings, what their attitudes are toward sharing space with others, and how they feel about modesty in their robes. This information may be available if you search for it, because others may have already conducted such research. Whether research has already been conducted or not, the heuristic use of generic E-B concepts, such as territoriality and privacy, helps to "get into" a plan and identify issues for further exploration.

    • *Generic issues: specific users.* Generic E-B issues applied to a particular plan will refer to particular users, user groups, and settings. For example, questions about territoriality and privacy applied to Good's building refer to the way patients in hospitals behave. Applied to Howell and Epp's problem, they refer to older persons' behavior in elevator buildings. Among the many user groups and settings that have been studied are teenagers in parks, students in schools, patients in hospitals, older persons in housing, families with children in housing, employees in offices, and visitors in any setting.

Research can be used to determine the tendencies of people in certain groups to respond in particular ways to generic issues, such as wayfinding, territoriality, and privacy. For example, one study seems to indicate that patients waiting in various states of undress in cancer-treatment clinics value social contact with relatives and other patients more than privacy from members of the opposite sex (Conway et al., 1977). The more information designers have on this topic, the better the design of such a facility can provide opportunities for social mixing and privacy to meet the needs of the greatest number of patients. Another example is that teenagers in schools tend to take over particular places as their "turf" more than other places: they use slightly hidden areas behind schools as hangouts or clubhouses, and they perch on available planters and walls to watch people in more active areas (Zeisel, 1976a). Designers can use data about teenagers to provide less-fragile furnishings and surfaces in those areas to accommodate such potentially positive informal activity while minimizing property damage to the school resulting from rough play.

• *Unique user-group needs.* Some issues are unique to certain users. For example, older people with limited muscular ability to control pupil dilation and contraction are particularly sensitive to the contrast between dark surroundings and bright light—including sunlight (Pastalan, Mantz, and Merrill, 1973). Designers who maximize southern sun to warm a building might unwittingly be making it uncomfortable for older residents to use that side of a building. As another example, teenagers take part in more show-off and challenge activity than other groups. A hung ceiling in a park's recreation room—meant to be convenient for many maintenance tasks—is likely to present teenage users with an opportunity to show off by seeing who can jump the highest and break one of the panels. The resulting maintenance problems may be worse than the ones the hung ceiling was meant to solve.

In sum, E-B research provides designers and investigators with the chance to put themselves into someone else's shoes without relying on well meaning but often-misguided empathy and intuition. Such research data include descriptions of (1) generic E-B concepts, (2) generic concepts referring to specific users, and (3) unique user-groups' needs.

Reading People into Plans

Research findings about groups of people provide data about what some people tend to do in a setting. Such data do not tell you how individuals with diverse wants and needs will actually use the setting. Nor can descriptions of environments be used to predict what anyone will or will not do. Environments enable and constrain activities; they can encourage some activities by making

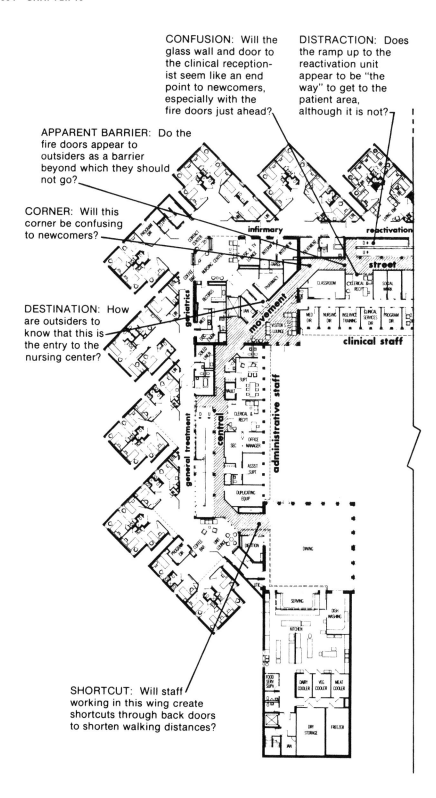

CONFUSION: Will the glass wall and door to the clinical reception-ist seem like an end point to newcomers, especially with the fire doors just ahead?

DISTRACTION: Does the ramp up to the reactivation unit appear to be "the way" to get to the patient area, although it is not?

APPARENT BARRIER: Do the fire doors appear to outsiders as a barrier beyond which they should not go?

CORNER: Will this corner be confusing to newcomers?

DESTINATION: How are outsiders to know that this is the entry to the nursing center?

SHORTCUT: Will staff working in this wing create shortcuts through back doors to shorten walking distances?

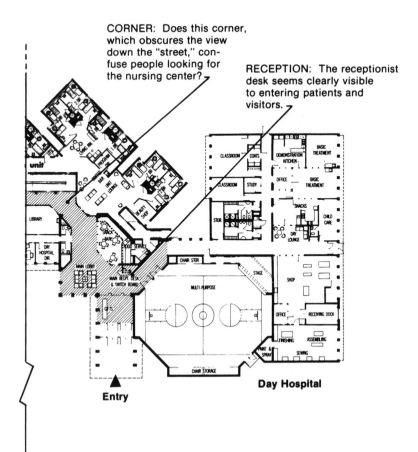

CORNER: Does this corner, which obscures the view down the "street," confuse people looking for the nursing center?

RECEPTION: The receptionist desk seems clearly visible to entering patients and visitors.

Entry

Day Hospital

Behavioral annotations raising wayfinding questions for future evaluation of the Norwood Mental Health Center, Wood County, Wisconsin. (Courtesy of Lawrence R. Good, Hougen–Good–Pfaller & Associates, Architects–Engineers.)

(From *Managing Vandalism*, by A. Scott, R. Fichter, and S. King. Illustrated by Kata Hall. Boston: Parkman Center for Urban Affairs, 1978. Used by permission.)

them easier to carry out and discourage others by making them difficult. For example, in Good's hospital, one visitor might find his way from the entry to the nurses' center with no difficulty while another gets hopelessly lost until a passing staff member gives her directions. If you want to use a plan to foresee some of the things that might eventually occur in a built environment, you must be able to imagine how different people using the environment will react to its various parts: If a nurse wants to relax, where will he go? If a visitor wants to relax, where does the hospital enable her to sit? To read people into plans in this way, three questions can be helpful:

- What *scenarios* does E-B research indicate particular users might enact in the setting: what will they want to do and need to do?
- What behavioral *side effects* will there be for particular users when they do what they want or need to do in the setting: what does the environment allow or force people to do, see, hear, smell, touch, and perceive on the way to their primary goal?
- What *physical elements* in the setting influence these reactions: what objects, barriers, and environmental attributes (such as size and shape)?

• *Research-based scenarios.* If you want to put yourself in someone else's shoes, one of the easiest people to imagine is a visitor trying to find his way. You probably have information to do this from personal experience in new places, especially if you are naturally curious and like to travel. If you ask yourself, "How would I know where to go if I were arriving here for the first time?" you will begin to look for and discover wayfinding clues in the design. You will begin to see places where paths are clear and places where they might be confusing. For example, in Good's mental-health clinic you might feel that the receptionist's desk is clear enough but that finding your way to the nurses' station might be confusing, since you will have to pass corners, a ramp going up to your right, a suite of offices to your left, and a set of doors in the hallway before even seeing the steps to the nurses' center. Using yourself as a reference point is generally not a good idea; it is difficult, if not impossible, to intuit accurately what others feel and do.

If you want the design decisions you make to have the effects you want in the eventual setting, you need to base scenarios on research as much as possible. To design on the assumption that patients in mental hospitals will spend most of their days in bed is not helpful, especially if research shows that they do not. Scenarios used in this way are aids to translating E-B research data into useful design information; they are not intended as marketing mechanisms based on explicit but fictitious views of how people might use an environment. Scenarios help to translate research data about what people want, how individuals or groups get what they want, needs people have and how they meet them, and particular perceptions people have—all the types of data this book's research methods can help to collect.

• *Behavioral side effects.* Research-based scenarios provide vehicles for reading into plans particular persons doing something: a patient who needs to go to the bathroom; a visitor who wants to find a nursing center; a nurse trying to relax during a hectic day. In different settings users would do these things differently. In one room a patient has to pass close to his roommate to reach the toilet; in the other both patients are forced to be seen by anyone sitting in the adjacent lounge. Good's nursing center is open on all sides to patients, visitors, and other staff members. To relax, nurses there might have to retreat into the nearby "records" room. In health care settings with some closed-off areas, staff can disappear more easily.

Only the number of possible scenarios limits the possible immediate behavioral and sensory side effects in a plan; in other words, there are no limits within the constraints research sets for possible scenarios. The environment that physical plans represent provides designers and E-B investigators with data to use to identify what is likely to happen when people use the environment. When, for example, a patient goes to the bathroom, you can read from lines on the drawing what kind of places he must pass through and what he will be likely to see, hear, smell, touch, and perceive on the way. The only question that remains is: What parts of the drawn setting are likely to be most helpful in making this determination?

• *Physical elements.* Plans are models of physical environments—you ought to be able to look at and do things to the two-dimensional drawing as if it were the real setting. Symbols represent objects:

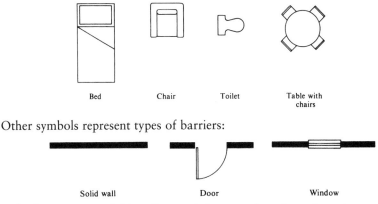

| Bed | Chair | Toilet | Table with chairs |

Other symbols represent types of barriers:

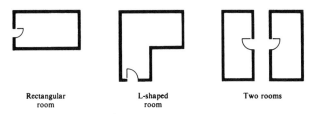

| Solid wall | Door | Window |

Still others represent field attributes of places, such as size, orientation, and shape:

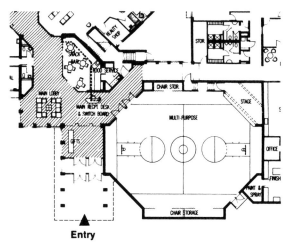

| Rectangular room | L-shaped room | Two rooms |

And some attributes of the environment, such as noise and light conditions, have to be inferred from the way symbols like the preceding ones are put together.

Entry

Identifying behavioral side effects: If a basketball game takes place in the multipurpose room and the doors are open, there might be much noise in the entryway. (Courtesy of Lawrence R. Good, Hougen–Good–Pfaller & Associates, Architects–Engineers.)

With knowledge of a handful of such symbols applied, for example, to Good's plan, you can begin to answer for yourself:

- What *objects* has the designer put into this plan to indicate how spaces are to be used? (Examples are chairs indicating visitors' lounge and a cafeteria counter indicating a place to eat.)
- What barriers have been provided between areas: what connections (glass between the entry area and the cafeteria; a ramp between the "street" and the "reactivation unit") and what separations (doors between entry and multipurpose gymnasium; wall between library and "street")?
- What *fields* does the designer set up by the way he plans and arranges spaces? (Shapes of various patient rooms; potential for noontime sun through the windows into the clinical staff offices.)

These are the same questions suggested in Chapter 9 to help designers understand the behavioral consequences of built environments.

As with any technique dependent on the skill of the person using it, everyone who analyzes the behavioral implications of plans will do it in her own way to meet her own purposes. If your purpose is to put yourself hypothetically into another person's shoes, you can do this successfully using your own intuition only for yourself as a user. At other times you must know your limitations and turn instead to E-B research.

DATA ARCHIVE UPDATE

Data archives are increasingly being mined with care, thoroughness, and insight—yielding practical E-B findings. The fact that so many studies have been carried out, models and analytic approaches developed, and theories proposed has created a new significant set of archives—books containing E-B findings, theories, and studies. In the past E-B researchers who identified a problem to study in a proposal or article had to look for references in sociology, anthropology, psychology, or one of the design disciplines. Archival studies now employ primarily E-B-referenced sources to elaborate problem definitions, theoretical approaches, analytic frameworks, methodologies, and analytic techniques, enhancing analysis sophistication and depth. One broad topic that has stayed in the forefront of environment-behavior as it has developed and matured is the implication physical environment has for specific crimes—car burglary, rape, prostitution, and arson among them. The availability of thorough archival crime data with clear physical environment referents has kept research focused on this topic. Another major development in archival methods is a plan analysis technique called Space Syntax explored at the end of this update.

After looking at three brief studies that elegantly demonstrate how much can be learned from thoroughly analyzing archival data, several more complex studies are described. The first set of studies deal with streetwalkers in San Diego, California; lost deer hunters in Nova Scotia, Canada; and baseball players. In each case, the authors selected their data sources because they were the most objective ones available and the researchers mined the archival data for all they were worth. The archival sources included data on the locations where streetwalkers were arrested, the place that the Nova Scotia Emergency Measures Organization found lost hunters, and players' recorded batting averages in domed and open stadiums.

Riccio (1992) wanted to understand one side effect of urban gentrification in San Diego, California—how it forced streetwalkers to change their solicitation behavior. Analyzing the location of arrests for prostitution in three sequential years of San Diego Police Arrest Records—a public data source— Riccio found that prostitutes who used to do business in traditional urban core and older urban waterfronts had moved to suburban commercial strips closer to their homes and where others complained more. In order to find out how these people selected the best location to engage customers—what specific physical features they looked for in a setting—Riccio offered a questionnaire to 100 prostitutes being held at the Los Colinas Correctional Center. Thirty-seven questionnaires were completed and returned.

These data made evident that prostitutes, like taxi cab drivers, need to be on the street where they can be seen by customers, that quick turnover contributes to their income, and that both cab drivers and prostitutes spend more time cruising than actually engaged with customers.

Most interesting, however, is the finding that unlike cab drivers, prostitutes face a dilemma when soliciting—they need to be seen and be invisible at the same time. They "also must be able to camouflage their profession or behavior to avoid being overly obtrusive for the general public, especially along suburban commercial strips. . . . [meanwhile] patrons [in automobiles] must be able to distinguish them from ordinary pedestrians." To achieve this chameleon-like appearance, streetwalkers choose locations where they can actively solicit one moment, and then quickly and discreetly blend "into the street scene when police are patrolling."

Where are these places? Bus stops and public telephone booths both provide opportunities to "blend in" by the streetwalkers merely sitting on the bus stop bench or picking up the phone. Another pattern that emerged is that streetwalkers choose to solicit near street corners and hotels—but not for the apparent reason. "Most hotels have parking lots for cars to pull into, whereas corners enable drivers to turn off the main thoroughfare to talk to soliciting women" (Riccio, 1992, pp. 564–55.) Because violent crime often follows "victimless" crime such as prostitution, the greater the predictability of such behavior, the greater is the chance of preventing violent crime.

Hill (1992) used three archival data sources in his study of older Nova Scotia hunters—records of land searches for lost persons maintained by Nova Scotia's Emergency Measures Organization, records of deer hunting licenses maintained by Nova Scotia's Department of Natural Resources, and census data. In Nova Scotia nearly 33 percent of all men over age sixteen hunt, and over 10 percent of all hunters are over sixty-five years old. These older hunters face a dilemma. Older people are often advised to engage in outdoor activities to maintain their health. Since they score worse than younger people on pen-and-pencil tests of spatial ability, this admonition may be sending seniors into danger.

The archives contained hard facts: of 338 reports of lost hunters the age range was sixteen to eighty-three years. In 213 cases, searchers rescued the hunters, in 116 incidents the subjects walked out of the woods on their own, and 9 incidents resulted in death.

Hill analyzed only archival data in determining if going into the woods to hunt was a healthy or dangerous past time for older people. He had many questions. Are older people disoriented by having to keep an eye on their prey—the deer—while maintaining a constant "fix" on their location in relation to home? Are proportionately more elders the subject of land searches than younger hunters? Are the paper-and-pencil tests on spatial ability more or less valid than actual "ecological" situations where elders need to find their way in places with which they are familiar—like the woods they have hunted in for many years? Archives held the answers to these questions—all of which is good news for elderly hunters wanting to continue recreational deer hunting.

> While elderly men constitute over 12 percent of people licensed to hunt deer . . . they become the subjects of only 6 percent of land searches for lost hunters. Moreover, lost elderly hunters were no less able than younger hunters to reestablish their orientation and walk out of the woods unassisted by searchers (Hill, 1992, p. 789).

Most deaths from hypothermia occurred among hunters aged fifty-one to sixty-seven and among the fifteen lost hunters over sixty-seven years old there were no such deaths. The data show that elderly hunters walk as far during the hunt as younger people and nevertheless remain safe. Hill explains that, like older chess players who play as well as younger players and older typists who type as fast as younger typists, older deer hunters develop alternative strategies in this outdoor activity. Older chess players consider fewer alternatives and make decisions to move more quickly. Older typists train themselves to scan more of the to-be-typed text while working so that they have more time to type each character. And older hunters tend to be more aware of landmarks they pass, knowing that they will otherwise have a more difficult time finding their way back home.

Goodman and McAndrew's (1993) use of five years of archival data in the Elias Baseball Analyst (Siwoff, Hirdt, and Hirdt, 1988) provide us with a data archive analysis touching on a lighter subject, albeit one with great financial consequences. Are domed or open stadiums better for baseball players' batting performance, and is real grass or artificial synthetic turf better for runners? Of the twenty-six teams studied, sixteen played in outdoor stadiums with natural grass, seven in outdoor stadiums with artificial turf, and three were housed in domed stadiums with artificial turf. No teams had a domed stadium with a natural grass playing field.

The archival data for each team included "number of home runs, batting averages, extra base percentage (percentage of hits that were not singles), stolen base percentage, and the number of errors" (Goodman and McAndrew, 1993, p. 122). These data showed that artificial turf was associated with significantly higher numbers of extra and stolen bases, and fewer errors, but neither higher numbers of home runs nor improved batting averages. Although the number of domed stadiums was small, making statistical analysis difficult, among all the stadiums with artificial turf, teams playing in domed stadiums had higher rankings for home runs and batting averages.

These studies demonstrate the rich store of data archives hold. The following studies show how archives can serve as the basis for complex and sophisticated environment-behavior research.

Lundrigan and Canter (2001) based their study of serial murderers' choice of where to bury bodies on archival data, as did Fritzon (2001), in her study of the relationship between arsonists' motives and the distance they travel to set fires. Both topics, while seemingly abstract and theoretical, contribute to the science and art of finding criminals who commit such acts. In both studies mean distances traveled by type of criminal are calculated, and both employ a form of statistical analysis and data display called SSA—Smallest Space Analysis—that "converts the associations among variables into distances plotted on a geometric map so that groups of thematically similar variables can be represented visually" (Fritzon, p. 50).

Lundigran and Canter start their research on serial murderers by employing content analysis of several sources to organize the data for each murder—a form of archival analysis first described in Webb et al.'s *Unobtrusive Measures* (1966). These sources included "newspapers and magazine articles, true crime books and academic texts" (p. 427). These data— particularly where each serial murderer lived and where they buried their victims—were triangulated for verification through interviews with people close to the criminal investigations.

The researchers wanted to explicate the inherent spatial logic of such offenses, even when the offender does not know there is one. It is not evident, for example, that serial murderers are aware they have a "criminal range" over which they operate (much like a bird has its own territory) and that because the general direction of sequential burial sites can be modeled, the sequence is more predictable than haphazard.

Based on their data analysis for each murder and murderer—murderer's home address, the sequence of the murder, and how far from previous burial sites and from the murderer's home the body was disposed—Lundrigan and Canter's findings and analysis are extremely helpful to investigators of serial crimes.

- Serial murderers appear to have one of three basic "criminal ranges" to which they keep consistently—less than 10 kilometers, 10 to 30 kilometers, and over 30 kilometers—and the home of each murderer can be found within that range.
- Each murderer selects his criminal range based on what he perceives to be a "safe" distance—especially for those with a smaller criminal range.
- Each murderer maintains "safety space" around his home that effectively acts as a buffer zone between body disposal sites and the offender's residence.

- The distance a particular offender selects as a safe distance from home is used in his or her calculating the distance necessary between sequential disposal sites in order to feel safe.
- Especially for those serial murderers who stay near home, the location of a previous disposal site substantially affects the choice of the subsequent site. "The offenders appear to be moving to different locations around the base for each subsequent site so that no two sites are in the same general area" (p. 429).
- Interestingly, serial criminals are not so different from the rest of us in their spatial choices. They too are influenced by basic human feelings of "familiarity, mental mapping and the psychological role of home" (p. 431).

All this came from imaginatively gathering data from old newspapers, magazines, and crime books!

A similarly intriguing set of results is found in Fritzon's archival data study of how arsonists select the location for their fire setting. In an earlier article published with Canter (Canter and Fritzon, 1998) the authors distinguished between acts of arson directed toward objects versus those toward persons, and those which were primarily expressive—to express a feeling and get attention—versus instrumental—those that served a purpose. Employing these characteristics, Fritzon developed a typology of four types of arson acts:

Types of Arson Acts		
	Property	*Person*
Instrumental	Damage	Destroy
Expressive	Display	Despair

She then used archival data from solved police files to determine different spatial patterns associated with the motivations of the four types. Before blindly relying on the quality of the archival data, Fritzon determined its biases, an important lesson to remember. If only solved crimes are included—as they were—those arson acts that are more difficult to solve, such as arson for profit, might be under-represented; and arson acts where the victim knows the arsonist are likely to be over-represented. Fritzon estimated that while these are biases of the data source, they were unlikely to affect the data she was planning to employ in her analysis—home address and address of the act of arson.

What did she find out about distances traveled by members of each group? The mean distance traveled for all arson acts was 2.06 kilometers, differing by type.

Types of Arson Acts		
	Property	*Person*
Instrumental	Damage 2.11 km	Destroy 6.24 km
Expressive	Display .54 km	Despair .56 km
	Mean = 2.06 km	

Expressive acts of arson—those carried out against oneself to draw attention to emotional distress, or against large public buildings for another type of attention—are carried out closer to home than instrumental acts. Those carrying out instrumental arson—either to conceal a crime, for peer acceptance, or to get revenge—traveled further. A spatial behavior model like this can provide important direction to arson investigators.

Space Syntax Plan Analysis

Plans—working drawings, schematic plans, and maps—represent a major source of archival data relating to the physical environment. A new and significant technique for plan analysis has been developed: space syntax. Space syntax combines topological with mathematical analysis to quantify attributes of the physical environment captured in two-dimensional plans. Employing space syntax analysis together with other environment-behavior methods such as observing behavior and interviewing enables researchers to develop models of behavior correlated with the characteristics of the plans. Because the plans can be described mathematically, attributes of different environments can be compared and predictive environment-behavior theory developed.

Space "syntaxticians" (Bafna, 2003) primarily develop two types of graphs to represent the sets of spaces they analyze, and analyze these in terms of particular elements.

TYPE OF MAP

- *Convex map:* A graph created by indicating each identifiable space as a node and the relationship between adjacent spaces as lines, with the sequence of linked nodes graphed, starting with the relationship between exterior and interior and then moving from the most common space to the spaces with the least number of connections—the ones deepest into the plan. From such a graph, qualities such as depth, connectivity, and rings are derived.
- *Linear or axial map:* A graph created by drawing the longest straight line possible between any two spaces—representing the longest sight line possible through a door, window, or other threshold—with each line represented in the graph as a "node" and each set of crossing lines as a "boundary" or connection between nodes.

ANALYTIC ELEMENTS

- *Boundary partition:* Boundary partitions are the edges of the spaces that define a node/space in a convex graph. In order to assign a node to a space for graphing, the analyst must decide what boundaries define that space. In the case of an office or home these would clearly be the walls of each room. In an urban streetscape, boundaries are less defined. An analyst generates definitions of boundary partitions to respond to the different degrees of spatial enclosure in each setting.
- *Depth:* The depth of one space from another can be calculated by counting the number of spaces through which a person would have to pass going from one space to another. Spaces with similar depth are seen as symmetric, while those with different depth are asymmetric. If the depth value of each node is calculated, an average depth—mean depth—can be calculated for a discrete set of graphed spaces

and when these are compared across several grouped spaces (an office, an urban neighborhood, a park), a comparative relative asymmetry can be derived.

• *Connectivity*: For a single space, the number of other spaces directly connected to it is its connectivity. In a convex graph, connectivity represents the number of other spaces directly accessible from it; for an axial graph, the number of axial lines that cross another axial line.

• *Rings, circuits, and chains*: Rings are representations of spatial configurations in which a person passing through a series of spaces would end up back at the original space. Different pathways in a ring or circuit have different derived characteristics and measurements such as depth and connectivity.

• *Degree of control*: This calculated characteristic implies a social or behavioral correlate to the physical relationships of spaces in plan. The degree of control a space has—or more precisely that a person in that space is expected to feel and have over social interactions—is by calculation inversely related to the depth of that space. If a person walking between two spaces has to pass through or by a third space, the person in the intervening space is assumed to have greater control.

• *Line of sight*: This is a second derived behavioral characteristic. The fact that every crossing set of axial lines represents the opportunity for people moving through a sequence of spaces to see into other adjacent spaces, the path itself can be seen as representing a sequential series of sight lines, and thus a particular set of visual experiences for users.

Depth and connectivity are straightforward descriptions of spatial relationships. While mean depth and rings still refer to physical space, they are derived characteristics of a larger set of spaces. Degree of control and line of sight are derived behavioral and social implications that are assumed to be linked directly to physical characteristics such as depth, rings, and axial connections. Research employing space syntax tests and elaborates these assumptions.

Space syntax is a useful addition to E-B plan and spatial analysis in that it enables spatial dimensions and characteristics that environment-behavior has long studied to be compared across settings. When linked to data from other E-B methods—behavioral observation, questionnaires, or other archival data—space syntax can serve as the basis for increasingly precise evidence-based hypotheses and eventually predictions of behavior in physical settings.

One exemplary use of space syntax plan analysis together with other data collection methods to study an environment-behavior phenomenon is Umut Toker's study of spatial relationships, unscheduled face-to-face interactions, and innovation in a university research center (Toker, 2005). Toker collected behavioral data through an activity log that scientists filled in along with a questionnaire, and then selectively employed space syntax plan analysis to augment his data analysis. The analysis focused on the way environment supports impromptu interactions, one of two significant contributors to productivity according to Brill (2001).

Pre-coded, self-administered activity logs the sixteen scientists in the study filled out for five consecutive weekdays elicited information on both pre-scheduled and coincidental face-to-face and electronic media contact—e-mail, phone calls, and in-office video conferencing. Toker selected activity logs to record behavioral data instead of direct observation to be able to identify "research related technical consultation," thereby avoiding the bias of an outside observer counting all contacts as equal. Locational data from the logs were eventually arrayed as behavior maps on floor plans.

Toker's questionnaire survey inquired about frequency of space use and locations where colleagues met. Open-ended questions addressed environmental likes and dislikes or "perceived environmental qualities." These data were then correlated with space syntax plan analysis calculations, identifying each space's configurational properties. Toker was particularly interested in the effect on interaction of "depth"—the minimal number of spaces a person has to pass through to reach a particular space. He also calculated the "global integration" of each space, the sum of that space's depth in relation to all other spaces in the Center, and its "local integration"— the total depth of a space from all other spaces within a limited number of steps of depth, usually three (Hillier and Hanson, 1984). Each space's visibility—the total area of space that can be seen from a point in that space—was also calculated.

Over 80 percent of all content-related communications were face-to-face and unscheduled. The higher the global configuration of an office in which someone worked, the greater the chance that person has of bumping into a colleague, and the higher the visibility from the office, the greater chance the office occupant has of making eye contact with others and thus the greater chance of non-office communications.

Toker's aim was to determine whether layout influenced the type and number of content-related contacts between scientists—to determine if certain environmental design characteristics can be seen as "precursors" to innovation. When he ran a straight correlation between visibility, depth, and content-related contacts, he found no correlation. But then Toker used his activity log data to identify what innovation calls "key communicators"—colleagues everyone seeks out because they are central to many scientific activities. When Toker omitted these two employees from the analysis, data showed that "higher configurational accessibility and visibility of cellular offices had [significant] positive correlations with higher numbers of unscheduled office visits." In other words, if you're an important person to speak with, it doesn't matter where your office is. People will find you. If you're new or junior, however, and you find yourself in an office on the beaten path, you are more likely to have professional contacts with your colleagues. Toker's use of multiple methods linked to space syntax analysis enabled him to explore these E-B phenomena at greater depth than a less coordinated methodology would have allowed.

The following case study of a Center for Multi-Handicapped Blind Children in Jerusalem employs archival analysis—primarily published sources—to augment a multi-method study to develop extensive design performance guidelines for a special user group.

Main upper-level entry.

CASE STUDY

THE JERUSALEM CENTER FOR MULTI-HANDICAPPED VISUALLY IMPAIRED CHILDREN
Ramot, Israel

The 35,000-square-foot Jerusalem Center for Multi-Handicapped Blind Children was built in 1991 in Ramot, Israel, a suburb of Jerusalem. Housing forty residential children, and serving twenty-five others who are brought to the Center on a daily basis, twenty full-time and twelve part-time staff work there, in addition to seven volunteers. The Center is primarily Jerusalem stone, a local material similar to Western Sandstone and gives the building a warm feeling. It has four stories, each with one or two major uses: the dormitory level, main entrance and classroom level, therapy and dining level, and the synagogue level where teachers' apartments and an outdoor playground are also located. Two open staircases connect the dormitory level to the main entrance level and an elevator that talks Hebrew serves all four levels.

Having hired project architect Adina Darbasi, who had local expertise but limited experience in designing for people with disabilities, Keren-Or decided to add to the team Wolfgang Preiser, an environment-behavior consultant and researcher, to develop design and planning guidelines for the project. The full project team also included liaisons from the client organization, New York–based Keren-Or, and the client's local representative in Jerusalem, Mr. Moshe Rips.

The consultant's task was to develop design performance criteria guidelines for the building. Research included analysis of archives to identify critical issues related to blindness in multi-handicapped children; site visits to precedent buildings from which exemplary design solutions could be distilled and adapted for the present project; on-site focused interviews with key informants about therapy and care of blind children in Israel; post-occupancy evaluation walk-throughs in existing facilities in Jerusalem serving blind children; focus group interviews with representatives of the client organization and the architect to troubleshoot and modify plans for the proposed future facility; and, finally, several post-occupancy evaluations of the completed facility, starting on opening day in 1991.

Keren-Or, a New York–based foundation, has as its mission the care and therapy of legally blind children who also have other physical or mental disabilities, or both. To maximize its effectiveness with limited resources, Keren-Or has developed a unique and humane philosophy of care, focusing on residential learning interactions. Meeting their mission and goal requires extensive staff and volunteer support, in addition to a building and gardens that enhance the life experiences of the children who live there.

Eight E-B research methodologies were employed to develop the project's design performance criteria.

1) *Archival and literature research:* Relevant literature Preiser had accumulated over the years and data he had previously collected while field-testing guidance systems for visually impaired persons proved invaluable in distilling key design features and guidelines. The archive, ranging in scale from product design and interiors to architecture and site design, helped design criteria for surface characteristics, dimensions, and color-coding, as well as general criteria for residential and training facilities for people with visual impairments.

2) *Focused interviews with walk-through probes:* Systematic observation and site visits to facilities serving persons with visual impairments in Germany and Switzerland permitted observation of successful and unsuccessful design features in use. These observation walk-throughs included a focused interview with the facility director and critical observations were documented by still photography.

3) *Individual focus interviews:* Focused interviews were conducted after the walk-through with key personnel, departmental supervisors at the facilities visited, and directors not previously interviewed.

4) *Plan annotation:* Environment-behavior annotations based on the site visit observations and interviews were recorded on plans of the visited facilities. These critique annotations, linked to the photographic documentation included both successful and unsuccessful design features.

5) *On-site observations:* In Jerusalem the E-B specialist carried out three strategic planning activities. First he evaluated Keren-Or's existing facility, housed in a large converted residential building. Included were systematic data on the operation through direct observation, still photography, and focused interviews with staff and some parents. Preiser also carried out a walk-through POE and interviews with the Director of the Jewish Institute for the Blind, and a walk-through POE of an unfinished building to assess its suitability for a project with such special requirements.

6) *Focus design recommendation sessions:* Based on his research, Preiser made specific short- and long-term strategic recommendations to Keren-Or's Board of Directors, the project team, and the architect. Intense political pressure to proceed with the project limited certain design modifications. For example, the decision was made to build on an extremely steep site that the City of Jerusalem had donated to the project, although this resulted in significant difficulties moving the children throughout the building.

7) *Opening day post-construction evaluation:* On opening day in 1991, Preiser conducted a walk-through evaluation that identified serious fire code violations and potential safety threats that were addressed.

8) *Post-occupancy evaluations:* At one and three years after occupancy, post-occupancy evaluations were carried out, resulting in numerous recommendations, many of which have been implemented. The conceptual framework and methodology for such evaluations can be found in Preiser (1996), Preiser, Rabinowitz, and White (1988), Preiser and Ostroff (2001), and Preiser and Vischer (2005).

The environment-behavior research resulted in general planning and design criteria for residential/training/educational facilities for the visually impaired, many of which were included in the building as designed and built.

EVIDENCE-BASED DESIGN GUIDELINES
FOR THE VISUALLY IMPAIRED AT KEREN-OR

- *Safety Codes:* For this vulnerable population, meeting safety codes is particularly critical, including fire codes, UBC and life-safety code, and ADA standards. These result in wider doorways, additional exits, and obstacles eliminated from emergency evacuation paths.

Rest period.

- *25 Percent Space Premium*: 25 percent more space is needed for this group of users when compared with persons who have primarily physical disabilities, because these students need to move around more to orient themselves to objects and furniture in their environment as well as to spaces, walls, and other built-in contextual elements. In addition, they tend to have a larger "space bubble" around them—a zone where they feel intruded upon by others.
- *Site Criteria*: Proximity to schooling, training, shopping, restaurants and cultural facilities is essential, therefore community facilities need to be within walking distance. A site near buses and other public transportation with little movement interference from traffic and congestion, is ideal. Outdoor sports and recreational activity amenities appropriate to the user group are also needed, and a residential appearance helps such a facility fit into the neighborhood.
- *Residential Scale*: Because it is home to students and staff, the building needs to appear and feel like a real home. To maintain hominess, plan spaces for training and educational activities apart from living areas; use a variety of forms, materials, and contrasting textures; and include natural materials and day lighting, residential spatial relationships, and colors. Recognizing regional architectural features adds to residential appearance.
- *Bedrooms*: Bedrooms must be large enough to accommodate residential furniture, any necessary special equipment, and circulation. Students need both personal space and protection for their belongings. Moveable furniture increases the feeling of control a blind student has.
- *Common Living Rooms*: More than average space is needed in common rooms for people with cognitive disabilities because of their larger "space bubble." "Open-plan" common area design provides ease of supervision on the one hand, and a feeling of togetherness on the other.
- *Bathrooms*: Bathrooms need to be usable with wheelchairs when the door is closed, and lateral transfer to the toilet from the wheelchair must be possible. In addition to meeting all ADA requirements, increased student control can be supported by lower mirrors; lavatories with lower controls; lever-type handles on sinks, doors, and lavatories; switches within reach of the wheelchair user; hard and smooth floor materials for wheelchair users; maximum door pull of eight pounds; choice between roll-in showers and bathtubs; and individual private showers and toilets.
- *Loop Guidance Handrails for Outdoor Spaces*: Handrails installed along a prescribed set of pathways allow able-bodied, visually impaired people to enjoy the outdoors on their own. Loop configurations that guide the user from one point in the system, through outdoor spaces, and back to the beginning support individual independence. Where pathways intersect, a crossbar mounted on the handrail indicates that the guidance system is interrupted ahead and the user will soon have a choice of direction.
- *Touch and Smell Gardens in Raised Planters for Wayfinding*: Visually impaired users can easily follow touch and smell gardens in raised planters arranged around the periphery of an outdoor space. Material with Braille labels and/or raised lettering that indicates the type of plant at a given location, help students even more when they are located at the top of three-foot-high planter boxes made of smooth material such as finished wood. A planter "shoreline" that loops from the entrance to the garden area and back after letting students explore the garden, and the sound and touch of a water element, such as a fountain, further aids wayfinding for the visually impaired person. Braille labels and

Stair safety gates.

raised lettering at the top of the planters indicating the type of plant at a given location help students even more.

- *Hallways*: An unambiguous single main hallway with secondary hallways branching off in clear, hierarchical fashion helps the visually impaired find their way.
- *Community Plan*: One way to create community in such situations is to organize group living spaces into "cottages" with one resident teacher or counselor assigned to and living in each cottage. Single-level cottages permit direct access from living spaces to an outdoor garden for each community group.
- *Window Safety*: For the visually impaired, especially those with cognitive difficulties, safety measures at windows are particularly important to prevent accidental falls. Using window stops and safety glass rather than grates helps maintain a residential image.
- *Fence Safety by Planting*: Planting thick, thorny shrubbery in front of perimeter fences, and on decks, terraces, naturally discourages visually impaired students from getting too close to fences, preventing climbing and accidents.
- *Stair Safety*: Pedagogically, residents need to learn to climb staircases by themselves because they will find staircases in regular housing and other multi-level buildings they use. On the other hand, stairs are dangerous for students with physical disabilities who mistakenly gain access. Lockable gates that indicate where a staircase begins can avoid accidents while enabling able-bodied, blind residents to use the staircases safely on their own.
- *Differential and Adjustable Height Fixtures*: When residents range in age from eighteen months to eighteen years each needs quite different amenity heights. Differentiated and adjustable height fixtures such as sinks, toilets, and water fountains enable each person to adapt the height of amenities to his or her needs. Visually impaired students may not know whether to reach up or down for an appliance, and if they have a physical disability, may not be able to do so.
- *Split Handrails*: A second handrail, installed at half-height below all regular height handrails, is particularly helpful for smaller children.
- *Tactile Art and Decor*: Artwork in such a building can provide wayfinding landmarks and stimulation in addition to presenting a friendly image for residents, staff, and visitors. Unique pieces of artwork on hallway and activity area walls

Hanging napping basket.

achieve this particularly well when they are sculptural, relief-type art that visually impaired people can touch and explore.

- *Colors for Residents with Residual Vision*: Bright and cheerful colors and distinctly color-coded floors contribute to sensory stimulation and way finding for residents with residual vision.

- *Tactile Flooring Clues*: Changing flooring material and texture near doorways, stairways, and other dangerous places warn residents and visually impaired visitors that they are approaching a doorway that might swing into their face or another intersection at which they need to pay particular attention.

- *Differentiated Door Hardware*: Emergency egress doors with textured doorknobs that are shaped differently from the standard hardware on safe interior doors can help residents differentiate one type of door from another. This empowers those students with the capacity to understand the difference between doors of different sorts.

- *Handrail Orientation Device*: Handrails mounted on all wall surfaces in hallways and other circulation spaces support both wayfinding and physical disability. Braille messages or even signals like upholstery nails inserted into the top of the handrail at strategic spots can indicate floor levels, room numbers, and other information.

- *Talking Elevator and Safety Keypad*: The first Hebrew-speaking elevator in the world was installed by Otis to provide orientation to students moving between floors. The children found it a wonderful place to play, but this raised safety issues. A coded keypad that staff could use to operate the elevator, but not unsupervised students, resolved this safety problem.

- *Orienting Interior Spaces*: In open-plan interior spaces, such as dining halls or assembly areas, bookshelves and other space-defining elements can help create smaller, more manageable spaces. A student entering a dining room divided by bookshelves or other "shoreline" guidance devices can proceed to her assigned seat at the dining table on her own. Such an environment permits users to compute their progress toward their destination without white canes.

- *Hallway Width*: Hallways no more than six feet wide make it easier for visually impaired persons to maintain their bearings, because wider hallways feel more like a place than a pathway. A narrower hallway provides more directional cues than one that is wider.
- *Hanging Napping Basket*: A basket-like device suspended from a single point in the ceiling has been found to be an ideal relaxation/napping place for small children while in the classroom.
- *Raised Doorknobs*: Door hardware moved from normal height to approximately six feet off the floor helps prevent children from leaving classrooms unattended during unsupervised moments. Staff can reach the doorknob, but children cannot.
- *Dutch Half-Doors*: Dutch doors in bedrooms that allow the top half to be kept open (swung into the room) while the bottom half is latched into the door frame help teachers acoustically and visually supervise children's bedrooms. They also provide cross-ventilation from air circulating between the windows on the outside of the building to openings in the interior atriums. This was particularly important at the non–air conditioned Center.

These evidence-based guidelines reflect a unique and humane philosophy of caring for multi-handicapped blind children. The focused E-B research carried out in similar facilities around the world, together with the knowledge of the "resident experts" who operate the Center, ultimately led to a high-quality environment. A series of ongoing follow-up POE visits identified additional inadequately addressed operational, functional, and psychological issues that were resolved through modifications. Although a flat site with direct access to the outside might have made a "cottage concept" design more possible, the present Center Director reports that the similarity of floor plans on each floor helps occupants orient themselves and find their way. The Center's mission and therapeutic philosophy is to encourage improved planning at future similar facilities elsewhere and for this reason it encourages post-occupancy evaluation and comparative analysis by others using these guidelines.

This case study is based on the work of Wolfgang F. E. Preiser, Ph.D., Professor of Architecture, School of Architecture and Interior Design, College of Design, Architecture, Art, and Planning, University of Cincinnati.

OVERVIEW

Archives of documents—from newspapers to institutional records and architectural plans—can provide E-B investigators and designers with readily available data about the past. Investigators who overcome potential problems of data access, completeness, and relevance have access to varied types of data: words, numbers, and nonverbal representations. Nonverbal representations—especially two-dimensional plans—remain a special source of data for E-B researchers who want to learn from people and apply what they find out about people to designing environments. In behavioral plan analysis, to foresee how others will react to an environment, designers and investigators have to use research to gain insight into other people's perspectives. For the same reason, you have to be able to read plans with these perspectives: to understand what effects elements in a particular plan will have on eventual users. These skills will enable designers to avoid imposing their own empathy and subjective intuition on their research data and on future users of environments they design.

In the next chapter we look at how a neuroscience and design approach provides insight into environment-behavior knowledge, concepts, and practice. The expanded E/B/N paradigm is applied to understanding existing E-B knowledge, and to defining directions for future study.

CHAPTER 14

ENVIRONMENT / BEHAVIOR / NEUROSCIENCE

This chapter demonstrates the relationship between neuroscience and environment-behavior in research and practice. The E/B/N approach is first applied to basic E-B concepts and used to analyze the impact of neonatal intensive care unit environments on premature babies. After a brief discussion of hypotheses and E/B/N design performance criteria, research employing internal state measurement approaches is reviewed, and an E/B/N design case study of an Alzheimer's assisted living treatment residence is presented.

Neuroscience and E-B Concepts
  Place, personalization, territory, and wayfinding

What Is the Real Difference between E-B and E/B/N?
  Fetal development and neonatal intensive care unit design

Constructing E/B/N Hypotheses and Design Performance Criteria—
Critical First Steps
  Elements of hypotheses that link neuroscience and E-B
  Selected examples of learning environments that support
  brain development and learning

Methods for Measuring Internal States
  Cortisol, blood pressure, fMRI

Case Study: Neuroscience Design for Alzheimer's Assisted Living
  A built environment that contributes to the treatment of its residents

NEUROSCIENCE AND E-B CONCEPTS

If a new paradigm is to further the discipline of environment-behavior studies, it must shed new light on old concepts and introduce new concepts, methods, theories, and models. Place, personalization, territory, and wayfinding are four topics that form the core of E-B theory and practice. They also play a central role in the evolution of the brain in all animals, including *Homo sapiens*. Therefore these concepts are particularly robust and strategic for exploring what a neuroscience perspective can add to traditional E-B approaches.

> *Four E/B/N Concepts*
> Place
> Personalization
> Territory
> Wayfinding

Place

Place—space that holds meaning—may be the most fundamental concept in environment-behavior studies. Research into the meaning and use of built places, naturally occurring places, and culturally important places is the basis of much E-B theory and practice. In the neurosciences, studies show that words and concepts that hold meaning are remembered and learned more profoundly than non-meaningful terms. This is likely to hold for "meaningful spaces"—places—as well.

Applying neuroscience concepts of non-semantic, semantic, and elaborative semantic meaning to space—terms developed to describe how people understand and interpret words—yields a potentially useful taxonomy of place. *Non-semantic* places are those we hardly know, like one of many street corners we pass on a trip downtown that holds no special meaning for us. We hold *semantic* knowledge of places that are set in our brains in context, but not in a context with deep personal or intellectual meaning for us. A place with semantic meaning might be a well-known vacation spot, such as Disney World in Florida, or the Piazza San Marco in Venice. An *elaborative semantic* place is one that is firmly embedded in a personally meaningful context. The homes we live in and those we grew up in evoke elaborative semantic memories, as do spiritual buildings such as mosques, synagogues, and churches. Defining *place* as space with meaning—semantic and elaborative semantic space—invites researchers to employ cognitive neuroscience methods and perspectives to determine precisely the types of places that hold the most meaning for users, places with deeper meaning for particular cultures, and what particular elements of those places inspire deep meaning in users (Kagan, 1997).

The concept of place is not new to cognitive psychology and neuroscience. Children's awareness of place is one of the earliest brain capabilities to develop. As psychologist Jerome Kagan and his colleagues point out (Herschkowitz et al., 1987), starting at the age of ten months children in unfamiliar settings begin to react to strangers and to the absence of their mothers (Gazzaniga, p. 59). For children to behave this way at such an early age, major changes in brain maturation must occur that enable them to distinguish familiar and unfamiliar places.

> Brain circuits are hooking up on a preprogrammed plan, and behavioral changes are automatically occurring in response to maturational shifts in the brain. Genetically programmed brain circuits are doing their job [to recognize the difference between places they know and those they do not] (Gazzaniga, p. 59).

Personalization

Personalization is the act we engage in to make a place our own—to reflect our personalities, our past, and our aspirations. Why do we do this? Is it merely because we feel good in our own places, or is there a more fundamental purpose? Neuroscience research suggests that there is a more profound reason. Memories of our past largely define our selves—who we believe we are. People with amnesia who cannot remember their pasts say that they do not know who they are, that they have lost their "selves" (Schacter, 1996).

Personalized environments that express who we are to the outside world also cue our memories and feelings about ourselves. Stimulating memories of our past through personalized environments reinforces a sense of who we are. We can call environmental cues that have these effects *environmental personalization memory cues*. For those with healthy brains, small environmental cues such as carrying a picture of family members in one's wallet can achieve this memory stimulation. However, environmental personalization memory cues grow in importance for people whose brains are not functioning as well, such as people living with Alzheimer's disease. For Alzheimer's residents, out of sight is often out of mind. With little working short-term memory, people living with Alzheimer's often feel lost and lack a "sense of self." Continual environmental reminders of their history and who they are can help them to overcome these feelings. Pictures of family members on the walls of their bedrooms and living rooms, framed reminders of their life's work and achievements, and a residential setting reminiscent of their previous homes help people living with Alzheimer's remain aware of themselves as people—people with pasts. Such personalized environments stimulate brain regions that this group of people cannot stimulate themselves. The same process takes place as we all age and becomes more important as our brains generate fewer memories of who we are that provide us with a sense of self. In the first twenty-five years of environment-behavior studies, there was speculation about such hypotheses, but researchers had only crude ways to test them. Newer neuroscience technologies provide researchers the opportunity to achieve much greater understanding.

Territory

Recognizing different types of *territory*, a skill closely related to place recognition, is an environment/behavior/neuroscience (E/B/N) concept essential to the survival of all species. The simplest cue to distinguishing one territory from another is when one moves from a familiar place to an unfamiliar one. Animals need to know the extent of their realm: where they can roam safely, where they can expect social support from others, and where predators are at a disadvantage. Studies of mammals, according to Kagan (2001), "have shown that the ability to distinguish territory is built in, genetic, and adaptive." If a young mammal wanders too far from the nest, it is likely to face dangers it cannot negotiate. The brains of certain animals are pre-set and hard-wired with an understanding of how far they can go safely, and how to get back home in the most direct way.

It is difficult, if not dangerous, to draw on territory studies of animals for lessons about humans because traditionally humans have wandered far from home, even moving between continents. An argument can be made, however, that a primary territorial marker for people is the sense that they have moved from a familiar to an unfamiliar environment. Thus the brain capability that children develop at the age of ten months to distinguish familiar and unfamiliar environments is probably the key to their ability to determine where their own territory ends and another begins.

Environment-behavior scientists need to find out how human brains process territorial information. Such neuroscience studies are likely to determine that, in addition to hard-wired, brain-based place definers, our brains also hold hard-wired territoriality definers and markers. Neuroscience studies can help us better understand the importance of territoriality to our survival and provide aid in defining the types of territorial markers that work best for people of different cultures and subcultures.

Wayfinding

Linking place and territory, *wayfinding* describes the mental and physical activities associated with finding the way to food and potential mates, avoiding predators, and getting home to safety. The ability to find our way also helps us explore new territories, survive when our food sources have dried up, read cues from others who wish us to follow, and negotiate new and urgent situations such as hospital admissions.

Studies of small mouse-like voles who can find their way without ever learning a route have shown that wayfinding is a hard-wired brain activity.

> Many processes that guide us—wayfinding processes—are mental activities, yet they are similar to low-level reflexes in being built-in adaptations fabricated by the brain when it encounters a challenge. . . . Examples of wired-in mechanisms found in animals are useful in thinking about this fact. Take the spatial behavior of the vole, that ugly little beast living in farm fields (Gazzaniga, p. 64).

Certain birds are born with an ability to recognize the winter night sky, demonstrating the same hard-wired wayfinding ability in their migratory patterns. Young birds who are kept inside, away from stars they might study on their own, or are separated from adult birds who might teach them about the stars, "migrate" south when they are put into a planetarium with the stars in the night sky artificially set for winter.

While it is unlikely that neuroscience will determine that humans are hard-wired to fly south in winter, it is certain to uncover which wayfinding cues hold greater meaning for humans and thus have greater effect—and that some may even be hard-wired.

> A moment's thought should tell you that your capacities for . . . navigating around in the world are built-in features of your brain. If each brain had to learn all the rules of just one complex mental skill [like wayfinding], people would be wandering around aimlessly in the dark (Gazzaniga, p. 171).

Cognitive science has already uncovered cue recognition information that designers can apply. Knowing that physical cues located below eye level are more readily processed and attended to than those located above it, wayfinding cues that designers place in our lower field of vision are likely to be most effective. Gazzaniga (1998) believes this trait has evolved from our need to identify predators and track our prey for food, with our ancestors being more likely to find tracks of prey and lurking predators on the ground and in bushes than up in the trees. As he points out:

> Through evolution we have tuned our attentional system to be more sensitive to objects in our lower visual field. This enhanced capacity to process information in our lower field is consistent with there being more connections to the parietal lobe from the part of the visual brain that represents the lower visual field (Gazzaniga, p. 99).

This is why military snipers waiting in ambush are less detectable when they position themselves in trees rather than on the ground. Further neuroscience understanding of such spatial abilities will help designers more effectively plan environments for wayfinding.

In sum, place, personalization, territory, and wayfinding are critical subjects for studying the convergence of environment-behavior and neuroscience approaches. Each provides fertile ground to explore how the neurosciences can provide additional insight for E-B researchers and practitioners. As we progress down this path, we must keep our eyes open for other critical concepts and approaches that are certain to emerge and enrich the field.

NEUROSCIENCE/DESIGN ARRIVING AT DIFFERENT DESIGN CRITERIA

There is no reason to add another science to those that are already part of environment-behavior if the only consequence is a slightly deeper interpretation of a few concepts and topics. This is not the case with the neurosciences, however. The promise is much greater. To identify how greatly the neurosciences contribute to E-B studies and design, we can look at the example of design of and research on neonatal units for premature infants.

A user-needs analysis of settings for these highly vulnerable babies focuses on avoiding the health dangers they face from being born too early and that place them in intensive care, and on providing them with qualities of life that will aid their healthy development. Such an analysis concentrates on the environmental needs that must be met so that nurses can watch for danger signs, doctors can respond quickly, and parents can give the children the family warmth they need. The result is an environment that has enough light for caregivers to see visual danger signs, alarms to alert nurses and others to physiological distress the baby may be experiencing, and areas that are large and private enough for family visits yet isolated enough to prevent infections from spreading. All this makes complete sense from any point of view—except the baby's. Taking into account what we know about brain development during this critical period in the child's life, a very different picture of need emerges.

Looking at fetal brain development tells us what the best environments for prematurely born babies are, and what actual damage can be wrought by using a pure E-B approach to study environments. The following discussion closely follows the research and analysis of Stanley Graven and his colleagues (1992).

The genetically determined process of fetal brain development comprises three major structural elements: sequence, timing, and stimulus.

• *Sequence*—there is a preset, hard-wired sequence of sensory development that dictates which senses develop first, which senses follow, and in what order.

• *Timing*—the sensory developmental sequence also has a temporal element; certain sensory abilities develop in the first trimester of pregnancy, others in the second, some just before a baby is born, and others after birth.

• *Stimulus*—the type of stimuli needed for healthy development at each stage is pre-set. It is either endogenous (generated by the fetus itself) or environmental (from the outside world) and of a particular type and intensity.

At the global scale of brain development there are three sequential stages. Early in fetal development, genetically encoded cells in the central nervous system and genetically driven biochemical processes guide neurodevelopment of the brain's basic structure, nerve tracks, the sensory organs, and all the basic pathways and connections that future functioning will employ. In the second stage of brain development, the genetic blueprint leads to emergence of the basic structures of the sense organs—the eyes and ears—including their connections via pathways to the central nuclei and the cortex. The visual and auditory cortices develop without any stimulation, but "in anticipation" of both the endogenous and environmental stimuli they will eventually receive, and that will continue to affect their development after the genetic blueprint is fulfilled. The third developmental stage occurs after birth, when environmental stimuli effect changes to the previously genetically guided pathways, memory circuits, and cortical neuronal connections. The answer to the question of nature versus nurture is evident in this process. Each has its place in the brain's development—and "its place" is clearly genetically encoded. Neither speeding up the process nor changing this sequence in any way improves development. Recent work by neuroscientist Fred Gage (Eriksson et al., 1998) has demonstrated that environmentally affected development continues longer into our lives than previously thought.

A finer-scale and more particular development sequence of the sensory systems takes place in the fetus parallel to this global development. The first senses to develop are touch, pain, position, and temperature sensitivity—the somatesthetic modalities. The middle ear systems that detect motion develop next—the vestibular modalities—with the chemosensory systems of smell and taste following soon afterwards. Between the twelfth and twenty-fourth week of fetal development these sensory systems are well established with their connections to midbrain and basal ganglia.

The last senses to appear—after the thirty-second week of gestation—are the auditory and visual modalities, and it is essential that these two develop in that sequence. First the fetus begins to develop systems by which it recognizes sound and vibration, then visual development takes place. Both occur without any external stimuli! This does not mean there are no stimuli at all—just no external ones.

The fetus senses sound and vibration during these important last months before birth. And during these important months, when the eyes, retinas, tracks, and visual cortex are developing, the fetus will generate its own "endogenous" stimuli during rapid eye movement (REM) sleep, preparing the cortex for the external visual stimuli it will get at birth.

When a baby is born, the anticipated external stimuli play their role in development. What she sees and under what conditions she sees it influence the development of her optic cortex. She needs "clear images" such as faces and objects positioned at a distance that keeps them in sharp focus, and "varying light levels" so that she can see the objects clearly and her eyes can develop correctly.

Each system has its own critical period during which the body's genes have programmed us to be extremely sensitive to external environmental stimuli that impact cortical neuronal connections and locations. During the critical period for the visual system that begins at birth, the things a baby sees and the light hitting her eyes stimulate optic cortex neurons to move into column relationships based on the visual images. During the critical period for the child's auditory system that begins about two months before birth and continues after birth and beyond, there are major changes to his auditory nucleus. Specifically, this is the period when the child develops the ability to discriminate between frequencies and recognize patterns.

We are genetically programmed to develop our auditory system before our visual system, to start these processes after the thirty-second week of gestation, and to anticipate external stimuli after about the fortieth week of development— after we are born. It should be clear from this explanation that premature infants emerging into an external environment for which they are ill prepared run an extremely high risk of having this development sequence disrupted.

The Confrontation between Environment and Development

Being born prematurely is a shock to an infant's systems. Being faced with an environment designed to save its life presents another type of shock. What is the baby faced with?

- Bright lights to help caregivers see what they are doing in emergencies
- Noisy equipment to monitor vital signs and identify distress
- Bright daylight
- Noise from air handling units managing air changes to reduce infections
- Communication system noise when staff members need to attend to an infant immediately
- Staff voices that are raised to be heard over the noise of the environment.

This may be an extreme scenario that is not found everywhere, but it is not infrequent. What are the health outcomes for a premature baby—a preemie—who lives her first months of life in such an environment? According to Graven and his team, the genetically programmed sequence is disrupted, the timing of the genetically programmed development process is upset, and external stimuli are inserted into the development process earlier than genetically anticipated and in much higher doses. The impact is often damaging to the auditory and visual systems, which are the last to develop.

Health Outcomes

Such an environmental onslaught has a major impact on both the auditory and visual systems. The baby's auditory system develops trouble with *frequency discrimination*. Later in life he has difficulty distinguishing between adjacent tones because the "bandwidth for the reception of sound" in his ear widens. For the rest of his life he has difficulty differentiating between adjacent tones with slightly different frequencies. A musical career that requires perfect pitch is out of the question.

Impacts on the visual system can also be significant. With few gentle faces at a nearby distance and in the correct amount of light intensity, and with exposure to overly bright lights for too long a period—wavelength, intensity, and duration—the eye grows too quickly, resulting in myopia.

It is not our goal to generate a set of design performance criteria for a healthy neonatal intensive care unit, but rather to demonstrate that if we want to meet Changeux's challenge to create brain-supportive environments, adding neuroscience perspectives and methods to those already in the environment-behavior arsenal makes good sense.

Formulating Testable E/B/N Hypotheses

To take advantage of the neurosciences in E-B research we must be able to generate joint E/B/N research hypotheses. The following model, developed in two workshops sponsored by the Academy of Neuroscience for Architecture (Zeisel et al., 2004; Whitelaw et al., 2005) indicates the discrete elements that constitute an E/B/N hypothesis: physical environmental characteristics, neuroscience dimensions, physiological factors, behavioral outcomes, and performance outcomes—with measurement techniques suited to each subject matter.

MODEL FOR E/B/N DESIGN RESEARCH HYPOTHESES

	DOMAINS OF STUDY			
Design	*Neurosciences*		*Environment-Behavior*	
	Variables in each domain			
Physical environmental elements	Neuroscience dimensions	Physiological factors	Behavioral outcomes	Performance Outcomes
	MEASUREMENT TECHNIQUES TARGETED TO SPECIFIC DISCIPLINES			
Measures describing the characteristics of environment such as plans and dimensions	Neuroscientific methods to measure this dimension such as PET scans, MRI, and ERP evoked potentials	Indicators of physiological reactions such as cortisol saliva tests and blood pressure readings	Behavioral observation and other measurements such as systematic observation, photography, and self-report	Paper and pencil test, performances, portfolios, expert judgment

Were we to turn the discussion of the relationship between environments in NICUs into a set of hypotheses for future research, we could use this model to generate a work product. It might look like this:

E/B/N DESIGN RESEARCH HYPOTHESES

The light and noise characteristics of neonatal intensive care units, if not controlled to respond to the developmental needs of premature infants, will have both immediate and long-term negative health impacts on the children's auditory and visual systems and associated behavioral and performance outcomes.

	DOMAINS OF STUDY			
Design	*Neurosciences*		*Environment-Behavior*	
	Variables in each domain			
Lighting intensity, duration, and frequency Sound levels	Neuronal development in auditory and visual systems	Characteristics of the eye and ear	Ability to discriminate frequencies Myopic vision	Hearing problems, lack of musical skills, learning and work problems
	MEASUREMENT TECHNIQUES TARGETED TO SPECIFIC DISCIPLINES			
Lux and decibel measures	PET scans, MRI, ERP evoked potentials	Physiological interventions— CAT scans	Auditory testing, vision tests	Test scores, school performance, job performance

E/B/N PERFORMANCE CRITERIA
DESIGN GUIDELINES

Hypotheses, informed guesses as to how several variables relate to each other, can be used to design research methodologies to study specific relationships among variables. Once research determines such relationships, this knowledge can be used in design to generate *performance criteria design guidelines.*

In design programming, the term *performance criteria* refers to the objectives a particular design element must meet in order for the entire design to meet its goals. E-B performance criteria generally define research-based user-needs that environmental design must meet in order to achieve greater effectiveness, performance, or efficiency. E/B/N performance criteria go deeper—they link environments with neuroscience research to support brain development and functioning.

For example, we could ask what neuroscience research tells us about learning behavior, and what performance goals might be generated for school or learning environment design that truly support the development and functioning of students' brains? The following table represents an effort to link research findings to possible design approaches. Although actual research is necessary, this exercise in generating hypotheses and performance criteria is useful in identifying the logical links that can be made between neuroscience, behavioral outcomes, and environmental design. The table below draws on specific findings in the literature about how the brain develops and learns to generate selected design performance criteria for a brain-responsive learning environment such as a school.

This table and chapter take a risky step into the unknown by linking neuroscience approaches to E-B concepts, hypotheses, and design performance criteria. To verify such connections and validate this paradigm shift, further linked E/B/N research is necessary. One way to achieve this is to employ research methods that measure the internal states of our minds and bodies, for example stress, mood, and focus of attention. The following section describes several research projects that have begun to do this.

Measuring Internal Behavior States

Observing behavior in E-B has generally meant watching people at work, at play, doing chores, and at home. The definition of "behavior" as it relates to environment has broadened to include the behavior of the human body, brain, and mind in response to specific environmental conditions. Studies to locate areas of the brain that are part of its environmental system with fMRI tests and measure stress by collecting samples of saliva cortisol and blood pressure readings are described in this section. Other methods, such as eye tracking machines and event related potentials (ERP) to measure focus of attention are likely to be developed and become more prevalent among researchers who adopt the E/B/N paradigm described above and in Chapter 7.

SELECTED E/B/N DESIGN PERFORMANCE CRITERIA
FOR LEARNING ENVIRONMENTS—A TRIAL EXERCISE

Brain Development—design to support the brain development of young children
   Social Challenges—complexity drives brain development
   Autobiographical Self Development—autobiographical information helps
     us define who we are
Focus on Learning—design to support children's brains in focusing on learning
   Distraction Principle and Tug of War Attention Mediators—distractions reduce
     learning effectiveness
Encoding Memories—design to support children's ability to remember what they learn
   Mnemonic Loci Learning—visualizing information in space aids recall
   Sleeping-on-it Consolidation—sleep helps set learning more firmly in the brain
Recall of Subject Matter—design to support children's ability to perform better on tests
   Visual Memory Reinforcement—visual contexts that reflect subject matter aid recall
   Elaborative Semantic Learning—meaningful environments set knowledge in
     memorable contexts
Individual Differences—design to support children's different learning needs
   Brain Clocks—different people learn better at different times of the day
   Multiple Intelligences—learning styles differ among people

GENERIC NEUROSCIENCE PRINCIPLE

Phenomenon Name and Research Description	*Design Performance Criteria*	*Design Options*
Brain Development design to support the brain development of young children		
Social Challenges Grappling with varied and complex social situations and relationships as we grow up is a driving force for the development and evolution of a complex brain (Changeux, 1985, p. 268).	Learning environments that provide the opportunity for a continuum of social and project situations—from individual to large group—contribute to brain learning.	Provide diversity in size of classrooms and study areas. Provide flexibility in such physical elements as seating, tables, and space dividers.
Autobiographical Self Development Everyone defines their "self" in termsof their life experiences—their past. People with certain amnesias say they have lost their "self"— they do not know who they are (Schacter, 1996).	In childhood learning and development, environments can reinforcea sense of identity and self when personal and family history is displayed.	In grammar school classrooms include a communal corner with photos of and objects that are important to students themselves, their families, and family histories.

Phenomenon Name and Research Description	Design Performance Criteria	Design Options
Focus on Learning design to support children's brains in focusing on learning		
Distraction Principle and Tug of War Attention Mediators When brain focus is on a learning task and attention is diverted, memory of the specifics of the learning experience is reduced, although people who are distracted do remember that they took part in the learning experience.	Learning environments that reduce alternative attention distracters, and thus help people focus on learning tasks at the moment of learning, support brain learning.	Consider the shape of rooms, lighting design, and visual relationships among students to minimize distractions.
Attending to and focusing on a particular topic requires a continual tug of war between distraction by many stimuli and obsession with one (Hobson, 1994).	Learning environments support brain learning when they help students attend to a single topic without becoming obsessed by it— while simultaneously blocking out distractions.	Provide flexible lighting—almost like stage lights— that can be used to "illuminate" the teacher and objects of a topic at one time, and the class during discussion at another time.
Encoding Memories design to support children's ability to remember what they learn		
Mnemonic Loci Learning Complex memories can be enhanced by visualizing vivid images in related physical places for each part of the memory—such as picturing a different field of colorful flowers in each room of your home to remind you of all your family members' birthdays.	Learning environments organized to reinforce the structure of conceptual relationships physically can increase recall of multiple-part concepts— such as the periodic table of elements or parts of sentence structure.	Consider physically organizing classroom entries, pathways, seating groups, and the relationship between teacher and students according to sentence structure elements in grammar class, the periodic table in chemistry, and so on. This can provide students with an immediate visual mnemonic locus.
Sleeping-on-it Consolidation Attention-relaxing states that rely on the aminergic rather than cholinergic brain system, such as sleeping and meditation, help people naturally organize into coherent whole concepts, what initially appear to be disparate bits of information. Sleep enables people to set what they learn more firmly in their brains (Hobson, 1994; Stickgold et al., 2000).	Learning environments that appropriately enable and encourage temporary mental "dropping out" support brain learning.	Include in the school places that are private enough for students to let down their "public" face without fear of ridicule— close ones eyes, sigh, just vegetate—perhaps with a built-in ledge to sit on.

Phenomenon Name and Research Description	*Design Performance Criteria*	*Design Options*

Recall of Subject Matter
design to support children's ability to perform better on tests

Visual Memory Reinforcement People remember events better when those memories include visual information about the physical setting or context of those events. The same region of the brain is involved with visual imagery and visual perception (Schacter, 1996, p. 23).	Environments that provide strong visual cues to associate with learning events will support recall of learned material.	Consider "stage set"-like classrooms in which the visible "props" and scenery change to be particularly appropriate to the subject matter being taught. This may be achieved through such items as lighting or operable cabinets.
Elaborative Semantic Learning The more learning environments associate knowledge being taught with a person's meaningful and familiar experiences, the greater the chance the person will remember and be able to recall the material learned (Schacter, 1996).	Learning environments that place learning events in a context of broader meaning enhance learning.	Plan walls in classrooms decorated with visual images related to the meaning of subjects. For example, include photographs of nuclear submarines, an atomic energy plant, and a mushroom cloud in the chemistry lab.

Individual Differences
design to support children's different learning needs

Brain Clock Clock genes have patterns that reflect varying circadian rhythms, enabling people to learn better at different times of day.	Learning environments support brain learning whenthey enable students to adjust when they learn certain subjects to their own internal learning clocks.	For subjects that can be learned interactively—using computers, videos, pre-recorded lectures, language, or conversations—locate and design places for such learning where students can choose when they want to study.
Multiple Intelligence Individual brains are differentially suited to process different types of information—mathematical, visual, linguistic, social, and emotional (Goleman 1995; Gardner, 1993).	Learning environments that accommodate different learning styles and do not force all students into the same style, support brain learning.	Design classrooms so that students can study in different ways without distracting other students.

Internal state behavior measurement has focused on stress, employing physiological measurements of blood pressure, pulse rate, and levels of the hormone cortisol in saliva. Future studies are likely to include measurement of mood and focus of attention as well. With the advent over several decades of non-invasive ways to measure brain activity—functional magnetic resonance imaging (fMRI) and PET scans—researchers are further able to specify where in the brain certain environment-related activities take place.

In one stress measurement study, Wener and colleagues studied the effects of a train system routing change on commuters when a direct train from New Jersey to New York City was added where formerly commuters had to change trains to get to the city (Wener et al., 2003). Because the research team had already begun collecting data from commuters on the original schedule, this change created a natural quasi-experimental design. While other transportation studies have measured elevated blood pressure levels, neuroendocrine hormone (catecholamines) processes, and elevated skin conductance as indicators of stress, the Wener team decided to incorporate measurement of salivary cortisol in their studies. Salivary cortisol is a psychophysiological marker that is sensitive for thirty to seventy-five minutes after a stressful event. It is "produced in the hypothalamic-pituitary-adrenocortical (HPA) system that is involved in complex biological processes implicated in the regulation of stress and emotion" (p. 524).

At the end of subjects' longer or shorter commute, Wener and colleagues handed twenty-nine pre-selected commuters a salivette—a plastic tube with sterile cotton in an inner container. Each subject chewed the cotton for thirty seconds before re-inserting it into the tube and returning it to the researcher, who labeled it and put it into cold storage.

Applying this method must take into account that our body's cortisol levels rise and fall diurnally, with a high peak between 6 and 7 A.M. followed by a steady and marked decline until 8 P.M., when cortisol rises again during the night. Measures therefore have to be compared to the natural circadian rhythm of cortisol levels in addition to the previous measurement. To establish a baseline for comparison with pre- and post-event measures, the researchers took measurements at subjects' homes at the same time of day as the experiment but on a weekend.

In a second stress-management study, Legendre, who was interested in daycare environmental features that reduced or elevated stress among toddlers, studied children in eight daycare centers—six in a Paris suburb and two in Budapest. Legendre took saliva samples from selected children at 7:30 A.M. when they awoke, then again at 9:30 and 10:30 A.M., and froze the samples before they were analyzed "by a competitive Enzymeimmunoassays in microtitre plate formats to measure unbound cortisol." The precision of such methodology is important for the standing of such data when compared to data from other disciplines.

Legendre's methods were part of a multi-method approach that also included observations of the physical environment, interviews with staff, and plan analysis. Stress measured in cortisol levels was his major independent variable. His study results determined that, although regulations in France empha-size the staff-to-child ratio as a measure of quality care (for children from one to three years old, a minimum of 1:8), three other conditions reduced stress among the children: groups of no more than fifteen with an average age difference of less than six months, a small team of no more than three to four adult caregivers, and playrooms in which each child has at least 5 square meters of space.

Wener's team also employed multiple methods—giving each commuter an editing task to be carried out during the trip to assess motivation, and brief questionnaires on self-perceived stress and spousal perception of stress. Although the research team assessed commuters having to change fewer times between transportation modes (car, train, walk), perceived predictability of the commute, and reduced commuting time, they found that only reduced commut-ing time appreciably affected reduced stress.

In a third stress-measurement study, Ulrich and his team selected blood pressure and pulse rates as measurements for their naturalistic field experiment on stress associated with television programming in a blood donor clinic wait-ing room. This choice was made partly because collecting these data could eas-ily be seen as part of the standard procedure in such a setting. Based on the the-ory that our brains have hard-wired memories of natural surroundings, and that environments that remind us of those places reduce stress more than other environments, Ulrich presented four conditions to 872 blood donors in the clin-ic at different times. They were: having the TV on with regular programming (talk shows, game shows, soap operas, and commercials, but no continuous news stations), playing a tape loop of an urban setting (either a traffic-free shopping mall or a pedestrian-free commercial street), playing a tape loop of an outdoor nature area (a park-like setting with trees or a flowing stream), or no TV at all. Between 198 and 260 blood donors were present under each of the four conditions. Just before they started waiting and after they had their blood drawn and blood pressure taken, subjects filled out a standardized self-report questionnaire with scales for measuring fear, arousal, anger/aggression, sadness, positive affect, and attentiveness/concentration.

Pulse-rate data revealed that situations including nature on the television were less stress-inducing than urban shows, and that the television being turned on at all caused more stress than leaving it off. The findings have the self-evi-dent implication that no television is better than

> the widely held assumption of healthcare providers—implied by their apparently pervasive practice of playing television continuously in waiting areas—that uncon-trollable daytime television is a restorative positive distraction for stressed health-care consumers (p. 40).

As important as this finding may be, the study also makes a major contri-bution to E-B methods by illustrating that:

> It is sometimes possible in real healthcare settings to perform research according to an experimental design, employ multiple measures of health outcomes, yet use procedures that are largely unobtrusive, have minimal impact on patients, and cause negligible disruption of the normal operations of the facility (p. 45).

Functional magnetic resonance imaging (fMRI) is a measurement tool increasingly making its way into environment/behavior/neuroscience studies. FMRI takes a continuous photograph of energy release in a subject's brain while she is presented with a visual or auditory stimulus, and can be used to identify specific brain behavior associated with the physical environment. Epstein and Kanwisher of MIT's Department of Brain and Cognitive Sciences, for example, carried out an experiment to locate those parts of the brain that respond to and manage inputs related to "place." In each of three sequential experiments, they showed different photos to subjects while photographing brain behavior with fMRI.

In one experiment subjects were presented photos of faces, objects, houses, and scenes—both intact and scrambled. Scrambled photos looked like puzzles with the pieces in the wrong place. The fMRI data identified a particular part of the brain near the hippocampus that appeared to be more activated by photos of intact scenes than by faces or objects—the parahippocampal place area, or PPA:

> a bilateral region of parahippocampal cortex straddling the collateral sulcus (including the posterior tip of the parahippocampal gyrus) and adjacent to the fusiform gyrus. This region does not include the hippocampus proper.

Results of the second experiment showed that the PPA responded more strongly to photos of furnished rooms, empty rooms, and outdoor scenes— "bare spatial layouts"—than to photos of the furniture from the rooms or familiar landmarks. To test what in the photos actually activated this area—the places, the context, or the enclosed space—the researchers presented subjects with photos of faces, objects, intact rooms (simple constructions of walls and floors), fractured rooms (each plane of the previous photo separated from adjacent planes), and fractured rooms with the elements rearranged. They found that photos of both intact and fractured but not rearranged rooms triggered the strongest PPA response, confirming their spatial-layout hypothesis for this part of the brain. As the researchers summarize:

> The difference in response must reflect the fact that the fractured rooms defined a coherent space, whereas the fractured + rearranged rooms did not. . . . [These findings] suggest that the PPA performs analysis of the shape of the local environment that is crucial to our ability to determine where we are (p. 600).

While research of this type is only beginning in environment/ behavior/neuroscience, the leap into E/B/N design has already taken place. The following discussion presents the process of developing E/B/N performance criteria for people living with Alzheimer's disease and a case study of an operating Alzheimer's assisted living treatment residence to illustrate the impact a neuroscience approach can have in evidence-based E/B/N design.

Developing E/B/N Design Performance Criteria for Alzheimer's Treatment Residences—A Strategic Research Opportunity

People with Alzheimer's disease need specially planned environments because, among other problems, they have great difficulty remembering physical environments and finding their way around in new settings. Although they know where they are when they are there—in a garden, in front of a picture, at a door—they cannot easily remember where they have been. Unless they see the destination, they may not remember where they are going or even what may be around a familiar corner. Well-designed physical environments for these people substitute for missing capabilities while directly supporting remaining skills. Brain-responsive environments also visually cue memories of their pasts to add to their autobiographical sense of self.

This population offers a window into the critical role environments play in cognitive mapping, memory, and self-awareness because the brains of people with Alzheimer's have such an extreme need for support in these areas. The approach described here demonstrates that design incorporating an under-standing of the brain's neuronal structure and processes leads to the most sup-portive setting. For this reason, design for people with Alzheimer's disease rep-resents what sociologist Robert Merton calls *strategic research material*:

> the empirical material that exhibits the phenomenon to be explained or interpret-ed to such advantage and in such accessible form that it enables the fruitful inves-tigation of previously stubborn problems and the discovery of new problems for further inquiry (1963).

With the onset and development of Alzheimer's disease, several parts of the brain are damaged, while other parts continue to function well into the dis-ease. Designing for this brain phenomenon is complicated and extremely rewarding: Those living with Alzheimer's in supportive environments are more functional because these supports help them to have a sense of place, know where they are going, walk with greater purpose, feel at ease where they are, have memories of their past, recognize their family, and appreciate their own achievements. Environmental design helps such users to be more aware of where and who they are, become less agitated and aggressive, be less fearful and disoriented, and act more independently (Zeisel et al., 2003; Zeisel and Raia, 2000; Zeisel and Tyson, 1999; Zeisel in Preiser, 2001).

What cognitive neuroscience findings can help designers create such envi-ronments? What types of environments are responsive to these findings? The table below presents the major brain deficits associated with Alzheimer's disease, along with design performance criteria that respond to these brain changes. Following the table and its analysis is an annotated plan with photographic illus-trations of an environment designed with these characteristics in mind.

The greatest environmental challenge people living with Alzheimer's face is that they lose certain types of spatial processing abilities and memories while others remain. For example, in a train station or on a busy street, the simple perception, "Where am I?" turns into brain noise rather than a clear brain sig-nal. The person becomes disoriented. If an environment requires a person to use all his spatial processing and memory functions to figure out "Where am I? Where have I been? What was the place like? Where am I going? And where after that?," whatever remaining memory functions he has are effectively dis-abled. It is just too much to ask patients' brains to process. People with

ALZHEIMER'S DESIGN PERFORMANCE CRITERIA RESPONSIVE
TO COGNITIVE NEUROSCIENCE

Brain atrophy	Brain deficit/capability
Parietal and occipital lobes	Loss of ability to hold a cognitive map; remaining ability to be in the present
Anterior occipital lobe & hippocampus	Out of sight out of mind; lack of safety without enclosure
Frontal lobe	Loss of sense of self; memories can be primed
Hippocampal loss and amygdala strength	Loss of ability to remember places visited in the recent past; remaining ability to hold on to moods, feelings, emotions
Hippocampus	Difficulty perceiving and processing new places; remaining hard-wired memories of home and hearth
Frontal lobe and motor cortex of the parietal lobe	Lack of self awareness of physical disabilities; natural sense of self control and independence
Anterior & medial temporal lobe, and parietal lobe losses; sensory cortex strengths	Loss of receptive and expressive language centers; remaining senses of smell, touch, hearing
Supra chiasmatic nuclei (SCN)	Loss of sense of time and circadian rhythms; remaining ability to sense nature, the passage of time, and the seasons out of doors

Design performance criteria	Possible design responses
Environments in which all the information needed to find ones way around is embedded in the setting rather than needing to be kept in mind—naturally mapped (Norman, 1990)	Clear destinations at the end of hallways; attention-getting lively and familiar wall decorations in hallways attention-getting llively and familiar wall hangings
Environments that are totally protected, with exit doors that are made less evident and with blocked views of what is beyond the enclosure	Camouflaged exit doors; electronically locked doors; windows with safety latches; high garden fences impossible to climb
Personal environments that provide residents with autobiographical cues of their past	Furniture and decorations that evoke memories of a person's culture, personal history, family, and achievements
Rooms and garden that evoke different and strong moods and emotions so that residents feel—and thus know—they have been somewhere else before getting to where they are	Varied common areas, each decorated to evoke a different mood and emotion—friendly living room, lively dining room, ceremonial entry foyer, relaxing front porch and garden
Significant places that focus on hard-wired memories such as food, warmth, social support, and nature	Environments that include strongly evocative residential elements such as fireplace, eat-in country kitchen, view out over garden
Environments that are prosthetic in that they naturally make up for losses in mobility and limb strength, and are safe yet not evidently institutional	Environments with rails to lean on in hallways, toilets high enough to get on and off with little arm strength, soft materials on the floor to cushion falls
Environmental messages and cues in non-verbal form that take advantage of multiple remaining sensory modalities at the same time	Environments in which smells of food, sounds of music, comforting soft materials are all orchestrated to indicate time for certain activities
Environments that provide contact with nature, weather, time of day, and plants—natural cues to the passage of time. Gardens that support residents' brain abilities	Gardens with clear pathways, lively planting areas, hard surfaces to walk on, benches to sit down, shady areas, trees, and plants

Note: Although several areas of the brain are usually affected for each brain deficit, areas of brain atrophy are presented as if these were the only areas affected. This oversimplification is presented for illustrative and descriptive purposes. Generally, although one area may be more affected than others, more than one associated area is often affected by the disease and influences behaviors and brain responses.

Alzheimer's can negotiate environments that edit out difficult wayfinding demands. "Where am I?" and "Where am I going that I can see?" are easily answered questions when perceived in a place with clear spatial landmarks and few alternative destinations.

Another damaged brain ability is the cognitive map. People living with Alzheimer's have difficulty holding in mind an explicit picture of any physical environment, much less a complex one with twists and turns. Most of us with less impaired memories can hold in the "map room of our brains" an image of places we have been and might want to go again. We hold in mind the instructions for an environment's use—much like we keep in mind the instructions for unlocking a door or starting a car. But we actually need a written instruction booklet when the microwave is too complicated or the VCR date-setting mechanism is too obscure.

Psychologist Donald A. Norman has named self-evident environments that need no instruction booklets "naturally mapped" (1990, pp. 75–80). For the brains of those living with Alzheimer's disease, environments that require holding instructions in mind, that are not naturally mapped, are upsetting, frightening, and create anxiety. *Pacing* and *wandering*, behaviors that are commonly considered disease symptoms, are results of this anxiety. Naturally mapped environments that reduce such behaviors raise the question of whether they are actually direct symptoms of the disease or secondary effects of confusing environments that have no self-evident destinations.

The disease affects sensory comprehension differently for different people. Sense of smell can be affected either early or late in the disease, as can finding words to express oneself—aphasia—and understanding the words of others. One caregiver tells the story of a woman who for two years had not explicitly recognized her son Ned when he was in her presence. Ned became accustomed to walking past his mother without even saying "hello." Once, however, a startling event occurred. Ned walked past his mother as usual, but this time she turned to the woman next to her and said: "That's my son Ned. He's wearing the same after shave lotion my husband wore every day for as long as we were married." Ned's grooming habits had primed important sense memories in her brain that day.

The disease may affect hearing and verbal comprehension as well, although music seems to be appreciated and understood far into the disease. The part of the brain that responds to gentle touch and soft fabrics also seems to remain functional. Because sensory comprehension capabilities are so varied, it is essential that environments for people with Alzheimer's be designed to communicate through as many sensory routes as possible. Smells of baking food communicate that it is time to eat better than a call to dinner. Sounds of music from the piano communicate better than a sign on the wall that it is time for a concert.

Another Alzheimer's disease deficit is that while people living with the disease hold memories in their brains of their personal and cultural pasts, they have difficulty priming themselves to recall these older memories. If asked about their childhood they describe it in great detail, but without being asked or being otherwise reminded, they do not seem to reminisce about childhood. Because our pasts are essential parts of our sense of self, caregivers for people living with Alzheimer's often discuss a person's family, past achievements, and places where that person has lived in order to cue memories. Old family furniture, photos, recordings of family members' voices, and old songs played on the piano all prime existing memories and provide residents with a sense of self they otherwise seldom experience. This is a still more profound contribution that environmental design for the brain can make to the lives of those with Alzheimer's disease.

How do these neuroscience principles apply to designing actual treatment settings for people with this particular disability? The following case study demonstrates the application of these principles. The photographs of particular design elements and the annotated plan of the residence further illustrate how the principles are reflected in the design.

E/B/N DESIGN CASE STUDY

AN ALZHEIMER'S ASSISTED LIVING TREATMENT RESIDENCE
Woburn, Massachusetts

This evidence-based project, located in a renovated hospital building in Woburn, Massachusetts, is an assisted living treatment residence for people living with Alzheimer's disease. It houses twenty-six people who are cared for by a twenty-four-hour staff, and serves several people who come to participate in

Garden and "front" porch, Hearthstone Alzheimer Care, Woburn, Massachusetts.

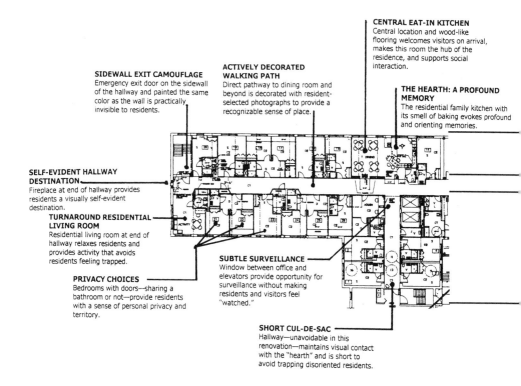

CENTRAL EAT-IN KITCHEN
Central location and wood-like flooring welcomes visitors on arrival, makes this room the hub of the residence, and supports social interaction.

ACTIVELY DECORATED WALKING PATH
Direct pathway to dining room and beyond is decorated with resident-selected photographs to provide a recognizable sense of place.

SIDEWALL EXIT CAMOUFLAGE
Emergency exit door on the sidewall of the hallway and painted the same color as the wall is practically invisible to residents.

THE HEARTH: A PROFOUND MEMORY
The residential family kitchen with its smell of baking evokes profound and orienting memories.

SELF-EVIDENT HALLWAY DESTINATION
Fireplace at end of hallway provides residents a visually self-evident destination.

TURNAROUND RESIDENTIAL LIVING ROOM
Residential living room at end of hallway relaxes residents and provides activity that avoids residents feeling trapped.

PRIVACY CHOICES
Bedrooms with doors—sharing a bathroom or not—provide residents with a sense of personal privacy and territory.

SUBTLE SURVEILLANCE
Window between office and elevators provide opportunity for surveillance without making residents and visitors feel "watched."

SHORT CUL-DE-SAC
Hallway—unavoidable in this renovation—maintains visual contact with the "hearth" and is short to avoid trapping disoriented residents.

Hearthstone Alzheimer Care
Woburn, Massachusetts

the program during the day. The self-contained residence is located on one floor and is secured with magnetic door locks that are deactivated by the fire alarm and coded push pads, limiting egress and access to those who can remember the code. The doors have no windows to the outside, and the facility's garden is surrounded by a tall decorative fence. These measures reduce potential agitation by preventing views to outdoor activities that might attract residents' interest and encourage them to leave.

The central pathway in the residence is a straight corridor from one end to the other with many wall hangings, providing residents an interesting and orienting walking path. These wall hangings include photographs residents have selected and thus understand, reminiscence shadowboxes with mementos of residents' lives, decorated boards announcing events, staff members' names,

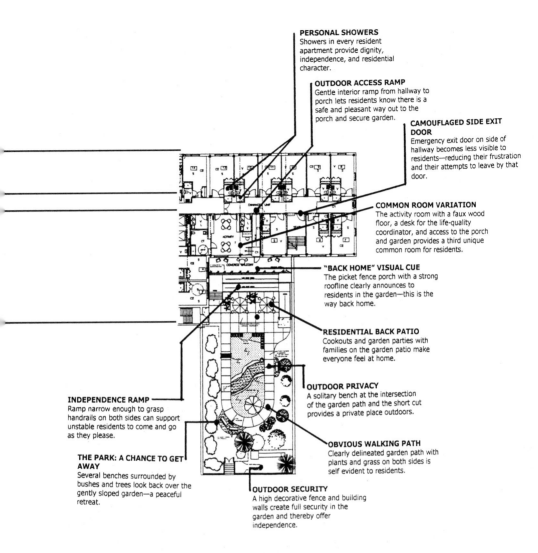

PERSONAL SHOWERS
Showers in every resident apartment provide dignity, independence, and residential character.

OUTDOOR ACCESS RAMP
Gentle interior ramp from hallway to porch lets residents know there is a safe and pleasant way out to the porch and secure garden.

CAMOUFLAGED SIDE EXIT DOOR
Emergency exit door on side of hallway becomes less visible to residents—reducing their frustration and their attempts to leave by that door.

COMMON ROOM VARIATION
The activity room with a faux wood floor, a desk for the life-quality coordinator, and access to the porch and garden provides a third unique common room for residents.

"BACK HOME" VISUAL CUE
The picket fence porch with a strong roofline clearly announces to residents in the garden—this is the way back home.

RESIDENTIAL BACK PATIO
Cookouts and garden parties with families on the garden patio make everyone feel at home.

INDEPENDENCE RAMP
Ramp narrow enough to grasp handrails on both sides can support unstable residents to come and go as they please.

OUTDOOR PRIVACY
A solitary bench at the intersection of the garden path and the short cut provides a private place outdoors.

THE PARK: A CHANCE TO GET AWAY
Several benches surrounded by bushes and trees look back over the gently sloped garden—a peaceful retreat.

OBVIOUS WALKING PATH
Clearly delineated garden path with plants and grass on both sides is self evident to residents.

OUTDOOR SECURITY
A high decorative fence and building walls create full security in the garden and thereby offer independence.

and resident snapshots. At the end of the walking path are a fireplace/hearth and a living room with a television set where resident meetings are held and small group activities are organized. In the middle of the path are a large dining room and residential kitchen, and at the other end of the residence is a room with a tile floor, where painting and other messy activities can be run.

The common rooms' decor is varied to stimulate different moods in residents' minds. The living room has carpet, a unique decorative border near the ceiling, and white flowing curtains. The kitchen/dining room has windows along one side, dining chairs and tables, a tile floor, and a residential kitchen with wooden cabinets and a breakfast counter. The common room adjacent to the porch and garden has less light and furniture more suited to activities such as painting, puzzles, and games. While residents may not remember the precise

Naturally mapped pathways and treatment garden landmarks,
Woburn and Marlboro, Massachusetts.

attributes of each room, their functioning amygdalae enable them to remember
the "feel" of each.

Bedrooms provide residents the opportunity for privacy and personalization surrounded by their personal furniture and mementos. All but six of the
twenty-six bedrooms have a dedicated bathroom, while each of the three two-
bedroom apartments has a common bathroom. Residents live with their own
furniture, wall hangings, and other decorations—all cues to improve memory
and reduce agitation.

Adjacent to the common room, a wide outdoor porch provides access to a
large therapeutic healing garden. The covered porch is wide enough to sit on and
provides a view over the garden. A gentle ramp leads down to the completely
enclosed garden a half level below. Designed with landscaped care and residential and wayfinding principles, it features a clear walking path, planting boxes,
benches, and landmarks to help orient residents (Zeisel and Tyson, 1999).

Each room in the assisted living treatment residence is scaled to feel residential—with the exception of the large dining room that can seat all twenty-six residents. The ceilings are low, the furniture residential in style, and unique decorative borders on the walls reflect the use of each room. The size of the residence
provides the opportunity for everyone who lives, works, and visits there to get to

Memory boxes remind everyone to see residents as people first.

Left: Residence kitchen-hearth.
Right: Personalized resident room.

know one other. While the number of residents is larger than a nuclear family, it is about the size of an extended family unit or a small residential community.

Because the residence is safe inside by virtue of its finishes and fixtures, and safe outside by virtue of secure doors and fences, residents are free to be as independent as their physical capacity allows. Staff members, secure in their knowledge that residents will not wander away, do not feel they have to follow residents around. The lean rails along the walls in each hallway even enable residents who might otherwise be unsteady on their feet to make their way to where they are going by themselves.

There are no strange sounds, views, or other sensory stimuli in the residence. Furniture is familiar, the arbor in the garden is the same as in many residential yards, and the photos on the walls present comforting and familiar sights. There is no public announcement system nor are there strange and shiny floors waxed to meet regulations for cleanliness, as might be found in long-term care institutions. The radio and television are not left on all day; specific programs are chosen and video- or audiotapes are played that present familiar shows and songs.

In sum, the design and layout of this residence for people living with Alzheimer's disease—its architecture, landscape, and interiors—are planned to

Alzheimer treatment gardens with raised beds, Woburn and Marlboro, Massachusetts.

Three-dimensional wall art and family board, Marlboro and Woburn, Massachusetts.

augment residents' memories and ability to function on their own. By taxing the parts of residents' brains that are still working well and relieving the parts that are damaged, the whole person is supported. Residents feel at home, as much in control as their age allows, and competent.

Using the E/B/N design paradigm focused the designers' attention on environmental design options that reflect what we know about the neuronal structure and activity of the brains of people living with Alzheimer's and their behavioral needs. Measurement of the effectiveness of this approach at Hearthstone at Choate and in similar settings will need to wait for post-occupancy evaluations that link environment to behavioral and neuroscience outcomes.

Marc Maxwell, AIA was architect/designer for this project. This case study is drawn from a decade of collaborative practice between Dr. Joan Hyde, CEO, Hearthstone Alzheimer Care, and John Zeisel.

OVERVIEW

This chapter operationalizes the environment/behavior/neuroscience paradigm. A neuroscience perspective is applied to fundamental environment-behavior concepts such as place, territory, wayfinding, and personalization. The case of neonatal intensive care unit design is used to demonstrate how the two paradigms can yield critically different design performance criteria. Research methods applicable to this type of research are demonstrated by reviewing several studies. A hypothetical case study for learning environments is employed to demonstrate how E/B/N hypotheses can be constructed, and how E/B/N design performance criteria can be generated from them. A case study of a building-in-use designed with an E/B/N approach—the Hearthstone Assisted Living Treatment Residence in Woburn, Massachusetts—illustrates how E/B/N and E-B can be integrated in actual design.

AFTERWORD

Several Invitations to Several Groups of Readers

— DONALD T. CAMPBELL

It gives me a special pleasure to invite several quite distinct groups of readers to this very fine book by my friend John Zeisel. Let me list all of you first before I explain why I extend each of these several invitations.

- Undergraduates, graduate students, and practitioners in architecture, industrial design, landscape architecture, interior design, and city planning.
- Policy scientists and program-evaluation professionals who are called upon to engage in E-B studies.
- Instructors in research methods in the E-B professions.
- Instructors in applied social-science research methods.
- Program-evaluation methodologists and advocates of an experimenting society.

For those of you who are or will be engaged in the professions of deliberate environmental change, and who do not at all aspire to be research methodologists even for your own field, this book has several distinct values. It invites you to treat each new project not only as an opportunity to apply the skill and wisdom you have already acquired but also as an exploration that can expand that skill and wisdom. From the title on—design itself as a mode of inquiry—it provides both inspiration and commonsense suggestions for learning from your innovations. It will encourage you to collaborate with your clients in still bolder explorations of alternatives that you and they might not otherwise dare try. It will even enable them and you to look with pride on a noble mistake—a mistake no more costly than the banalities you might otherwise commit in the name of timidity—for risking such mistakes is part of your duty to add to the wisdom of the profession you utilize.

This book does a remarkable job of teaching the whole scope of social-science methods, from philosophy of science to doorstep interviewing, without the prerequisites that would exclude many designers from the usual text (statistical methods, formal experimental design, sociological and psychological theories of human behavior, formal courses in philosophy of science). Zeisel's mode of instruction is to start where you are, with a concrete problem you understand, and to illustrate the methodological alternative in that setting before presenting it in abstract terms. Not only will this training help you to become practitioners of environmental change and intelligent readers of research literature, it will also be a resource for low-cost, informal ways of learning more from your own practice—even through efforts so obvious but so neglected as a two-year-later interview or a questionnaire directed to the occupants of a new environment you have designed.

Most of you have esthetic as well as utilitarian goals. This book will help you tell how well you and your client have done for all types of goals. Some of you will want to develop a unique personal style or "signature." Why not make it also a *tested* style, instead of stubbornly persisting in self-defeating idiosyncrasies? There are plenty of intelligent idiosyncrasies and intelligent versions of your favorite thematic emphasis.

This book can also bring home to you how ambiguous and equivocal most judgments of effect in natural situations are, how many recurrent "optical illusions" and illusions of judgment make our own evaluations of outcomes misleading in ways both overly encouraging and overly discouraging. Greater awareness of the equivocality of inference will help you become a subtler judge of your project's impact.

This awareness will also, I hope, make you a more self-confident critic of studies presented as definitive social science applied to your area. You, with your site-specific wisdom, are the most competent critic of such studies. You can generate the most relevant and plausible "threats to validity" for a particular study in your field or on your project. Properly understood, this book will help you to keep from being mystified by computer output and elaborate statistical massagings based upon inappropriate assumptions and inadequately controlled and often irrelevant data, so that you will not be cowed into suppressing your doubts and your wise alternative explanations of the outcomes. (I hope it also leads you to demand graphic presentation of the data in its least massaged form as one of the final data presentations.)

Those of you already teaching research methods for the environmental-change professions can improve your teaching by supplementing your present statistical-tools-and-abstractions-first textbook with this text, which reverses the order and presents the need for methodology in concrete settings of obvious professional relevance to your students. It will motivate your students to recognize their own need for the difficult and esoteric skills you must also teach in your more advanced courses. For those of you who are already practicing quantitative, experimental, and quasi-experimental program-evaluation methods and are now called upon to apply your skills in an environment-behavior setting, this book provides both an entré into the specifics of that arena and a review in that setting of methodological maxims you already know. For those professionally practicing *qualitative* ethnographic evaluation, the book will likewise serve to remind you of the need for judgmental discussion of threats to validity and alternative explanations, which cannot be avoided by abandoning quantification and formal procedures. Teachers of applied social-science research methods for any setting will find that the concrete explicitness of the "treatment variables" and settings makes the examples in this book especially useful for conveying general methodological points.

The arenas of deliberate environmental change have a particular relevance for those of us in the field of program evaluation and those who would like our society to become able to learn more about the experiments it undertakes. In our wholesale application of our present techniques to "programs" of all types, an early self-confidence that we knew how to do it and could evaluate any program is being seriously undermined. The frustrations and ambiguities we encounter are chilling the motivation for reform by tempting many in our profession to abandon the goal of impact assessment and thus to abandon the image of an experimenting society. Two major aspects of the problem that have precipitated this loss of heart are the ambiguity and instability of our notions about what the "program" or "reform" consists of and the patent implausibility in many cases of the idea of a program package that could be identified as such for dissemination to other settings. "Community Mental Health Clinics," "Head-Start," "Follow Through," and "Decentralized Decision Making" have all proved to be elusive and unreplicable reforms. And these are among the more specifiable reforms. Governmental tendencies to label what is in actuality only topic-specific revenue sharing as though novel, specifiable alternatives to present practice were involved, and to accompany these with calls for immediate evaluations, have further confused the program-evaluation profession. These are not settings in which we can learn our trade.

In contrast, the innovative alternatives of the deliberate environmental-change professions provide experimental "treatments" that are concrete, often precisely replicable, and subject to precise reexamination as new theoretical understandings focus attention on different attributes. These are the sorts of reforms and programmatic alternatives through which we can improve our competence in the science of program evaluation and in the development of methodology for the experimenting society.

The slum-clearance and public-housing projects of the 1930s were striking social experiments for which we have no formal outcome records (although we have some insightful retrospective speculations). At that time, the architects, builders, and social planners thought they knew what they were doing; they were not aware that they were experimenting with one alternative among many possible ones. We missed that chance. Now we can only look with regret at the row after row of identical highrises, all repeating the same mistakes, and wish that there had been a deliberate variation in the alternatives generated by the planners and architects, plus outcome measures. When the great Model Cities programs came along in the 1950s and 1960s, Congress and the Washington administration, influenced by the ideology of social experimentation, set aside funds specifically for evaluation. But when the local Model Cities administrators went to colleges and universities for help in evaluation, the skills were not there. Nor did the Model Cities administrators understand how to implement their innovations so as to optimize impact assessment. No book that I know of will do more than this one to ensure that, when the political will to redesign our cities next returns, we will be ready to learn from our experiments.

Donald Campbell, the renowned social science methodologist, wrote this comprehensive "invitation" to readers of the first edition of my book in 1981. For those who have now read the revised edition, his words can be seen as a continuing invitation to put into practice its message.

REFERENCES

Abernathy, E. M. "The Effect of Changed Environmental Conditions Upon the Results of College Examinations." *The Journal of Psychology* 10 (1940): 293–301.

Alexander, C. *Notes on the Synthesis of Form.* Cambridge, MA: Harvard University Press, 1964.

Altman, I. *The Environment and Social Behavior.* Monterey, CA: Brooks/Cole, 1975.

Altman, I., P. A. Nelson, & E. E. Lett. *The Ecology of Home Environment.* Washington, DC: U.S. Department of Health, Education, and Welfare, 1972.

Altman, I., D. Stokols, J. F. Wohlwill, A. Rapoport, M. Powell Lawton, C. M. Wermer, A. Wandersman, E. H. Zube, K. Christiensen, S. M. Low, & A. Churchman. *Human Behavior and Environment 1–13* (1980–1994). Kluwer: New York.

Amarel, S. "On Representations of Problems of Reasoning About Actions," in D. Michie (Ed.) *Machine Intelligence* 3. New York: American Elsevier, 1968.

Archea, J., & A. H. Esser. "Man-Environment Systems: A Statement of Pur¬pose." *Man-Environment Systems* 1, no. 2 (January 1970).

Archer, L. B. "The Structure of the Design Process," in Broadbent, Geoffrey, & Ward (Eds.) *Design Methods in Architecture.* London: Lund Humphries for the Architectural Association, 1969.

Argyris, C. *Learning in Design Settings.* Mimeo, Harvard Graduate School of Education, 1977.

Asimov, M. *Introduction to Design.* Englewood Cliffs, NJ: Prentice-Hall, 1962.

Bafna, S. "Space Syntax: A Brief Introduction to its Logic and Analytical Techniques," in R. C. Dalton & C. Zimring (Eds.) *Environmental Cognition, Space, and Action, Special Issue of Environment & Behavior* 35, no. 1 (January 2003). Thousand Oaks, CA: Sage.

Banning, J. H. "Brick and Mortarboards: How Student Union Buildings Learn and Teach." *College Services Administration* 23, no. 3 (2000): 16–1.

Barker, R. *Ecological Psychology.* Stanford, CA: Stanford University Press, 1968.

Barnett, H. G. *Innovation: The Basis of Cultural Change.* New York: McGraw-Hill, 1953.

Barton, A., & P. F. Lazarsfeld. "Some Functions of Qualitative Analysis in Social Research," in G. J. McCall, & J. L. Simmons (Eds.) *Issues in Participant Observation.* Reading, MA: Addison-Wesley, 1969.

Bechtel, R. B. *Enclosing Behavior.* Stroudsburg, PA: Dowden, Hutchinson & Ross, 1977.

Bechtel, R. B., & A. Churchman. *Handbook of Environmental Psychology.* New York: John Wiley & Sons, 2002.

Bell, P. A., J. D. Fisher, & R. J. Loomis. *Environmental Psychology.* Philadelphia: W. B. Saunders, 1978.

Bell, P., T. Greene, J. Fisher, & B. Andrew. *Environmental Psychology, Fifth Edition.* New York: Harcourt Brace, 2000.

Blau, P. M. "The Research Process in the Study of the Dynamics of Bureaucracy," in P. E. Hammond (Ed.) *Sociologists at Work.* New York: Basic Books, 1964.

———. *The Dynamics of Bureaucracy.* Chicago: University of Chicago Press, 1963.

Boulding, K. E. "Foreword," in R. M. Downs, & D. Stea (Eds.) *Image and Environment: Cognitive Mapping and Spatial Behavior.* Chicago: Aldine, 1973.

———. *The Image: Knowledge in Life and Society.* Ann Arbor, MI: University of Michigan Press, 1956.

Bowns, C., & M. Francis. *Urban Wildlife Preserve Post-Occupancy Evaluation.* University of California, Davis: Center for Design Research, 1998.

Brand, S. *How Buildings Learn: What Happens After They're Built.* New York: Viking Press, 1994.

Brecht, M., & W. F. E. Preiser. "Tactile Directories for Building Interiors as Orienting and Way- Finding Aids for the Visually Impaired: A Prototype." *Proceedings of the 24th Annual Meeting of the Human Factors Society* (1980): 405–407.

Brill, M. *Disproving Widespread Myths About Workplace Design.* Jasper, IN: Kimball International, 2001.

Broadbent, G. "Creativity," in S. Gregory (Ed.) *The Design Method.* London: Butterworth, 1966.

Broadbent, G., & A. Ward (Eds.). *Design Methods in Architecture.* London: Lund Humphries for the Architectural Association, 1969.

Brolin, B. C. "Chandigarh Was Planned by Experts, but Something Has Gone Wrong." *Smithsonian 3,* no. 3 (June 1972): 56–63.

————. *The Failure of Modern Architecture.* New York: Van Nostrand Reinhold, 1976.

Brolin, B. C., & J. Zeisel. "Mass Housing: Social Research and Design." *Architectural Forum 129* (July/August 1968): 66–71.

Brower, S. *The Design of Neighborhood Parks.* Baltimore, MD: City Planning Commission, Dept. of Planning, 1977.

Brown, B., D. Perkins, & G. Brown. "Place Attachment in a Revitalizing Neighborhood: Individual and Block Levels of Analysis." *Journal of Environmental Psychology* 23, no. 3 (2003): 259–271.

Bruner, J. S. *Beyond the Information Given: Studies in the Psychology of Knowing* (J. M. Anglin, Ed.). New York: Norton, 1973.

Buckner, J. "The Development of an Instrument to Measure Neighbourhood Cohesion." *American Journal of Community Psychology* 16: 771–791.

Campbell, D. T. "Quasi-Experimental Designs," in H. W. Riecken, & R. F. Boruch (Eds.) *Social Experimentation: A Method for Planning and Evaluating Social Intervention.* New York: Academic Press, 1974.

————. "Degrees of Freedom and the Case Study." *Comparative Political Studies* 8, no. 2 (July 1975): 178–193.

————. "Qualitative Knowing in Action Research." Kurt Lewin Award Address, Society for the Psychological Study of Social Issues, meeting with American Psychological Association, New Orleans, 1974. (Revised version: Campbell, D. T. "Qualitative Knowing in Action Research," in M. Brenner, & P. Marsh (Eds.) *The Social Contexts of Method.* New York: St. Martins, 1978.)

————. "Reforms as Experiments." *American Psychologist* 24, no. 4 (April 1969): 409–429. Reprinted with modifications in F. G. Caro (Ed.) *Readings in Evaluation Research Second Edition.* New York: Russell Sage Foundation, 1977.

Campbell, D. T., & D. W. Fiske. "Convergent and Discriminant Validation by the Multitrait-Multimethod Matrix." *Psychological Bulletin* 56, no. 2 (1959): 81–105.

Campbell, D. T., & J. C. Stanley. *Experimental and Quasi-Experimental Designs for Research.* Chicago: Rand McNally, 1966.

Canter, D. *The Psychology of Place.* London: Architectural Press, 1977.

Canter, D., & K. Fritzon. "Differentiating Arsonists: A Model of Firesetting Actions and Characteristics." *Legal and Criminological Psychology* 3 (1998): 73–96.

Carp, F. *A Future for the Aged: Victoria Plaza and its Residents.* Austin, TX: University of Texas Press, 1966.

Changeux, J.-P. *Neuronal Man.* Princeton, NJ: Princeton University Press, 1985.

Chapin, F. S. "An Experiment on the Social Effects of Good Housing." *American Sociological Review 5* (1940): 868–878.

Chipuer, H. M., G. H. Pretty, E. Delorey, M. Miller, T. Powers, O. Rumstein, A. Barnes, N. Cordasic, & L. Laurent. "The Neighbourhood Youth Inventory: Development and Validation." *Journal of Community and Applied Social Psychology* 9 (1999): 355–368.

Christopherson, D. G. "Opening Address: Discovering Designers," in Jones, J. C., & D. G. Thornley (Eds.) *Conference on Design Methods.* Oxford: Pergamon, 1963.

Churchman, C. W. *The Design of Inquiring Systems.* New York: Basic Books, 1971.

Cimprich, B. "Development of an Intervention to Restore Attention in Cancer Patients." *Cancer Nursing* 16 (1993): 83–92.

Conway, D., J. Zeisel, & P. Welch. "Radiation Therapy Centers: Behavioral and Social Guidelines for Design" (report). Washington, DC: National Institutes of Health, 1977.

Conway, D. *Social Science and Design: A Process Model for Architect and Social Scientist Collaboration.* Washington, DC: American Institute of Architects, 1973.

Cooper-Marcus, C. *House as a Mirror of Self; Exploring the Deeper Meaning of Home.* Berkeley, CA: Conari Press, 1995.

————. "St. Francis Square: Attitudes of its Residents." *AIA Journal* 56 (December 1971): 22–27.

————. *Easter Hill Village.* New York: Free Press, 1975.

————. "Residents' Attitudes Toward the Environment at St. Francis Square, S.F." (Working Paper #126). Berkeley, CA: Institute of Urban and Regional Development, University of California, 1970.

Cooper-Marcus, C., & P. Hackett. "Analysis of the Design Process at Two Moderate-Income Housing Developments" (Working Paper #80). Berkeley, CA: Institute of Planning and Development Research, University of California, 1968.

Cooper-Marcus, C., & M. Barnes (Eds.). *Healing Gardens: Therapeutic Benefits and Design Recommendations.* New York: Wiley, 1999.

Cook, B. E. "Initial Evaluation of Koffinger Place, Pleasanton, California." Berkeley, CA: Hirshen & Partners, Architects, 1973.

————. "Survey Evaluation for Low-Cost Low-Rent Public Housing for the Elderly, Pleasanton, California." Berkeley, CA: Hirshen & Partners, Architects, 1971.

Cook, T. D., & Donald T. Campbell. *Quasi-Experimentation: Design and Analysis Issues for Field Settings.* Chicago: Rand McNally, 1979.

Damasio, A. R. *Descartes' Error: Emotion, Reason, and the Human Brain.* New York: G. P. Putnam's Sons, 1994.

Davis, G., & V. Ayers. "Photographic Recording of Environmental Behavior," in M. William (Ed.) *Behavioral Research Methods in Environmental Design.* Stroudsburg, PA: Dowden, Hutchinson & Ross, 1975.

Day, K. "Assault Prevention as Social Control: Women and Sexual Assault Prevention on Urban College Campuses." *Journal of Environmental Psychology* 15 (1995): 261–281.

Devlin, A. S., & J, Bernstein. "Interactive Way-Finding: Map Styles and Effectiveness." *Journal of Environmental Psychology* 17 (1997): 99–110.

Downs, R. M., & D. Stea (Eds.). *Image and Environment: Cognitive Mapping and Spatial Behavior.* Chicago: Aldine, 1973.

Duffy, F. *The New Office.* London: Conran Octopus, 1997.

Eberhard, J., & B. Patoine. "Architecture with the Brain in Mind." *Cerebrum* 6, no. 2 (Spring 2004): 71–84.

Ellis, W. R., Jr. "Planning, Design and Black Community Style: The Problem of Occasion-Adequate Space," in W. J. Mitchell (Ed.). *Proceedings of the Environmental Design Research Association, Third Annual Conference, EDRA-3.* Stroudsburg, PA: Dowden, Hutchinson & Ross, 1972.

———. "The Environment of Human Relations: Perspectives and Problems." *Journal of Architectural Education* 27, nos. 2 & 3 (June 1974): 11–18, 54.

Epp, G., D. Georgopulos, & S. Howell. "Monitoring Environment-Behavior Research." *Journal of Architectural Research* 7, no. 1 (March 1979): 12–21.

Epstein, R., & N. Kanwisher. "A Cortical Representation of the Local Visual Environment." *Nature* 392 (April 1998): 598–601.

Eriksson, P. S., E. Perfilieva, T. Bjork-Eriksson, A.-M. Alborn, A-M., C. Nordborg, D. A. Peterson, & F. H. Gage. "Neurogenesis in the Adult Human Hippocampus." *Nature Medicine* 4, no. 11 (1998): 1313–1317.

Eshelman, M. "Communication Between the Visually Handicapped and the Built Environment: Summary Project Report." Albuquerque, NM: University of New Mexico, School of Architecture and Planning, December 1983.

———. "Southwest Institute for the Visually Handicapped." Albuquerque, NM: University of New Mexico, School of Architecture and Planning, December 1983.

Farbstein, J., & M. Kantrowitz. "Design Research and Post-Occupancy Evaluation: A Team Assists the US Postal Service," in D. Evans, Ed. *A/R Architecture/Research 1.* Washington, DC: American Institute of Architects, November 1991.

———. "Design Research in the United States Postal Service," in M. Conan & C. Zimring (Eds.) *Designing and Managing Public Buildings.* New York: Butterworth Architecture, 1992.

Felipe, N. J., & R. Sommer. "Invasions of Personal Space." *Social Problems* 14, no. 2 (1966): 206–214.

Festinger, L. S., S. Schachter, & K. Back. *Social Pressures in Informal Groups.* New York: Harper, 1950.

Finnie, W. C. "Field Experiments in Litter Control." *Environment and Behavior* 5 (1973): 123–144.

Foz, A. T. K. "Some Observations on Designer Behavior in the Parti" (Master's Thesis). Cambridge, MA: Department of Urban Studies and Planning, Massachusetts Institute of Technology, 1972.

Francis, M. "A Case Study Method for Landscape Architecture." *Landscape Journal* 19, no. 2 (2001): 15–29.

———. *Urban Open Space: Designing for User Needs.* Washington, DC: Island Press, 2003.

Francis, M., & J. Rice (Eds.). *The Healing Dimensions of People-Plant Relations.* Blacksburg, VA: People-Plant Council, 1994.

Fried, M. "Grieving for a Lost Home," in L. J. Duhl (Ed.) *The Urban Condition.* New York: Basic Books, 1963.

Fried, M., & P. Gleicher. "Some Sources of Residential Satisfaction in an Urban Slum." *Journal of the American Institute of Planners* 27, no. 4 (1961): 305–315.

Fritzon, K. "An Examination of the Relationship Between Distance Traveled and Motivational Aspects of Firesetting Behaviour." *Journal of Environmental Psychology* 21 (2001): 45–60.

Galtung, J. *Theory and Methods of Social Research.* New York: Columbia University Press, 1967.

Gans, H. J. "The Potential Environment and the Effective Environment," in H. J. Gans (Ed.) *People and Plans.* New York: Basic Books, 1968.

———. *The Levittowners.* New York: Pantheon, 1967.

———. *The Urban Villagers.* New York: Free Press, 1962.

Gardner, H. *Frames of Mind: The Theory of Multiple Intelligences.* New York: Basic Books, 1993.

Gazzaniga, M. S. *The Mind's Past.* Berkeley, CA: University of California Press, 1998.

George, A. L. "Quantitative and Qualitative Approaches to Content Analysis," in I. Pool (Ed.) *Trends in Content Analysis.* Urbana, IL: University of Illinois Press, 1959.

Gerlach-Spriggs, N., R. E. Kaufman, & S. B. Warner. *Restorative Gardens: The Healing Landscape.* New Haven, CT: Yale, 1998.

Gifford, R. *Environmental Psychology: Principles and Practice, Third Edition.* Colville, WA: Optimal Books, 2002.

Goffman, E. *Behavior in Public Places.* New York: Free Press, 1963.

———. *The Presentation of Self in Everyday Life.* New York: Doubleday, 1959.

Goleman, D. *Emotional Intelligence: Why it Can Matter More Than IQ.* New York: Bantam Books, 1995.

Good, L., & W. Hurtig. "Evaluation: A Mental Health Facility, its Users and Context." *AIA Journal* 67, no. 2 (February 1978): 38–41.

Goodey, B. *Perception of the Environment.* Birmingham, England: Centre for Urban and Regional Studies, University of Birmingham, 1971.

Goodman, G. H., & F. T. McAndrew. "Domes and Astroturf: A Note on the Relationship Between the Physical Environment and the Performance of Major League Baseball Players." *Environment and Behavior* 25, no. 1 (January 1993): 121–125.

Gordon, W. J. J. *Synectics: The Development of Creative Capacity.* New York: Harper & Row, 1961.

Gordon, M. T., & S. Riger. *The Female Fear.* New York: Free Press, 1989.

Gould, S. J. "This View of Life: Bathybius Meets Eozoon." *Natural History* 87, no. 4 (April 1978): 16–22.

Graven S. N., W. W. Bowen, Jr., D. Brooten, A. Eaton, M. N. Graven, M. Hack, L. A. Hall, N. Hansen, H. Hurt, R. Kavalhuna, et al. "The High Risk Environment, Part I. The Role of the Neonatal Intensive Care Unit and the Outcome of High Risk Infants." *Journal of Perinatology* 12 (1992): 64–172.

Guebbels, H., C. Knapen, & B. Lochtenburg. *Onrustgevoelens bij jonge vrown ten aazien van kriminaliteit en het bald dat za hebben van verkrachting*. Leiden, Holland: Rijksuniversiteit, 1978.

Guerra, G. "A Geometrical Method of Systematic Design in Architecture," in Broadbent, Geoffrey, & Ward (Eds.). *Design Methods in Architecture*. London: Lund Humphries for the Architectural Association, 1969.

Günter, R., R. Wessel, & J. Günter. *Rom-Spanische Treppe*. Hamburg: Germany: VSA-Verlag, 1978.

Gutman, R. *People and Buildings*. New York: Basic Books, 1972.

Habraken, J. *Supports: An Alternative to Mass Housing*. New York: Praeger, 1972.

Hall, E. T. *The Hidden Dimension*. Garden City, NY: Doubleday, 1966.

Hammond, P. E. (Ed.). *Sociologists at Work*. New York: Basic Books, 1964.

Harding, J. R. "Heuristic Elicitation Methodology and FRM Acceptability." Paper presented at the World Health Organization Conference on Cross-Cultural Research Methods and Instruments and FRM Acceptability, Geneva, Switzerland, 1974.

Harding, J. R., & J. M. Livesay. "Anthropology and Public Policy," in G. McCall & G. Weber (Eds.). *Social Science and Public Policy: The Role of Academic Disciplines in Public Analysis*. Port Washington, NY: Associated Faculty Press, 1984: 51–85.

Heimessen, C. F. H., & D. de Jonge. "Eindexamencandidaten over Woningen en Mensen." Delft: Centrum voor Architectuuronderzoek, Afdeling der Bouwkunde, Technische Hogeschool Delft, 1967.

Hershkowitz, N., J. Kagan, & K. Zilles, K. "Neurobiological Bases of Behavioral Development in the First Year." *Neuropediatrics* 28 (1997): 296–306.

Hill, K. A. "Spatial Competence of Elderly Hunters." *Environment and Behavior* 24, no. 6 (November 1992): 779–794.

Hillier, B., & J. Hanson. *The Social Logic of Space*. Cambridge, UK: Cambridge University Press, 1984.

Hillier, B. & A. Leaman. "How Is Design Possible?" *Journal of Architectural Research 3*, no. 1 (January 1974): 4–11.

Hillier, B., J. Musgrove, & P. O'Sullivan. "Knowledge and Design," in W. J. Mitchell (Ed.). *Proceedings of the Environmental Design Research Association, Third Annual Conference, EDRA-3*. Stroudsburg, PA: Dowden, Hutchinson & Ross, 1972.

Hobson, J. A. *The Chemistry of Conscious States: How the Brain Changes its Mind*. Boston: Little, Brown and Company, 1994.

Hoogdalem, H. van. "Some Conceptual Tools for the Analysis of Man-Environment Systems." *Delft Progress Report 2* (1977): 249–256.

Howell, S. C. *Designing for Aging: Patterns of Use*. Cambridge, MA: M.I.T. Press, in press.

Howell, S., & G. Epp. *Shared Spaces in Housing for the Elderly*. Cambridge, MA: Design Evaluation Project, Department of Architecture, Massachusetts Institute of Technology, 1976.

Hutt, C. *Crowding Among Children*. Reading, UK: University of Reading, 1969.

Hyman, H. *Survey Design and Analysis*. New York: Free Press, 1955.

Ittelson, W. H., L. Rivlin, & H. M. Proshansky. "The Use of Behavioral Maps in Environmental Psychology," in H. M. Proshansky, W. Ittelson, & L. Rivlin (Eds.) *Environmental Psychology: Man and His Physical Setting*. New York: Holt, Rinehart & Winston, 1970.

Jacobs, J. *The Death and Life of Great American Cities*. New York: Vintage Books, 1961.

Jones, J. C. *Design Methods: Seeds of Human Futures*. London: Wiley, 1970.

Jones, J. C., & D. G. Thornley (Eds.). *Conference on Design Methods*. Oxford: Pergamon, 1963.

Jonge, D. de. "Images of Urban Areas, Their Structure and Psychological Foundations." *Journal of the American Institute of Planners 28* (1962): 266–276.

Kagan, J. (2001). Personal communication.

———. "Temperament and the reactions to unfamiliarity." *Child Development 68* (1997):139–143.

Keller, S. "Design and the Quality of Life in a New Community," in J. M. Yinger & S. J. Cutler (Eds.) *Major Social Issues: An Interdisciplinary View*. New York: Free Press, 1978.

———. *Twin Rivers: Study of a Planned Community*. National Science Foundation (Grant NSF G1 41 311), 1976.

Kitsuse, J. I., & A. V. Cicourel. "A Note on the Uses of Official Statistics." *Social Problems 11* (1963): 131–139.

Koestler, A. *The Act of Creation*. London: Hutchinson, 1976.

Koestler, A., & J. R. Smythies. *Beyond Reductionism: The Alpbach Symposium*. London: Hutchinson, 1969.

Korobkin, Barry J. *Images for Design: Communicating Social Science Research to Architects*. Cambridge, MA: Architecture Research Office, Harvard Graduate School of Design, 1976.

Kuhn, Thomas S. *The Structure of Scientific Revolutions, Second Edition*. Chicago: University of Chicago Press, 1970.

Kulhavy, R. W., L. C. Caterino, & F. Melchioro. "Spatially Cued Retrieval of Sentences." *The Journal of General Psychology 116* (1989): 297–304.

Kuo, F., & W. Sullivan. "Aggression and Violence in the Inner City: Effects of Environment via Mental Fatigue." *Environment & Behavior 33*, no. 4 (July 2001): 543–571.

Kuo, F. E., & Taylor, A. F. "A Potential Natural Treatment for Attention-Deficit/Hyperactivity Disorder: Evidence From a National Study." *American Journal of Public Health 94* (September 2004): 1580–1586.

Kupritz, V. W. "Privacy in the Work Place: The Impact of Building Design." *Journal of Environmental Psychology 18*, no. 4 (1998): 341–356.

Ladd, F. C. "Black Youths View Their Environment: Neighborhood Maps." *Environment and Behavior 2* (June 1970): 74–99.

Laing, A., F. Duffy, D. Jaunzens, & S. Willis. *New Environments for Working: The Re-design of Offices and Environmental Systems for New Ways of Working*. London: Construction Research Communications, 1998.

Lakatos, I. "Falsification and the Methodology of Scientific Research Programmes," in I. Lakatos, & A. Musgrave (Eds.). *Criticism and the Growth of Knowledge*. Cambridge, UK: Cambridge University Press, 1970.

Lakatos, I., & A. Musgrave (Eds.). *Criticism and the Growth of Knowledge*. Cambridge, UK: Cambridge University Press, 1970.

Lang, J., C. Burnette, W. Moleski, & D. Vachon (Eds.). *Designing for Human Behavior.* Stroudsburg, PA: Dowden, Hutchinson & Ross, 1974.

Lazarsfeld, P. F., & M. Rosenberg. *The Language of Social Research.* New York: Free Press, 1965.

Lazarsfeld, P. F., W. Sewell, & H. Wilensky (Eds.). *The Uses of Sociology.* New York: Basic Books, 1967.

Le Corbusier. *Towards a New Architecture.* New York: Praeger, 1965.

LeDoux, J. *The Emotional Brain: The Mysterious Underpinnings of Emotional Life.* New York: Simon & Schuster, 1996.

Lefkowitz, M., R. Blake, & J. Mouton. "Status Factors in Pedestrian Violation of Traffic Signals." *Journal of Abnormal and Social Psychology* 51 (1955): 704–706.

Legendre, A. "Environmental Features Influencing Toddlers' Biomedical Reactions in Day Care Settings." *Environment and Behavior* 35, no. 4 (2003): 523–549.

Lenihan, K. J. *85 Vistas* (research report). New York: Bureau of Applied Social Research, Columbia University, 1966.

Lewin, K. *Field Theory in Social Science.* New York: Harper & Row, 1951.

Lockwood, R. *News by Design: A Survival Guide for Newspapers.* Denver, CO: Quark Press, 1992.

Lundrigan, S., & Canter, D. "A Multivariate Analysis of Serial Murderers' Disposal Site Location Choice." *Journal of Environmental Psychology* 21 (2001): 423–432.

Lynch, K. *The Image of the City.* Cambridge, MA: M.I.T. Press, 1960.

Madge, J. "Housing: Social Aspects," in D. Sills (Ed.) *International Encyclopedia of the Social Sciences* 6 (1968): 516–517. New York: Macmillan & The Free Press.

Manis, M. *Cognitive Processes.* Monterey, CA: Brooks/Cole, 1966.

Marans, R., & S. Ahrentzen. "Developments in Research Design, Data Collection, and Analaysis," in E. H. Zube & G. T. Moore (Eds.) *Advances in Environment, Behavior, and Design.* New York: Plenum Press, 1987: 251–277.

Markus, T. A. "The Role of Building Performance Measurement and Appraisal in Design Method," in Broadbent, Geoffrey, & Ward (Eds.) *Design Methods in Architecture.* London: Lund Humphries for the Architectural Association, 1969.

Matchett, E. "Control of Thought in Creative Work." *The Chartered Mechanical Engineer* 14, no. 4 (1968).

McCall, G. J., & J. L. Simmons (Eds.). *Issues in Participant Observation.* Reading, MA: Addison-Wesley, 1969.

Merton, R. K. "Multiple Discoveries as Strategic Research Sites," in N. W. Storer (Ed.) *The Sociology of Science.* Chicago: University of Chicago Press, 1973: 371–82.

———. *Social Theory and Social Structure.* New York: Free Press, 1957.

Merton, R. K., & P. Kendall. "The Focused Interview." *American Journal of Sociology* 51, no. 6 (1946): 541–557.

Merton, R. K., et al. "Crafttown and Hilltown." Unpublished mimeo, 1960.

Merton, R. K., M. Fiske, & P. L. Kendall. *The Focused Interview.* New York: Free Press, 1956.

Michael, S., B. Hull, & D. Zahm. "Environmental Factors Influencing Auto Burglary." *Environment & Behavior* 33, no. 3 (May 2001): 368–388.

Michelson, W. *Man and His Urban Environment.* Reading, MA: Addison-Wesley, 1970.

———. (Ed.). *Behavioral Research Methods in Environmental Design.* Stroudsburg, PA: Dowden, Hutchinson & Ross, 1975.

Mintz, N. L. "Effects of Esthetic Surroundings: II. Prolonged and Repeated Experience in a 'Beautiful' and an 'Ugly' Room." *Journal of Psychology* 41 (1956): 459–466.

Mitchell, W. J. (Ed.). *Proceedings of the Environmental Design Research Association, Third Annual Conference, EDRA-3.* Stroudsburg, PA: Dowden, Hutchinson & Ross, 1972.

Montgomery, R. "Comment on Rainwater's Fear and House as Haven in the Lower Class." *Journal of the American Institute of Planners* 32, no. 1 (January 1966): 30–35.

Moore, C., G. Allen, & D. Lyndon. *The Place of Houses.* New York: Holt, Rinehart & Winston, 1974.

Moore, R. "Children at Play." Film study presented at conference of Environmental Design Research Association, Blacksburg, VA, 1973.

Morison, E. *From Know-How to Nowhere.* New York: Basic Books, 1974.

Moser, G., & Corroyer. "Politeness in the Urban Environment: Is City Life Still Synonymous with Civility?" *Environment and Behavior* 33, no. 5 (September 2001): 611–625.

Myerson, J. (Ed.) *Design for Change: The Architecture of DEGW.* Basel: Brookhauser, 1998.

Nahemow, L., & G. Downes. "Collaboration in Architectural Design: A Case Study of the Oxford Home for the Aged." *Journal of Architectural Research* 7, no. 2 (August 1979).

Nasar, J. L., & K. M. Jones. "Landscapes of Fear and Stress." *Environment and Behavior* 29, no. 3 (May 1997): 291–323.

National Bureau of Standards. *The Performance Concept: A Study of Its Application in Housing.* Washington, DC: U.S. Dept. of Commerce, 1968.

Newman, O. *Defensible Space.* New York: Macmillan, 1972.

Norman, D. A. *The Design of Everyday Things.* New York: Doubleday/Currency, 1990.

O'Doherty, E. F. "Psychological Aspects of the Creative Life" in J.C. Jones & D. G. Thornley (Eds.) *Conference on Design Methods.* Oxford: Pergamon, 1963.

Olson, R. V., B. L. Hutchings, & E. Ehrenkrantz. "'Media Memory Lane' Interventions in an Alzheimer's Day Care Center." *American Journal of Alzheimer's Disease* 15, no. 3 (May/June 2000): 163–175.

Orleans, P. "Differential Cognition of Urban Residents: Effects of Social Scale on Mapping," in R. M. Downs, & D. Stea (Eds.). *Image and Environment: Cognitive Mapping and Spatial Behavior.* Chicago: Aldine, 1973.

Osborn, A. F. *Applied Imagination.* New York: Scribner's, 1963.

Osgood, C., G. J. Suci, & P. H. Tannenbaum. *The Measurement of Meaning.* Urbana, IL: University of Illinois Press, 1957.

Ostrander, E., & J. Groom. "The Coolfont Design Process Model: A Finer Grain Look," in W. Preiser (Ed.) *Programming for Habitability*

(Monograph Series). Urbana, IL: Department of Architecture, University of Illinois, 1975.

Paivio, A. *Mental Representations: A Dual Coding Approach.* New York: Oxford University Press, 1986.

Parsons, T., & E. Shils (Eds.). *Towards a General Theory of Action.* Cambridge, MA: Harvard University Press, 1951.

Passini, R., C. Rainville, N. Marchand, & J. Yves. "Wayfinding and Dementia: Some Recent Research Findings and a New Look at Design." *Journal of Architectural and Planning Research* 15, no. 2 (1998): 133–151.

Pastalan, L., R. K. Mantz, & J. Merrill. "The Simulation of Age Related Sensory Losses: A New Approach to the Study of Environmental Barriers," in W. Preiser (Ed.) *Environmental Design Research. Proceedings of the Fourth Environmental Design Research Association Conference 1.* Stroudsburg, PA: Dowden, Hutchinson & Ross, 1973.

Patton, M. Q. *Qualitative Evaluation and Research Methods.* Beverly Hills, CA: Sage Publications, 1990.

Payne, S. *The Art of Asking Questions.* Princeton, NJ: Princeton University Press, 1951.

Perin, C. *With Man in Mind.* Cambridge, MA: M.I.T. Press, 1970.

Piaget, J., & B. Inhelder. "The Gaps in Empiricism," in A. Koestler, & J. R. Smythies. *Beyond Reductionism: The Alpbach Symposium.* London: Hutchinson, 1969.

Polanyi, M. *Personal Knowledge: Towards a Post-Critical Philosophy.* Chicago: University of Chicago Press, 1958.

———. *The Tacit Dimension.* Garden City, NY: Doubleday Anchor, 1967.

Polya, G. *How to Solve It: A New Aspect of Mathematical Method.* Princeton, NJ: Princeton University Press, 1945.

Popper, K. R. *Objective Knowledge: An Evolutionary Approach.* London: Oxford University Press, 1972.

———. *Conjectures and Refutations.* London: Oxford University Press, 1963.

Preiser, W. F. E. "A Combined Tactile-Electronic Guidance System For Visually Impaired Persons in Indoor and Outdoor Spaces," in E. Chigier (Ed.) *Design For Disabled Persons.* Tel Aviv, Israel: Freund Publishing House, Ltd., 1988.

———. "Design Guidelines: Center for Multi-Handicapped Blind Children," in W. F. E. Preiser & E. Ostroff (Eds.) *Universal Design Handbook.* New York: McGraw-Hill, 2001.

———. "POE Training Workshop and Prototype Testing at the Kaiser Permanente Medical Office Building in Mission Viejo, California, USA," in G. Baird et al. (Eds.) *Building Evaluation Techniques.* London, UK: McGraw-Hill, 1996.

———. (Ed.). *Environmental Design Research. Proceedings of the Fourth Environmental Design Research Association Conference.* Stroudsburg, PA: Dowden, Hutchinson & Ross, 1973.

Preiser, W. F. E., & J. C. Vischer. *Assessing Building Performance.* Oxford, UK: Elsevier, 2005.

Preiser, W. F. E., & Ostroff, E. (Eds.). *Universal Design Handbook.* New York: McGraw-Hill, 2001.

Preiser, W. F. E., H. Z. Rabinowitz, & E. T. White. *Post-Occupancy Evaluation.* New York: Van Nostrand Reinhold, 1988.

Pretty, G. H., H. M. Chipuer, & P. Bramston. "Sense of Place Amongst Adolescents and Adults in Two Rural Australian Towns: The Discriminating Features of Place Attachment, Sense of Community and Place Dependence in Relation to Place Identity." *Journal of Environmental Psychology* 23 (2003): 273–287.

Proshansky, H. M., W. Ittelson, & L. Rivlin (Eds.). *Environmental Psychology: Man and His Physical Setting.* New York: Holt, Rinehart & Winston, 1970.

Rainwater, L. "Fear and the House-as-Haven in the Lower Class." *Journal of the American Institute of Planners* 32, no. 1 (January 1966): 23–31.

Ramachandran, V. S., & S. Blakeslee. *Phantoms in the Brain: Probing the Mysteries of the Human Mind.* New York: William Morrow and Company, 1998.

Rapoport, A. "Facts and Models," in Broadbent, Geoffrey, & Ward (Eds.) *Design Methods in Architecture.* London: Lund Humphries for the Architectural Association, 1969.

———. *House Form and Culture.* Englewood Cliffs, NJ: Prentice-Hall, 1969b.

Regnier, V. A. *Assisted Living Housing for the Elderly: Design Innovations from the United States and Europe.* New York: Van Nostrand Reinhold, 1994.

Reizenstein, J. "Linking Social Research and Design." *Journal of Architectural Research* 4, no. 3 (December 1975): 26–38.

Riccio, R. "Street Crime Strategies: The Changing Schemata of Streetwalkers." *Environment and Behavior* 24, no. 4 (July 1992): 555–570.

Richardson, S. A., B. S. Dohrenwend, & D. Klein. *Interviewing: Its Forms and Functions.* New York: Basic Books, 1965.

Robinson, I. M. et al. "Trade-off Games," in W. Michelson (Ed.) *Behavioral Research Methods in Environmental Design.* Stroudsburg, PA: Dowden, Hutchinson & Ross, 1975.

Roethlisberger, F. J., & W. J. Dixon. *Management and the Worker.* Cambridge, MA: Harvard University Press, 1939.

Ruesch, J., & W. Kees. *Nonverbal Communication.* Berkeley, CA: University of California Press, 1970.

Runkel, P. J., & J. E. McGrath. *Research on Human Behavior.* New York: Holt, Rinehart & Winston, 1972.

Saegert, S., G. Winkel, & C. Swartz. "Social Capital and Crime in New York City's Low-Income Housing." *Housing Policy Debate* 13, no. 1 (2002): Fannie Mae Foundation.

Saile, D., J. R. Anderson, R. Borooah, A. Ray, K. Rohling, C. Simpson, A. Sutton, & M. Williams. *Families in Public Housing: An Evaluation of Three Residential Environments in Rockford, Illinois.* Urbana, IL: Committee on Housing Research and Development, University of Illinois, 1972.

Sanoff, H. *Community Participation Methods in Design and Planning.* New York: John Wiley and Sons, 2000.

———. *Methods of Architectural Programming.* Stroudsburg, PA: Dowden, Hutchinson & Ross, 1977.

Sanoff, H., & G. Barbour. "An Alternative Strategy for Planning an Alternative School," in G. T. Coates (Ed.) *Alternative Learning Environments.* Stroudsburg, PA: Dowden, Hutchinson & Ross, 1974.

Schacter, D. L. *Searching for Memory: The Brain, the Mind, and the Past.* New York: Basic Books, 1996.

Schon, D. A. "The Design Process." Cambridge, MA: M.I.T. Press, 1974.

Schwartz, N. H., & R. W. Kulhavy (1981). Map Features and Recall of Discourse. *Contemporary Educational Psychology 6:* 151–158.

Scott, A., R. Fichter, & S. King. *Managing Vandalism.* Boston: Parkman Center for Urban Affairs, 1978.

Shaw, M. E., & J. M. Wright. *Scales for the Measurement of Attitudes.* New York: McGraw-Hill, 1967.

Simon, H. A. *The Sciences of the Artificial.* Cambridge, MA: M.I.T. Press, 1969.

Siwoff, S., S. Hirdt, & P. Hirdt. *The 1988 Elias Baseball Analyst.* New York: Macmillan, 1988.

Snyder, L., & E. Ostrander. *Research Basis for Behavioral Program: The New York State Veterans Home, Oxford, New York.* Ithaca, NY: Dept. of Design and Environmental Analysis, Cornell University, 1974.

Sommer, R. *Personal Space: A Behavioral Basis for Design.* Englewood Cliffs, NJ: Prentice-Hall, 1969.

Spradley, J. P. *The Ethnographic Interview.* New York: Holt, Rinehart and Winston, 1979.

Stea, D. "Architecture in the Head: Cognitive Mapping," in J. Lang, C. Burnette, W. Moleski, & D. Vachon (Eds.) *Designing for Human Behavior.* Stroudsburg, PA: Dowden, Hutchinson & Ross, 1974.

Steinfeld, E. *Barrier Free Design for the Elderly and the Disabled, Part Three: Programmed Workbook.* Syracuse, NY: All University Gerontology Center, Syracuse University, 1975.

Stickgold, R., J. LaTanya, & A. J. Hobson. "Visual Discrimination Learning Requires Sleep After Training," in *Nature Neuroscience 3,* no. 12 (December 2000): 1237–1238.

Strauss, A. & J. Corbin. *Basics of Qualitative Research: Grounded Theory Procedures and Techniques.* Newbury Park, CA: Sage, 1990.

Stubbs, S. "Attention to its Users: Successful Programming and Reprogramming of H.E. Butt Headquarters in San Antonio." *Architecture,* December 1989.

Theodorson, G., & A. Theodorson. *A Modern Dictionary of Sociology.* London: Methuen, 1970.

Toker, U. "Workspaces for Knowledge Generation: Facilitating Innovation in University Research Centers." *Journal of Architectural and Planning Research 22,* no. 4 (2005).

Turner, J. "Housing as a Verb," in J. F. C. Turner & R. Fichter (Eds.) *Freedom to Build.* New York: Macmillan, 1972.

Tyson, M. M. *The Healing Landscape: Therapeutic Outdoor Environments.* New York: McGraw Hill, 1998.

Ulrich, R. S., R. F. Simons, & M. A. Miles. "Effects of Environmental Simulations and Television on Blood Donor Stress." *Journal of Architecture and Planning Research 20,* no. 1 (spring 2003): 38–47.

Underhill, P. *Why We Buy: The Science of Shopping.* New York: Simon & Schuster, 2000.

Valentine, G. "Images of Danger: Women's Source of Information About the Spatial Distribution of Male Violence." *Area 24,* no. 1 (1992): 22–29.

Van der Ryn, S., & M. Silverstein. *Dorms at Berkeley: An Environmental Analysis.* New York: Educational Facilities Laboratories, 1967.

Vischer, J. "Case Study: Can This Open Space Work?" *Harvard Business Review* (May–June, 1999).

———. "Strategic Workspace Planning." *Sloan Management Review 37,* no.1 (Fall 1995).

———. *Environmental Quality in Offices.* New York: Van Nostrand Reinhold, 1989.

———. *Workspace Strategies: Environment As A Tool For Work.* New York: Chapman and Hall, 1996.

———. *Space Meets Status: Designing Building Performance.* London: Spon Press, 2005.

Wampler, J. "'La Puntilla' Design Awards." *Progressive Architecture* (January 1968).

Webb, E. J. et al. *Unobtrusive Measures.* Chicago: Rand McNally, 1966.

Weiss, R., & S. Bouterline. *Fairs, Exhibits, Pavilions and their Audiences.* New York: IBM Corp., 1962.

Welch, P. *Hospital Emergency Facilities: Translating Behavioral Issues into Design* (Graham Foundation Fellowship Report). Cambridge, MA: Architecture Research Office, Harvard Graduate School of Design, 1977.

Welch, P., J. Zeisel, & F. Ladd. "Social Dynamics of Property Damage in Boston Park and Recreation Facilities." Mimeographed Report, Cambridge, MA: Architecture Research Office, Harvard University, 1978.

Wener, R. E., G. W. Evans, D. Phillips, & N. Nadler. "Running for the 7:45: The Effects of Public Transit Improvements on Stress." *Transportation 30* (2003): 203–220.

Whitehouse, S., J. Varni, M. Seid, C. Cooper-Marcus, M. J. Ensberg, J. Jacobs, & R. Mehlenbeck. "Evaluating a Children's Hospital Garden Environment: Utilization and Consumer Satisfaction." *Journal of Environmental Psychology 21* (2001): 301–314.

Whitelaw, A., J. Dyck, R. Carter, E. Lehew, J. Zeisel, K. Meairs, & N. Rottle. "Report on Spatial Competence in Schools: San Diego Workshop on Neuroscience and K-6 School Design," San Diego, CA: Academy of Neuroscience for Architecture, 2005.

Whyte, W. F. "The Social Structure of the Restaurant." *American Journal of Sociology 54* (1949): 302–308.

———. *Street Corner Society, Revised Edition.* Chicago: University of Chicago Press, 1955.

———. *The Social Life of Small Urban Spaces.* New York: Municipal Art Society of New York, 1980. (film)

Wicker, A. W. *An Introduction to Ecological Psychology.* Monterey, CA: Brooks/Cole, 1979.

Wilner, D. et al. *Housing Environment and Family Life.* Baltimore, MD: Johns Hopkins Press, 1954.

Wilson, R. L. "Liveability of the City: Attitudes and Urban Development," in F. S. Chapin & S. F. Weiss (Eds.) *Urban Growth Dynamics.* New York: Wiley, 1962.

Wiseman, F. *Hospital.* Boston: Zipporah Films, 1970. (film)

Yinger, M. J., & S. J. Cutler (Eds.). *Major Social Issues: An Interdisciplinary View.* New York: Free Press, 1978.

Young, M., & P. Willmott. *Family and Kinship in East London.* London: Routledge & Kegan Paul, 1957.

Zeeuw, G. de. "Andragogisch Verbeteringsonderzoek: Commentaar op Problemen" ("Andragogical Improvement Research: Comments on Problems"). Serie Commentaar No. k. Mimeo. Amsterdam: Institut Wetenschap der Andragogie, 1978.

Zeisel, H. *Say It with Figures, Fifth Edition.* New York: Harper & Row, 1968.

Zeisel, J. *Inquiry by Design.* New York: Cambridge University Press, 1984.

———. "Evidence-based Design in Coordinated Health Treatment," in A. Dilani (Ed.) *Design & Health III—Health Promotion Through Environmental Design.* Stockholm: International Academy for Design and Health, 2004: 35-43.

———. "Life-Quality Alzheimer Care in Assisted Living," in Benjamin Schwartz & Ruth Brent (Eds.) *Aging, Autonomy, and Architecture: Advances in Assisted Living.* Baltimore, MD: Johns Hopkins University Press, 1999.

———. "Building Purpose: The Key to Measuring Building Effectiveness," in *The Impact of the Work Environment on Productivity.* Washington, DC: Architectural Research Centers Consortium, Inc., 1985.

———. "Fundamental Values in Planning with Non-Paying Clients," in B. Goodey (Ed.) *Interpreting the Built Environment.* Oxford, UK: Pergamon, in press.

———. "Negotiating a Shared Community Image." *Ekistics 42,* no. 251 (1976): 224–227. (b)

———. "Symbolic Meaning of Space and the Physical Dimension of Social Relations: A Case Study of Sociological Research as the Basis of Architectural Planning," in J. Walton & D. Carns (Eds.) *Cities in Change.* Boston: Allyn & Bacon, 1973. (a)

———. "Technology Is Not Enough." *Progressive Architecture 54,* no. 6 (June 1973): 109–112. (b)

———. "Universal Design to Support the Brain and its Development," in W. F. E. Preiser & E. Ostroff (Eds.) *Universal Design Handbook:* New York: McGraw-Hill, 2001.

———. *Sociology and Architectural Design.* Russell Sage Social Science Frontiers Series, no. 6. New York: Free Press, 1975.

———. *Sociology and Architectural Planning* (Ph.D. thesis). Chicago: University Microfilms, 1971.

———. *Stopping School Property Damage: Design and Administrative Guidelines to Reduce School Vandalism.* Arlington, VA: American Association of School Administrators; New York: Educational Facilities Laboratories, 1976. (a)

Zeisel J., J. Hyde, & S. Levkoff. "Best Practices: An Environment-Behavior (E-B) Model for Alzheimer Special Care Units." *American Journal of Alzheimer's Care & Research.* Waltham, MA, 1994.

Zeisel, J., & M. Maxwell. *Functional Reprogramming: The H-E-B Case Study,* in F. E. W. Preiser (Ed.) *Professional Practice in Facility Programming.* New York: Van Nostrand Reinhold, 1993.

Zeisel, J., & M. Maxwell. *Programming Office Space: Adaptive Re-use Programming for the H-E-B Arsenal Headquarters.* Paris: Corporate Space and Architecture, International Symposium Papers, Plan Construction et Architecture, 1992.

Zeisel, J., & P. Raia. "Non-pharmacological Treatment for Alzheimer's Disease: A Mind-Brain Approach." *American Journal of Alzheimer's Disease and Other Dementias 15,* no. 6 (November –December 2000).

Zeisel, J., & M. Tyson. "Alzheimer's Treatment Gardens," in C. Cooper-Marcus & M. Barnes (Eds.) *Healing Gardens: Therapeutic Benefits and Design Recommendations.* New York: John Wiley & Sons, 1999.

Zeisel, J., & D. Rhodeside. "A Social/Physical Diagnosis of Gund Hall." Unpublished research report, 1975.

Zeisel, J., & M. Griffin. *Charlesview Housing: A Diagnostic Evaluation.* Cambridge, MA: Architecture Research Office, Harvard Graduate School of Design, 1975.

Zeisel, J., C. Fay, P. Milner, P. Noyes, & P. Russell. "Report on Calming Environments." *Woods Hole Workshop on Neuroscience and Health Care Design.* San Diego, CA: Academy of Neuroscience for Architecture, 2004.

Zeisel, J., J. Hyde, & S. Demos. *Low-Rise Housing for Older People: Behavioral Criteria for Design.* Washington, DC: U.S. Government Printing Office, 1978.

Zeisel, J., J. Hyde, & L. Shi. "Environmental Design as a Treatment for Alzheimer's Disease," in L. Volicer & L. Bloom-Charette (Eds.) *Enhancing the Quality of Life in Advanced Dementia.* New York: Taylor and Francis, 1999.

Zeisel, J., P. Welch, & V. Parker. *Independence Through Interdependence: Congregate Living for Older People.* Boston: Department of Health and Human Services, Massachusetts Department of Elder Affairs, 1984.

Zeisel, J., N. M. Silverstein, J. Hyde, S. Levkoff, P. M. Lawton, & W. Holmes. "Environmental Correlates to Behavioral Outcomes in Alzheimer's Special Care Units." *The Gerontologist* (October 2003).

Zinnes, D. A. "Documents as a Source of Data," in R. C. North et al. *Content Analysis.* Evanston, IL: Northwestern University Press, 1963.

Zube, E. H., R. W. Marans, & G. T. Moore. *Advances in Environment, Behavior and Design 1–4* (1987–1997): New York: Kluwer.

INDEX